THEORIES OF THE SELF

THEORIES OF THE SELF

Jerome David Levin, Ph.D.
New School for Social Research
New York, New York

⊙HEMISPHERE PUBLISHING CORPORATION
A member of the Taylor & Francis Group
Washington   Philadelphia   London

USA	Publishing Office:	Taylor & Francis 1101 Vermont Avenue, N.W., Suite 200 Washington, DC 20005-3521 Tel: (202) 289-2174 Fax: (202) 289-3665
	Distribution Center:	Taylor & Francis 1900 Frost Road, Suite 101 Bristol, PA 19007-1598 Tel: (215) 785-5800 Fax: (215) 785-5515
UK		Taylor & Francis Ltd. 4 John Street London WC1N 2ET, UK Tel: 071 405 2237 Fax: 071 831 2035

THEORIES OF THE SELF

Copyright © 1992 by Jerome David Levin. All rights reserved. Printed in the United States of America. Except as permitted under the United States Copyright Act of 1976, no part of this publication may be reproduced or distributed in any form or by any means, or stored in a data base or retrieval system, without the prior written permission of the publisher.

1 2 3 4 5 6 7 8 9   E B E B   9 8 7 6 5 4 3 2

This book was set in Times Roman by Hemisphere Publishing Corporation. The editors were Kathleen Porta and Lisa Speckhardt; the production supervisor was Peggy M. Rote; and the typesetters were Darrell D. Larsen, Jr., Linda Andros, and Sandra Watts. Cover design by Michelle Fleitz.
Printing and binding by Edwards Brothers, Inc.

A CIP catalog record for this book is available from the British Library.

∞ The paper in this publication meets the requirements of the ANSI Standard Z39.48-1984 (Permanence of Paper)

Library of Congress Cataloging-in-Publication Data

Levin, Jerome D. (Jerome David)
    Theories of the self / Jerome David Levin.
        p.   cm.
    Includes bibliographical references and index.
    1. Self—History.   2. Self psychology—History.   3. Self (Philosophy)—History.   I. Title
    BF697.L4125   1992
126—dc20   *92-12864*
                                                                      CIP

ISBN 1-56032-260-8 (case)
ISBN 1-56032-261-6 (paper)

*In memory of my father, **Nathan Levin***

Where is she now? Yes,
seek the snows of yesteryear!
It is easily said:
but how can it really be,
that I was once the little Resi
and that I will one day become the old woman. . .
The old woman, the old Marschallin!
"Look you, there she goes, the old Princess Resi!"
How can it happen?
How does our dear Lord make it so?
While I always remain the same.

Hugo Von Hofmannsthal
Libretto for *Der Rosenkavalier*

Contents

Preface

This book grew out of a long-standing interest in the self, its conceptual eluci-
dations and its experiential reality. Originally that interest was philosophical and
theoretical, being a topic I pursued many years ago in the philosophy department
of McGill University; more recently, it has had a more directly "practical" import
for me in my clinical practice as a psychoanalyst and psychotherapist. I have
learned much about the vicissitudes of the self, its psychopathology, and the ame-
lioration of that psychopathology from my patients. I am grateful to them. I have
also had the opportunity to teach a course on "Theories of the Self" to students
young and old at the New School for Social Research. My classes, with their
mutually enriching mix of traditional undergraduates, adult students, and older
students from the New School's Institute for Retired Professionals, have provided
a forum for multigenerational, intellectually stimulating, intense and deeply felt
discussions of the self that illuminated the questions raised in this book. My students have taught me a great deal and I am in their debt.

My wife Ginny has long been my primary source of intellectual stimulation.
Her creatively critical contribution to our dialogue goes back to our "Freud
fights" when I was in analytic school, and has continued to challenge and stimu-
late me to this day. This book owes much to her.

I am grateful to Eugene Beresin, M.D. of the Massachusetts General Hospital–
Harvard Medical School Department of Psychiatry for his brilliant lectures on
Winnicott, to which I am indebted.

Sue Morgan and Virginia Wray transcribed and put onto disk a long and complicated text with all of its "visions and revisions." Lisa Speckhardt, production
editor, efficiently and cheerfully superintended the conversion of disk into book. I
am grateful to them.

I thank Ellyn Allison and C. Fred Alford, Professor of Government at the
University of Maryland, for reading and commenting on the manuscript. Their
suggestions were invaluable.

Last, but certainly not least, I would like to thank my editor at Hemisphere,
Ron Wilder. Ron's blend of urbanity, decency, intelligence, and competence is
hard to come by and makes him a pleasure to work with.

Although this is primarily a book about the history of an idea, it also draws
upon subjective experiences of self—personal encounters with human
inwardness—my own and those of my patients.

Jerome David Levin
New School for Social Research

1

Historical Prelude

For the ancient Hindus, the Atman was the Brahma: the Self Immanent was the Self Transcendent. For modern man, the very existence of a self has become problematic. From the 17th century on, there has been a powerful conflict between those who think that the self is either an illusion or a "grammatical fiction" and those who think that the self is our one indubitable datum, our only certainty. In our own time, the logical positivists view the self as a "meaningless" concept, while the phenomenologists view the self as the "ground" of any possible experience. Historically, it has been the empiricists who have cast doubt on the substantiality of the self, while the rationalists have affirmed its centrality in human experience. Clearly there is a problem—indeed a mystery—here. Philosophers, theologians, psychologists, and just plain folks have struggled to define and elucidate the nature of the self. It is a topic that intrigues people. The self to which we think we are so close eludes definition and, indeed, becomes more elusive as we attempt to grasp it. It has certainly eluded the long progression of philosophers and psychologists. The empiricists and the rationalists of the 17th and 18th centuries were succeeded by the German idealists of the 19th century and the existentialists of the 20th century, all of whom had much to say about the self, but none of whom came up with entirely satisfying answers to its dilemmas. Contemporary psychoanalytic theorists are no less intrigued by the self and no more in agreement as to its nature. Which theory comes closest to the truth? What is this self that is so elusive? Is it an illusion? An organizing principle? A synthesis? Something experienced? Something substantive? Something that unfolds? Something that paradoxically develops only in relationship with others? Whatever the ontological status of the self may be, we do have a sense of self. How do we develop this sense? Can this process misfire? Is there a pathology of the self? If so, can anything be done to ameliorate that pathology? This book is an attempt to answer these questions.

Our experience of ourselves is paradoxical. We experience our selves as coherent and fragmented, as the same and as different, as ongoing and as disparate, as known and as unknown, as mundane and as esoteric. An adequate theory must be able to account for continuity as well as discontinuity, both of which are intrinsic to our experience of self. The same is true for the other antinomies of the self experience. Is there a theory that does so? I don't think that there is. What about the unconscious? How does this primarily 20th-century notion impact on the various accounts of the self and its vicissitudes? Why the contemporary obsession with narcissism? We have never been so preoccupied with self as we are during a time when the very existence of a self is called into question by so many. Depersonalization is no longer so much a psychiatric diagnosis as it is a normative experience and a theoretical stance. The problematic nature of the self has become a central concern of the contemporary mind.

This book traces the history of the concept of the self from the philosophical controversies of the 17th century to the psychoanalytic controversies of the present day. This historical approach permits the explication of the major ways self has been accounted for or dismissed as illusionary. Along the way it attempts to give some tentative answers to the baffling questions left unanswered by both the philosophical and the psychological traditions. After exposition and criticism comes integration. I hope to cull what is valid in the competing philosophical, psychological, and psychoanalytic analyses of the self and integrate them into a view of the self that is both developmental and relational.

The theorists of self themselves had selves, and the history and experiences of those selves are not without relevance to the theorists' conceptualizations of self. Neither are their cultural and historical situations—what has been called the *existential context*. Accordingly, I shall have something to say about their lives as well as their theories.

In the course of our discussion, we are going to encounter a number of terms that refer to the self or aspects of it. They have not been used in any uniform or consistent way in either the philosophical or the psychological traditions, and that inconsistency further confuses an already confusing subject matter. These terms and the concepts they denote are *self, mind, consciousness, identity, personality*, and *self-concept*. I could give my own definitions now, but that would be to prejudge the very issue, the nature of the self, that for the present must remain indeterminate and continue to remain so until we have understood the very different ways in which self has been understood by our various authors. Suffice it to say that I do not wish to define *self* as either a bodily or a mental phenomenon, as either awareness or unconscious process, as either the sense of who we are or the relatively enduring traits we call personality, nor yet as the description we give of who we are. That is, I do not wish to prejudge to what extent self is, or is not, mind, body, both, consciousness, identity, personality, or self-concept. Definitions are prescriptive as well as descriptive. They are decisions—decisions I do not wish to make at this point. To do so would be to beg the question. Rather, I will try to clarify how, and to what extent, each of our authors understands self in relation to the related concepts just enumerated and defines them in the context of their specific use. But it is well for you, the reader, to keep in mind this inherent confusion and to ask yourself at a given point whether self is appearing in the guise of mind, of consciousness, of body, of identity, or of personality and to ask, "Is this theorist able to justify his decision as to the nature of self?"

Having just said that I do not wish to define *self* at this point, I find that nevertheless I must define it to the extent that we know what we are talking about. This is paradoxical, but then so is the self.

The self is the ego, the subject, the I, or the me, as opposed to the object, or totality of objects—the *not me*. *Self* means "same" in Anglo-Saxon (Old English). So *self* carries with it the notion of identity, of meaning the selfsame. It is also the *I*, the personal pronoun, in Old Gothic, the ancestor of Anglo-Saxon. Thus, etymologically *self* comes from both the personal pronoun, *I*—I exist, I do this and that—and from the etymological root meaning "the same"—it is the same I who does this, who did that. All that sounds unproblematic, but this is far from the case.

As I have said, the self is elusive. Now you see it, now you don't. What is this slippery something we are trying to grasp? Is it a psychosomatic existence? Is it a verbal representation? Is it an organizing principle around which experience accretes? Is it substantial—indeed, the most substantive thing there is? Is it a kaleidoscope, a "mere" stream of thought and feeling? Does it evolve? Is it static? Is it something that unfolds? Is it an illusion? Is it a cybernetic program? Is it an act of synthesizing, or that which is synthesized? What is the ontological status of the self, and what is its phenomenal reality? Over the course of human history these questions have been pondered and answered in myriad ways. Charles Taylor (1989) and Julian Jaynes (1976) believe that not only the concept of the self but the self itself has evolved and changed over historical time, and this may be so.

For the ancients, the self was eternal, but for us the very existence of the self is in doubt, and this doubt constitutes a deep narcissistic wound, an affront to our pride that diminishes our self-esteem. When the ancient Hindus said the Atman was the Brahman, the Self Immanent was the Self Transcendent, they were adumbrating a notion of a self as the ground of reality, a ground that is both within and without us. The self within is that part of us that is beyond the reach of time. This is a notion found in many cultures. The self in this sense is something like what is usually denoted the soul. For the Hindu sages, the task of man is clearing the delirium of desire and aversion so that this self, in its pure essence, can be experienced. This self is equated with a void, with Nirvana, with the eternal and transcendent in the universe; it is the Divine within, not in a personal sense but in a transpersonal one. Taoism and Buddhism have similar beliefs. The Biblical concept of the self is rather different. It is more personal. When God, speaking from the burning bush, says, "I Am who I Am," He is asserting personal identity, personhood being a more Western notion. The Hebrew notion of the soul always carries with it overtones of individuality. This notion differs importantly from the Eastern notion of self as something to be achieved or at least gotten in contact with. The self in Eastern traditions is that which must be uncovered by letting go, by nonaction, by detachment. Only then does the self within coalesce with self without, the identity of the self immanent with the self transcendent become manifest. This is paradoxical in two senses: separation leads to union, and inaction brings about profound change. There are similar ideas in the Western tradition, but the emphasis is rather different.

Western civilization is said to be the product of the interaction of two cultures, the Hebraic and the Hellenistic. The ancient Greeks invented philosophy and science as we know them. At first they were exclusively concerned with giving an account of the cosmos, with "natural philosophy"—what we would call *cosmology* or *physics*. Socrates changed that when he made the investigation of man and his inner life the central philosophical task. Without using the word *self*, Socrates exemplified and delineated the search for it through introspection and dialectic—through the interpersonal pursuit of truth. Thus, Socrates' implicit notion of the self is relational; the self is discovered in the process of discourse and dialogue with others. He also contributed the idea of a Daemon—an inner force that goads and drives—as a constituent of self. Socrates also elucidated, with unequaled sensitivity, the idea of cosmic alienation—of man not being completely or fully at home on this earth. Echoing the oracle at Delphi, Socrates defined the central task of the philosopher, and indeed of each of us, as self-knowledge. "Know yourself," said the oracle, an injunction echoed in Socrates' judgment that "the unexamined life is not worth living." Implicit in this is the notion that there is a complexity and mystery about the self, that the self is a largely unexplained continent, the rivers, fields, and mountains of which are unknown to us. The idea is that there is an unconscious component of the self that can only become conscious through "therapy," the therapy of philosophical dialogue.

Plato, whose Socrates depicted in his *Dialogues* is the Socrates we know, further developed the notion of the self as soul, but made an important new contribution. He was the first to describe the self as conflictual, as being constituted by what Freud called "agencies of the mind." Plato, like Freud, described a tripartite model of the self in his dialogue *Phadeus* (1961a) using the metaphor of the chariot driver trying to control two spirited steeds. The chariot driver represents reason and control, a function akin to that of Freud's ego; one steed represents appetite and is a close relative of Freud's id, while the other steed represents ambition (i.e., the pursuit of narcissistic gratification). The second horse is also to be understood as the "spirited" part of the self. There is no parallel to Freud's superego in Plato's model. The chariot driver is in perpetual need of establishing control over his horses. Self here is split and in constant conflict between opposing forces and tendencies.

Plato, in a manner akin to yet different from the Hindu sages, also saw the chariot driver as the rational part of the psyche (soul or self), which is the unchanging part of self that is potentially in contact with that which is eternal. In the *Republic* (1961b) and elsewhere, he identified that part of self that is permanent with a certain kind of knowing, a knowing through the mind rather than through the senses. So cognition of a special sort, and the import of that cognition, comes to characterize the self, a self that is trapped in "the prison house of the body." So far we have seen self as the transpersonal Self potentially having identity with the ultimately real; the self as personhood; the self as a mystery, as largely an unknown whose nature must be discovered through introspection; and finally the self as divided within itself, characterized by dynamic tension between its constituents.

The Stoics introduced the notion of nonattachment into Western thought. They equated the self with the *Logos*, the eternal pattern embedded in the universe and within us. For the Stoics, who were much concerned with the "slings and arrows of outrageous fortune," the concept that nothing could injure the good man was reassuring. It gave them some solace from the pain of this life. They saw suicide as the ultimate freedom; man could always free himself by refusing to play. Death anxiety was strong and conscious in the Stoics, whose view of the self and its ultimate freedom was a way of dealing with that anxiety. The Roman poet Lucretius wrote a long meditation on death and the reasons for not fearing it. He attacked superstition and the notion of an afterlife in his scientific-philosophical poem *On The Nature of Things* (Lucretius, 1951). In contradistinction to those Eastern and Western philosophers who believe that the self is in some way eternal, the enduring part of us that can bond with that which endures out there, Lucretius is a naturalist who accepts the composite nature of the self, viewing it as being composed, as is everything else, of atoms in patterns: with the dissolution of the patterns comes the dissolution of the self. The atomistic metaphysics (partly borrowed from Epictetus) in *On the Nature of Things* is the first materialistic epiphenomenal account of the self in the Western tradition. That is, the self is seen as a manifestation of matter in motion. There is a whistling-in-the-dark aspect to Lucretius's reiterated belief that death anxiety is irrational and without foundation, but there is something enduring in his view that science—rational knowledge—can dispel fear and lead to its mastery.

With St. Augustine, the fourth-century Christian philosopher, the self becomes self-consciously problematical. For the first time, the questions "What is the self?" and "What am I?" are asked in the context of a psychological autobiography. Augustine's *Confessions* (1961) constitutes the foundation of the Western introspective autobiography. In it he clearly recognized the power of childhood experience in the shaping of personality and identity; the uniqueness and loneliness, indeed the estrangement, of the self; the epigenetic nature of the self; and the role of unconscious ideation and affect, which are, for the first time in the Western tradition, explicitly discussed. In addition, Augustine has a keen sense of the incompleteness of the self, of the need for relatedness, which, in his case, is predominantly relatedness to God. "I am not at one complete until I am one with Thee," says Augustine (1961, p. 11), projecting the preverbal urge for symbiotic union with the mother onto the cosmos (whatever the ontological status of God, that is the dynamic of Augustine's longing). Augustine also makes the self central insofar as he has the notion of cognition as the basis of personal identity. He anticipates Descartes's "I think, therefore I am" but doesn't develop it. Nevertheless, he recognizes that his own very existence is problematic and must be established.

In the interval between the end of the classical era and the beginning of modernity in the 17th century, there was a defocusing on the self and much more emphasis on man's relationships within a hierarchy, with man as a link in the "great chain of being." Man is seen as fitting into a notch, fulfilling a preordained role in structures social, economic, political, ecclesiastical, and cosmic. The Renaissance and Reformation changed that, and the role of the individual self again came to the forefront of Western thought. Indeed, modern philosophy starts with the self, albeit construed as solipsistic cogitator.

2

The 17th Century: Rationalism and Empiricism Encounter the Self

René Descartes (1596–1650), scientist, mathematician, and philosopher, was one of a handful of 17th-century innovators who shaped the modern world. His innovations changed the way humankind understood itself and its relation to the cosmos. The self that emerges from his philosophizing is indeed strange. Descartes's interests were dual: one being the quest for certainty that led him to engage in *radical doubt*, that is, doubting all that can be doubted to determine if there are any certainties, any indubitable knowables, upon which to erect an edifice of systematic science; the other being the securing of a place for scientific knowledge, which for Descartes is mechanistic and deterministic, apart from, and free from, dogmatic and theological considerations. In a time of persecution of free thought he sought to separate and isolate science so it could proceed without any conflict with the powers that were. He succeeded in doing so. Thus, the nature of the self that emerges from his philosophizing is tangential to his intellectual goals, to the main thrust of his thought. Nevertheless, the Cartesian self is an uncanny notion that has been widely influential. Indeed, his theory of the self resonates down the centuries to find a strong and unique response in, and attunement to, the thought of our time.

Descartes was a solitary. After years of wandering as a volunteer on the fringes of the Thirty Years' War, he found himself alone in a small Bavarian town. Although the story may be apocryphal, it is said that he sat in a large Dutch oven and tried to doubt everything that he could possibly doubt. He related this experience in his *Discourse on Method* (1637/1951a) and *Meditations on First Philosophy* (1642/1951b). In them, he tells how he decided to engage in radical doubt and to hold all received opinions up to scrutiny to see if any could withstand his test of indubitability. First he considered tradition, the opinions of his schoolmasters, and the texts he had read. None held up. The authorities contradicted each other; none of his received knowledge was beyond doubt. Continuing his radical doubting, he concluded that sense knowledge, the belief that there was an external world, and the reality of his corporality could also be doubted—doubted in the sense that their negation was not self-contradictory—or to put the same thought positively, that their nonexistence was logically possible although not logically necessary. Finally he tried doubting that he was doubting, cogitating, or thinking and found that he could not, for the very doubt that he was doubting implied a doubter. Doubt is a form of thought, thinking implies a thinker. He had arrived at his famous *cogito, ergo sum*—"I think, therefore I am." Thinking is, here, mental activity of any sort—any cognition. Logically it should include affect, but Descartes is significantly silent about this. So modern thought starts with the disembodied, solitary thinker, lacking body, external world, and relationships—or at least not certain of their reality. All this self can know is that it is knowing—thinking. Descartes's self could be a character in a Beckett play. Bertrand Russell argued that Descartes had concluded more than he was entitled to from his data and his method. According to Russell, the only certainty is thinking now, and not that a thinker is doing the thinking. For Descartes, however, the self in this stripped, solipsistic sense does have existence and reality, and he knows that with certainty. Small pickings at best, but it does give us one certain proposition, the contrary of which is self-contradictory. Once he has his one certainty, Descartes is able to prove to his satisfaction that there is a God who will guarantee the veracity of his "clear and distinct" (1637/1951a, p. 2) ideas. Then he brings back the external world and goes on to build a dualistic ontology in which there are two substances: extended substance and thinking substance. Descartes never solved the problems raised by his radical dualism, such as how the two substances interact, but his metaphysical schema does give him a way to secure a place for a science, albeit a science that mathematizes nature and strips it of sensuous qualities. Cartesian science includes mechanistic psychology, which views the psyche as a piece of clockwork. Although Descartes states that he accepts the teaching of the Catholic church, there is really no place for soul in his system. Science can now be pursued without fear of persecution, but at what a cost. Descartes's self is devoid of affect, relationships, or development; it is a solitary knower, a pure subject. There is a bitter paradox here: Descartes's whole system stands on his indubitable knowledge of his existence, his *I am*, his selfhood, but he has traded certainty for vacuity. His *I am* is vastly different from the Burning Bush's *I am*; it is subject without object, computer program without data, existence without feeling. It is self as inferred, not as experienced. This is depersonalization with a vengeance, a view of self that can't help but be impoverishing and narcissistically wounding, yet that has had an incalculable influence on subsequent Western thought.

Descartes wasn't aware of the existential implications of his disembodied, unrelated, alone self. On the contrary, he felt exhilarated that he had started science on its way and had solved many of the questions of philosophy. He did, however, have a dream in 1619 that he interpreted as an augury of good fortune, but that is obviously suffused with anxiety. It was reported in Maxime Leroy's (1929, as cited in Freud, 1927/1969) biography of Descartes. Leroy sent the dream to Freud for his comments. Freud thought that the dream thoughts were not far from Descartes's consciousness, although the more obscure parts of the dream represented the more deeply unconscious, probably sexual, latent meaning of the dream. Freud also thought that Descartes's difficulties in moving represented inner conflict. Here is the dream (or dreams) as told by Leroy. They were dreamt while Descartes was in a state of perplexity and about to embark on his adventure in radical doubt.

> *Then during the night, when all was fever, thunderstorms, panic, phantoms rose before the dreamer. He tried to get up in order to drive them away. But he fell back, ashamed of himself, feeling troubled by a great weakness in his right side. All at once, a window in the room opened. Terrified, he felt himself carried away by the gusts of a violent wind, which made him whirl round several times on his left foot.*
>
> *Dragging himself staggering along, he reached the buildings of the college in which he had been educated. He tried desperately to enter the chapel, to make his devotions. At that moment some people passed by. He wanted to stop in order to speak to them; he noticed that one of them was carrying a melon. But a violent wind drove him back towards the chapel.*
>
> *He then woke up, with twinges of sharp pain in his left side. He did not know whether he was dreaming or awake. Half-awake, he told himself that an evil genius was trying to seduce him, and he murmured a prayer to exorcise it.*

He went to sleep again. A clap of thunder woke him again and filled his room with flashes. Once more he asked himself whether he was asleep or awake, whether it was a dream or a day-dream, opening and shutting his eyes so as to reach a certainty. Then, reassured, he dozed off, swept away by exhaustion.

With his brain on fire, excited by these rumors and vague sufferings, Descartes opened a dictionary and then a collection of poems. The intrepid traveller dreamt of this line: "Quod vitae sectabor iter?" Another journey in the land of dreams? Then suddenly there appeared a man he did not know, intending to make him read a passage from Ausonius beginning with the words "Est et non". But the man disappeared and another took his place. The book vanished in its turn, then re-appeared decorated with portraits in copper-plate. Finally, the night grew quiet. (Freud, 1929/1961, pp. 200–202)

Clearly, the embarkation on the journey into radical doubt aroused great anxiety in Descartes. There is a feeling of things being out of control in the dream. He is swept by forces of the storm, no doubt representing his inner storm, and Freud is on the money in pointing out the conflict, in the dream, between the forces of left and right, between thought and feeling, between instinct and reason. It is interesting that the "evil demon," who plays a role in Descartes's philosophical writings as intellectual deceiver, makes an appearance in the dreams as moral seducer. Descartes's dreams of 1619 reveal the human emotional cost, concealed behind a facade of cool urbanity, of the new scientific philosophy. Descartes's philosophical concerns with certainty and reality testing are direct derivatives of his existential crisis and its representation in his dream.

Descartes's younger contemporary, Blaise Pascal (1623–1662), who was also a triple-threat thinker—philosopher, scientist, and mathematician—was exquisitely aware of the existential implications of the Cartesian self. His reaction to the implications of the scientific revolution of the 17th century was horror, in spite of the fact that he was a participant in that revolution. Protesting against the self as pure intellectualization, he exclaims that "the heart has its reasons which Reason knows not." Reacting to humankind's displacement from its hitherto secure place in the great chain of being between the angels and the animals, Pascal sees that the new instrumentation provided by the telescope and the microscope has revealed man's insignificance in the scale of things, his aloneness in the vastness, indeed the infinitude, of space, and he cries out, "These infinite spaces terrify me" (1670/1966, p. 47); "The eternal silence of these infinite spaces fills me with dread" (1670/1966, p. 67); and "When I consider the brief span of my life absorbed into the eternity which comes before and after . . . the small space I occupy which I see swallowed up in the infinite immensity of space, spaces of which I know nothing and which know nothing of me, I take fright and am amazed to see myself here rather than there: there is no reason for me to be here rather than there, now rather than then" (1670/1966, p. 48). Continuing, he cries out, "I want the God of Abraham, Isaac, and Jacob, not the God of the philosophers" (1670/1966, p. 95). That is, Pascal wants a personally meaningful God not the God of Descartes who validates the truth of clear and distinct propositions in mathematics and science. Pascal was reacting to the radical contingency of the self, its arbitrariness, its "throwness" (to borrow a term from Heidegger), and its estrangement—all strikingly contemporary motifs. Pascal goes on to say,

Man is only a reed, the weakest in nature, but he is a thinking reed. There is no need for the whole universe to take up arms to crush him: a vapor, a drop of water is enough to kill him. But even if the universe were to crush him, man would still be nobler than his slayer because he

knows that he is dying and the advantage that the universe has over him. The universe knows none of this. (Pascal, 1670/1966, p. 95)

This heroic defiance is one way that Pascal deals with his cosmic anxiety. The second way he deals with that anxiety is through passionate belief in a mystical form of Christianity. The thinking reed is Pascal's way of regaining some self-esteem in the face of nothingness and insignificance. It is reminiscent of Job's "I will maintain my own ways before Thee" in response to God's omnipotence, although it has a different focus. Ironically, it is thinking in a broad sense of consciousness that is Pascal's way of responding to the emotional implications of Descartes's cogitating—and only cogitating—self lost in the vastness of space with which he cannot even make contact.

The experience of cosmic anxiety, of dread of the infinite empty spaces of the universe, is far from unique to Pascal. I remember lying on my back on the flagstone balustrade of the Junior Balcony at the University of Pennsylvania dormitories, feeling myself being pulled into the infinite regression of endless space. As anxiety welled up, I looked at the stars and thought, "You are but hydrogen into helium fusing without possibility of knowing it, while I am mightier than you because I do know it." Long before I had heard of Pascal, I was reacting to cosmic anxiety much like he did in his concept of the thinking reed. More recently, one of my patients had to limit his hobby of gazing through his telescope because it engendered too much Pascalian cosmic anxiety.

In the history of philosophy, Descartes is usually classified as a rationalist, in fact as the founder of modern rationalism. He is so classified because of the primacy in his system of reason as the only reliable source of veridical, certain knowledge. In Descartes's epistemology, the proper use of reason leads us to clear and distinct ideas that are self-validating. His model is mathematics. Descartes is aware of the importance of experimentation and observation, but they are peripheral to his understanding of how science works. Furthermore, he is a believer in innate ideas; that is, he believes that the self comes into the world with knowledge already imprinted on it. This is an idea as old as Plato's doctrine that "knowledge is reminiscence," but assumes a characteristically modern form in Descartes. Reason, properly used, brings to consciousness innate ideas that are already imprinted, and their clearness and distinctness serve as guarantors of their truth.

In a sense, Descartes's thinking subject, his I, is an innate idea. Descartes is characteristically suspicious of the reliability of the senses as a source of knowledge or as a basis of doing science, and that places him squarely in the rationalist camp. Descartes doesn't question the sufficiency of sensory knowledge for everyday living, but he does give it an inferior role in scientific methodology. In stripping matter of *secondary qualities*—taste, smell, color, and so forth—and reducing it to extension—matter in motion—he mathematizes nature. He does the same thing to the self—here seen as thinking substance rather than as extended substance—it is depersonalized, deindividualized, and dequalified; that is, it is stripped of qualities, leaving thought as the self's only attribute. As I said above, Descartes is not emotionally threatened by his conceptualization of thought and being (unless his dream indicates otherwise), while Pascal is very much so. Part of their different reactions to the same state of affairs has to do with their temperaments. Descartes, the solipsistic contemplator in the Dutch oven, was, after all, a soldier, courier, and man of the world who had a series of liaisons and, indeed, a natural child whom he lost. Although he didn't marry, he enjoyed vigorous good health and won adherents, thereby gaining much narcissistic gratification. He was an ambitious man who enjoyed seeing his ambitions fulfilled, while Pascal was unworldly, sickly, tormented in both mind and body, and sexually repressed, or at least unexpressed. His reaction is anxiety, not exhilaration, at the new position of the self in relation to the universe that was corollary to the rise of science. Pascal's mother died when he was 3, and one wonders how much of his terror before the eternal silence of those infinite spaces had its origin in the toddler's devastation at his mother's eternal silence and in the emptiness of the "vast" spaces in which that toddler must have searched for and yearned for her without ever finding her.

Descartes was the child of a family of successful middle-class professionals; although we don't know much about his early life, it seems to have been unproblematic. He was educated in the best school in France, La Flèche, which was run by the Jesuits, and went on to receive a degree in law. He looked about the world, such as it was: in his youth was an aide de camp to various participants in the Thirty Years' War, and he eventually returned to Paris before settling in Holland, where he published circumspectly so as not to get in trouble with the church authorities. He succeeded, and went on to enjoy considerable renown and respect. Given his basic sense of security he was able to engage in radical doubt; indeed, he wrote that he felt compelled to doubt—to doubt everything that can be doubted, including the reliability of the senses, the trustworthiness of reason, and the existence of the external world. He doubted in order to be certain. Better to know nothing than to have false belief. He worried that he might be fooled by an evil demon who was trying to deceive him into believing, for example, that he was awake while he was in fact dreaming, a state of affairs prefigured in his dreams of 1619. If such were the case, there would be no possibility of knowing anything to be true; that is, it would be impossible to both know the truth and know that you know it as long as the demon remains in the realm of possibility. Descartes's doubt is a meditative technique, a form of thought therapy to cure the mind of excessive reliance on the senses or on received ideas. So, in this sense, Descartes is a "dark enlightener," as Yovel (1989) calls those thinkers who destroy false belief systems. He is one of those thinkers who sweeps away the cobwebs of custom and belief and, in so doing, takes away some of our security. In Descartes's case, he undermines old belief systems, including beliefs about the nature of self, which had provided ontological security, a sense of relatedness to the cosmos, for the educated classes of Western Europe.

In his state of radical doubt, Descartes does finally find something to rely on, the principle of natural light, and herein comes to the fore his rationalism. It was the clearness and distinctness of the cogito that validated the existence of the self, from which Descartes generalizes that, if he can know something as clear and distinct in the light of nature, then he can be sure of it. Descartes's natural light is strangely parallel to the Quakers' belief that the light of nature validates moral insight. It is its rationalistic equivalent, and it is a thoroughly Protestant notion, Descartes's Catholicism notwithstanding. The idea that each man can arrive at truth through meditation, rather than by following authority, would not have been conceivable before the Reformation.

Descartes's task is to try and set a foundation upon which the science of the 17th century could build. What he does, once he finds something that is self-evident, the self, is to see what kind of ontology he can build. He winds up with a dualistic view of the world. There are two substances: extended substance and thinking substance. Each substance is self-sufficient. Particular things and particular minds are real by virtue of their partaking of extension and of thought, respectively. From another point of view substances are substrates in which qualities adhere. What we perceive of the external world are its primary and secondary qualities. The primary qualities are really matter in motion. Material things are defined by their positions in space and their extension. For Descartes these primary qualities are "real," that is, actually resident in matter, while the secondary qualities are unreal in the sense that they do not appear in nature but are our contribution to perception. Descartes believed that there are innate ideas whose truth, as long as they are clear and distinct and seen in the light of natural reason, is self-evident, and guaranteed by an omnipotent God. This is a strange belief for a radical skeptic. The way Descartes arrives at his belief in the certainty of clear and distinct ideas is by "proving" the existence of a God who will not deceive him. This God guarantees the certain truth of certain kinds of thought and becomes a God who validates mathematics and physics, but who has none of the qualities of the comforting God whom Pascal was looking for in his cosmic terror. Descartes tells us that, for all his radical doubt, he is going to follow the customs and adhere to the beliefs of his environment. His doubt is theoretical and philosophical, but does not extend to practical matters. Accordingly, he remains a practicing Catholic. That, however, does not seem to influence his philosophical system. Descartes's true religious convictions are unknown; perhaps he was simply protecting himself from persecution, or perhaps he was a sincere believer, as his more recent biographers believe.

Let's return to Descartes's *cogito, ergo sum*—I am thinking, I exist; I think, therefore I am—and try to analyze what kind of proposition it is. Descartes maintains both that it is a self-evident mental intuition and that it is a proven inference. Historically, it has been regarded as both, although most philosophers have considered it a proof. We have seen Russell's criticism of that proof, in which he maintains that all Descartes can legitimately say is that thinking is occurring now and that the I is gratuitous. Can there be thought without a thinker? Or, to turn that around, does thought necessitate a thinker? Logical necessity does not compel us to conclude that there is a thinker, and there is nothing self-contradictory in the proposition "thinking does not imply a thinker." Russell is right. However, Descartes does not only rely on *cogito, ergo sum* as a valid and self-evident inference in positing the certainty of the existence of the self. On the contrary, he affirms that everyone can intuit that he exists as a thinker, thinking, here, including all of cognition—willing, judging, doubting, and affirming. It is this direct intuition, not mediated by logic but rather validated and, so to speak, certified true by its clearness and distinctness that is, in the last analysis, the ground of the one certain belief that is to be the foundation of all knowledge. One could question this. After all, clearness and distinctness are remarkably subjective criteria of truth. When clearness and distinctness of a thought don't mean that its contrary is self-contradictory but rather that it is intuitively self-evident, one man's clearness and distinctness need not be another's. But Descartes does not see this. For him the clearness and distinctness of a thought make it self-validating for all, and the propositions so validated have universal conviction and certainty.

Descartes does raise a problem about the nature of the thinker, about the thinking self, when he writes "you do not know whether it is you yourself who thinks or whether the world soul in you thinks as the Platonists believe." However, Descartes is really not much worried about this question and does not take it seriously, nor is he concerned with the world soul. Rather, his interest lies in the certainty of his existence as a thinker because that knowledge is clear and distinct and serves as a model for, and criterion of, all knowledge. "I think, therefore I am" is a paradigm of scientific truth.

Descartes has remarkably little to say about the nature of the self. Given the way he arrives at the certainty of the self, this is hardly surprising. One of the few things he does say is, "I recognized that I was a substance whose essence or nature is to think and whose being requires no place and depends on no material thing" (1642/1951b, p. 26). Here we see very clearly the insubstantiality of the Cartesian self, its disembodied nature as a thinking self, as pure mind.

Material things are also substances for Descartes, but they are extended substances. For the scholastics (i.e., the medieval philosophers), substances were concrete entities (i.e., particular things), but not so for Descartes. He writes, "By substance we can understand nothing else but a thing which so exists that it needs no other thing in order to exist" (1642/1951b, p. 75). Strictly speaking, given Descartes's definition of substance, there can be only one substance, God, who has two attributes, thought and extension. Spinoza (1677/1951), Descartes's successor in some ways and very much his own man in others, defined substance as "that which is the cause of itself" (of which there can only be one) and developed a metaphysical system in which God or Nature, the one substance, has infinite attributes of which we can know only two, thought and extension. For Descartes there are two substances, thinking substance and extended substance. As Descartes puts it, there are two created substances that need the concurrence of God to exist. That is, if God wasn't continually creating us as a thinking substance and the world as extended substance, both world and self would cease to exist.

The radical subjectivism that is so central to Descartes's thought has become so characteristic of modern thought that we don't recognize how much of who we are, and of how we conceptualize who we are (with all of the problems, limitations, and illuminations of that conceptualization), we owe to him. When he wrote, "I resolved to seek no other knowledge than that which I find within myself, or perhaps in a great book of nature," and continued, "I reached the decision to study myself" (1637/1951a, p. 6), he was adumbrating the inwardness of modernity— anticipating the self-conscious self-absorption of our own time.

Descartes's thought has another, more objective aspect: his elucidation of a method of scientific problem solving, which sounds almost like a computer flow chart. The method includes a number of steps, the first of which is to never accept as true anything but that which is self-evident (i.e., clear and distinct); the second, to divide the problem up into manageable bits; third, to think about them in an orderly fashion, breaking down the complex into a series of simple steps; and finally, to enumerate and review the results to see that no error occurred. So to speak, he builds in a feedback loop in his review step. This methodology is related to, but not identical with, the geometric method, which is purely deductive. Descartes was indeed influenced by the example of mathematics, which alone seemed to give certain knowledge, and was himself a great mathematician, the founder of a branch of mathematics, analytic geometry, in which algebra and geometry are seen to be capable of representing the same truths, to be isomorphic in modern language. This method of geometry, somewhat modified, becomes the method of philosophy for him. It was the certainty, clarity, and distinctness of mathematical proofs that served as the model for conscious truth seeking and led to the *cogito*—a strange path to the self.

Once Descartes established his one certainty, himself as solitary thinker, he needed to bring God back into the universe as the guarantor of the truth of clear and distinct ideas. The way he does this is an old one going back to St. Augustine. Descartes gives a modern twist to Augustine's "ontological proof" of the existence of God. Once he has established his certain existence as thinker, he realizes that among his thoughts is the thought of an absolute perfect being. However, he himself is not perfect, is not omniscient or omnipotent, so he cannot be the cause of this thought of perfection since every effect needs a sufficient cause. At least that was the belief of the scholastics, the medieval philosophers, whom he had studied at La Flèche and whose thought he had unconsciously carried over into his not as radical as he believed radical doubt. He argues that since it is more perfect to exist than not to exist, and since God is a perfect being, existence must be one of God's attributes. Furthermore, God must have put the thought of a perfect being in his mind, since as an imperfect being he could not be a sufficient cause of the idea of perfection. Bertrand Russell wrote that the ontological proof was one of the great scandals of philosophy because it seems in many ways to be *prima facie* absurd, yet that logically he could not quite see what was wrong with that proof. It is not logically fallacious, nor is it technically invalid. Descartes is, however, satisfied with his proof, and once he has established the existence of a good God simply uses Him as a guarantor of the truth of mathematical physics and of his style of philosophizing. Descartes is now free to go ahead and pursue science in his rationalistic way, without fearing the opposition of the church, which he goes out of his way not to offend. Using a traditional proof of God's existence didn't hurt his case, nor did his cautious affirmation that in ordinary matters of belief and custom it is wise to follow the ways of the society one lives in, which is precisely what he did.

Once God is back in His Heaven, if that is where He is, Descartes uses Him to establish the truth of clear and distinct ideas, including the idea that the external world exists. The result is an odd system indeed, in which the solitary self becomes the foundation for a kind of disembodied mathematical view of the universe in which the truth of that mathematical system is ultimately guaranteed by a God who is proved by an argument about logical necessity. Neither the thinker nor the Deity seems to have any sort of affective life. This is not a God one would or could love, fear, or worship, and this is not a self that seems to have feelings, although feeling states are certainly part of thinking as Descartes uses the term.

We can now see quite clearly what Pascal was reacting against. He, too, was a great mathematician, the founder of the scientific study of probability, an experimentalist, and no mean physicist in his own right; he was a multifaceted genius, who, almost in passing, started the public transportation system in Paris. He was temperamentally very different from Descartes. He suffered a lot of loss in his life. There was the early death of his mother and the later death of a beloved sister. He himself was always sickly, his existence always threatened, and although he had what is called his "worldly phase," he was essentially an unworldly man. Pascal became attracted to Jansenism, a form of mystical Catholicism to which his sister had converted. In a way it was she who converted him; however, his reaction to the new world view of the 17th century (including its view of the self), which was abject terror, predisposed him to that conversion. The Pascalian self is the thinking reed looking with fear and trembling at the immensity of the universe and taking the gamble of religious belief. Probability rather than certainty, feeling rather than thought, as primary categories distinguish Pascal's thought and understanding of self from that of Descartes.

It is no accident that Descartes's major contribution to mathematics was analytic geometry, which relates and shows the structural identity (isomorphism) of the clear and distinct sciences of algebra and geometry, while Pascal's major contribution to mathematics was the theory of probability, which deals with the random and chance. It is almost as if Descartes were groping for a model for the interaction of the realm of extension and the realm of thought by demonstrating the underlying unity of two apparently disparate branches of mathematics, while Pascal was attempting to work through his terror and anxiety by demonstrating that the apparently random and merely probable was also lawful and capable of rational understanding.

Descartes died on a visit to Christina, Queen of Sweden, where he had been appointed advisor to court. He was not able to take the Nordic winter, but, as far as we know, he was in a cheerful and confident frame of mind until his final illness. Descartes's body was shipped back to France. With almost perfect symbolism for the man who bifurcated nature into thought and extension, the head arrived severed from the body, and is buried apart from it. It is almost as if the problems raised by his dualistic metaphysics pursued him into his grave.

Pascal didn't have it so easy. Probably suffering from tuberculosis, he died young after many years of progressive weakness and illness. In the end his interest was in his Christian faith and his wager that a God existed and in his passionate commitment to that faith. His self is a self of fear and trembling; a self acutely aware of cosmic insignificance; a self, like that of St. Augustine, that is desperately trying to reconnect to some sort of loving, caring outwardness, to something in that vastness that so diminishes and terrifies him that will validate the thinking reed that he knows the universe can snuff out at any time.

So, having seen something of the self as understood by the great rationalist, Descartes, and the emotional reaction of Pascal to that understanding, we are going to go on to look at some different views, those of the empiricists. Before we do so, we might summarize the journey we have taken so far. We started with the idea of the self as that which is the same, that which endures, and went on to the Eastern idea of the self as the God within and to the Hebraic notion of self as the personality of God. In Plato, and the Greeks in general, we see the self as psyche, as mind or as spirit, and as something enduring that is the rational part of the mind, and as such is identified, or potentially can be identified, with the eternal. In this conception, the relationship between the self (or parts of the self) and the most permanent object of consciousness, which is for Plato the "Form of the Good," allows us to reach a stable relationship with that which is not mutable. We are enduring insofar as we relate to the eternal. The Platonic notion of self also highlights its inner division and conflict. We went on to see the personalization of the self in Hebrew scriptures when God describes himself as "I am who I am," where once again the self is essentially relational. It is a person relating to a person, or relating to God. That is also true for the ancient Hindus, with their distinction between the immanent indwelling self and the transcendent self. That immanent indwelling self is to be distinguished from the psychophysical self. It is a kind of transcendental self, and again there is an identification here between self as in-dwelling and self as transcendent that is reminiscent of Platonism. Connecting with the reality behind the changing world of appearances and sensations was the goal of the early philosophical theorizing of both East and West. They both sought, and both inferred, the existence of a soul-like enduring self as subject commensurate with an eternal object in an attempt to link the permanent with the permanent. A relational concept of self indeed.

This way of thinking was taken over by early Christianity, and we saw how St. Augustine developed it in his autobiography. However, his *Confessions* are more deeply subjective and more deeply personalized than previous writing about the self. In St. Augustine we have a new emphasis on the importance of the self and of the individual as the child of God, so the self becomes something of supreme importance.

In the Middle Ages, the importance of the individual diminishes, and there is relatively little interest in the self as such. What there is tends to be expressed in medieval political theory, in which the state is seen as organic and the self is defined in terms of its contractual relationships. Here the self is situated not only, or even primarily, in terms of its position in a worldly hierarchy, but more saliently as part of the great chain of being in which it occupies a secure and defined place. That security was lost as the Ptolemaic geocentric world view broke down and the Copernican heliocentric world view replaced it. At the same time, the universality of Catholicism was challenged by the rise of Protestantism. The economic, reli-gious, philosophical, metaphysical, and political vision of the High Middle Ages was coming to an end, and the corresponding institutions that expressed and em-bodied that vision were no longer stable or beyond question. The Renaissance and the Reformation changed the world forever. The former redirected attention to the individual and the self, and the latter made each man the judge of truth. The emphasis was now on inwardness, on the internalization of conscience, as exem-plified and taught by Martin Luther. Simultaneously, there was a dramatic increase in privacy, in the potential for aloneness, in all but the lowest classes.

The old synthesis broke down in the 17th century, to be replaced by the rise of individualism. That individualism was exciting. It led to new opportunities for many people, but it was also threatening because it was achieved at the cost of relatedness. It is no accident that the existence of the self becomes problematic at precisely the time when self becomes self-conscious and intensely aware of sepa-rateness. Nor is it an accident that Descartes seeks certainty at precisely a time when the cosmological, social, political, and religious certainties of the medieval world view ceased to be tenable. In premodern conceptualizations, the self had been seen as safely coherent and enduring, deriving its stability from its relation-ship to God, but now something else was required as a cement. The old verities were no longer certain, and the unity of the self, itself, was now problematical. The 17th century was the time of the rise of the bourgeoisie and of capitalism. That entailed a fragmentation of the old social fabric, a breakdown of the great chain of being, events that paralleled the rise of Protestantism and the concomitant end of the Church Universal. The fragmentation of society and the fragmentation of the self are contemporaneous. The rise of materialistic philosophy—for exam-ple, in Thomas Hobbes's writings, which maintain that the only reality is matter in motion—is another manifestation of this new world view. Although it hearkens back to Lucretius and the Greek Atomists, materialism is given a new impetus and is very much in the air in the 17th century. Materialism, Protestantism, and individualism were the raw materials that Descartes used to fashion his world view and to arrive at the solipsistic thinking self. That self as pure thinker now needed a way to connect with the other reality, matter in motion.

Discord followed the breakdown of the geocentric picture of universe and the rise of the heliocentric one. Galileo was condemned by the Inquisition for supporting the heliocentric theory. Freud wrote that mankind experienced three narcissistic wounds—deep injuries to self-esteem: Copernicus's demotion of man from the center of the universe to a resident of one of nine planets of a minor star; Darwin's demotion of man from the product of God's special creation to but another animal; and Freud's own demonstration that instead of being master in his own house, man was the plaything of unconscious forces. The response to narcissistic injury is rage and anxiety. The 17th century, which felt the full impact of the first narcissistic injury, demonstrates plenty of both.

Contemporaneously with the abandonment of the geocentric world, alienation and estrangement become dominant themes in writers as diverse as Pascal, writing from a religious point of view, and Montaigne, writing from a humanistic point of view. Now man is no longer at home in a comprehensible universe but is, on the contrary, alienated and estranged in a better understood (at least from a scientific point of view) but less humanly inhabitable universe. The phenomenal self, Pascal's thinking reed, becomes central in thinking about self precisely as the non-phenomenal self, the indwelling self tied metaphysically to something eternal, loses its credibility and is no longer tenable.

The world is no longer viewed as a vale of tears, a preparation for eternity, but as something valuable for its own sake. There is, however, a price to pay for this new humanism and this worldliness, namely cosmic loneliness.

Paul Tillich (1952) maintains that the predominant anxiety of the Middle Ages was fear of condemnation, while the predominant anxiety of modern times is fear of meaninglessness. This is congruent with the new emphasis in the 17th century on the self and its problematical status.

We now turn to another point of view that emphasizes experience rather than reason. The view that knowledge comes through the senses rather than through abstract thinking is called empiricism. The empiricists replaced the primacy of reason with the primacy of the senses. Empiricism stands in opposition to rationalism. Roughly speaking, rationalism is a Continental European phenomenon, while empiricism is an English, and later an American, phenomenon. The more radical empiricists maintain that the senses are the only sources of knowledge; less radical empiricists allow reason a subsidiary role in their epistemologies.

When the English physician, political theorist, man of affairs, and philosopher John Locke (1632–1704) wrote "nothing is in the mind that wasn't first in the senses" (1690/1959, p. 123), he became the founder of modern empiricism. Locke, like Descartes, was the son of a lawyer. His father was caught up in the English civil war, in which he backed Cromwell. Locke, like Descartes, grew up in a world in which the traditional order was under assault but, unlike him, looked not for certainty as a basis for both knowledge and personal security, but to probable knowledge and mutual tolerance of differing opinions. Descartes reacted to the twin threats of dogmatism and meaninglessness by looking for certitudes that could be agreed on by all men; Locke's goals were more modest, but perhaps more livable. Though he studied Greek and moral philosophy at Oxford, looking toward taking holy orders, Locke graduated in medicine. As a physician, he was both exposed to the new science and socialized into a pragmatic, observational, applied science. Locke, however, practiced little, being quickly drawn into the world of diplomacy and public affairs. Toward the end of the century, he retired from public life and turned toward philosophy. He published his masterpiece, *An Essay Concerning Human Understanding*, in 1690 (Locke, 1690/1946). It was preceded by his great political tracts, including *Letters Concerning Toleration* (Locke, 1667/ 1959), which argued for freedom of thought in an age when men killed each other for their beliefs and opinions. The political Locke importantly influenced Jefferson, and many of his ideas are embedded in the American Constitution and Bill of Rights. This, however, is not the Locke who interests us here; rather, we are interested in Locke the technical philosopher.

Book 1 of the *Essay* is concerned with refuting the notion of innate ideas. Descartes for all of his skepticism had reintroduced innate ideas into his system. In a sense, all clear and distinct ideas are innate, or at the very least the test of certitude, clarity, and distinctness is itself innate, a built-in given. Locke feared that any epistemology that allowed a role for innate ideas as a source of knowledge would open the doors to speculative metaphysics and dogmatic theology, precisely what he wanted to deny credibility. (When my wife and I acquired a Newfoundland puppy, who we called Freud, we were told that all Newfoundlands have an innate desire to please. When he proved to be sweet but recalcitrant and quite willful, I told my wife that unfortunately he was a Lockeian, not a Cartesian, Newfoundland. She looked puzzled.)

Locke tells us that the idea for the essay started with a friendly discussion in his rooms at Oxford about various metaphysical questions. He tells us that the group of friends decided that, before such ultimate concerns could be meaningfully addressed, it was first necessary to determine the limits of knowledge: what it was possible to know and how it might be known. To do so, it was necessary to examine the nature of, and limits of, our instrument of knowing, the human Understanding. To fail to do so could lead to unwarranted claims, dogmatically held, and to bloody conflict and repression. This, after all, had been the history of the 17th century. The task of examining the Understanding critically was given to Locke, and 20 years later he published the result. Hence, the thrust of the essay is critical—throwing away the debris of fanatical belief and dogmatic certitude. It is of some interest to note that the origin of the essay is social; its impetus came out of dialogue and out of interpersonal interaction, in contradistinction to both the impetus and the execution of Descartes's *Principles* and *Meditations*, which emerged from solitary contemplation. Their respective origins both exemplify and determine their ambience and not a little of their conclusions, or at least there is a reciprocal (dialectical) relationship between their social-solitary genesis and their views of self, world, and the possibility of knowing either or both.

After demonstrating, by a variety of arguments, that innate ideas, including the idea of the self (as innate), do not exist, Locke postulates that the Understanding (the mind) starts as a blank slate (*tabula rasa*) or, in an alternate metaphor, as an empty cabinet needing to be furnished. Nothing (including the idea of the self) is in the mind that was not first in the senses.

Let us then suppose the mind to be, as we say, white paper, devoid of all characters, without any ideas: how comes it to be furnished? Whence comes it that vast store which the busy and boundless fancy of man has painted on it as an almost endless variety? Whence has it all the materials of reason and knowledge? To this I answer in one word, from EXPERIENCE. In that all our knowledge is founded; and from that it ultimately derives itself. Our observations employed either, about external sensible objects, or about the internal operations of our mind perceived and reflected on by ourselves, is that which supplies our understanding with all of the materials of thinking. These two are the foundations of knowledge from whence all of the ideas we had, or do naturally have, do spring. (Locke, 1690/1959, Vol. 1, pp. 121–122)

Having cleared the decks—refuted the existence of innate ideas—Locke goes on to examine what ideas furnish the cabinet, are written on the blackboard, on the (initially blank) slate. He finds that they are of two kinds: ideas of sensation and ideas of reflection. The two are distinguished by their degree of clarity, immediacy, and force. Either can be simple or complex, unitary or composite. Ideas of sense (sensation) come from the external world through the senses. The cabinet is furnished, the blank slate is written upon, by, and only by, sense experience. I have the idea of *red*, I have it by seeing red. That is a simple idea of sensation. If I see something is red and round, that is a complex idea of sense. It is in my mind because it came from the external world by means of vision, a sensory mode. Ideas of sense can be highly complex, but this doesn't change their origin. Clearly, Locke's use of the word *idea* differs from Plato's. For Plato, ideas are archetypes—universals known only through ideation; through thought, not through the senses. The ontological status of Platonic ideas is problematic, but they are certainly real, in fact the only really real reality, for Plato. Perhaps Plato's *forms*, another word he uses for *archetypes*, are, in fact, ideas in the mind of God. At least his Christian interpreters have so viewed the Platonic ideas. Not so for Locke; when he says ideas, he means just that, ideas: sensations, perceptions, and so forth in the minds of men, in the Understanding. Ideas can also arise from reflection on the operations of the mind—by introspection. These Locke calls *ideas of reflection*, which arise from the *internal sense*, an organ of perception just as much as the eye or the ear. Ideas of reflection too can be simple or complex. Both ideas of sense and ideas of reflection are thoughts. Ideas of reflection are insights into the operation of the mind. The *Essay* itself is a complex idea of reflection. As Locke's successor David Hume put it, all knowledge concerns either matters of fact (ideas of sensation) or relations of ideas (ideas of reflection). These are the only sources of our knowledge. Having completed the critical task of the *Essay*, Locke goes on to examine the status of abstract ideas, of concepts, and concludes that they are generalizations from particulars. In this respect he is a modern nominalist. (In medieval philosophy, those who held that concepts, like Plato's forms or ideas, existed apart from the particulars that embodied them, were called *realists*, and those who held that general terms were but names for collections of particulars [*cat* was but a name for *Tabby, Felix*, etc.] and for their commonalities were called *nominalists*.)

This brings us to Locke's discussion of identity. *Identity* is an abstract term, a concept. Locke feels certain that he has accounted for conceptual knowledge as abstraction from ideas of sense and ideas of reflection. Identity is a complex idea of reflection. He goes on to give an account of this particular idea of reflection and, in so doing, arrives at the concept of personal identity, which is his version of the self. In doing so, he is one of the first to explicitly recognize and acknowledge the problematical nature of personal identity, of the self. I realize that personal identity and self are not necessarily identical, but there is certainly a close relation-

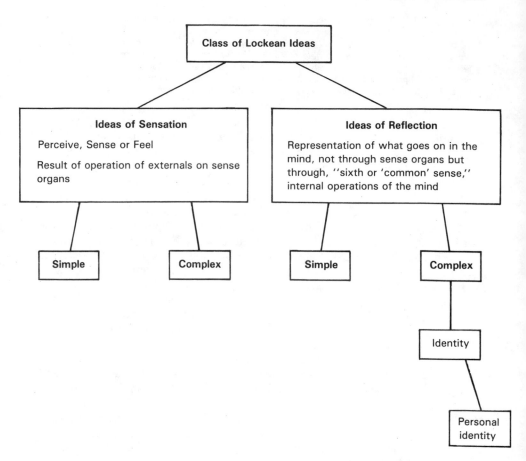

ship between the two. To have a self is to have an identity, although selfhood may entail more than identity. In any case, Locke's discussion is primarily of personal identity.

The concept of personal identity entails two distinct notions: one's identity as something particular—as a man or woman, as an artist or scientist, or as a child or an adult—and one's identity as being the same person, as having continuity, ongoingness, and relatedness to past states of being. Locke is interested in the second notion of identity and doesn't deal with the particulars of personal identity or with the relationship between these particulars and one's more global sense of sameness, of identity. You may ask, Does the Cartesian self have identity? The Cartesian self is consciousness, and Descartes doesn't raise the question of the sameness of that consciousness across time. It is Locke who first raises that question.

Locke recognizes four kinds or types of identity. The first is logical identity. A is A. This he takes from Aristotle's logic. A thing is identical with itself and with no other, and so is a thought. The second kind of identity is the identity of an object continuing through time, for example, a stone seen today and seen tomorrow is the same stone. It endures, and this is its identity. The third kind of identity is the identity of organization, exemplified by plants and animals. Their identity is organic, consisting of the organization and the relationship of their parts, which remains the same, although the constituents of those parts are in constant flux. Their atoms change, but the relationships of the succeeding atoms to each other do not change. The fourth kind of identity is personal identity. As I noted above, the very word *self* comes from the Anglo-Saxon word used for *same*. Since *self* means "same," the concept of personal identity is implicit in the concept of self. To have a self is to be the same. Of course, our experience of ourselves is as both continuous and discontinuous, as both unitary and composite, as both consistent and inconsistent, and as both cohesive and fragmented. Any theory of the self, if it is to be convincing, must account for both sides of these antinomies of the self. Locke is aware of this and struggles, not particularly successfully, to do so. This is hardly surprising since he was the first to clearly see and delineate these difficulties.

According to Locke, personal identity, the self, is the *I* that accompanies all consciousness. Intuition of our existence accompanies every thought. I accompany every thought. We have identity (i.e., are self-identical) in several senses. One is as an organism, as creatures whose material constituents change, but whose relations of parts—organization—does not change. Of course, logically we are we, A is A, at any given moment. When we see, hear, smell, or reflect, we know that we do so; our knowing it is data, just as much as the sensation itself, and is inseparable from it. Self-consciousness necessarily accompanies consciousness. Perceptions perish as they occur; indeed, Locke defines time as "perpetual perishing" (1690/1959, p. 265). Yet I am also aware of continuity in time. Identity, a sense of self, depends on consciousness and memory and on the self-consciousness that is concomitant with each idea, and with the memory of consciousness in the past. Our identity is not disturbed by breaks in consciousness. I also exist as a body, as a person, and as an immaterial substance that underlies the vicissitudes of time, but these do not constitute my identity. Rather, Locke says that memory bridges gaps in consciousness, and it is my memory of being the same person that is the basis of my personal identity. So it is either immediate self-consciousness or memory of a similar self-consciousness in the past that leads me to believe that I endure, that I have continuity in time, and that I am the same self now as I was in an earlier stage of my life. Breaks in consciousness don't disturb the sense of enduring personal identity because memory bridges them.

For our purpose, Locke has done several important things in his discussion of personal identity and of the self. First, he has connected the consciousness of self with the body and its sensations. Personal identity consists of the enduring organization of one's organism as well as in self-consciousness. So we are no longer in Descartes's world in which the *cogito*—the self—is pure thought without material existence, since the realm of extension in which matter exists and the realm of thought in which I exist are dichotomous. For Locke the "withness of the body" is intrinsic; my sensations and my feelings are now part of myself, and are not ethereal, detached, floating, and unanchored, as they are in the Cartesian self.

Next Locke asserts that we are always aware, or at least potentially aware, of our selfhood. He asserts this as a matter of fact, not as a conclusion of thought. For him self-consciousness is a datum, originating in what he calls the common sense, or the sixth sense, which gives us information about what happens in us just as the five senses give us information about what is happening outside of us. Third, he recognizes that our continuity as persons, as selves, is problematical, and not a given. Since we are not always conscious, and self for Locke is always conscious, there are discontinuities in our experience as self. These are bridged by memory. In a sense, our knowledge of the sameness of the self is no different from our knowledge of the sameness of the stone. Both depend on memory and on comparison to establish the identity of yesterday's stone with today's and of yesterday's self with today's. Locke is aware of the possibilities of unconscious ideation, but he doesn't want to allow it for two reasons: first, it might be a back door for reintroduction of innate ideas, and second, it isn't empirical, because for him an unconscious idea is neither an idea of sense nor an idea of reflection, the only sources of knowledge. Locke's criticism of the unconscious as a notion without epistemological foundation is a recurrent one in the history of thought. Memory, of course, consists of stored ideas that are not necessarily in awareness. The unconscious, in this sense, Locke does admit into his system. The data stored in Locke's memory is what Freud called preconscious rather than dynamically unconscious; that is, the contents of memory can be made conscious and used in mental operations such as comparison by an effort of will or attention; they are not repressed, nor are they unavailable in principle.

Consciousness is a tricky, complex concept. Its meanings include simple awareness, awareness of the display of sensa, awareness that it is I who am aware, and awareness of some of the specificity of the I who am aware. When Locke is talking about consciousness, he is usually talking about the awareness that it is I who am aware, which he calls self-consciousness. But he doesn't make the distinctions in the meaning of consciousness that I do, and his meaning is not always clear.

Locke is aware of the difficulties posed by such phenomena as multiple personalities and loss of consciousness in amnesia, and he worries them but fails to solve the dilemmas they cause for any theory of the self. Locke solves some of the problems of sameness within discontinuity through the concept of substance, of an underlying substrate to which, or in which, ideas occur. But his account of personal identity is independent of any notion of substance. Whether we are one or more than one substance is an empirically unanswerable question for Locke so he drops it and turns to consciousness and memory, not enduring underlying substance, to account for our idea of personal identity. Characteristically, Locke's discussion is highly practical. He is concerned with such questions as legal responsibility, and accountability in the afterlife, when he talks about our many selves and the continuity of personal identity. Should a man be held responsible, in this life and the next, for acts committed when he wasn't himself? asks Locke. He decides not. In Locke's account of the role of memory in establishing the continuity of personal identity through comparison and the judgment of identity, his inert *tabula rasa*, his passive cabinet of the mind, becomes highly active. Here the operations of the mind approximate what the psychoanalysts would call the "synthetic functions of the ego."

C. Fred Alford (1991), writing from the point of view of a political theorist, sees the Lockeian self very differently. Alford is interested in the relation of the Lockeian self to property, a concept central to Locke's political philosophy, seeing property as a self-object, as an extension and constituent of self. This is a psychoanalytic notion to which we will return.

To sum up, Locke understands the self in at least two ways: as the enduring organization and structure that remains through development and change in the material constituents of the body and as the self-consciousness that accompanies every idea and that memory allows us to establish as the same self-consciousness that accompanied our previous ideas. It is a self that is active, in part given, and in part created through thought, the operations of the mind. It is pattern and perception, relation of parts and ideas of reflection. It also has aspects that Locke knows he cannot account for.

For Locke, self in the sense of self-consciousness is a given, an idea of sensation or reflection, as the case may be. It is a matter of fact, in the same sense that "the pencil that I am now writing with is hard" is also a matter of fact. Not so for our next theorist of self, Locke's successor David Hume. Hume's main contribution to the theory of self is the intuition that there isn't any. He takes Locke's claim, that awareness of self is a given, seriously, and looks for it. He says that he can't find it; therefore, if that is what the self is, then self is an illusion.

3

David Hume: The Self as Illusion

David Hume (1711–1776) is a fascinating figure in the history of thought. Usually classified as a skeptic, he spent little time in philosophy, abandoning it at the age of 29 in the belief that he had said what he had to say about its problems and questions. He thought he had found philosophical truth. He spent the rest of his life writing the history of England from a Tory point of view and a more popular account of his philosophy. The son of a lawyer who wished him to be the same, Hume tried business, diplomacy, and then became the librarian of the University of Edinburgh Law School. His simplified, popular account of his philosophy did indeed sell much better, but it did not bring him the recognition or financial reward he craved.

Philosophy in the 18th century was not written for a specialized academic audience. The reign of the professors came later. Hume, like many of his contemporaries, was a gentleman scholar who wrote for an educated lay audience. Except for lacking the means, he was typical of the type. Hume supplemented his resources with civil service and diplomatic and academic pursuits. Being a Scot, Hume was somewhat of an outsider in English society, and perhaps his skepticism in intellectual matters bears some relationship to the natural skepticism of a provincial toward the mores and conventions of the capital, although Hume was a conservative in politics. Be this as it may, Hume was influenced by the atmosphere of the University of Edinburgh, particularly by the thought of his friend, the great economist Adam Smith. What Hume was skeptical about was the claims of reason.

Hume shared and exemplified the 18th-century distrust of "enthusiasm." Enthusiasm had led to dissension, persecution, and civil war. The 18th century would have none of it. I find this skepticism admirable in politics and religion, but problematic when applied to our topic, the self. Hume embodies a contradiction, or at least a deep conflict, between the distrust of enthusiasm—passionately held convictions—and the recognition of the power of emotion (which he calls sentiment) in human life. Indeed, this belief in the primacy of the passions is one of the cornerstones of his philosophy. There is also a conflict between his epistemological skepticism, his questioning of the grounds of our belief that we really know what we think we know, and his intellectual ambitions, which are nothing less than to put what we would call social science, or perhaps psychology, on as firm a basis as Newtonian physics, by discovering the general laws that regulate human thought and action.

Hume's temperament was congruent with his philosophizing. He wrote the following self-obituary, or "funeral oration" as he called it, of himself during his final illness. It is remarkably calm and dispassionate for a man on his deathbed.

To conclude historically with my own character I am, or rather was (and that is the style I must use when speaking of myself which emboldens me the more to speak my sentiments), I was I say a man of mild disposition, of command of temper, of an open, social and cheerful humor, capable of detachment but little susceptible to enmity, and of great moderation in all my passions. Even my love of literary fame, my ruling passion, never soured my temper, not withstanding my frequent disappointments. My company was not unacceptable to the young and careless as well as to the studious and the literary; and as I took a particular pleasure in the company of modest women, I had no reason to be displeased with the reception I met with from them. In a word though most men, otherwise eminent, have found reason to complain of calumny, I never was touched, or even attacked by her baleful tooth; and though I wantonly exposed myself to the rage of both civil and religious factions, they seem to be disarmed in my behalf of their wonted fury. (Hume, 1775/1911a, p. viii)

To me, Hume sounds like Henry Higgins here: contemplative, above it all, a bit silly, except he is, here, facing death with aplomb and aristocratic calm.

Hume set out to apply the experimental method of reasoning to human affairs, to parallel Newton's experimental method. As the heir of the 17th-century scientific revolution and of the empiricism of Locke, Hume was, like Freud and Marx after him, looking for extremely general truths about human beings. He set out to do for humanistic study—social science—what Newton had done for physical science. Being a strict empiricist, he did this by examining how the mind works. Hume was not actually as empirical as he thought, and clearly some of what he thought he saw when he examined the operation of the mind was more determined by a priori ideas or assumptions than by observation. In short, his psychology doesn't really stand up, not because his method is too empirical, but because it is not empirical enough. Be this as it may, what Hume thought he observed as mental contents were actually *perceptions*. He also calls them *objects of the mind*. Percepts are atomistic. They are discrete. Percepts are not connected to each other. They are essentially sensations—sensations such as sounds, colors, pressures, tastes, odors, and other tactile quallae. Each is an entity in itself, experienced as itself. Hume divided perceptions into two classes: impressions and ideas. Hume's impressions are much like Locke's ideas of sensation. They are mental contents. Locke divides ideas into ideas of sensation and ideas of reflection. Hume divides objects of the mind (perceptions) into impressions and ideas.

The impressions are felt or experienced. They are of two kinds: (a) impressions of sensations that, like Locke's ideas of sensation, are the result of the external world acting on the sense organs and (b) impressions of reflection, which are memories and fantasies. Hume had difficulty distinguishing the two—not in prac-

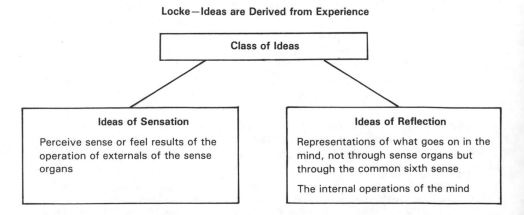

Locke—Ideas are Derived from Experience

Class of Ideas	
Ideas of Sensation Perceive sense or feel results of the operation of externals of the sense organs	**Ideas of Reflection** Representations of what goes on in the mind, not through sense organs but through the common sixth sense The internal operations of the mind

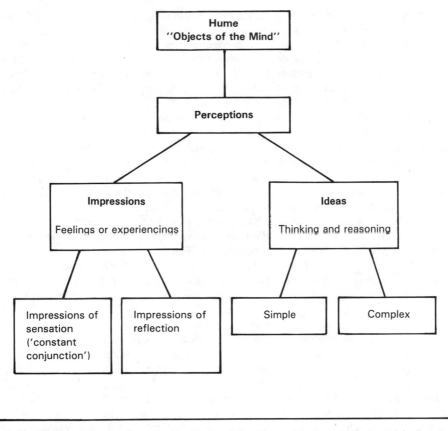

Hume
"Objects of the Mind"

Perceptions

Impressions	Ideas
Feelings or experiencings	Thinking and reasoning

| Impressions of sensation ('constant conjunction') | Impressions of reflection | Simple | Complex |

Judgments—aesthetic, moral, and intellectual are the results of sentiments and feelings.

tice, but in theory—and finally fell back on vividness and immediacy to distinguish impressions of external reality (sensations) from impressions of reflection. The issue here is reality testing, and Hume's differential doesn't really work. Descartes's demon could be fooling him, and some sensations are faint while some memories are vivid and intense. In the *Treatise* (1738/1911b) Hume recognizes this and has recourse to impressions of sensations carrying their own labels; they just feel different than ideas of reflection. From a logical standpoint this is obviously unsatisfactory. However, from Hume's point of view this isn't too important. He believes that the claims of reason are highly inflated and the motive of his philosophizing is to expose the fragility and limitations of human reason. He is skeptical not because he doesn't believe that we have practical knowledge sufficient for living everyday life, but because he distrusts the claims of the philosophers. He wants to be reasonable rather than rational, and in the final analysis relies on sentiment and custom to validate a great deal. It is feeling and sentiment that determine human action. Belief is "nothing but a more vivid and intense conception of any idea." It is a difference in feeling. He goes on to say, "Reason is . . . the slave of the passions, and never pretends to any other office than to serve and obey them" (1738/1911b, p. 12). Here Hume is again anticipating Freud, not only in reaching for extremely general principles on which to found a science of human behavior, but, more saliently, in demonstrating how thin a reed is reason and how little it determines our actions—how little influence it really has over human life. Hume demonstrates this with his epistemological analysis, and Freud does it through clinical analysis; both men use their respective analyses to build a structural theory of the workings of the human mind. In Descartes's schema man was free, free to will what he wanted—most desirably the rational—while nature was mechanistic. Not so for Hume, who wants a science of man that in the end is just as mechanistic as Descartes's nature. Hume's science of man discredits man as the "rational animal." Hume does this by looking at the origin of our beliefs and by examining their foundation in reason. Generally speaking, Hume finds that the alleged foundation in reason is wanting and falls back on the genesis of ideas and beliefs in feelings, sentiments, and customs.

For Hume, perceptions include ideas as well as impressions. Hume's ideas are unlike either Locke's or Plato's; they are neither the general class of mental contents (Locke) nor the archetypes of particulars (Plato), but rather are mental operations. Ideas are both the objects of and constituents of our thinking and reasoning. They are not psychological, like Locke's ideas of reflection, but logical. Ideas are relations for Hume. Mathematical proofs are the purest case of the Humeian idea. Mathematical ideas have relations to each other. Once we know the meaning of addition and the meaning of number, we know that $2 + 2 = 4$. We know it by reasoning about the relation of (here, mathematical) ideas.

Hume now has his epistemological schema. There are impressions of sensation, impressions of reflection, and ideas. These are the only sources of human knowledge. He is, if anything, even more radically empirical than Locke. Sensations and impressions are not really connected; they are atoms of experience. In his famous analysis of causality, Hume says that we perceive no "real" connections between impressions; rather, we infer connections because in the past the impressions have always been in "constant conjunction." However, there is absolutely no rational reason to believe that this will be the case in the future. We never perceive the connection between impressions.

> There is nothing in any object, considered in itself, which can afford us a reason for drawing a conclusion beyond it; so that even after the observation of the frequent or constant conjunction of objects, we have no reason to draw any inference concerning any object beyond those of which we have had experience. (1738/1911b, p. 139)

He goes on to say,

> Whenever any individual of any species of objects is found by experience to be constantly united with an individual of another species, the appearance of any new individuals of either species naturally conveys the thought of its usual attendant. (Hume, 1738/1911b, p. 93)

Observation of constant conjunctions leads to "unity in the imagination" (1738/1911b, p. 93). Hume now has his equivalent of Newton's Gravitation. The association of ideas is the force that relates atomistic impressions. They are associated by constant conjunction, habit, and custom. The objects of the mind, impressions, come from the outside, from the memory, or from the imagination, which can form complex ideas à la Locke, and are related, operated on, by the laws of association. Hardly a rational procedure or a rational notion of the working of the mind. In working with ideas, the mind is somewhat more rational, but it can only determine the relationships among its own ideas (concepts), which have no intrinsic application to the world (to external reality). Perceptions (atoms) and association (force) constitute our mental life, along with conceptual reasoning, which is essentially tautological (i.e., only makes explicit inherent meanings). Now Hume has his psychology based on principles of great generality.

Hume has another model for science, for his psychology, besides Newton. That he found in the writings of his friend and later colleague at the University of Edinburgh, Adam Smith. Adam Smith, the first of the classical economists, viewed man as atomistic. In his economic function, each man acts in his own self-interest and tries to maximize his profit. This is admittedly a far more "rational" account of man than Hume's. But is it? Is self-interest rational? In a sense, yes, but not in another sense, because it is driven by passion. In that sense, Smith's view of man is rationally irrational, just as Hume says reason is the slave of the passions. Furthermore, Smith has his gravitational force, which he calls the "invisible hand." This hand is the "market" and its laws. The invisible hand somehow "rationalizes" the atomistic, solipsistic, nonsocially motivated economic life of each isolate, so that the seemingly discordant individual notes turn out to be felicitously harmonious. The result is maximum productivity that accrues to the general good. Individualism is, in the final analysis, socially beneficent through the efforts of the invisible hand. Finally, Adam Smith theorizes about the specialization of labor—again an isolating, atomistic activity in which the individual laborer never completes the gestalt, never sees the product as a whole—as a way to maximize productivity. Each turn of the screw on the primitive production lines of the 18th century is an atom of economic productive reality, however fragmenting and alienating such labor may be, and somehow the atoms make a bigger pie. Whatever one may think of Smith's sweeping analysis of, and apology for, capitalism (he was not unaware of the inequities inherent in it), there is clearly some connection between the social forces that he both depicts and rationalizes in his theory and Hume's view of the human mind and its operations. The association of ideas is not only Hume's force of gravitation; it is his invisible hand. The economic activity of the medieval guild member is clearly different from the economic activity of a factory production worker, and so are the accounts of human nature that emerge from the two disparate social-economic schemes. One is organic, with intense connectiveness, while the other is atomistic and alienated, with no intrinsic connection between workers, just as there is no intrinsic connection between Hume's impressions. Clearly, there is a reciprocal relationship between ideology (including philosophy) and social reality. Each determines, at least in part, the other. Although it is true that Adam Smith did not publish his masterpiece, *The Wealth of Nations* (Smith, 1776/1936), until 1776, the year of Hume's death, the two men knew each other, and Hume must have been conversant with Smith's ideas. Ultimately, one could view Hume's epistemology and Smith's economics as reflections of the same social, intellectual, and economic conditions—as part of the same Zeitgeist.

Hume was nothing if not consistent. He drew the logical conclusion from his philosophizing, his epistemology, and wrote, "Does a book contain matters of fact or reasoning about the relation of ideas. If not, consign it to flames."

This brings us to Hume's analysis of the self. Given his skepticism and his analysis of experience as discontinuous, it is hardly surprising that the self does not fare very well in Hume's hands. For him, there are only two ways that we could know the self, as an impression (i.e., as a datum of experience) or as a relation of ideas. Clearly that self is not a relation of ideas, so it is either experiential (i.e., an impression of sensation or of reflection) or unknowable. It is logically possible that the self could exist, but that we could not know it. Hume's is an epistemological, not an ontological, skepticism; that is, his doubts are about human nature, the potentiality of the human mind for the acquisition of rational knowledge, not about the existence of things themselves. For Hume, however, this isn't a real issue; he is interested in what we can know, not in what we cannot know. Since Hume implicitly eliminates the self as a relation of ideas, he is left to determine if we have an impression of the self. He does this so succinctly and precisely that I will let him speak for himself:

> For my part, when I enter most intimately into what I call myself I always stumble on some particular perception or another, of heat or cold, light or shade, love or hatred, pain or pleasure. I can never catch myself at any time without a perception, I can never observe anything but the perception. When my perceptions are removed for any time as by sound sleep, so long am I insensible of myself, can I truly be said not to exist. . . .
>
> I may venture to affirm to the rest of mankind that they are nothing but a bundle or collection of different perceptions, which exceed each other with an incredible rapidity, and are in perpetual flux and movement. . . .
>
> The mind is a kind of theater, where several perceptions successively make their appearance; pass, repass, glide away, mingle in an infinite variety of postures and situations. . . . The comparison of the theater must not mislead us. There are the successive perceptions only, that constitute the mind; nor have we the most distant notion of the place where these scenes are represented, or of the materials of which it is composed. . . .
>
> Memory alone acquaints us with the continuance and extent of this succession of perceptions, . . . it is to be considered, the source of personal identity . . . [memory gives us], that chain of causes and effects, which constitute our self or person which [we] extend and fill in the gaps. (Hume, 1738/1911b, p. 238)

Hume is indeed incisive. Are you merely a bundle of perceptions? Is all flux and flow like Locke's time as perpetually perishing? Hume says look and see what you find. It is an empirical test. Can you find yourself? Is the mind (here, the self) a show taking place in a theater that doesn't exist, as in Hume's trenchant metaphor? If Hume is right, the self is an illusion, at least from an epistemological point of view. If there is a self, we can't know that there is one, and for all practical purposes Hume has decimated the self. The Humeian self has been called a "bundle self": the self as a bundle of impressions. There is no cord holding the bundle together, so there is no self but the perceptions themselves, and this is no self at all. What are we to conclude from this? In a little more than 100 years, we have gone from Descartes's notion of the self as thinker, as cogitator, as the one self-evident, indubitable reality to Hume's annihilation of the possibility of knowing the self. Has Hume merely slain a late scholasticism, a residual from medieval philosophizing, the self as substance, as the putty in which experience inheres or adheres? I don't think so; I believe that Hume has done more than slain a chimera of interest only to technical philosophers of a certain persuasion. That would be interesting, but essentially a move in a Mandarin game. Rather, Hume is clearly stating that we have no experience of a self. We have experiences, but no experience of the experiencer of these experiences. There is something existential about Hume's conclusions; there is an eeriness to the theater that doesn't exist that is the locus of my experience. This is more than an academic game; it is a reassessment of what it means to be human.

Hume doesn't mean to say that there is no experience of personal identity, but that is something different than a substantial self. By personal identity, Hume doesn't have anything arcane in mind, simply the subjective experience, the idea (of reflection), that we are the same, that we have continuity over time. In this he follows Locke; when he introspects, he doesn't find a self, but he does find the "idea" of personal identity. He then asks what is the source of this idea, and answers that it is memory alone that gives us a sense of personal identity. We extend ourselves forward in imagination and use imagination to fill in the gaps in past experience. Essentially we create a continuity that doesn't exist in the impressions themselves and consolidate a sense of identity—the closest Hume comes to allowing us a self. It is resemblance, contiguity, and causation (or the illusion of it) that are the raw materials that memory (and imagination) use to build a sense of ongoingness, of continuity, and of identity. This is strikingly similar to the function of feeling, sentiment, and habit, rather than reason or experience, in generating our expectations of order, causality, and ongoingness in the external world. In the end, both self and world, or at least our belief in them, are irrational (i.e., not based on reason or given in experience). For Hume, I, although I don't exist, am constituted, insofar as I am constituted, by the activity of my memory. Personal identity is, for Hume, the result of what a psychoanalyst would call the synthetic function of the ego. The self is illusion; identity is a construct.

Hume is hard to refute. When you introspect, do you find yourself, or at least a self? I don't. So my contention that I do have a self either is erroneous or has some other basis. Of course, when I introspect, I do not find that my perceptions are individual atoms, so perhaps Hume is empirically wrong; the interconnectedness is a given, or is at least more of a given than Hume would allow. Be that as it may, it is hard to read Hume's analysis of the notion of the self without feeling yourself (pardon the expression) disappearing.

Hume's analysis of the self brings to mind the story of the philosopher and the theologian, with Hume playing the role of the philosopher and those who uphold the substantiality of the self, particularly of the self as substance, as a substrate of experience, as the theologian. The two esteemed gentlemen are engaged in debate. The theologian says to the philosopher, "You are like a blind man looking for a black cat that isn't there in a coal bin at midnight." "Agreed," says the philosopher, "but you would have found it." Hume would rather grope in the dark and fail to find the cat than demonstrate under the theologian's illumination that the cat, who really isn't there, is there: skeptic versus believer, with the skeptic paradoxically upholding the value of the truth, no matter how disconcerting. Hume is one of those modern thinkers who has been described as a "dark enlightener." The dark enlighteners are all those who expose the futility and illusionary qualities of our most cherished beliefs. Kant, on his critical side; Nietzsche, Marx, and Freud also belong to the ranks of the dark illuminators.

Hume's elimination of self as experience has been historically influential. The logical positivists, the contemporary heirs of the empirical tradition, agree with Hume that the self is illusion. Some of them have described the self as a "grammatical fiction" arising from mistaking the grammatical subject, the *I*, for an existent. This has reverberations in the ideologies of the modern collectivities. It is ironic that one spin-off of the individualistic notions of the 18th century, already paradoxical in Hume, has been the obviation of the self as individual existence in those collectivities. In Arthur Koestler's (1941) novel *Darkness at Noon*, a story about the Russian purge trials, the protagonist, Rubashov, is an idealist who sees himself as existing only to actualize the historical mission of the Party. He regards himself as a grammatical fiction, the *ontos on*, the real reality being history, the Party, and the masses. In the course of the novel, he is destroyed by the Party to which he has given his life and, in the course of his humiliation and destruction, discovers that that grammatical fiction, himself, is indeed real. Koestler's novel is poignant. Rubashov pleads guilty as a last contribution to the Party and to history. His self-immolation is partly motivated by guilt; he has destroyed many grammatical fictions in the course of his career in the Party. Ironically, his final repudiation of that self-immolation, his discovery that the grammatical fiction is real, coincides with his physical destruction by the regime in which he tried to submerge his egoism and individuality. He regains his individuality just as he loses his life.

Hume certainly did not intend to justify the destruction of the individual by collectivities, but ideas have consequences, and it is perhaps no accident that the century that has been so taken with Hume's style of philosophical analysis, our own, should have produced such extraacademic interpretations of the self as a grammatical fiction, subservient to the aims of the state. I say this knowing that Hume's intellectual heirs are, for the most part, liberal and humanistic in their politics and ethics. Nevertheless, there seems to me to be a connection between proofs that the self doesn't exist and ideologies that act on that proof.

4

Immanuel Kant:
The Self as Transcendental Unity

Immanuel Kant (1724–1804) is simultaneously one of the most difficult and one of the most intriguing and stimulating of philosophers. He is also one of the most human. Kant was the son of a poor saddle maker. His family had emigrated from Scotland to East Prussia several generations before Kant's birth. He grew up and lived almost all of his life in Königsberg, a member of the Hanseatic League, a group of Baltic seaports important in commerce from the Middle Ages on. Königsberg was not only a lively commercial center, it was also a university town. For a relatively small place, it was cosmopolitan and had a good-sized educated class. The adult Kant's friends included resident English businessmen and other representatives from the world beyond the flat plains of East Prussia. Kant's family were Pietists. The Pietists were a Protestant denomination that emphasized simplicity, moral duty, and inwardness: spirituality rather than ritual. The Pietists were humanistic, intense, peaceful, and loving, at least in their ideals and frequently in their practice. They could also be stiflingly rigid and self-righteous. Kant wrote that Königsberg was a town in which one could travel without traveling. In his mature theory of the mind, Kant held that all experience was filtered through the apparatuses of the mind, much as the experience of the world had to pass through Königsberg. Kant was educated at the local school and continued at the university where he studied philosophy and science. After graduation, he spent several years as a tutor—the only time he left his native town. He returned to his alma mater as a lecturer at age 30, and remained there for the rest of his life. His academic advance was slow, and he suffered from poverty. He finally became a full professor in his late 40s. Kant was a man of extraordinarily regular habits: the people of the town were said to set their watches by his daily walk. One day Kant didn't emerge from his house at the usual time. All Königsberg was aghast. Kant didn't take his walk that day because he was reading Rousseau's *Emile*. Kant was sympathetic toward the French Revolution, at least before the Terror, and Jean Jacques Rousseau was his favorite author.

Kant was a liberal in politics and religion. Kant's values, ethics, and sensibilities were congruent with the ideals of the anticlerical, antiauthoritarian principles of the European Enlightenment, the great 18th-century intellectual revolution that planted the seeds of tolerance, democracy, reasonableness, and liberalism, which he reflected, embodied, and in part created. His inwardness and moral seriousness were derived from tradition, from his Pietist upbringing, while his critical, iconoclastic, probing philosophizing was derived from the contemporary and forward ethos of the Enlightenment. For all his solitary scholarliness, Kant was an urbane man who enjoyed socializing with the Königsberg merchant community. He is said to have twice considered proposing, but each time tarried so long that the lady married another, and he remained a lifelong bachelor. He was a popular and lively lecturer. His presentations were both humorous and clear, but the same cannot be said for his philosophical writings, which are often turgid, ponderous, and academic. Late in his life Kant's views on religion got him into difficulties with the Prussian authorities, and he agreed to write no more on that topic. Kant's tolerance was reflected in his friendship with the German Jewish Enlightenment thinker, Moses Mendelssohn. Mendelssohn was snubbed by as great a man as Goethe because of his Jewishness, but not by Kant. Kant lectured on many subjects: physical geography, meteorology, pedagogy, and physics, as well as metaphysics and logic. His early writings were mostly scientific, and although imaginative and often prescient, they are no longer of much interest. In philosophy, he was a follower of Christian Wolfe, a disciple of Leibniz, who taught a dogmatic, almost scholastic (in the sense of medieval scholasticism) rationalism that made what Kant would later call "uncritical" claims for the ability of reason alone to discover truth, especially metaphysical truth (truth about the ultimate nature of things). Then Kant read Hume, who remained second only to Rousseau as his favorite author, and was "awakened from my dogmatic slumbers." A great deal of Kant's philosophizing is an attempt to refute Hume's skepticism about the possibilities of veridical knowledge. Hume, as we have seen, demolished the rational foundations of causality and the belief in the existence of the substantive self. Once having read Hume, Kant couldn't return to Wolfian dogmatic rationalism, but neither could he accept Hume's refutation of the possibilities of scientific knowledge. Kant's answer was his "critical philosophy," which established, at least so he thought, what could and could not be known and how it was known by the human mind. Thus, the main thrust of Kant's technical philosophizing was epistemological. He was looking at both the limits of, and the possibilities of, human knowledge, in the spirit of, but from a different vantage point than, Locke. In the course of his critical epistemological inquiries, he had important, novel things to say about the nature of the self. Before we can understand his understanding of the self, we need to understand something of his view of the mind and how it works.

The first of Kant's critical works to reflect his post-Humeian awakening from his dogmatic slumbers was his *Critique of Pure Reason* (1781/1990). Kant was disappointed by its reception. Its style is so forbidding that few read, and fewer understood, it. Kant revised it, and also wrote a sort of popularization of it: his *Prolegomena to any Future Metaphysics that Will Be Able to Present Itself as a Science* (1783/1953). We are about to see what Kant had to say about mind and about self in his first *Critique*. He followed the first critique with the *Critique of Pure Practical Reason* (1786/1949a), a treatise on the possibility of moral knowledge; the *Critique of Judgement* (1793/1952), a work on aesthetics; *Religion Within the Limits of Reason Alone* (1793/1949b), which got him in trouble with the authorities; and *Perpetual Peace* (1795/1986), in which he proposed a world federation based on the principles of the Enlightenment.

The purpose of the *Critique of Pure Reason* is to determine how science is possible. Clearly science was successful; it did work in the sense of generating predictions that were verifiable and verified. Yet Hume had shown that there is no rational ground to believe that any antecedent entailed any consequence, that there were any causal connections in nature. As we have seen, Hume thought that he had demonstrated that just as there are no intrinsic connections between the sequential presentation of impressions and ideas in the theater that doesn't exist, which is our mind, there is no intrinsic connectiveness, no substantive self, in the recipient of those representations. Kant realized that Hume's destructive analysis vitiated the possibility of scientific knowledge based on reason and replaced it with habit, custom, and sentiment. This Kant found unacceptable. That wasn't science, that was faith; yet the science of the 17th and 18th centuries had solid accomplishments that metaphysics had to account for. Physics did exist, yet clearly could not on Hume's premises, so Kant asked, How is physics possible? Further, Kant saw that Humeian epistemology not only made science impossible, it also rendered experience itself inexplicable. For Kant, metaphysics described the requirements for any possible experience. In this sense the *Critique of Pure Reason* is metaphysical. Metaphysics cannot, however, describe what cannot be experienced by the senses (e.g., God, immortality, freedom, or morality), although there may be other reasons to believe in them. That is why Kant's metaphysics is critical: it describes only the conditions necessary for experience; it doesn't, unlike traditional, precritical metaphysics, say anything about what cannot be experienced. Kant's metaphysics is *transcendental*, to use his technical term, in the sense that it transcends, is a condition of, is logically but not necessarily temporally, prior to any possible experience. Kant starts by analyzing Hume's categories of judgment. To Hume, all judgments (knowledge) are either matters of fact (e.g., the table is red) or relations of ideas (e.g., 2 + 2 = 4). The first is empirical; the second, logical. Matters of fact are a posteriori, after experience. Relations of ideas are a priori; they do not depend on experience, although they are elicited by it and perhaps in some sense derived from it. Matters of fact are synthetic: they synthesize, or make connections, as between table and redness. Relations of ideas are analytic in the technical sense that their conclusions are contained in their premises. They merely elucidate our concepts. Logically, though not necessarily psychologically, they tell us nothing new. Analytic judgments also tell us something about the meaning of our concepts—in this example, about the meanings of addition, number, and equality. However, given these meanings, the conclusion is entailed in the premises. If the calculations in our mathematical example were highly complicated, the conclusion would tell us something we didn't know before (i.e., it would be psychologically novel), but would nevertheless be entailed in its premises and in that sense would not tell us anything that was not "contained" in the left side of the equation. As we will see, Kant's analysis of intellectual judgment—or, if you want to depsychologize the argument (i.e., move it from the analysis of thought to the analysis of language) of propositions—is considerably more complex than Hume's. It has two dimensions: analytic-synthetic and a priori-a posteriori (empirical). This makes it possible for Kant to consider the antecedents of, logic of, and truth value of four kinds of judgment:

Analytic a priori   ~~Analytic a posteriori~~
Synthetic a priori   Synthetic a posteriori

I have put a line through analytic a posteriori because it is self-contradictory: in analytic propositions a conclusion is entailed in the premises, for example, tall men are tall, and no experience is necessary to confirm this. You don't have to look at tall men to confirm that tall men are tall. That leaves three classes of judgment. The analytic a priori is no problem. By definition analytic judgments are a priori. They tell us nothing new about the world; they only spin out the meanings inherent in our concepts. They are relations of ideas. In 20th-century terminology, they are tautological. The synthetic a posteriori also presents Kant with no problem. There is no way to determine whether or not a cat is gray except to look at it; such knowledge about the state of affairs in the world is never given a priori. As we shall see, Kant doesn't have Hume's difficulties with the connectedness of impressions, but even Hume would not have problems with "the cat is gray" as long as the necessity of its grayness is not part of our claim to such knowledge. The real problem comes with the category of synthetic a priori judgments. When Hume says (of a book), "Does it contain matters of fact or reasoning about the relationship of ideas? If not consign it to the flames," he is eliminating the possibility of the synthetic a priori. Kant (at least the critical Kant) also wants to demonstrate that the claims of the old style metaphysics—with their obscurity, dogmatism, and implicit, when not explicit, support for authoritarianism of various stripes—are excessive and without foundation, but he believes that Hume has thrown out the baby with the bath water and that logic, mathematics, and physics consist of synthetic a priori judgments. Earlier, I used arithmetic as an example of an analytic a priori judgment, which I believe it is. Not so for Kant, who held that arithmetic is synthetic a priori; that is, it tells us something new about the world, not merely about how we use (mathematical) language, without consulting experience. Most subsequent philosophers have disagreed with Kant on this. Be that as it may, Kant did believe that a good deal of our knowledge is synthetic a priori. His first *Critique* was not only an attempt to answer the question "How is physics (science) possible?" it was also an attempt to answer the question of how synthetic a priori judgments are possible. That is so, because for Kant, logically grounded knowledge of the world is only possible if synthetic a priori judgments exist and give verifiable knowledge of what is the case. It is going to turn out that one of the transcendental conditions of such synthetic a priori judgment is the existence of a self that is real, ongoing, and continuous rather than unreal, sequential, and atomistic. The argument is both about the nature of experience and about the nature of the self.

Essentially, Kant's answer to the question of how synthetic a priori knowledge is possible is to make the connectiveness intrinsic by putting it inside our heads. The mind works by filtering the *manifold of sense* (i.e., that which is empirically given in experience) through the categories of the Understanding. Knowledge is not something that is passively received; we are not blank slates to be written on by experience, nor are we empty cabinets to be filled; rather, we are constitutive of both experience and knowledge. We are active in cognition. In the words of Kant's near-contemporary, the Romantic poet William Wordsworth, "The world is half created and half perceived." There are no givens in experience; everything we know is processed by, refracted through, the prism of the Understanding. The transcendental (i.e., necessary for and logically prior to any possible experience) condition of knowledge is the active input from, the structuring by the Understanding, of the manifold of sense. Kant called this his Copernican revolution. Just as Copernicus moved the center of the solar system from the earth to the sun, Kant moved the locus of knowing from the world to the mind. In a sense, Kant's journey was in an opposite direction—from anthropocentric to "remotepocentric" for Copernicus and from world centered to mind centered for Kant—but his "revolution" was no less profound for that. Kant summarized both the critical (i.e., limiting) and affirming aspects of his analysis as follows:

Thoughts without content are empty, intuition without concepts are blind. . . . These two powers or capacities cannot exchange their functions. The understanding can intuit nothing, the intuition can think nothing, only through their union can knowledge arise. (1781/1990, p. 1)

Kant's use of *intuition* is unfortunate: what he is talking about is something strikingly similar to Hume's impressions, except that these impressions are already actively organized so that sensations (the raw materials given in the manifold of sense) are experienced as perceptions.

Now knowledge is possible because any experience whatsoever is organized by us, and we can only experience the world in the way that we experience it, and that way is invariant. This is a kind of subjectivism, but it is not solipsistic, nor personally unique. All humans experience the world causally, for example, because causality is one of the categories of the Understanding. We cannot experience things as disconnected because we intrinsically connect them. It is as if we always wore blue-colored glasses so that the world always appeared blue. If that were the case, we would not need to experience future events as blue in order to know that they were blue; they would be blue and could be known to be blue transcendentally (i.e., before they, or anything else for that matter, was experienced).

Kant thought that we process sensory input, structure the manifold of sense, in two ways, which he called the *aesthetic* and the *categorical*, respectively. Let us see what Kant's aesthetic consists of.

In the *Critique of Pure Reason*, Kant uses *aesthetic* in a sense different from its ordinary usage. His "aesthetic" (theory of the function and nature of art and of what constitutes beauty) is contained in his *Critique of Judgement*, while the "Transcendental Aesthetics" of the first *Critique* is a demonstration that space and time are subjective in the sense that they are "forms of intuition" under which the manifold of sensation is organized. For Kant, sense experience is not a pure given, something coming from the outside that inscribes on a receptor; on the contrary, the receptors (the senses) themselves organize any possible sensations spatially and temporarily. Thus, any experience whatsoever must be spatial and temporal, must have a location in space and in time. Instead of blue glasses, we wear spatial-temporal glasses that cannot be removed. The forms of space and time are transcendental in Kant's sense of being logically antecedent to any possible experience. According to Kant, the pure intuition of the outer senses is space (i.e., outer sensations are organized spatially), while time is the pure intuition of inner sense (i.e., any introspective sensation is organized temporally; it is preceded by something and followed by something). Kant's arguments to prove that this is so are elaborate, obscure, and difficult. Their exposition and evaluation are beyond the scope of this book. Later philosophers have split in the degree, if any, to which they have been persuaded by Kant's analysis. However, the subjectivity (this subjectivity is not personal, it is universal, built into each and every human mind) of time and space receives some support from modern relativity theory, but there it is the perspective of the observer, which could be an instrument, that organizes space and time rather than a mental structure.

Once he has established his transcendental aesthetics, Kant draws the reasonable conclusion that we can only know the world as we know it, that is, under the aspects of space and time, and not as it is itself. The world as we know it Kant calls the *phenomenal* world; the world in itself he calls the *noumenal* world.

Phenomenal reality is spatial-temporal; noumenal reality is, according to Kant, whatever else it may be, not spatial-temporal (not in space and in time). Since he argues that what he calls the *ding-an-sich*, the thing-in-itself, is unknowable, I don't see how he can consistently say anything whatsoever about it, including that it is not spatial-temporal in nature, but he does.

After his analysis of sensory representation in the transcendental aesthetic, Kant proceeds to subject the Understanding to a similar analysis. For Kant, the mental apparatus—the mind—has three aspects: the Senses that contribute the pure intuitions of space and time; the Understanding that contributes the categories—extremely general conceptual schemata—by which, or perhaps better *through which*, any experience whatsoever is organized; and finally the Reason, which provides the synoptic vision, the integration and capacity for self-awareness and self-criticism.

In the section of the first *Critique* called "Transcendental Logic," Kant comes up with a table of categories: of quantity, of quality, of relation, and of modality. All experience must be organized by the four categories, which explicitly include causality under relation. So Hume's analysis that there is no necessary connection between things, nothing within them that constitutes them, becomes irrelevant, since the connections are necessarily supplied by the Understanding. It is as if we had replaced our blue spectacles with unremovable bifocals, one lens of which organizes sensations into spatial-temporal perceptions and the other of which organizes perceptions into categories. Since phenomenal events are causally determined, or at least experienced as causally determined, there is no freedom in the phenomenal realm; the noumenal world is not causally connected and is a realm of freedom. Just as Kant argued that the thing-in-itself is outside space and time because the mind is the source of their spatial-temporal organization, he argues that noumena, things-in-themselves (including the self-in-itself), are free because causality (determination) is contributed by the Understanding. As with space and time, I don't see any reason to say that real connections cannot reside in things-in-themselves just because the mind makes connections. By definition we can't know noumena, so we can't know what they aren't, any more than, given Kant's premises, we can know what they are. This brings us to Kant's analysis of the self. First, however, I would like to say something about what Kant calls the *transcendental dialectic*.

In the transcendental dialectic, Kant demonstrates what results when a rationalist thinker using reason alone attempts to draw conclusions about matters beyond the limits of experience. Such reasoning ignores Kant's demonstration that thoughts without sensations are empty and results in what he calls the *antinomies of reason*: mutually contradictory statements such as "the world has a beginning in time and the world does not have a beginning in time." Both conclusions can be proved by metaphysics. To push reason beyond its legitimate realm is to come up with contradictions and absurdity. The transcendental dialectic is the destructive part of Kant's philosophizing in which he demonstrates that the traditional proofs of God's existence, along with the traditional claims of metaphysics (knowledge about that which we do not and cannot experience) is illusionary. Kant is clearing the forest of the accumulated tangle of the weeds of generations of pretension and dogmatism much as Descartes, Locke, and Hume did in their respective ways. Here the *Critique* is indeed critical. The result is to free the human mind of the bonds of ignorance raised to certainty, and from all the catastrophic consequences flowing from each and all dogmatisms, inflicting their certainties on "nonbelievers" and "heretics."

Having demonstrated the antinomies (i.e., mutually contradictory conclusions) that come from the misapplication of reason, Kant turns back to what we can know and the conditions of that knowledge. One of those conditions is the existence of the self as an enduring and substantive entity. Kant says that "the . . . unity of conscious . . . [is] a condition under which every intuition must stand *in order to become an object for me*. For otherwise . . . the manifold would not be united in one consciousness." This is analytic because "all my representations must be subject to that condition under which alone I can ascribe them to an identical self as my representations" (Kant, 1781/1990, p. 112). Kant, here, seems to be equating the self and consciousness, but he does not do this consistently.

So much for Hume's demonstration that the self is an illusion, that it doesn't exist. Hume says, look for it and you can't find it. Kant says, don't bother to look for it, you could not have any coherent experience whatever, and you do have some, unless you have a self that is in some sense a unity. This too is transcendental in the sense that existence of the self is logically antecedent to any experience that makes sense. If the self is merely a grammatical fiction that denotes a flow of discontinuous impressions, there could be no experience of coherence or of continuity, and there is one. Although Kant doesn't think so, this is a combination of an empirical (the world does make sense) and a logical (it couldn't if we didn't cohere) argument for the existence of a self-identical self. Kant goes on to say,

> It must be possible for the "I think" to accompany all my representations for otherwise something could be represented in me that could not be thought at all, and that is equivalent to saying that the representation would be impossible, or at least would be nothing to me. (Kant, 1781/1990, p. 117)

So to speak, the function of the self is synthetic, not in Hume's sense that habit and memory give us a sense of personal identity, but much more in the spirit of the modern psychoanalyst speaking of the synthetic function of the ego. Here the self is active, is constitutive of experience, just as are the *categories of the understanding*. There is a reciprocal and dialectical relationship between the intelligibility of the world and the logical necessity for the existence of the self as enduring and creative. It is both the synthesizer and the synthesized. In a famous phrase, Kant speaks of the *transcendental unity of the apperception*. *Apperception* for Kant is self-consciousness; so the *transcendental unity of the apperception* means that a unified awareness of self and an awareness of the self as unified is logically antecedent to any experience whatsoever that can be experienced as mine, and there is no other kind of experience. Kant himself defines the transcendental unity of the apperception as "that self-consciousness which, while generating the representation 'I think' (a representation which must be capable of accompanying all other representations), cannot itself be represented by any further representation" (Kant, 1781/1990, p. 119).

Kant goes on to say that time is the form of the inner sense, just as space is the form of the outer senses, and "in introspection I am at times aware of myself and perceive myself after the fashion of an object, that is to say under the form of time, though not of space, and under the unity of pure apperception" (Kant, 1781/1990, p. 119).

As a result of this analysis, Kant now has two selves: the phenomenal (empirical) self that I sometimes can catch in introspection, and a noumenal self. The vicissitudes of the phenomenal self are the subject matter of scientific psychology, which may be either experimental or introspective. The phenomenal self is, in principle, knowable and is, to some extent, known. It is knowable through the inner sense as the temporal sequence that is me.

For Kant, there is a noumenal self in addition to the phenomenal self. The noumenal self is a self-in-itself, which is the *I am* that transcendentally must accompany every thought. The noumenal self is unknowable. It is thinkable but not known. The self-in-itself that becomes the *transcendental ego* in 19th- and 20th-century philosophy is without specifications; it is a purely logical condition of thought. In this way it seems much like Descartes's *cogito*, which also lacks specification, yet it is more than that. In his moral philosophy, Kant manages to say a great deal about the noumenal self that he can't say in his epistemological work. In the *Critique of Pure Practical Reason* (Kant's attempt to answer the question, "How is moral knowledge possible?"), the noumenal self is seen as free, that is, outside the realm of necessity, and as potentially immortal. It becomes something like the traditional soul, although a soul whose existence is not established by illegitimate use of reason, in the manner of the old metaphysics. Kant believes there are two realms, that of necessity and that of freedom. The noumenal self—the *I am* that must necessarily accompany every intuition—is free from the causal order, although it is the ground of my experience of that causal order. Being outside of the causal order, it is not knowable. The empirical self, on the other hand, is part of the causal order of nature and is thoroughly knowable. Although Kant didn't himself write psychology, he believed that science can explicate the richness and complexity of the empirical self.

In one of the epigrams that shine through the turgid prose of the critiques, Kant says, "Man as noumenon is free; [while] man as phenomenon is part of the causal order of nature." In the *Critique of Pure Practical Reason*, Kant demonstrates to his satisfaction that the moral sense, which exists just as scientific knowledge does, requires that man be free and concludes that, in some sense, man stands outside of all causal chains. His critics have suggested that Kant tried to undo his critical analysis of the limits of reason in the *Critique of Pure Reason* in his ethical works and that they are not persuasive.

Kant's notion of the self is much richer than either Descartes's or the empiricists'. It is both a unity and a unifier; it is, in one respect, potentially knowable and in another respect, a free, albeit unknowable, moral agent.

To return to Kant's epistemology, the function of the Understanding is to structure the "output" of the manifold of sense by subsuming that output under Kant's categories. Kant derived his categories from Aristotle's logic; living in a time when there was no geometry except the Euclidean and no logic but the Aristotelian syllogistic, Kant assumed that those categories were universal and intrinsic to the operation of all minds. That is, Kant assumed that the categories of Euclidean geometry and Aristotelian logic were universal and characteristic of all minds. We now know this not to be true and Kant's categories are merely of an antiquarian interest, but the notion that experience is shaped by indwelling schemata of the mind is perfectly valid. For Kant the categories are prewired or, to change the metaphor, the software is eternal and invariant. Current scientific knowledge seems to suggest that the software is not invariant, although not easily modified, and that it is partly genetically programmed and partly laid down by early experience or, more precisely, by the internal representation of early interpersonal interactions, which are modifiable by later experience, although not easily. There is a built-in inertia in the system that makes it resistant to change. This is perhaps what Freud meant by (or is intrinsic to what he meant by) the "repetition compulsion." There is a dialectical (reciprocal) relationship between mind shaping experience and experience shaping the structural and structuring functions of the mind. The developmental psychologist Jean Piaget, who liked to call himself a *genetic epistemologist*, spoke of this dialectical relationship as assimilation (the shaping of sensory input by cognitive schemata) and accommodation (the shaping of cognitive schemata by sensory input). But these are cybernetic and psychoanalytic interpretations and modifications of Kant's salient and basically valid notion of the Understanding shaping the manifold of sense. The manifold of sense is simply the array of raw sensa (sense data) provided by experience antecedent to any perceptual or cognitive processing.

The *reason*, for Kant, is that part of (i.e., functional output of) the mind that is self-reflection and is capable of subjecting its operations to critical analysis. It is the part of the mind that made it possible for the critiques to be written. Ideas are to the reason what concepts are to the Understanding. The reason's application of ideas permits us to philosophize and to look at how we think and to reason about the conditions necessary for that thinking. The result is Kant's a priori transcendental comprehension of the aesthetic shaping of the manifold under the forms of space and time and the categorical shaping of the manifold by the Understanding. The reason is also the source of whatever synoptic vision or overall integration we may attain of our metaphysical conditions (i.e., our way of being as abstract scientists and as moral beings, enactors of pure reason and of practical reason).

The most famous part of the first critique is the transcendental dialectic, in which Kant demonstrates that reasoning about matters of which we have no experience leads to absurdity. However, the destructive critique in the transcendental dialectic produces a paradoxical result. According to Kant, any claim to knowledge, particularly metaphysical knowledge, that goes beyond experience leads to contradictory conclusions, which he calls antinomies. The antinomies demonstrate that we land in absurdity when we try to "prove" through logical deduction that God exists or, on the contrary, that God doesn't exist; that the universe has a beginning in time or that the universe doesn't have a beginning in time; that the universe has a boundary, or that the universe doesn't have a boundary; and so forth. So to speak, ultimates can't be proved or known through the use of pure (i.e., theoretical) reason. As Ludwig Wittgenstein said, "About that which we can not speak, we must be silent." But Kant doesn't agree. On the contrary, he says that since we can neither prove nor disprove metaphysical ultimates, we should be guided by the requirements of practical reason, by that which is necessary to act morally in the world and to hope. Kant is, in this sense, a pragmatist. Kant's argument brings to mind the story from the Buddhist scriptures in which Buddha's disciple Ajunta asks the Master, "Does the world have a beginning in time? Does the world have a limit in space?" and the rest of the Kantian antinomies. In each case, the Buddha remains silent. Finally Ajunta asks, "Master, why don't you answer my questions?" The Buddha replies, "The answer to these questions makes not for salvation." Kant would have told Buddha's disciple, "My son, I am glad you asked these questions; their self-contradictory, antithetical solutions demonstrate the impotence of reason to answer them, forcing us to seek answers elsewhere, therefore, paradoxically leading us to salvation."

In being allowed to look, and in looking, elsewhere, Kant asked, "What is necessary for me to act morally?" For him the moral is a given, a datum of experience, as certain as any other datum. Further, it is something that I experience within me. For Kant, the postulates of practical reason are God, freedom, and immortality. He has gone an awfully long way to arrive at what most men believe without having written the two critiques. Kant's position is somewhat like William James's, when James, after considering whether the existence of free will or determinism can be demonstrated and concluding that they cannot, states that his first act of free will will be to believe in free will. So Kant, in a dialectical rapprochement, has managed to say something about that which we cannot know, the noumenal world of the thing-in-itself, or at least that part of it that constitutes the self-in-itself. Kant, unlike Wittgenstein, is not silent about that of which we cannot speak and, having first demonstrated that pure reason can say nothing about these matters, now demonstrates that practical reason, although it cannot demonstrate, can postulate the a priori conditions of a moral world within. Hence Kant's famous conclusion that man (i.e., the self) is, as phenomenon, part of the determined order of nature, but as a noumenon is free.

In a sense, Kant has not really answered Hume; rather, he does an end run around him. Kant does not look for the self, as does Hume, and find it (or not find it); rather, he asks what are the necessary conditions of coherent experience and of a science that successfully explains and predicts, each of which exist, and concludes that the transcendental unity of the apperception is that condition. Since self-consciousness must accompany every mental act, he concludes that the self must exist. Kant's argument is metaphysical in his sense of metaphysical (i.e., an explanation of the transcendental ground of experience), while Hume's argument is empirical—go and look.

Two of Kant's successors are worth mentioning at this point: Johan Gottlieb Fichte and Arthur Schopenhauer. Gottlieb Fichte (1762–1814) turned Kant's Transcendental unity of the apperception into a radical subjectivism. Fichte speaks of the Ego that "posits" itself. Kant's noumenal self doesn't postulate itself. Fichte is a typical romantic in his exultation of an extreme individuality that creates itself. Fichte was also a rabid German nationalist, and there is an inconsistency between his self-positing Ego (whatever that means) and his romantic inflation of the self as unique individual and Romantic authoritarianism. Fichte is usually seen as a proto-Fascist.

Schopenhauer (1788–1860) returns to Kant's phenomenal self, renaming it the *self as presentation*. The self as presentation stands under the forms of perception and the Understanding. Kant's noumenal self becomes Schopenhauer's *self as will*, which is the self-in-itself understood as irrational force. Schopenhauer anticipates both Freud's theory of the instincts and the worship of force in modern totalitarianism. Apart from its political anticipation, Schopenhauer's notion of the self as blind striving underscores a real aspect of the self ignored by both the rationalists and the empiricists. It is a notion that has found much support in 20th-century thought.

To return to Kant, it has been said that he is an empirical realist, but a transcendental idealist. This is true of both his epistemology and his account of the self. Kant's moral theory is derived from his analysis of the self and from his Enlightenment values. He himself doesn't think that he is offering value judgments, but rather that he has demonstrated that we have intuition of what is right. The abstract summary of that right is given in Kant's renowned categorical imperative. He phrases it several ways: My action is moral if, and only if, "I can also will that my maxim should become a universal law"; and "act as if the maxim of your action were to become through your will a *universal law of nature*." He goes on to say, "Man is an end in himself," therefore "act in such a way that you treat human beings both in your own person and in the person of all others, never as a means only but always equally as an end" (1785/1959, p. 47). There are logical problems both with Kant's arguments for his moral conclusions and with their universal application that may entail conflicts Kant didn't see, but their nobility is self-evident. They embody the Enlightenment at its best. I believe that there is a dialectical (two-way) relationship between Kant's analytic establishment of the substantiality, and the centrality in knowing and experiencing, of the self and the endurance of that self and Kant's dictate of "practical reason" that each person is an end (i.e., intrinsically valuable) in himself or herself. It is the Enlightenment's defiance of the claims of all collectivities, religious or political, to subjugate or sacrifice the claims of the individual to some "greater good." This is not a romantic exultation of radical individualism as in Fichte, for each individual must take into consideration the desirability of universalizing his or her actions. There are problems with this, but it is a notion congruent with human dignity.

Kant asked and, to his satisfaction, answered three questions: What can I know? What ought I to do? and What may I hope? At the end of his first critique he said, "I never cease to respond with awe and wonder when I contemplate the two certainties, the starry sky above and the moral law within." One could do worse.

5

G. W. F. Hegel: The Dialectic of the Self

The selves of Descartes, Locke, Hume, and Kant are rather schematic and abstract. This is true of Descartes's self as cogitator, of Locke's self as synthesis of memory, of Hume's self as illusion, and of Kant's noumenal self as the *I think* that must accompany all of my perceptions. This is less true of Kant's phenomenal self, but he himself does not concretize the potential richness of the empirical self. This is not the case for our next thinker about self, Georg Wilhelm Friedrich Hegel (1770–1831). Hegel's concept of self is complex, dynamic, and far from clear. Hegel's self develops, and that development proceeds only through conflict. Thus, Hegel's self is epigenetic and conflictual. Further, the realization (development) of the Hegelian self depends on its externalization, on *praxis* (the action of the self on and in the world) that results in cultural products: thoughts, works of art, social and political institutions, religions, and philosophies that Hegel calls *concrete universals*. The self only becomes the self through action. That which is externalized is then internalized, and the self that becomes itself in interaction with other selves and in the projection onto the world of its inwardness reintegrates that which flowed out to reach its next stage of development. No longer abstract thinker, detached observer, patched-together identity, grammatical fiction, or prerequisite of any possible experience, this self unfolds, acts, creates, develops, struggles, and finally identifies with the results of its actions, creations, developments, and struggles. A dynamic view of self, indeed.

The man who so conceived self was hardly himself dynamic. Hegel's life was singularly uneventful. He started as a tutor and ended as a university professor, serving as an editor and high school principal en route. So bland was his life that he has been referred to as "secretary to the Absolute," the Absolute being the highest categorical concept in his philosophical system. Hegel came from an upper middle-class family in Stuttgart, Germany. Little is known of his formative years, except that he was a middling student. He went on to study theology at the University of Tübingen. He spent his 20s as a private tutor for a number of aristocratic families, finally turning to philosophy in his early 30s when he became co-editor of the *Journal für Philosophie*. His co-editor was Friedrich Schelling, who developed a "Philosophy of Nature" in which Nature is seen to be an "Odyssey of the spirit," which has some parallels in Hegel's thought. Schelling taught a mystical, romantic interpretation of religion. The two men ended as bitter rivals. While editing the philosophy journal, Hegel was writing his first major work, the *Phenomenology of Mind* (1807/1931). He mailed the manuscript to his publisher just as Napoleon's troops were assaulting Jena, so the theory of development through conflict was itself launched in the midst of conflict. Hegel, like most intellectuals of his generation, had been an admirer of the French Revolution, and he was sympathetic toward Napoleon, whom he saw as the representative of progress even though the French Emperor was attacking Germany. Hegel fled from the chaos of battle and became an increasingly conservative newspaper editor in Bamberg, after which he was appointed director of the Gymnasium—the European classical high school—in Nuremburg. While headmaster he developed his philosophical "system," first expounded in his *Science of Logic* (Hegel, 1812–1814/ 1929b). The *Logic* established his reputation, and he was successively appointed professor of logic at Heidelburg University and at the University of Berlin. His influence while at the University of Berlin was enormous. Students came from all over Europe and beyond to study under him, and European intellectual history in the second half of the 19th century would have been radically different if he hadn't shaped the thinking of so many. He himself became increasingly conservative, even reactionary, during his Berlin years, and wound up deifying the Prussian state. However, some of his followers interpreted his thinking in a revolutionary way, leading to a split between the "Left Hegelians" and the "Right Hegelians." If the ceaseless striving of spirit unfolding itself is interpreted as ongoing, the implications are revolutionary; if, on the other hand, the process is held to end in Hegel's System, the implications are justification of the status quo and conservatism. Hegel himself ended as a Right Hegelian. Hegel is the first of our thinkers about self who married and had a family. Becoming a professor, a civil servant of the Prussian state, an apologist for that state, and a contented bourgeois householder, the implicitly revolutionary Hegel became a harbinger of Victorian smugness.

Hegel published relatively little in his lifetime; the *Phenomenology of Mind* (1807/1931), the *Logic* (1812–1814/1929b), and the *Encyclopedia of the Philosophical Sciences* were his chief works. After his death, his students published his lectures as the *Philosophies of Religion, Aesthetics, Law, and History*. For our purposes, the *Phenomenology* and the lectures on the philosophy of history (Hegel, 1837/1929a) are the most important. Hegel is extraordinarily difficult to read and interpret. His prose is a thicket of neologisms and technical terms; his style is epigrammatic at its best, but at its worst, it is turgid, obscure, arcane academese. German students are said to read him in English translation, the English being more intelligible. In spite of this, Hegel's school of thought, in its various interpretations, dominated philosophical thought for three quarters of a century. That school is generally called *idealism*. It is idealistic in the sense that mind or spirit (i.e., the realm of ideas) is the ultimately real for its adherents.

The *Phenomenologie des Geistes* (1807) is a remarkable work. A phenomenon is that which appears, hence phenomenology is the study of what appears. The common German word *Geist* is difficult to translate. It means both *mind* and *spirit*. Hence, Hegel's book is a treatise on the manifestations of the mind, the spirit, or both. It is a history of the *forms of consciousness*. As such, it is an account of the vicissitudes of the human mind and its thought processes. On one level, it is not about the individual self at all, but about the way spirit, as incarnated in human consciousness, has manifested itself in history. However, on another level, at least implicitly, the *Phenomenologie* is about the individual self and its vicissitudes. At least, some commentators have so interpreted it. For our purposes, Hegel's analysis of spirit will be regarded as an analysis of self. If ontogeny recapitulates phylogeny—if the development of the individual recapitulates the development of the (human) race—then there is no conflict between the two interpretations. In German literature there is a tradition of the *Bildungs Roman*, the novel of spiritual and sensual education of a young protagonist. Hegel's contemporary and acquaintance, Goethe, initiated the *Bildungs Roman* tradition with *The Sorrows of Young Werther*. Hegel's *Phanomenologie* is a *Bildungs Roman* of the human spirit.

A few more words about *Geist*. *Geist* is both individual minds and what Hegel variously calls *Spirit* and the *Absolute*. The Absolute seems to be something trans-human or at least more than human, something like the traditional transcendent Judeo-Christian God. It is and it is not. *Geist* is not transcendent; it is immanent—indwelling. There is no Absolute apart from its manifestations in nature and its unfolding in human history. The Absolute may exist somewhere as potential, and although Hegel seems interested in this possibility, its realization is in human history. The theory of immanence holds that there is no creator apart from his (its) creation and that the creation is ongoing. So to speak, God (the Absolute, the Spirit) comes into being in human consciousness, especially self-consciousness. History is the process of spirit becoming aware of itself. Self-awareness or self-consciousness is the culmination of the process. At first there is nature, inert, existing only *in-itself* (i.e., without consciousness); later there is consciousness, and finally *being-for-itself*, self-consciousness or self-awareness. The unfolding of the absolute, the phenomenology of Spirit, is the acquisition of self-consciousness not through introspection (or not only or primarily so), but through the production of cultural products: art, science, religion, economic and political institutions, law, and, at the highest level, philosophy. The Spirit becomes aware of itself by individual human beings becoming self-aware of that which they individually and humankind collectively have produced through action. *Self-consciousness* in Ger-man also means *self-accused*, so there is an element of guilt in self-awareness, perhaps because Hegel believed that conflict between self-consciences is inevita-ble. For Hegel, as Susan B. Anthony says in Virgil Thomson's *The Mother of Us All*, "Life is strife." Spirit is as Spirit does, but only when Spirit is aware of what it does. Furthermore, *Geist* is in conflict with itself and with other conscious-nesses. In our terms, the self is its own consciousness of what it does through action, that awareness never being without conflict both within itself and in its relation with other selves.

For Hegel, *The Truth is the Whole*, and all previous philosophies suffer from one-sidedness. They are not wrong; rather, they are incomplete. Their error is that they do not see that incompleteness. Thus, empiricism has something valid to say, and so does rationalism, but neither is the whole story; hence, neither is the truth. Hegel is striving to build a system that will encompass all previous *Weltanschauung* (world views), each of which has its own validity. To understand a philosophical system, a work of art, a religion, or a culture (or, I would say, a person), we must feel ourselves into that cultural product's point of view. These manifestations of Spirit, these actualizations of itself at a given development of *Geist*, which Hegel calls *concrete universals*, cannot be understood from the outside, from a hostile or critical standpoint, but only through empathy, through assuming the point of view of that concrete universal or cultural product or the point of view of that individual consciousness. In our terms, Hegel is saying that the self at any point of development has a *Weltanschauung*, a way of experienc-ing and creating a world, that has validity but is not Truth, because each and every *Weltanschauung* is limited and biased, is a partial view and mistakes that partiality for totality.

Selves and their manifestations, including our own selves, cannot be understood by a purely intellectual process, but only by empathy, by feeling ourselves into, by feeling with that which we are trying to understand, be that ourselves or another. Veridical perception of consciousness in all its subjective and objective manifestations, as self-consciousness and as cultural product, is only possible through empathy. We must understand before we criticize.

There is something playful in understanding; I play a role to understand a point of view. Hegel is recommending a kind of psychodrama of ideologies in which I play skeptic, stoic, empiricist, and rationalist successively as I trace within myself the development of Spirit objectified in these concrete universals of thought.

The same is true of each developmental phase of the self. I cannot understand my point of view as a child except by becoming a child again or by playing at being one. This side of Hegel implies a certain compassion of the self for itself. Even the actions that I now most regret and repudiate once made sense, once reflected a stage of development that was necessary and inevitable.

So much for the validity of each developmental stage, of each philosophical system, of each *Weltanschauung*. Yes, each is valid within its own terms, but each is a distortion, each is guilty of what Alfred North Whitehead called the "fallacy of misplaced concreteness," of taking the part for the whole. This being the case, any proposition or standpoint will generate its opposite or antithesis. For example, empiricism pushed far enough is self-contradictory and leads to Humeian absurdity, to a skepticism that cannot really be lived; this in turn generates a neorationalistic philosophy, which in its turn also becomes one-sided and generates its own absurdity. Thesis generates antithesis, which in turn generates a higher synthesis. That synthesis is itself a one-sided viewpoint, albeit one that encompasses more reality than its antecedent thesis and antithesis. The synthesis in turn stands as a thesis generating its antithesis, leading to yet a new synthesis, *ad infinitum*, or at least continuing until Hegel created his System.

Hegel developed this *dialectical logic*, which the American Hegelian Joshua Royce called a logic of passion, most fully in his *Logic*, which is not a treatise on logic but more of what would have traditionally been called metaphysics. In it, Hegel starts with the concept of Being, the most general of possible concepts: so general, in fact, that Being is without definition or characteristics. Being generates its antithesis, Nothing, which is implicit in it. In a sense, Being and Nothingness are codeterminous. In another sense, Being's lack of internal distinctions, articulations, and spaces necessitates its antithesis, Nothing. If there was only Being without Nothing, there would be no world at all. The synthesis of Being and Nothing is Becoming. Process and history begin. Hegel goes on to elaborate an extremely complex System a priori, by spinning out his logic. He calls this *dialectic*. Dialectic takes each position to its extreme or turns it into its opposite. Each extreme leads to a contradiction; hence, the emergence of the opposite.

The self has a similar dialectical development. The self, for Hegel, is historical both phylogenically and ontogenically. It evolves. Furthermore, development occurs through conflict between thesis and antithesis. The results of our actions are not what we expect. "The moving power of human passions which produce unintended results and in that way sudden reversals" (Hegel, 1837/1929a, p. 368) is what drives history.

Hegel's theory of truth is worth comment. Most theories of truth are variants on the correspondence theory of truth. A statement or proposition is true if, and only if, it corresponds to a set of affairs. "The pencil I write with is red" is such a true proposition since it corresponds to a set of affairs—my pencil being red. Hegel wouldn't deny this, but his is a coherence theory of truth. A system is truer than another system if it accounts for more of reality, if it organizes more data into a coherent picture. The truth is the whole, and my truth is never whole, but approximates it by successively taking into account more and more of reality.

In tracing the dialectic of the unfolding of spirit, Hegel looks at the history of human consciousness as objectified in philosophical systems and *Weltanschauung*. His range is impressive, yet his selection is itself partial and limited in ways that Hegel does not see. Among these concrete universals are *skepticism*; *stoicism*, which he calls the unhappy contrite consciousness; *traditional morality* (custom), or *Sittlichteit*; *rational moralittät* (*moralittät*), which he attributes to Kant; and *Spirit alienated from itself*. His history of the forms of consciousness proceeds dialectically, each one-sided view generating its antithesis, which in turn leads to a new synthesis, until Spirit finally becomes conscious of itself in Hegel's System. If the history of the forms of consciousness does indeed come to an end in Hegel, which is one reading of his meaning, then the social, intellectual, and political implications of his System are conservative, however, if the process continues as given Hegel's premises it should, the social, intellectual, and political implications of that System are either evolutionary or revolutionary.

In this tracing of the history of consciousness Hegel tells us that it is a rational process and postulates that Reason is the ground of all things. Although the unfolding of the Absolute is a temporal process, this unfolding is a logical, or logically necessary, progression, and Hegel's interest lies in its logical rather than its temporal structure. For Hegel, whatever is, is logically necessary, and could not be otherwise. This constitutes its rationality. In his *Logic*, Hegel tries to demonstrate the rationality of the process that is the universe. In effect he deduces the world and everything in it, including human history, from the dialectic of Being and Nothing. In Hegel, the transcendental method, the a priori elucidation of the prerequisites of experience, which Kant used critically, becomes an excuse for the reintroduction of metaphysics—a reintroduction with a vengeance. Hegel is all too ready to tell us about the thing-in-itself, and to tell us in extensive detail.

Related to the dialectic is the notion of *Aufheben*. This is a German verb that has three antithetical meanings: to annul or destroy, to preserve, and to exalt. When a culture, an idea, an institution, an art form, or a developmental stage in the existence of our individual self is *Aufgehoben*, it is annulled, preserved, and transcended at the same time: annulled as it passes into its opposite and preserved as it passes into a new state of being. It is destroyed, transcended, and incorporated simultaneously. This is an epigenetic theory of self, in which each earlier stage of development is contained in, finds representation in, is a living presence in, each higher (later) stage of development.

In his *Philosophy of History* (1837/1929a), Hegel states that "The Real is Rational and the Rational is Real." What he means is that whatever exists, exists because of logical necessity; that is, what comes into being is entailed in and necessitated by its antecedents in the same way as the conclusion of a syllogism is entailed in its premises. Logical necessity also means that what is could not be otherwise. According to Hegel, "the cunning of Reason" (1837/1929a, p. 380) uses human passion to "bring forth that which is ripe in the womb of time" (1837/1929a, p. 377). Men believe that they are fulfilling their personal desires when actually they are the instruments of the Absolute's self-realization. Hegel is here anthropomorphizing Reason. His intention may be metaphorical, but this anthropomorphizing of Reason points to a difficulty that runs throughout Hegel's System. The characteristics he attributes to Spirit, the Absolute, and the World Soul are human characteristics, and his theory may have more to do with projection than with logical deduction. That is, Hegel seems to be projecting human motives onto the totality of things understood as the Absolute. According to Hegel, history is tragic because it takes no account of human purpose or desire. But not to worry, this is perfectly all right because it is "necessary." This part of Hegel seems to me to be nonsense. He justifies anything and everything. As Ivan asks in *The Brothers Karamazov*, can children being tortured be part of God's (the Absolute's) plan? Of course, Hegel's Absolute doesn't have a plan, but is merely "rational." But one wonders, in what sense was the Holocaust rational? Was it logically necessary?

Hegel says that the rationality of being is not such as to allow us to predict the course of events. As his famous aphorism says, "The owl of Minerva flies only at night," so that we gain wisdom, or at least understanding, only after the event. That may be true, but Hegel also seems to say the opposite, that he can understand and indeed deduce a priori, that which is logically necessary. Either Hegel is a Monday-morning quarterback calling the plays after the game, or his System is not rational and driven by necessity. History is certainly tragic but it isn't made less so by its necessity. Hegel might agree, but he is, nevertheless, writing a theodicy, a justification of the ways of God to man. This part of Hegel seems to me either mistaken or pretentious. His theodicy is no more convincing than any of the others. Not so his psychological dynamics.

One of the most famous and most insightful parts of the *Phenomenology* is the "Dialectic of Master and Slave." In it, Hegel shows that, insofar as the Master cannot be Master without the Slave, the Slave is master of the Master, and the Master a slave to his dependence on the Slave. The Slave is master of the Master because the Master cannot be master without him. Hegel is here depicting a dialectical role reversal. Hegel certainly is onto something here, but he misses something, too. As psychologically sound as his analysis is, the power relationships remain, and the slave can be flogged by the master, but not the master by the slave.

Hegel's rather forbidding technical terms *Being-in-itself* and *Being-for-itself* have resonated down the years and played an important role in European intellectual history. Being-in-itself is thingness, the way of being of a rock or stone: solid, stolid, self-identical, and not self-aware. According to Hegel, Being-in-itself exists for Being-for-itself. Being-for-itself is self-awareness; it is consciousness of Being-in-itself and Being-for-itself. That is, it is self-conscious. For Hegel, self-consciousness is not something added to consciousness but is intrinsic to Being-for-itself. To be conscious is to be self-conscious. Of course, this is but another version of the distinction between mind and matter; however, in Hegel, the distinction is given a new twist. First, both are aspects of Being. Although Hegel does not say so, this is reminiscent of Spinoza's one Substance, which he calls Nature or God, which is the cause of itself (Hegel's Being) and which has infinite attributes, only two of which, extension and thought, are known to us. Hegel was indeed influenced by Spinoza, yet his understanding is different. Being-in-itself is characterized more by solidity and self-identity than by extension, and Being-for-itself is characterized more by self-reflectedness than by thought. The self-consciousness of Being-in-itself is a uniquely Hegelian contribution, as is his description of what happens when a Being-for-itself meets another Being-for-itself, each trying to reduce the other to a Being-in-itself, a thing that is the object of the reducer's consciousness. Hence, conflict is inevitable, indeed ontological (i.e., built into the structure of Being). For Hegel, Being differentiates itself into Being-in-itself and Being-for-itself, but a reintegration is then possible to create Being-in-itself-for-itself. Hegel does this by assimilating Being into thought. In his system, self-consciousness (Being-for-itself) includes consciousness of inanimate, un-self-aware Nature (Being-in-itself). Self-consciousness comes in gradations from the inchoate to the fully self-aware. In fact, Hegel believes that the achievement of full self-consciousness is the task of philosophy. He views his own philosophy as the culmination of human thought in which Being becomes conscious of itself. Hence, he concludes that "Thought and Being are One," moving from Spinoza's pantheistic monism to philosophical idealism, the belief that thought is the ultimate reality.

Hegel states that "Spirit is the Idea which has returned to *itself* from *otherness* and *self-estrangement* from a state of being not itself." Although couched in rather forbidding language, this is an extremely important notion. Hegel is describing what psychoanalysts call *projective identification*: the projecting outward of an aspect of self, which is either unacceptable or in need of protection from some other aspect of self, that is then identified with and reintrojected. Thus, in part, the self becomes the self by passing through otherness and self-estrangement before returning to itself.

Furthermore, Hegel sees that development (of the spirit or of the self) is a process of differentiation and integration. What starts as an undifferentiated matrix (pure Being, the neonate) undergoes differentiation in the process of becoming, and in turn integrates that into which it has differentiated through projection, action, and creation, reclaiming it and making it part of its internal structure. The integration is once again unitary, a plenum, but no longer without internal structure. The product of integration is in turn differentiated, and the products of that differentiation are in turn reintegrated, in an ongoing process terminated only by death. This is the dialectic at work as self or, better yet, the self as dialectical process. In that process the self is continuously *Aufgehoben*: destroyed, preserved, and transmuted.

According to Hegel, the ego (the I or self) is Being-for-itself; that is, Being conscious not only of objects but of itself. I as subject can have myself as object. Therefore, I am for myself, but a stone is not for itself—it is only for me; that is, its being is a Being-for-others. In philosophy I realize that others can only have being, for me, as objects of my subjectivity (my consciousness). Consciousnesses are in conflict with each other. It seems that another can only be an object (in itself) for me, but this seems to contradict what Hegel says about empathy, the understanding of art works, philosophical systems, and historical periods by entering into their points of view.

Hegel believes that in philosophy the Spirit sees the world as a manifestation of Thought, that is, of itself. The world is only an aspect of self. Thought's object, the world, is identical with the self as subject. Subject and Object are identical. Philosophy is finally a union of subjectivity and objectivity, and the Idea returns to itself. A psychoanalyst would see evidence of infantile grandiosity, a belief in the omniscience of thoughts, and a failure to complete the developmental tasks of separation-individualization (differentiation) in this equation of Thought and Being. It is almost as if after brilliantly enacting the developmental processes of differentiation and integration and the psychological mechanism of projective identification and projecting them onto the Absolute, Hegel regressed to predifferentiation, to symbiosis, in his various attempts to reconcile conflict in a higher synthesis.

In addition to the self as developmental, evolutionary, and conflictual, Hegel emphasizes the activity of the self and the self's coming to self-consciousness through that activity. In consciousness, I am aware of the object that is not the self, but in self-consciousness the mind's object is itself. The activity of the mind is the realization of the self. I gain a sense of self *when I feel that I act*. For Hegel, the philosophical idealist, that action is thought, but it need not be. So now the self is the feeling of volition, most powerfully felt in thought, that accompanies the dialectic of conflict, differentiation, and integration that constitutes both spirit and self. This Hegelian self is a far richer and less abstract self than the selves of Descartes, Hume, Locke, and Kant.

Hegel's most consequential disciple was Karl Marx. Marx was certainly not an uncritical disciple. On the contrary, he turns the dialectic on its head and makes human productivity and human labor and its products the material basis of existence, the ultimate reality. For Marx, it is that material base that undergoes the dialectical transformation that constitutes human history. Marx is a philosophical immanenist (one who believes that all value and meaning comes from human activity) in a much more profound and consistent way than Hegel. For Marx, there is no meaning or significance apart from human relations and human action, which he calls *praxis*, impacting on and transforming nature—no Absolute, no Spirit made self-conscious. For Marx, Hegel's concrete universals—art, religion, law, constitutions, the state, and philosophy—are epiphenomena of man's material and economic conditions. Marx is out to demystify Hegel's System and to undercut its politically conservative and reactionary implications.

Marx is an extremely complex, often obscure, thinker, who is economist, social critic, philosopher, and prophet rolled into one. For our purposes, I want only to highlight one concept he took from Hegel and developed in a new way. That is the concept of alienation. Hegel spoke of Spirit alienated from itself. Marx spoke of men being alienated from themselves by social forces that take the fruits of their labor away from them and turn the products of that labor into commodities controlled by other men. What Marx is saying about the self is that the self does not exist in isolation, but only as a part of a family, a social class, and a society at a given level of development, both technologically and in terms of the organization of production. In the present stage of that development, which he called capitalism, alienation is inevitable. Following Hegel, Marx sees the self producing concrete universals—goods, services, and cultural products—that are the objectification of that self. Ideally, that objectification, those cultural and economic products, would be reintegrated, used by the selves that produced them, and their labor would not be alienated. But that is not what happens in the present stage of development of the means of production. On the contrary, labor is alienated and self is stripped of its own manifestations. The products of that labor take on a life of their own in opposition to their creators, and man is caught up in what Edmund Wilson (1940/1972, p. 340) calls "the dance of the commodities." Under such conditions, the self cannot be unitary or integrated, and deformation of the self is intrinsic to living under such conditions. For Marx, both worker (proletarian) and owner (capitalist) are rendered less than human by their mutual relations. Each is deformed, distorted, and left insecure and incomplete because the reintegration of self objectified is not possible. Further, the proletariat and the capitalist class, who stand in relation of thesis and antithesis, are in irreconcilable conflict. According to Marx, the contradictions inherent in capitalism must lead to its destruction. Once again, conflict comes to the fore as constitutive of self: conflict both within the alienated self and between selves that are alienated and the selves who alienate them.

For our purposes, Marx's contribution is to emphasize, as none of our previous thinkers about self have done, that the self always exists in a social context. There are no selves solipsistically thinking, nor are there selves synthesizing themselves in isolation, nor are there Transcendental Egos accompanying each act of thinking apart from the social relations that define them. Marx's self is much less abstract. It is always determinate of and determined by social reality. There are no selves that are not members of communities and of social classes, and that membership importantly determines the nature of those selves. At present, the self is not only determined by its social (class) relations and its relations to the means of production, it is alienated a priori by those social (class) relations. According to Marx, there is no self apart from its social relations and there is no self that is not alienated from itself, that is, not torn by the asymmetry of the distribution of power and wealth. Marx thinks that he is being descriptive, not prescriptive, here, but that is not so. He is making a normative statement about what self should be and thereby introduces the notion that self can be healthy (not alienated) or sick (alienated), and he implicitly makes the value judgment that the alienated self is pathological. We have come a long way from Descartes's self as lone cogitator to Marx's self that has no existence apart from its social relations and its relationships to products generated by its transformation of nature through labor.

6

Søren Kierkegaard: The Self as Dread

Søren Kierkegaard (1813–1855) went to Berlin to study under Hegel and learn the System. He returned to his native Copenhagen and declared, "The System is magnificent; it is like a perfectly designed and constructed castle, the only problem is that I don't live in the castle, I live in the privy." Much of Kierkegaard's philosophizing can be seen as a reaction to Hegel. Kierkegaard's rejection of the dominant philosophical doctrine of his time was typical of him. Søren didn't cotton to much of anything that was accepted by his contemporaries. He wrote, "In our time everyone wants to make things easier, especially the professors who write handy compendiums, so I will take as my life work making things more difficult."

As we have seen, for Hegel, Thought and Being are one. The Absolute that becomes manifest (actual) in human history is rational in the sense of being logically necessary; all of Being, everything that is, is grounded in rationality, in logical necessity. The System demonstrates this. Kierkegaard responds, yes, that's fine and dandy, but what does that have to do with me living in my odoriferous outhouse? Indeed, what does the System have to do with any human being struggling with his or her particularity? How does it help me, for example, to know that my being tortured is logically necessary and is transparently grounded in the rationality of the Absolute? Hegel's rationality has nothing to do with human purpose. (Hegel agrees, but isn't upset by this. Kierkegaard is.) Paradoxically, Hegel's rationality is much more like the classical Greek *Ananke* (Necessity)—the blind will of the gods, against which we struggle in vain. To say that the brute facticity of life is rational is nonsense. Fatedness isn't rationality. It isn't Hegel the theodicist and philosophical idealist who is persuasive. On the contrary, Hegel is much more convincing in his awareness of the irrationality of history and of the indifference to human concerns in the unfolding of the Absolute, and in his emphasis on the centrality of conflict and aggression in human history and interpersonal relations. Hegel's synthesis is an attempt to make the conflict disappear by absorbing it into a "higher unity," and in that way Hegel's System is a theodicy, an explanation of the ways of God to man. Kierkegaard doesn't think much of theodicies. He would have agreed with A. E. Housman that "Mead does more than Milton can to explain the ways of God to man." Housman, of course, is thinking of Milton's *Paradise Lost* in his famous couplet. According to Kierkegaard, the trouble with the System, or any other explanation of the way things are, and the reason why they have to be that way is that the individual existent gets lost. There is no place for the self as lived rather than as related to the totality of things. Kierkegaard didn't want to be part of the System, of any system philosophical, religious, social, or political. He wrote that he wanted to be remembered as "The Individual" and have that engraved on his tombstone.

What sort of man was "The Individual"? A strange one. Søren Kierkegaard was born and lived his life, with the exception of some time in Berlin spent studying Hegelian philosophy, in Copenhagen. He was the son of a self-made man who had come to the Danish capital from a bleak, impoverished area of Jutland. The morose father, even when he had become wealthy, retained the bleakness of his early environment, which he had internalized. In a moment of despair, he, the father, had climbed a hill and cursed God; his consequent guilt never left him. Søren grew up in a gloomy, sin-obsessed home, dominated by his depressed, guilt-ridden, albeit prosperous, father. Søren's relationship with his father was the most powerful and enduring emotional relationship of his life. His father, who had been married previously, married his servant—who became the mother of his children—with unseemly haste after his first wife's death. We do not know Søren's feelings about his father's first wife, nor his reaction to his father's quick remarriage to the woman who became his mother, but we do know how another melancholy Dane reacted to his mother's hasty remarriage; this is certainly a different case, yet one remarriage somehow echoes the other. In any case, Søren brooded about what appeared to be family secrets.

Michael Kierkegaard believed in and practiced a dour Protestantism that emphasized guilt and damnation. In his adult life Søren pilloried the liberal Christianity, upbeat and self-congratulatory, that had become the dominant strain of religion in Denmark. In some sense, this was an unconscious identification with his father, whose life-style and values he had consciously repudiated. During his adolescence, there were frequent deaths in the family as Søren lost sibling after sibling, until only one brother remained. The father interpreted these visitations as manifestations of Divine wrath and as punishment for sin. Søren's darkest suspicions were confirmed. In the central trauma of his life, Søren discovered that his father had been carrying on an affair with his servant, Søren's mother, whom he had more or less raped, while his first wife was still alive. Furthermore, his father felt, perhaps at least partly correctly, that his infidelity had killed the woman he loved and whom he continued to love throughout his life. So his father, the idealized incarnation of piety and respectability, was indeed doubly damned: for cursing God and for murder. Søren's disillusionment was profound; he broke with his father and went through a phase of rebellious "worldliness."

If this twisted religiosity wasn't enough of a burden, young Kierkegaard also had to cope with deformity: he walked with a crab-like gait, hunched and deformed from a childhood accident, falling out of a tree. Was it the tree of knowledge the young Kierkegaard fell out of? At least in his unconscious it was. In spite of all this gloom, Kierkegaard's swift intelligence and rapier wit gave him a certain social presence. He had held his own at school and at the university. Kierkegaard became a man about town, frequenting the theaters and the cafes—even visiting a brothel. He became a feature of Copenhagen's intellectual life, playing to strength, so to speak, and built a reputation of being a "character." He was both admired and ridiculed. In his mid-20s he fell in love with an adolescent girl, Regine Olsen. In the second of his spiritual crises, the first being the traumatic disillusionment with his father, he broke off his engagement and renounced Regine Olsen. In *Fear and Trembling* (1843/1941b) he wrote of Abraham's sacrifice of Isaac as an heroic act, describing Abraham as a *Knight of Faith*. The parallel of his "sacrifice" of Regine is as intended as it is obvious. Søren saw his giving up of the possibility of marriage as a spiritual act. Nevertheless, later in life he wrote, "If I had had faith I would have married Regine." He remained obsessed with her, or at least with his decision, the rest of his life. Regine, on the other hand, seemed to have casually forgotten him, marrying another and rarely mentioning him after he became famous.

In a state of deep depression, Søren fled to Berlin. Hegelian philosophizing proved to be a poor antidepressant, and he returned to Copenhagen to play the gay bachelor while writing his "psychological works." It is with his psychological works that we are concerned. Published under pseudonyms, such works as *Either/Or: A Fragment of Life* (1843/1944b), *Fear and Trembling* (1843/1941b), *The Sickness Unto Death* (1849/1944c), and *The Concept of Dread* (1844/1944a) are early exemplifications of what became known as *depth psychology* (i.e., of a psychology concerned with unconscious as well as with conscious phenomena). Kierkegaard's psychological works have much to say about the nature of the self.

Kierkegaard found himself at war with the increasingly liberal bourgeois culture of Denmark. He hated the modern church, the professors, the social reformers, and the "levelers." He was appalled by the revolutions of 1848, finding in them confirmation of his worst fears. He anticipated and abhorred the mass societies of the 20th century, but in so doing he became something of a reactionary. Although primarily a religious philosopher, his social criticism points backward; its social, political, and economic implications are regressive. Søren's concerns are with spirituality, with the inner life, not with political philosophy or economics per se, but his distaste for the life he saw around him led to no redeeming social vision, but only to what seems to me a morbid religiosity. His father, with whom he was by now reconciled, won out. Wealthy, comfortable, and an increasingly acerbic intellectual, Kierkegaard mocked the established church and all the other official comforters from the Hegelian popularizers to the liberal prime minister. He was completely blind to the ravages of the Industrial Revolution, the growing proletariat, or the social or economic inequalities of Europe. In a sense, his quarrel was more with Norman Vincent Peale than with Marx or the Utopian socialists, but there is a blindness to other than spiritual suffering in his spiritually aristocratic inwardness.

Kierkegaard was a great admirer of Socrates. He wrote his dissertation on Socratic irony, and he saw himself as fulfilling a Socratic role. He, like Socrates, wandered about the marketplace of his hometown challenging the comfortable and comforting ideas of his fellow citizens. "Everyone makes things easier, I will make them harder." His work was "calculated to make people aware," and he didn't write books "to be perused during the afternoon nap." He disturbed his fellow citizens' un-self-aware complacency by challenging the unexamined, indeed often unconscious, assumptions by which they lived their lives of "quiet desperation." Like Socrates, Kierkegaard relied heavily on irony in carrying out his self-appointed task. Kierkegaard projects some of his bitterness onto Socrates: "Why, I wonder did Socrates love youths, unless it was because he knew men" (1849/1944a, p. 193). His identification with Socrates was deliberate and self-conscious. Kierkegaard described his chosen role as that of "gadfly," which is of course Plato's Socrates' self-description. Like Socrates, he was an existential radical and a sociopolitical reactionary: one who pushed himself and his fellows toward inward depths while supporting traditional authoritarian social structures. Furthermore, in his hostility toward and attacks on the "Establishment," Kierkegaard invited, but did not succeed in provoking, a similar fate.

The last phase of his life, following yet another spiritual crisis, which led him to formulate his mission as the destruction of the established church of Denmark, brought him a sense of fulfillment. The products of his final crisis—his religious works, both devotional and critical—were published under his own name, unlike his psychological works, which appeared under pseudonyms. Becoming a pamphleteer, he exhausted himself writing invective, collapsed in the street, and died at the age of 47. It is said that, in his final outburst of rage, he finally escaped his lifelong depression.

What did this tormented, guilt-obsessed man have to say about the nature of reality and the nature of the self? Before we can evaluate what Kierkegaard believed to be true about the self and the world, we need to understand his doctrine of truth. Of our various writers about self, his is the most sustained defense of the nonrationality, indeed the irrationality, of human life as lived, and of the consequent futility of reason as a guide to understanding that life. His theory of truth is congruent with his suspicions about the rationality of the world.

Kierkegaard's theory of truth has more to do with passion than with thought. He holds that *Truth is Subjectivity*. Although Kierkegaard has no quarrel with science and its empirical truth seeking, science's kind of objectivity and universal truth don't interest him. In fact, one of his books is entitled *Concluding Unscientific Postscript* (1846/1941a). "Truth is subjectivity": what does that mean? Clearly, this is neither a correspondence theory (a proposition is true if, and only if, it corresponds to a state of affairs; e.g., the proposition "the cat is on the mat" is true if, and only if, the cat is on the mat), nor is it a coherence theory (a proposition is true if, and only if, it is consistent with, or can be reconciled with, the totality of knowledge, in Hegelian terms, the System; e.g., the proposition "the cat is on the mat" can be true only if cats are the sort of things that can be on mats). Kierkegaard is interested in neither correspondence nor coherence, though he would not deny them their place in scientific theory or in daily life. What he is interested in is the truth as lived, truth as personal commitment, truth as passionately held belief. It is human commitment to it, its subjective quality, that makes the truth true; otherwise it is empty abstraction. Kierkegaard is, here, as almost always elsewhere, focused on the particular, the individual, or the concrete rather than on the general, the universal, or the abstract. Even the truth of Newton's Laws comes from the passionate commitment of Newton and other men to the belief that these laws are true. This is not rational, or at least not necessarily rational. For Kierkegaard, the most important thing is his commitment to Christianity, his decision made in "fear and trembling" to believe. Christian belief is not rational belief; the Incarnation is a mystery not illuminated by Reason. Tertullian, the early church father, wrote, "*Credo ad absurdum*": "I believe because it is absurd." Kierkegaard doesn't quite subscribe to this, but he isn't too far from it. He doesn't say, I believe because it is absurd, but he does say, even if what I believe is absurd, it is true if I believe it passionately enough. Kierkegaard is clearly on the side of those who believe that feeling is a better guide to action than thought, at least better than abstract thought. Here Kierkegaard, with his focus on the individual, particularly the individual as heroic truth seeker, is clearly part of the early 19th-century Romantic reaction to the Enlightenment thinking of the 18th century. There is something of Hume here, but without his skepticism and distrust of enthusiasm; Kierkegaard is much closer to the Pascal of "the heart has its reasons."

There is something deeply dangerous about Kierkegaard's view of what makes the truth true. How is passionate commitment to Hitler and National Socialism to be distinguished from Kierkegaard's passionate commitment to Christ and Christianity? By Kierkegaard's criteria, they are equally true. Even allowing for rhetorical and polemical exaggeration and provocation, the doctrine that truth is subjectivity is hard to take seriously. Nevertheless, Kierkegaard is onto something here. Perhaps life and being are absurd in the sense of being *brute facticity*—of being that which cannot be explained. The world and the things in it are brutally factual, and that is all that can be said about them; they simply are. Why is there something rather than nothing? Can Being be deduced? Hegel thought so; Kierkegaard did not. We do indeed live in the outhouse much of the time. Taken as a statement that there is no truth apart from the human beings who believe that truth, Kierkegaard's doctrine that truth is subjectivity makes some sense. Subjectivity doesn't determine the truth value of propositions, but those propositions are indeed embedded in the belief systems of particular human beings and assume their significance from being part of these passionately upheld belief systems. Kierkegaard does not quite take William James's position that truth is determined by the "cash value" of a belief, or Christ's that "By their fruits Ye shall know them." After all, he is an early 19th-century religious philosopher, highly critical of Enlightenment thinking, not a late 19th-century pragmatist. Nevertheless, there is something of the pragmatist in Kierkegaard that he himself would not be comfortable with, even though the absolutist in him undercuts his pragmatic side.

In a more sympathetic mode, at least to me, Kierkegaard is extolling reflection—thinking infused with feeling—in contradistinction to abstract thought. He argues that reflection is closer to the *individual's concrete existence* than is pure dispassionate reason, and because it is, it (meaning reflection) is a better vehicle to discover some kinds of truth. His reflections were not only of inward reality. Throughout his career, he reflected on the world around him and found it not to his liking. He is certainly a prescient social critic of the mass societies of modern times. He is the enemy of every collectivity and every facile comforter. His social criticism is essentially in the service of his commitment to the sanctity of the inner life and, for all of its narrowness, highlights the ways in which societies facilitate the escape from self, and the confrontations with self, that, for him, gives life its significance.

Kierkegaard's first book, *Either/Or: A Fragment of Life* (1843/1944b), starkly summarizes his philosophy both in its title and in its content. There is no reconciliation of opposites, no absorption into a higher unity; it is either/or, and what man must do is choose. It is said that the urchins of Copenhagen followed Søren through the streets chanting "neither/nor." *Fear and Trembling* (1843/1941b) builds on and concretizes the insights of *Either/Or*. In retelling the story of Abraham and Isaac, Kierkegaard tells the story of Søren and Regine. For them there was no reconciliation in a higher unity. He either married her or he did not. In either case, he made his decision in fear and trembling, as did Abraham. Abraham is characterized as a knight of faith, a category Kierkegaard creates to contrast with the tragic hero. The tragic hero fails through a flaw; the knight of faith engages in tragic actions because they are entailed by his faith, not because he is flawed. The central point is that reason does not help man's fate, the human condition; on the contrary, "one thing is needful": a decision, a leap of faith. There is no avoiding that decision, although we can repress our awareness of the necessity for one. In his antiphilosophic, individualistic stance, Kierkegaard echoes Luther when he states, "Whoever wants to be a Christian should tear the eyes out of his reason." In a similar vein, Luther had written, "Reason is a whore."

One cannot but wonder how much unconscious hostility toward Regine is present here. After all, she is identified with Isaac who is to be sacrificed, and God did not intervene to announce that her sacrifice was not required. Had Kierkegaard expected him to? Here Kierkegaard is identifying himself with Abraham, the knight of faith, who is doing the sacrificing. But his identification is neither so simple nor so unambiguous. If he is Abraham, he is also Isaac being sacrificed by his fearsome father. Kierkegaard's deeply neurotic conflict with his father is embedded in this conflictual identification with Abraham and with Isaac. After all, his father had not spared him the sacrifice of his innocent belief in his father's purity, or protected him from traumatic disillusionment.

Kierkegaard is often regarded as the first *existentialist*. I once knew a man who told me he was an existentialist. I asked him what he meant by that and he replied, "An existentialist is someone who sits alone in a room and meditates on the meaninglessness of life." That man was my patient in a psychiatric rehabilitation program, but he wasn't so far off. Existentialism, about which I will have more to say in a later chapter, is not a particular doctrine, but rather a way of philosophizing and a way of looking at the world that emphasizes extreme states, estrangement, singularity, and the limitations of reason. It is the philosophy of the privy, not of the castle. On the technical side, the central doctrine of existentialism is that existence precedes essence. This is not the nominalism (the doctrine that universals are but names and have no reality apart from particulars) of a logician; it is a statement that there is no a priori human nature apart from what we become. We are our acts. According to Kierkegaard, "The only 'thing-in-itself' which cannot be thought is existence, and this does not come within the province of things to think." This is the existentialist position in a nutshell. If the existentialists, including Kierkegaard, were logically consistent, they could say nothing about the human condition or about the nature of the self. Any such statement has to be a statement about essence—the essence of being human—and essence does not precede concrete existence. Nevertheless, all the existentialists, starting with Kierkegaard, manage to say a great deal about these topics.

One of the essentials of the self, which on Kierkegaard's own premises has no essence, that he discusses are the *Stages on Life's Way* (1845/1940). This is a developmental schema that is simultaneously a parody of the Hegelian dialectic and an unconscious adaptation of it. In this schema, the first stage is the *aesthetic*, the naive enjoyment of the senses, of art, of nature, and of the good life. The aesthete lives for pleasure, novelty, and enjoyment. He or she may develop into a connoisseur of the beautiful. Kierkegaard is fully aware of the appeals of the aesthetic life. He himself has lived it. His criticism of it isn't moral or ethical, nor does he stand in judgment on it. Rather he sees the problem with the aesthetic stage as dialectical. A life of pleasure leads to its antithesis, boredom and satiation, and is ultimately unsatisfactory on its own terms; it ceases to be pleasurable and becomes painful. The synthesis of pleasure and boredom is morality, and the next stage is the *ethical*. In the ethical stage of development, one lives for duty, for official and family responsibilities, and for fulfilling one's duties as worker, marital partner, parent, and citizen. Ideally the aesthetic is *Aufgehoben*, annulled, preserved, and transformed, and is now encompassed in the ethical. But Kierkegaard has a finer sense of the irreconcilability of differing ways of being human than does Hegel; the degree of "Aufgehobenness" in Kierkegaard's developmental scheme is open to question. At any rate, the ethical, too, generates its antithesis, wooden dutifulness—routine, unfeeling, dead fulfillment of duty. Kierkegaard probably has Kant in mind here, but he is primarily describing one way of being human, of existing and being. Having lived out the aesthetic and ethical stages and having experienced their limitations and self-generated contradictions, where is one to go? According to Kierkegaard, the next, and highest, stage is the *religious*. The religious is characterized neither by pleasure seeking nor by responsible action; rather, it is characterized by a nonrational leap of faith, a decision to believe: in Kierkegaard's case, the decision to be a Christian. In *Fear and Trembling*, Kierkegaard raises a terrifying question, "Is there a teleological suspension of the ethical" (1843/1911, p. 64), a putting aside of the dictates of morality (e.g., "Thou shalt not kill"), for the sake of an ultimate concern (e.g., obedience to God)? *Teleology*, from the Greek *telos*, end, is the study of final ends; hence, *teleological*, "in the service of, or because of, an ultimate purpose." Both the paradigm of Abraham and Isaac and his personal relinquishing of Regine raise this question. Kierkegaard worries it at length, and on balance seems to decide that there is such a suspension of the ethical. Presumably, in ordinary circumstances, there is both pleasure (beauty) and responsibility in the religious state, and in this sense they are *Aufgehoben* into it. But they do not characterize the religious stage. The leap of faith does.

Having lived through all too many "teleological suspensions of the ethical," through all of the 20th-century movements that have sacrificed the present for the future, that have put ends above means, that have murdered millions for the eschatological fulfillment of one or another Messianic dream, we at the end of the bloodiest century in history must reject any teleological suspension of the ethical. Kant's "treat every man as an end in himself," whatever its problems in practice, looks awfully good to me. None of this vitiates Kierkegaard's insight into three distinct ways of being human, of living life, nor of his description of the dialectical relationship between those stages as ways of being.

Kierkegaard contested both the philosophical dualistic legacy of Plato (and of Descartes) and the popular conception of the soul or self as substance, a thing comparable to the body. The self, in this traditional philosophical and common-sense view, is the permanent stuff to which things happen. The traditional categories are substance and accident. In this view, the self is the substance in which accidents adhere. Kierkegaard will have nothing of such substantiation—turning into a substance or underlying substrate—of the self. Nor can Kierkegaard accept Hegel's notion of the self as developing self-consciousness. For Kierkegaard this is still too rationalistic, too much a fluidization of Kant's transcendental unity of the apperception. What I mean by this is that Hegel's self is still a logical category, indeed a logical necessity a priori, albeit a dynamic one. It is in motion but it is still a kind of stuff. Kierkegaard likes the dynamism and self-consciousness, but not the rationality, of the Hegelian concept of the self. Having rejected self as mind or thinking substance, and having rejected self as Hegelian rational process, Kierkegaard offers his own understanding of the nature of the self. His formulation is prolix and in some ways inconsistent, but integral in its insistence on the primacy of emotionality, as the self as something experienced in certain feeling states. He says,

The self is essentially intangible and must be understood in terms of possibilities, dread, and decisions, when I behold my possibilities I experience that dread which is the "dizziness of freedom," and my choice is made in "fear and trembling." I am what I choose. (1849/1944a, p. 55)

Self is man deciding, and reason doesn't help. In his discussion of the self, the meaning of Kierkegaard's notion of truth becomes clearer. The truth of my existence is not propositional or logical, not objective but subjective. The closest thing in Kierkegaard to Hegel's absolute idea is the individual man's subjectivity. Consistent with his understanding of self and of truth, Kierkegaard writes, "The conclusions of passion are the only reliable ones," and "What our age needs is not reflection but passion."

What I find valuable in this is the notion of the "dizziness of freedom," of the vertigo that accompanies the idea that I have choices and that I am responsible for those choices. I see that clinically all the time. When people become more free— less neurotically constricted, less compulsive, less addicted—they also become more anxious. What Kierkegaard has come up with, although he doesn't quite say it, is the notion of the self as freedom, as existential, not as rational potentiality. Whatever the ontological status of the self, experientially it is free. At least in certain moods, I am aware that I experience myself as agent, as free, as maker of decisions, and chooser of choices. That is, whatever the ultimate truth about the free will-determinism question, I cannot live my life without experiencing myself as, at least to some degree, a free agent, and there is inescapable anxiety associated with that freedom. I think Kierkegaard is on target here; I do indeed discover me when I make choices and experience the Kierkegaardian dizziness. Kierkegaard's belief that choosing in fear and trembling is the only self-experience is contrary to fact, but it is indeed a central self-experience.

Kierkegaard is a psychologist of dread (anxiety) and despair (depression) *par excellence*. He was the first to distinguish between dread (anxiety) and fear. When I am afraid, I am afraid of something—of losing my job, of illness, of a snake, of loss of love, or of the truck bearing down on me. Anxiety, on the contrary, has no object; it is dread of . . . nothing, of I know not what. The objectlessness of anxiety is what makes it so terrifying, and so difficult to deal with. My biologically preprogrammed response to fear is fight or flight, to combat the danger or to remove myself from it. But I can neither fight nor run from my dread. Kierkegaard saw this clearly. He also saw that both dread and despair can be unconscious. He wrote that man may be in despair without knowing it. He would very much agree with his also-solitary contemporary, Henry David Thoreau, that "most men live lives of quiet desperation."

Kierkegaard describes despair as *The Sickness Unto Death*. He goes on to say that only man can despair because only he has a spirit, and concludes from this that the self is spiritual. This seems to contradict his earlier conclusion that the self is its choices, but perhaps there is no contradiction. I suppose spirit (whatever that may be) can make anxious choices. Kierkegaard formulates his notion of self as spirit in the following way:

Man is spirit. But what is spirit? Spirit is the self. But what is the self? The self is a relation which relates itself to its own self, or it is that in the relation [which accounts for it] that the relation relates itself to its own self; the self is not the relation but [consists in the fact] that the relation relates itself to its own self. Man is a synthesis of the infinite and the finite, of the temporal and the eternal, of freedom and necessity, in short he is a synthesis. A synthesis is a relation between two factors. So regarded man is not yet a self. . . the self is constituted by another—the Power *that constitutes it . . . by relating itself to its own self and by willing to be itself the self is grounded transparently in the Power which posited it. (1849/1944c, p. 146)*

There seem to be at least three notions here. One is that the self is reflexive. It consists in the act of relating itself to itself. Since to Kierkegaard there is no substantive self, it is the relating, not the relation, that is salient. But there is a problem here. How can you relate without relata? If I have a relation with myself and that self is the relationship, then what am I relating to? Is this an infinite regress? If, by relationship to myself, Kierkegaard means self-awareness, then there is no problem, but he doesn't seem to want to say, or merely say, that. He gets out of this dilemma by abandoning his existentialism for essentialism in characterizing man (the self?) as the synthesis of a series of opposites. Then the self becomes the act of synthesizing the paired opposites: finite and infinite, temporal and eternal, and freedom and necessity. Now the self is the self-awareness of the act of unification. It is the awareness of relating these antinomies to each other. Kierkegaard calls both the relating and the relationship spirit and identifies spirit with the self. He then introduces an entirely new notion—the incompleteness, indeed irreality, of the self merely as synthesis ("so regarded man is not yet a self"), without that self being made real (actual) by another, the Power that constitutes it. This seems to mean that there is no self without God, and that by relating myself to myself, by being reflexive and by choosing to be the self that I become (since there is no self that I am), I do indeed achieve a selfhood that is validated by a power other than myself. This sounds like the Hindu Atman (the self within) is the Brahman (the self without), but Kierkegaard isn't a mystic and I don't think that is what he wants to say. For him, God is always other, so that the self within is not the self without. Rather, Kierkegaard seems to be saying that without the decision to be a Christian, or at least the decision to believe, there is no self. I don't quite know what to make of this third aspect of the Kierkegaardian self, but the notion of the self as affectively aware self-consciousness; of the self as potentiality, that becomes rather than is; of the self as reflexively relating to itself; and of the self as the synthesizer and synthesis of opposites makes perfect sense and enriches our concept of the self. So does Kierkegaard's realization that all, or at least most, of this can be unconscious. Affect, fantasy, and belief can all be unconscious. Kierkegaard's belief that awareness—consciousness—of self-activity is desirable is normative and not descriptive. Descriptively, he is perfectly cognizant of the role of unconsciousness process.

In fact, for Kierkegaard both dread and despair can be unconscious. However, since selfhood requires self-awareness, it is desirable that that dread and despair become conscious. Kierkegaard saw his role as facilitating that consciousness. Singleness of purpose, "to will one thing," is prerequisite to self-awareness. However, singleness of purpose is difficult to achieve because of the dialectical nature of human existence and human awareness. For example, there is a dialectical oscillation between "despair at not willing to be oneself" and "despair at willing to be oneself" (1849/1944c, p. 128). Kierkegaard is here doubly essentialistic: first he is, against his own formulation, talking about a oneself that appears to be substantive, although the oneself, that one wills and doesn't will to be, could be potentiality—angst-permeated decision. Perhaps more important, he seems to be saying that such an oscillation is intrinsic to being human. This is the case because despair is not something that happens to one—to me—from outside like a disease one contracts; it is not like a bacillus that I contract that sickens me; rather, it is something that happens from within, that is intrinsic. Despair, Kierkegaard's sickness unto death, is in this regard much like Freud's death instinct that resides within every living thing. Similarly, dread is not something that happens to me; rather, it is the anxiety concomitant with the realization that one is (I am) insubstantial, not a thing. Dread is my response to the realization that I am free, and that in some sense what I do with that freedom can have no rational justification (i.e., lacks any sort of logical necessity).

Dread, like despair, may be conscious or it may be unconscious, but in either case it is inescapable. To be unaware of being in despair is to be in despair. Dread and despair are ontological in the sense of being structural components of self. To turn the potential into the actual (i.e., to make choices) is to lose potentiality, and there is a type of neurotic who can't fully live because he or she can't stand to lose potentiality. Choice is paradoxical in the sense that it is both eternal and nonannullable and renewed each living moment.

When Kierkegaard says that one is either in despair at knowing that one is in despair or in despair at not knowing that one is in despair, he is making despair ontological (i.e., intrinsic to the human condition). He holds the same to be true of dread (anxiety). So far he is merely being descriptive, descriptive of conscious and unconscious ways of being. But when he comes down on the side of consciousness, he is a moralist enjoining his fellows to greater self-awareness. Here he is both the protopsychoanalyst elucidating the power of the unconscious, and the inevitability of its being acted out if not brought to consciousness, and the religious traditionalist giving a new psychological twist to the ancient injunction "fear of the Lord is the beginning of wisdom."

Kierkegaard's self is a whole individual who feels and acts as well as thinks. That is why Kierkegaard's Subjectivity includes both objectivity and subjectivity as rooted in concrete human existence. The self is the "intermediate determinant" between psyche and soma and relates itself to both; however, it does not actually exist; it is only that which it is to become. "The self is reflection" and "generally speaking, consciousness, i.e., consciousness of itself, is the decisive criterion of the self"; in fact, "the more consciousness, the more self." Kierkegaard's individualism is not egotistic or narcissistic; rather, it is relational in both relating itself to itself and relating itself to the Power that constitutes it. Kierkegaard explicitly warns against narcissistic self-absorption and schizoid withdrawal, which he calls Shut-Up-Ness and characterizes as morbid inwardness. He himself spent his life fighting a tendency toward such morbid inwardness and shut-up-ness, which were both causes of, and consequences of, his lifelong depression. He was only partially successful in coming to terms with and overcoming that part of himself.

The dialectical nature of the self makes it possible to lose oneself in a false transcendence or in an empty concreteness; to succumb to a facile mysticism that gives an illusion of fusion with the totality of things, thereby denying one's uniqueness, separateness, and individuality; or to become a cipher in the crowd. To become either infinitized or finitized is to become less of a self. Authenticity of the self requires remaining aware of the opposites that constitute the self.

Oddly, Kierkegaard's notion of the self ends up not so very far from that of his hated and rejected alter ego, Hegel. For Hegel, the self is the "act of referring its contents to the unity of itself." Consciousness of this operation is the self. "The being of mind [here the self] is its act and its act is to be aware of itself." The difference between Hegel's and Kierkegaard's notion of self is essentially the level of anxiety in their respective formations. Hegel is aware of anxiety, but it is *Aufgehoben* into Reason; not so for Kierkegaard, for whom the self *is* anxiety. Kierkegaard's great contribution to the theory of self is his emphasis on affectivity, albeit only painful affectivity. Kierkegaard is far more aware than Hegel that unities are both tenuous and suspect. It is the act of unifying, not the unification, that is salient. These differences are important, but both emphasize selfhood as activity, that activity being self-reflection. For all the complexity of his thought about self, Kierkegaard essentially restates his hero Socrates' injunction that "the unexamined life isn't worth living," but as an ontological not a normative proposition. "The more consciousness, the more self," implies that self is not given, but is achieved, and that some have more self than others.

7

William James: The Multiplicity of the Self

William James (1842–1910) was exquisitely sensitive to the complexities of life, self, and world. Always suspicious of reductionist, overly schematic, psychological, and philosophical conceptualizations, he spoke for the "multiverse" in contradistinction to the universe. He himself was a multiverse: artist, naturalist, writer, experimentalist, theorist, physiologist, psychologist, and philosopher; tormented depressive, metaphysical optimist, neurotic enmeshed in his family of origin, urbane man of the world, introverted introspectionist, and warmly involved tender husband, teacher, and father. A multiverse, indeed, who would have gladly endorsed his father's friend Emerson's observation that "consistency is the hobgoblin of little minds."

William James was born into an extraordinary family. His father, Henry James, Sr., was wealthy, unemployed, brilliant, neurotic, and physically disabled, and knew every thinker and artist of consequence on both sides of the Atlantic. Henry Sr. was the son of an Irish Protestant emigrant who made a fortune by investing in the Erie Canal. The father was an adherent of the Calvinist God of predestination and damnation. Henry Sr. grew up preoccupied with religious guilt and later suffered a "religious crisis." Although less enthralled to a punitive God, William underwent a similar crisis and remained preoccupied with religious questions all of his life. As an early adolescent, Henry Sr. was heating a balloon to get it to rise when some turpentine he had spilled on his leg ignited. He was badly burned, and the leg was amputated above the knee. So William grew up with a disabled father, which must have had something to do with his writing about phantom limb phenomena and bodily intactness. Henry Sr. recovered, although his physicality and free roaming in nature were forever curtailed. He turned to things of the mind, attended Union College in Schenectady, not far from his native Albany, where he was something of a dandy and youth about town, and went on to Princeton Theological Seminary in an apparent attempt to placate his now-dead father. But the dour God of Presbyterianism was not to claim his allegiance. He left the seminary, moved to New York City, married, and became the father of William. When William was 2, the family moved to England, the first of many relocations, transatlantic and domestic. Here, William's father had some kind of breakdown, which he later called a "vastation." William was to suffer virtually the same symptoms, so I defer my account of them for a generation. Whatever the exact nature of the vastation, it profoundly affected Henry Sr. He remained a shattered human being, his confidence gone, awaiting a new encounter with the abyss. Insofar as he understood what had happened to him at all, he experienced it as some sort of religious crisis. One wonders what it was like for little William to live in a home permeated with fear. He continued to live in that anxiety-permeated ambiance until his father discovered the Swedish mystic Swedenborg. Somehow, reading Swedenborg "cured" him, or at least gave him a God other than the terrifying introject of his father projected onto the cosmos. Henry Sr. did not become an "orthodox" Swedenborgian, but he did become a religious philosopher who incorporated Swedenborgian principles into much of his writings. He published his many works at his own expense. He carried the master's works wherever he wandered throughout his peripatetic life.

So William was born into and grew up in an eccentric, troubled, yet vital and wonderful household. His parents had a gift for friendship, and at one time or another the intellectual elite of two continents dined with them. The conversation was unbridled. The atmosphere of William's home was self-consciously free, open, and challenging. No opinion was safe from attack. His mother, Mary, was formidable in her own way. Henry Jr. called her the cornerstone of the arch that was the family. Strong-minded, she had her own ways of exercising control. Both William and Henry had difficulties separating from her. Rivalry was intense, particularly William's with his younger brother Henry, who was to become a distinguished man of letters. It has been said that William was a psychologist who wrote like a novelist, while his brother Henry was a novelist who wrote like a psychologist. It has been further suggested that William should have been the novelist and his brother the psychologist. Be that as it may, they had a sibling rivalry of monumental proportions that never abated; there was also a deep love between them. There were two younger brothers who never recovered from their experiences in the Civil War, and a sister, Alice, who was sickly and emotionally troubled and who died relatively young. The family roamed across the Continent, went back to the United States, then turned around and returned to England. In the course of his boyhood and adolescence, William James crossed the ocean many times. Perhaps the father's restlessness and constant travel were compensation for his physical immobility. Under the circumstances, William's education was irregular, often a month in one school, a year in another. However, what he lacked in classroom experience he more than made up for in his exposure to high culture, the opportunity to acquire French and German, and contact with the most innovative minds of the time. Visitors reported that dining at the James's was an education in itself.

Eventually the family settled in New York, and William received some more regular schooling. He had his difficulties relating to his school fellows, which he dealt with by playing the tough guy in contrast to the more sedate Henry, to whom he bragged, "I play with boys who curse and swear." A major part of William's difficulties came from the fact that his father had neither socially recognized role nor sanctioned identity. William and Henry Jr.'s peers' fathers were professionals and businessmen; their father was a disabled conversationalist. When Henry asked, "What shall I say you are?" the father replied, "Say I'm a philosopher, say I'm a seeker for truth, say I'm a lover of my kind, say I'm an author of books if you like; or best of all just say I'm a Student." This being obviously unsatisfactory, he relented to the extent of saying, "Well, you can tell them I'm a writer." But the problem of identity, of who one's father was, of who one was, went deep with William and with Henry. All of his life, William was sensitive to questions of identity and identification, and the diffuseness of his personal self-concept is reflected in and embedded in his theory of the self. James's microcosm becomes his macrocosm; the multiverse is in part a compensation for the lack of a universe. There were more visits abroad, and eventually he studied at what was to become the University of Geneva. While at the university, it became time for William to "choose" a career. He decided that he would become a painter, and his father objected, not for the usual reasons that artists starve or that the artistic life is too unconventional, but rather because he saw the choice of any career as too restrictive, as a diminution of the potential of the self. This was but an extension of the father's theory of education, that there should be no restrictions placed upon the freedom of the mind. In a twist on Kierkegaard's dizziness of freedom, he saw any narrowing—which, of course, is entailed in choosing to actualize one rather than another potentiality—as a loss. Some people can't make decisions because the burden of choice is too anxiety provoking; others choose unnecessarily because openness is too anxiety provoking. It is to the latter that the father objected. What he wanted was for Willie to remain a "student," a thinker without qualification. In a sense that is exactly what William did do, but not immediately. Papa finally relented, and the family returned from Europe so that Willie could study under one of America's leading artists, William Hunt, in Newport, Rhode Island. James was a talented artist, and the sharpness of his eye was later reflected in the sharpness of his prose. He remained a superb descriptive artist in his incarnations as psychologist and philosopher; however, he decided he didn't quite have it as a painter, or at least that he would never really be first rate, and left Hunt to enroll at Harvard to study science. Willie's interests were in chemistry, anatomy, and what was then called natural history—ecologic and taxonomic descriptive biology. While at Harvard, James became overtly neurasthenic—neurotically incapacitated. Neurasthenia was a new nosological category, having recently been formulated by the American psychiatrist Mitchell Weir. It afflicted intellectually overworked young men and was characterized by ennui, psychosomatic symptoms, lassitude, anxiety, and depression. Freud classified neurasthenia as an "actual neurosis"; that is, one caused by lack of sexual satisfaction rather than by intrapsychic conflict. Freud's notion was that of toxicity (sexual energy that was neither discharged nor sublimated) gone sour, so to speak, and poisoning the bottling- and bottled-up young man. Weir, who was famous for his "rest cure" for emotional illnesses (neuroses), thought differently. Be that as it may, William certainly lacked sexual outlets.

He went off on a trip to the Amazon with the Harvard naturalist, Louis Agassiz. The trip did not go well for him, and he returned to Harvard to study medicine. His illness forced him to take a leave of absence, during which he studied in Europe, principally in Germany. His illness also exempted him from service in the Civil War. James's personal crisis corresponded to his country's crisis, and the two were certainly not unrelated. There was a civil war within as well as without William James. Neither Henry Jr. nor William served in the war, although both their younger brothers did, as did most of their friends, including Oliver Wendell Holmes, Jr. The younger James brothers participated in the horrors of the attack on Fort Wagner, which was vividly depicted in the film *Glory*. Neither brother entirely recovered from the trauma of combat, becoming drifters, drinkers, and ne'er-do-wells. Both William and Henry were guilt-ridden by their nonparticipation in the war. Many years later, William wrote of the necessity for a "moral equivalent of war" that would draw on the idealism and commitment of youth without destroying them. President Kennedy cited that James essay when he founded the Peace Corps. James finally completed his internship at Massachusetts General Hospital and received his MD. Shortly thereafter, his neurasthenic depression reached its nadir, being encapsulated in the following overwhelmingly intense experience that James reported in the *Varieties of Religious Experience* (1902). There he attributed the experience to a "French correspondent," but it was his own.

> *The worst kind of melancholy is that which takes the form of panic fear. Here is an excellent example, for permission to print which I have to thank the sufferer. The original is in French, and though the subject was obviously in a bad nervous condition at the time of which he writes, his case has otherwise the merit of extreme simplicity. I translate freely.*
>
> *"Whilst in this state of philosophical pessimism and general depression of spirits about my prospects, I went one evening into a dressing room in the twilight to secure some article that was there; suddenly there fell upon me, without any warning, just as if it had come out of the darkness, a horrible fear of my own existence. Simultaneously there arose in my mind the image of an epileptic patient whom I had seen in the asylum, a black haired youth with greenish skin, entirely idiotic, who used to sit all day on one of the benches, or rather shelves against the wall, with his knees drawn up against his chin, and the coarse grey undershirt, which was his only garment, drawn over them enclosing his entire figure. He sat there like a sort of sculptured Egyptian cat or Peruvian mummy, moving nothing but his black eyes and looking absolutely non-human. This image and my fear entered into a species of combination with each other. That shape am I, I felt potentially. Nothing that I can possess can defend me against that fate, if the hour for it should strike for me as it struck for him. There was such a horror of him, and such a perception of my own merely momentary discrepancy from him, that it was as if something hereto solid within my breast gave way entirely, and I became a mass of quivering fear. After this the universe was changed for me altogether. I woke morning after morning with a horrible dread in the pit of my stomach, and with a sense of the insecurity of life that I never knew before and that I have never felt since. It was like a revelation; and although the immediate feelings passed away, the experience has made me sympathetic with the morbid feelings of others ever since. It gradually faded, but for months I was unable to go out in the dark alone.*
>
> *In general I dreaded to be left alone. I wondered how other people could live, how I myself had ever lived, so unconscious of that insecurity beneath the surface of life. My mother, in particular, a very cheerful person, seemed to me a perfect paradox in her unconsciousness of danger, which you may well believe I was very careful not to disturb by revelations of my own state of mind. I have always thought that this experience of melancholia of mine had a religious bearing. (James, 1902, p. 156)*

William James, like his father before him, experienced a panic attack. Modern psychiatry understands such experiences as neurochemical disturbances to be treated with tricyclic (so called because of their molecular structure) antidepressants. The vulnerability to such attacks is held to run in families, so the psychiatrist would not see William's attack as, at least in part, an identification with his father or as a consequence of similar preoccupations and psychic conflicts, but rather as a result of genetically transmitted neurochemical vulnerability. James himself discusses neurology in his book on religion, but he, and I, would maintain that the neurochemical correlatives of a thought or a feeling do not determine its meaning. Also, it is well known that the same psychological symptoms can be the outcome of diverse etiological processes and pathways, so that one person's panic attack may be primarily neurochemical in origin while another's may be primarily psychodynamic in origin. It is worth noting that both Freud and modern organic psychiatry would attribute William's symptom to somatic sources, but that Freud would be interested in meanings and conflicts, while the contemporary organicist would not.

James himself understood his experience as a religious crisis, not so much in his father's sense of terror of a Calvinistic God as in the loss of meaning inherent in (for him) the mechanistic, deterministic explanations of human behavior that he had encountered in his scientific studies. Whatever the more personal, intrapsychic and interpersonal factors underlying his neurotic incapacitation, the loss of meaningfulness weighed heavily upon him. Scientific explanation, such as the neurochemical account of panic, robbed the inner life of human significance, and this reductive scientism, the prevailing *Weltanschauung* of his milieu, weighed heavily upon him. In fact, he became so depressed that "thoughts of the pistol, the dagger, and the bowl [to catch the blood]" never left him. How close to suicide he came during his period of suicidal ideation, we cannot be sure, but both the despair and the risk were real. He later wrote that no man is entirely educated unless he has had the realization that he can take his own life and has decided to live. When James said *realization*, he did not mean mere intellectual awareness but the deep emotional conviction that suicide is a real option.

Of course, his experience was one of vulnerability as well as one of meaninglessness. It is worth noting that James felt that he could not communicate his terror to his cheerful mother. For all the openness in the family, some things could not be discussed. James came out of his depression (insofar as he did) in a characteristic way. As a consequence of reading the French philosopher Charles Renouvier, he came to the conclusion that the arguments for or against determinism—or to state the alternative, for or against free will—were equally inconclusive. Somewhat in the spirit of Kant's reaction to his antinomies, but coming from a more emotional than logical position, James decided that reason was of no help in deciding whether or not he was a free agent. Furthermore, Renouvier convinced him that mind could affect body, just as body could affect mind. That did it for James. He wrote, "My first act of free will, shall be to believe in free will." He went on to say, "My belief, to be sure, can't be optimistic—but I will posit life . . . the self-governing resistance of the ego to the world" (Perry, 1935, p. 121). The corner had been turned. By sheer effort of will, James began his recovery from a decade-long depression.

His illness culminating in his crisis was "overdetermined," as the analysts put it. That is to say, it had many causes: James's identity diffusion; his repressed hatred of his simultaneously loved brother, Henry; his reaction to the carnage of the Civil War and guilt over not fighting in it; his sexual repression; his inability to successfully rebel against his overtly liberal, overtly generous, yet smothering parents; his shock over the loss of his young, beautiful, beloved cousin, Minnie Temple (immortalized as Millie Theale in his brother's novel *The Wings of the Dove*), an event that made death real to him; and his existential despair over the absence of meaning, agency, and belief in his life. James dealt with his illness by an act of will and by an intellectual analysis; one wonders what sort of person he would have developed into if he had also had the benefit of insight into the emotional and interpersonal roots of his neurasthenia.

James remained a semi-invalid living in his parents' home for several more years. At the age of 30, he emerged from his cocoon to teach at Harvard. His first appointment was as an instructor in anatomy and physiology. He subsequently became a professor of psychology, founding the first laboratory of experimental psychology in America (Wundt founded a similar laboratory at the University of Leipzig in the same year, 1874), and wound up as a professor of philosophy. Thus, his professional evolution was from artist, to chemist, to naturalist, to physician, to physiologist, to psychologist, to philosopher. It was an epigenetic development, with each later stage latent in each earlier stage, and each later stage incorporating the earlier stages. In a sense he was a philosopher all along. His most important works are *The Principles of Psychology* (1890/1983); *Varieties of Religious Experience* (1902); "Does Consciousness Exist?" (1904/1912a), an essay in which he first develops the philosophical positions he called *neutral monism* and *radical empiricism*; *The Will to Believe* (1896/1956); and *Pragmatism, a New Name for Some Old Ways of Thinking* (1907/1912c). *Essays in Radical Empiricism* (1912b) and *A Pluralistic Universe* (1909) were published posthumously.

James finally married at the age of 38. His marriage was a happy one and so was his family life. Although he continued to be plagued by emotional pain, he functioned and functioned magnificently, creative and productive in three fields. He also had a gift for friendship. James was loved by his students, his colleagues, his friends, and his family. Toward the end of his life, he met Freud on the latter's visit to the United States to receive an honorary degree from Clark University in 1909. Freud recounted how James, now really physically ill, had an attack of angina during a walk they took together. Freud was impressed by James's calm, grace, and acceptance in the face of not-distant death as he asked his European visitor to walk on while he recovered. Freud commented, "I hope I will show as much courage when it comes to be my time to die."

Eric Erikson, the psychoanalytic theorist who directed our attention to the process of achieving an identity, to the problematic nature of that identity, and to its psychopathological correlative "identity diffusion," used James as a case history of a lifelong identity confusion. He cited a late dream of James's to illustrate the problems of identity confusion in the last stage of life. Here is James's (as cited in Erikson, 1968, pp. 205–207) account of that dream.

> *I despair of giving the reader any just idea of the bewildering confusion of mind into which I was thrown by this, the most intensely peculiar experience of my whole life. I wrote a full memorandum of it a couple of days after it happened, and appended some reflections. Even though it should cast no light on the conditions of mysticism [which James was then investigating], it seems as if this record might be worthy of publication, simply as a contribution to the descriptive literature of pathological mental states. I let it follow, therefore, as originally written, with only a few words altered, to make the account more clear.*
>
> *San Francisco, Feb. 14, 1906. —The night before last, in my bed in Stanford University, I awoke at about 7:30 a.m. from a quiet dream of some sort and whilst "gathering my waking wits" seemed suddenly to get mixed up with reminiscences of a dream of an entirely different sort which seemed to telescope, as it were, into the first one, the dream very elaborate, of lions and tragic. I concluded this to have been a previous dream of the same sleep; but the apparent mingling of two dreams was something very queer, which I had never before experienced.*
>
> *On the following night (Feb. 12/13) I awoke suddenly from my first sleep, which appeared to have been very heavy, in a middle of dream, in the thinking of which, I became suddenly confused by the contents of two other dreams that shuffled themselves abruptly in between the parts of the first dream, and of which I couldn't grasp the origin. Whence come these dreams? I asked. They were close to me, and fresh, as if I had just dreamed them; and yet they were far away from the first dream. The contents of the three had absolutely no connection. One had a Cockney atmosphere, it had happened to someone in London. The other two were American. One involved the trying on of a coat (was this the dream I seemed to awake from?), the other was a sort of nightmare and had to do with soldiers. Each had a wholly distinct emotional atmosphere that made its individuality discontinuous with that of the others. And yet, in a moment, as these three dreams alternately telescoped into and out of each other, and I seemed to myself to have been their common dreamer, they seemed quite as distinctly not to have been dreamed in succession, in that one sleep. When then? Not the previous night, either. When, then, and which was the one out of which I just awakened. I could no longer tell: one was as close to me as the other, and yet they entirely repelled each other, and I seemed thus to belong to three different dream-systems at once, no one of which would connect itself either with the others or with my waking life. I began to feel curiously*

confused and scared, and tried to wake myself up wider, but I seemed already wide-awake. Presently cold shivers of dread ran over me: am I getting into other people's dreams? Is this a "telepathic" experience? Or an invasion of (double) or (treble) personality? Or is it a thrombus in a coronary artery? And the beginning of a general mental "confusion" and disorientation which is going to develop who knows how far?

Decidedly I was losing hold of my "self" and making acquaintance with a quality of mental distress I had never known before, its nearest analogue being the sinking, giddying anxiety that one may have when, in the woods, one discovers that one is really "lost." Most human troubles look toward a terminus. Most fears point in a direction, concentrate toward a climax. Most assaults of the evil one may be met by bracing oneself against something, one's principles, one's courage, one's will, one's pride. But in this experience all was diffusion from a center, and foothole swept away, the brace itself disintegrating all the faster as one needed its support more direly. Meanwhile vivid perception (or remembrance) of the various dreams kept coming over me in alternation. Whose? whose? WHOSE? Unless I can attach them, I am swept out to sea with no horizon and no bond, getting lost. The idea roused the "creeps" again, and with it the fear of again falling asleep and renewing the process. It had begun the previous night, but then the confusion had only gone one step and that seemed simply curious. This was a second step— where might I be after a third step had been taken?

At the same time I found myself filled with a new pity for persons passing into dementia with Verwirrtheit, *or into invasions of secondary personality. We* regard them as simply curious; *but what* they *want, in the awful drift of their being out of their customary self is any principle of steadiness to hold on to. We ought to assure them and reassure them that we will stand by them, and recognize the true self in them, to the end. We ought to let them know that we are with them and not (as too often we must seem to them) a part of the world that but confirms and publishes their deliquescence. [italics added]*

Evidently I was in full possession of my reflective wits; and whenever I thus objectively thought of the situation in which I was, my anxiety ceased. But there was a tendency to relapse into the dreams and reminiscences, and to relapse vividly; and then the confusion recommenced, along with the emotion of dread lest it should develop further.

Then I looked at my watch. Half-past twelve! Midnight, therefore. And this gave me another reflective idea, habitually when going to bed, I fall into a very deep slumber from which I never naturally awaken until after two. I never awaken, therefore, from a midnight dream, as I did tonight, so of midnight dreams my ordinary consciousness retains no recollection. My sleep seemed terribly heavy as I awoke tonight. Dream states carry dream memories—why may not the two succedaneous dreams (whichever two of the three were succedaneous) be memories of twelve o'clock dreams of previous nights, swept in, along with the just-fading dream, into the just-waking system of memory? Why, in short, may I not be tapping in a way precluded by my ordinary habit of life, the midnight stratum of my past?

This idea gave me great relief—I felt now as if I were in full possession of my anima rationalis. . . . *it seems therefore, merely as if the threshold between the rational and the morbid state had, in my case, been temporarily lowered, and as if similar confusions might be very near the line of possibility in all of us.*

James is here describing what has been called the "fragmentation of the self," with its concomitant terror. For Erikson the most salient point about James's account is his reassertion of his professional identity in his objectification and analysis of his experience. For me, the most salient aspect of James's report is his empathy—for others suffering similar experiences and ultimately for himself. Of course, that empathy was part of his professional identity.

James's theory of the self is primarily contained in his *Principles of Psychology*, but his chapters "The Sick Soul" and "The Divided Self" in *Varieties of Religious Experience* in which he recounts his "crisis" are also pertinent, as are his thoughts in his essay "Does Consciousness Exist?"

In the *Principles*, James describes a multiself constituted by an empirical self, or me—consisting of three components, the material self, the social self, and the spiritual self—and by the pure ego.

Schematically:

The empirical self or me   *The pure ego*
The material self
The social self
The spiritual self

Additionally, a complete description of self according to James must include not only the constituents of that self, material, social, and spiritual, but also the feelings and emotions that they arouse, which he denotes *self-feelings*, and the actions they promote, which he denotes *self-seeking* and *self-preservation*.

The Empirical Self, or Me, is what each of us calls *me*. James claims that we know perfectly well what he means, and that each of us has a perfectly coherent experience of self. To deny this is to engage in a metaphysical game and not to be truly empirical. The essential fact is some sort of experience of selfhood. However, James goes on to say that the line between *me* and *mine* is not clear, that is, our identity is not confined to our bodily and mental self. My children, my fame, my reputation, my home, and the products of my work are emotionally invested by me, and are experienced as part of me. It is interesting that James, who wrote of the "Bitch Goddess success," included fame in his list of qualities experienced as *mine*. According to him, the self always seems to be involved in acts of intentionality; that is, I am always conscious of something. James borrowed the idea of the intentionality of consciousness from the Viennese psychologist and philosopher Franz Brentano, whose work he respected. Sigmund Freud, who studied under Brentano, developed Brentano's concept of intentionality into his doctrine of cathexis, the investment of self and others with emotional energy, which is very close to James's notion of the self encompassing all that is mine.

James is quite cognizant of the necessity for emotional investment and involvement of and with the constituents of self. Here he is quite in agreement with Freud. Simply put, if I don't love it, it isn't mine; it isn't a part of me. James points out that even the body can be disowned or disavowed, as when the mystic dismisses his body as a "prison house of the soul." It is only by emotional investment that things, including my body, become part of the self. The me is fluctuating material as my emotional investments change. James concludes that "In its widest possible sense—*a man's Self is the sum total of all that he CAN call his*" (1890/1983, p. 273). This is a completely new notion in our history of theories of the self. The boundaries of the self are here quite altered. The closest approach to James's notion hitherto examined is Hegel's concept of the self being constituted by identification with the concrete universals that that self has produced, but Hegel's notion is abstract and metaphysical, while James's is *haimish* and human. Let us look more closely at the constituents of the self.

The major constituents of that self are the Empirical Self (or Me) and the Pure Ego. The empirical self is tripartite: material, social, and spiritual. The *material self*, as it is usually constituted, is primarily a bodily self. It is my body with all of my awarenesses of that body. There is a certain ambiguity in James's inclusion of the body as a constituent of the material self. Is it my body in all of its physicality sitting here writing, or is it only my sensations of body that constitute self? For James, who later denies that there is a mind-body dichotomy, this is a distinction without a difference. But my body as a material thing is different from my body as experience. I don't know that James thought about this ambiguity in his discussion of self in *The Principles*, but I suppose his answer would be that there is only one body, which can be experienced in a variety of ways, and that all of those ways are a part of self. However, as James points out (see earlier), nothing is part of the self unless it is emotionally invested, cared about. So the body may be peripheral to self, or even experienced as nonself, or, as is generally the case, be experienced as more central to the self-experience, although it is not, for most people, at the core of the self. This is an extraordinary notion and a new one in our discussion of self. James is saying that we have many self-experiences that differ in their saliency and centrality, and that their degree of saliency is determined by my affective relationship to that constituent of self. Is there a paradox, or even a logical contradiction, here? Does there not have to be a self to select the constituents of self that constitute it, antecedent to that selection, if James is correct? I am not sure. James does not explicitly conceptualize the self in the cathetic terms I use above, but it is implicit in his discussion of self. What does clearly emerge is the centrality of affectivity, not with Kierkegaard's emphasis on boundary states of despair, dread, and fear and trembling, but rather with the emphasis on ordinary, everyday, ongoing, caring for: valuing of some parts of self more than others, so that a hierarchy of selves is established. James's self is a feeling self, even though those feelings and feelingful choices are not ordinarily in awareness.

For most of us, *body* is an important part of self. According to James, so is everything that I identify with my selfhood, an identification not necessarily conscious at any point in time, but always potentially conscious. He singled out clothes, citing the old joke about the self consisting of my body, my soul, and my clothes. James is, here, highly aware of the symbolic significance of social presentation—of the role one's uniform plays in one's view of self. James's friend, Justice Oliver Wendell Holmes, was once asked if wearing those judicial robes made any difference. Holmes replied, "It damn well better." Holmes was saying that the robed presentation of self, with the robe symbolizing fairness and justice, should change the robed experience of self in such a way that the wearer's commitment to fairness and justice is enhanced. Put differently, the robe, at least ideally, changes the robed one's self-concept, which in turn changes his or her behavior so that it is congruent with the altered self-concept. James would entirely agree. Of course, the robe also changes one's social self, the way one is perceived and evaluated by others, but more of this later. The material self includes not only body and clothes, but all of our possessions: home, books, records, boat, and car, for example. Look at the way many people identify with their cars: James is onto something here. The products of my labor are also part of my material self: the things I have built and the money I have earned. Again, these things are more or less central to self depending upon how much they are cared about. James, who as a child was forever relocating, put great emphasis on one's home as a part of self, as something that is loved, enhanced, and experienced as part of self, even to the degree of feeling that one's self is being attacked if one's home is violated, disparaged, or criticized. James also includes under the material self other people insomuch as they are "my possessions." He explicitly talks about family, parents, wife and babes. Though he speaks of them as possessions, he is not unaware of their independent selfhood; rather, here he is speaking of their relationship to me, their existence as a part of me.

In the *social self*, the other side of the coin, my existence for others is highlighted. When those we love (however possessively) die, part of our very selves is gone. Loss entails a "shrinking" of ourselves—again, an entirely new notion of self. This is what a psychoanalyst would call an object-relational notion of self. (Objects are so called because they are the objects of my thoughts and feelings, objects in relation to me as subject. Objects usually are, but need not be, people; the term *object relations* encompasses both interpersonal relations and intrapsychic relations in which I relate to my internal objects, i.e., my mental representations of others.) Implicit in James's notion is the more love, the more self; the more loss, the less self. Freud has similar notions, but because he has the concepts of identification, incorporation, and internalization to work with as well as an explicitly cathetic model, he is able to develop this much more fully. But Freud's statement that "the ego [self] is the precipitate of abandoned object relations" is closely related to, albeit different from, James's notion of loss of loved ones as loss of self. Freud is offering a psychological alternative to James's notion of the self diminished by loss, namely the psychological incorporation of those who have been lost (see Chapter 8). James, like John Donne, believes that each person's loss diminishes me, at least if I love him or her.

So the self, just in its material self, is much more than just my body; it is everything, animate and inanimate, that I care about, everything that I invest with emotion, everything that I experience as mine. Furthermore, the material self is not a given, eternally immutable; on the contrary, it is in a constant state of variably rapid flux.

The social self extends the object-relational aspect of James's conceptualization of self. Since James is, here, as in his discussion of the material self, writing from the viewpoint of the self, his discussion is necessarily narcissistic in the sense that other people are not so much regarded as selves-in-themselves as selves-for-me. Even when others are seen as autonomous in their freedom to evaluate me, the emphasis is on my experience of those evaluations and on the importance of esteem from others for my self-esteem. I do not believe that this says anything about James being particularly narcissistic, but rather, it is ineluctably entailed by his topic being the self—rather than social relations.

In his notion of the social self, James brings to the forefront the centrality of our need for recognition from others. One wonders what Descartes's lonely cogitator would think of this aspect of James's conceptualization of self. James states that, "man has as many social selves as he has significant others" (1890/1983, p. 281). (As far as I know, James is the originator of the now much overused term *significant others*.) Here again we have the paradox, or perhaps the contradiction, of the self that is constituted, at least in part, by the evaluation of significant others, choosing, apparently antecedent to the constitution of that self, who shall be significant for it. Be that as it may, for James we do have some freedom in arranging our hierarchy of significant others, but we are not entirely free in this respect. One's boss is a significant other, as are one's parents, whether or not one wants them to be, although we do have some say in how significant they are for us. In fact, much of psychotherapy can be understood as helping the patient rearrange his or her hierarchy of significance (of others) and in most cases attenuating that significance. James points out that how I feel and how I experience myself is importantly determined by how my significant others treat me. The most significant of the significant others is the person I am in love with; he or she can change my whole state of being with a smile—or with a sneer. My social self, my "other-reflected" perception of self and, conversely, my presentation of self to others, may be harmonious or may be conflictual. Since I play many roles and elicit many different responses, it is likely that my social selves will not be altogether harmonious or consistent. The degree of integration of the social selves varies from person to person, but some degree of "splitting," of disharmony between social selves, is usual. The social self is both what I am to others and what I am for others. The notion of social role is implicit in James's discussion of the social self, as is the variability of the social selves—the selves that I am for others—that are elicited by and, in contemporary language, fed back to me. James postulates an ideal social self that is the possibility of recognition by an ideal other. He points out that we can, and frequently do, give up actual (present) approbations for potentially "higher" (i.e., more valued) approbations from more highly regarded significant others. In this quest for a self through others, we seek an ideal spectator. James's notion here is similar to Freud's notion of the ego ideal, but Freud's ideal other has become internalized and is, in part, an internalized parent, and, as such, is an heir of the past, while James's ideal spectator is an elusive figure, a spectator of the future. We give up present glory to seek the esteem of an ideal other, to consolidate an ideal social self.

James puts a lot of stress on his "Bitch Goddess" success, here wearing the garment of "fame and honors" in his development of the social self. My social self is importantly the degree of fame and honor I can garner for myself. Here James is generalizing what is personally important to him, although he is doubtlessly also generalizing from his experience of the "superstars" who gathered around his parents' table and who served with him on the Harvard faculty. He is also giving tremendous power to his critics and to his public. Whatever the role of his personal bias in his conceptualization of the social self, there is no doubt that what I am for me is importantly determined by what I am for others, and that James was the first to incorporate this insight into a theory of self.

The *Spiritual Self* is my inner subjective being; it is my psychic facilities and disposition. The spiritual self is the most enduring and intimate part of the self. It is that which we seem to *be*. The spiritual self is our core self. It is more central to our being than is the material or social self. It includes our ability to argue and to discriminate (nobody but James, having grown up in the family he did, would have included the ability to argue among the core attributes of the self), our moral sensibility, our conscience, and our will. It is these that are the relatively enduring attributes or constituents of self that make me, me. James goes on to say that if these attributes of self are altered, we are *alienated*. James is using *alienated* in its 19th-century medical sense; to become alienated in that sense means to become psychotic. Indeed, a psychiatrist was called an *alienist*. That is interesting in what it implies as a notion of mental illness. To become mentally ill, or at least psychotic, is to have one's core self, that which discriminates, evaluates, or acts, irreversibly altered. One thinks of James's description of his almost "losing it," as the current argot would have it, during his terminal dream reported earlier. James points out that the traditional categories of the mind—judgment, perception, and so forth—are abstractions. Not so the spiritual self; it is concreteness itself, that which most gives me the sense of being me.

Concretely, to use James's term, the spiritual self is the "entire stream of our personal consciousness" (1890/1983, p. 284), or the present segment of it. The stream is concrete existence in time. It is Kant's "inner sense," the direct perception of the flow of time within. In *The Principles*, James's chapter "The Stream of Thought" immediately precedes the chapter "The Consciousness of Self." The notion of the stream of thought or, as it is better known, the *stream of consciousness*, is one of James's most widely disseminated and important contributions. The stream of personal consciousness has a unity of a particular kind. That unity is the *process* itself. As Alfred North Whitehead, who was in some ways James's disciple, put it, "the process is the reality." The continuity of the process is directly experienced just as is its discontinuity. Insofar as we are in contact with our spiritual selves, *we think of ourselves as thinkers* and we identify ourselves with *thoughts and thinking as such*, not with the objects of thought. James is here using *thought, think*, and *thinking* in the same way in which Descartes uses *cogito*, that is, to mean any mental activity whatever—thinking, feeling, sensing, doubting, affirming, and so forth. For James there is no separation of thought and thinker. On the contrary, they are one. James notes that *it thinks* has a grammatical structure parallel to the grammatical structure of *it rains*, and that there is no more need to postulate a thinker apart from thinking than to postulate a rainer apart from raining. James is not here denying the personal nature of thought, the "me-ness" of my thinking and of my experiencing of the stream of thought; on the contrary, he is affirming it. What he is denying is the duality of subject and object and the idea that there is some sort of substance or stuff called consciousness, to which or in which thoughts occur or adhere. Consciousness is a succession of thoughts— thinking itself, not some kind of *stuff* that undergoes modifications. There is no substrate of mental activity; there is only the activity itself; the thought and the thinker are one. James expanded the ideas implicit in this conceptualization of the stream of consciousness into an ontology he calls neutral monism (see below). The stream of consciousness is characterized by its flow, which is not even, and in which the immediate past is still part of the present segment of the stream, which also anticipates that which is about to follow. James's conceptualization of the stream of consciousness owes something to Locke's conceptualization of time as perpetually perishing. There are eddies and pools and rapids and dead waters within the stream, and the qualitative experience of the flow can only imperfectly be captured by words. We all know what the experience is, but we can at best metaphorically allude to it, not directly communicate it.

James goes on to discuss what he calls the *subjective life*, which is characterized by *feelings of agency*. The portion of the stream felt by all people as the innermost center within the subjective life is the *self of all the other selves*, or, to put it differently, the core self (my term). The self of all selves is the active element in consciousness. It is "that Spiritual something that goes *out* to meet qualities and contents which seem to come *in*. . . . *It is what welcomes or rejects*." It is the "home of interest," that within us "to which pleasure and pain speak." It is the "source of the will." The core self is somehow connected with "the process by which ideas or incoming sensations are 'reflected' or pass over into outward acts, . . . a sort of junction at which sensory ideas terminate and from which motor ideas proceed, forming a kind of link between the two" (1890/1983, p. 285). This self-of-selves aspect of the spiritual self seems to reside between the afferent and the efferent, and in that way it shares some characteristics with Freud's ego, that part of the mind in his structural model that delays and decides. At the neurological level, the core self would appear to reside in the interneurons (those between the afferent and the efferent pathways).

Viewed not from within the stream nor from the experience of agency, the spiritual self can be defined somewhat differently as a "center around which experience accretes" (James, 1890/1983, p. 285); it is something permanent as opposed to changing, yet it changes and it is those changes. One might say that the flow of the spiritual self is slower than the flow of what it experiences, or at least that there is a feeling of ongoingness that is somehow the essence of the spiritual self. James maintains that all—except defenders of abstract philosophical systems—would agree that there is a central or core self around which experience accretes. But what is this core? The soul? An imaginary being denoted by the pronoun *I*? Or something in between the self as soul and the self as grammatical fiction? James responds to this by asking, "How does the central *nucleus* of the self *feel*?" (1890/1983, p. 286). For him the central part of the self is *felt*, which is consistent with his highlighting the affectivity of the material and social selves. The core self is not merely rational, nor is it the sum of our memories, nor is it the sound of the word *I*, but *par contra* something directly experienced. James is, here, flatly contradicting Hume, and he, like Hume, appeals to experience to validate his claim. But James's empiricism, at least in his eyes, is more thorough. It is a radical empiricism, an empiricism that examines experience completely without a priori assumptions such as the assumption that experience is intrinsically atomistic.

What James has to say about a direct sensible acquaintance with the central spiritual self is surprising. What he says is that acts of attending, ascertaining, negating, and so forth are felt as movements of something in the head. The "self of selves . . . consists mainly in the collection of these peculiar motions in the head or between the head and the throat," and "our feeling of spiritual activity is really a feeling of bodily activity whose exact nature is usually overlooked" (1890/1983, p. 288). So the self of selves is, as experienced, the sum total of usually unattended-to muscular tightenings around my Adam's apple that accompany my voluntary mental activities. A strange notion of the self, to say the least. It finds echoes in its general approach, if not in its particulars, in both Whitehead's insistence on "the 'withness' of the body" in all ideation, indeed in all experience, and in Freud's notion that "the ego is first and foremost a bodily ego" (1923/1961, p. 26).

I find James unconvincing here. There are indeed proprioceptive sensations that accompany mental acts, but I can see no reason to maintain that they constitute my self of selves. But I can see that James is being shrewd in telling Hume that he is looking for the self in the wrong place. It isn't in the empty theater that doesn't exist, but it is part of my experience—an experience that James in his philosophical mode maintains is neither bodily nor mental, but something antecedent to both.

James's insistence on the bodily nature of the self or selves brings to mind James's theory of emotion. Known as the James-Lange (nobody knows who Lange is) theory of emotion, it maintains that we are sad because we cry and that we are happy because we smile, not the reverse. It is the proprioceptive feedback from our tears or our facial muscles in the smile that we interpret as the emotions of sadness and happiness. Intriguing as this is, it is probably wrong, or at least only part of the truth about emotions. The expression of emotion appears to be preprogrammed in all mammals and is primarily mediated by a part of the brain called the hypothalmus, while the experience of emotion is a limbic function, the limbic system being a subcortical region of the brain. Most probably there is a cognitive labeling of preprogrammed emotionality, which is, at least partially, learned. Emotional experience is partly an interpretation and not merely given by one's physiological state. James, of course, had theoretical reasons for putting forth this theory of emotions, but the affective source of this theory of affectivity resides in James's self-conscious striving to overcome his depression. He was one of the first to advocate "act as if" ("act as if you are happy and you will be happy"). Or as the Alcoholics Anonymous slogan has it, "Fake it until you make it." This is quintessentially Jamesian, and perhaps it is no accident that the founder of Alcoholics Anonymous, Bill Wilson, was powerfully influenced by James's *Varieties of Religious Experience* and incorporated some of its conclusions into the Alcoholics Anonymous literature.

James also discusses what he calls the *nuclear self*, another aspect of the spiritual self. The nuclear self is that intermediary between ideas and overt acts discussed above. It lives in the interneurons and the cortex. James speaks of two kinds of physiological acts: adjustments and executions. The nuclear self consists of the adjustments collectively considered. The adjustments are what meet what comes in. The executions are responses to incoming stimuli; they too are part of the self, but they are experienced as less intimate; they are the more shifting aspects of self. The nuclear self—our adjustments collectively considered—is the gatekeeper of the mind, whose activities necessarily accompany any mental activity, and is, in that sense, a constant. That is why it is a nucleus; it is always there, and this feeling is all that I know of self. Anything more said about the self is guesswork and metaphysical speculation.

For all the complexity of this theory of James's, its basic thrust is simple: it is radically empirical. It looks to experience to determine what experiences come branded with my brand and are experienced as me. James stresses this in his summary statement of his hierarchy of selves—material, social, and spiritual—in which the key notions are affect and agency: "The words ME and SELF, as far as they arouse feeling and connote emotional worth, are Objective designations—ALL The Things in the stream of consciousness which have the power to produce excitement of a particular sort" (1890/1983, p. 304).

There can be rivalry and conflict between the material, social, and spiritual selves. The degree of harmony or dissension between them is an empirical question, the answer to which varies from person to person and for the same person at different stages of his or her life. There is also rivalry between potential selves. There are many potential selves but only one can be actualized. There is a sense in which the self is chosen and created.

In *The Varieties of Religious Experience* James discusses in great detail and with exquisite specificity the "Divided Self, and the Process of Its Unification" (1902, pp. 163–185). He does this by using case material derived from both his own life and the writings of others. He is prescient in relating lack of integration of the self to psychopathology, but he refuses to be reductionistic and sees value and insight as well as pain in the divided self. His cures are religious cures, integration through belief and through conversion experiences of various sorts.

Having described the constituents of the empirical self, James goes on to discuss *self-feeling* and *self-seeking* and *self-preservation*. There is no self without a feeling about that self. We always love or hate ourselves more or less. We experience both self-complacency and self-dissatisfaction. Our self-esteem has a baseline (high or low) and fluctuations from that baseline. In a neat formula, James says that self-esteem equals successes divided by pretensions, so that we can raise our self-esteem either by accruing successes or by lowering our pretensions. Self-seeking and self-preservation engender the feelings of anger and fear. Self-seeking includes the desire to be recognized and spiritual self-seeking as well as material self-seeking. I identify with my body, or any other aspect of self, because I love it, not vice versa; and if I love it, I seek to preserve it. This is much like Spinoza's notion of *conatus*, the striving of all living things to preserve themselves.

That brings us to *The Pure Ego*. The Pure Ego is the abstract "I think" which, like Kant's transcendental ego, must logically accompany every thought. It is also the source of our sense of personal identity. It is the judgment of sameness. The proposition "I am the same" is logically and epistemologically equivalent to the judgment "the desk is the same." A *subjective* synthesis is a bringing together in thought. An *objective* synthesis is an actual unity. Some sort of synthetic form is necessary to all thought. "Only a connected world can be known to be discon-nected," reasons James, in perfect parallel to Kant's argument for the transcenden-tal apperception of the ego. The sense of personal identity is an objective synthe-sis. I am the same self that I was yesterday. My feelings of bodily self and spiritual self (in subliminal muscle movements and in thought) have a characteristic warmth that experiences of the not-me lack; some experiences come with our own brand. Whatever resembles that which has the self-brand on it is ME. Because I have memory, indeed memories, of experience carrying my brand, I can determine what is self and what is not self.

The pure ego is the subjective synthesis of the stream of thought that is different at each instant, yet that each instant thereof is appropriated from the preceding thought. The present content of the stream contains the immediate past contents of the stream, which in turn contains its immediately past content, so that there is a sense in which the entire stream of my consciousness is a unity. "Each thought *hugs to itself* and adopts all that went before . . . stands as a representative of the entire stream" (1890/1983, p. 378). Furthermore, "If the passing thought be the directly verifiable existent that no school has hitherto doubted it to be, then *that thought is itself the thinker*" (1890/1983, p. 324). Therefore, I am unity. That is, if the stream of thought is unity, and I am the stream of thought, then I must be a subjective synthesis—a unity. The sense of personal identity, of the sameness of me at different times, is exactly like other perceptions of sameness between phenom-ena. Similarity is an attribute of continuity.

There is an "unbrokenness in the *stream of selves*," but this unity does not preclude a plurality in the selves in other respects. How much unity there is in fact is an empirical question. Resemblance among the parts of a continuity of feelings (especially bodily feelings) experienced along with things widely differ-ent in all other regards then constitutes the real and verifiable personal identity that we feel. It is this sense of the continuity of the bodily experience, of the continuity of the stream of thought, and of the continuity of the experience of the central adjustments of the nuclear self that constitutes our personal identity; they are kernels to which the represented parts of the self are assimilated, accreted, and knit together.

James's stream of consciousness found literary embodiment in the works of writers as diverse as James Joyce and Virginia Woolf. Earlier novelists such as Laurence Sterne in *Tristram Shandy* had tried to depict Locke's and Hume's "asso-ciation of ideas" in the sequence of thoughts occurring in their characters, but there is nothing comparable to Molly Bloom's stream of consciousness soliloquy in Joyce's *Ulysses* before James.

William James described himself as a "metaphysical democrat"; he wished to exclude no aspect of experience from his psychologizing and philosophizing. He is also a democratic self theorist, so inclusive that he becomes prolix and at times confusing. But what he sees is the case: our experience of self is enormously complex; it does include material, social, and what he calls spiritual aspects. Some experiences *do* come stamped "mine," and some do not. The central experiences of self are primarily affective. The experience of agency is central to the self-experience. Each moment of experience does, in some sense, incorporate and represent all past experience, and in this way forges a unity of—synthesizes—my experiences. The degree of integration of the plurality of my selves isn't determined a priori, and it is indeed an empirical question. Finally, the experience of discontinuity does presume continuity.

William James is identified with two important philosophical doctrines: neutral monism and pragmatism. The first is a metaphysical or ontological theory, the second a theory of truth. Neutral monism is the conclusion he draws from his radical empiricism. It is the doctrine that there is only one kind of stuff in the world, which James calls *experience* and which can be organized in such a way that it is experienced by us as material; alternatively, it can be organized in such a way that it is experienced by us as mental or spiritual. He gives the example paint, which is material in the tube and spiritual in the painting and yet the same paint. In "Does Consciousness Exist?" he demolishes the notion that consciousness is a thing, some kind of stuff, different from material stuff. What it is is one way of organizing the only stuff there is. James is, here, the heir of Spinoza with his doctrine of one substance, Nature or God, having infinite attributes of which we can only know two, thought and extension. But Spinoza is a strict determinist, and in many ways his system is static; not so James's. For James, the universe is a multiverse open to novelty, with an infinitude of nodal points within it that can be experienced as either mind or matter.

Pragmatism is James's theory of truth. It says roughly that if it makes me happy and doesn't hurt anyone else, it is true. He views beliefs as instruments, the truth value of which is determined by their consequences. "By their fruits ye shall know them" is a sentiment with which James would wholeheartedly agree. James came upon pragmatism when he realized that metaphysically ultimate questions are rationally unanswerable, so that we are free to choose our beliefs. Given that, why not choose the ones that bring happiness? In a characteristically American way, James asks, "What is the cash value of a belief?" In an important sense, James is uninterested in whether or not God exists; what he is interested in is whether or not belief in God brings happiness. Pragmatism is a formalization of his own path out of his neurasthenia. It has obvious difficulties as a theory of truth. James divided thinkers into "the soft minded and the tough minded." He is both, but in his theory of truth he was clearly among the tender minded.

I will close my discussion of William James by quoting a letter he wrote to his wife not long after their marriage (James, 1920/1980, p. 109):

I have often thought that the best way to define a man's character would be to seek out the particular mental or moral attitude in which, when it came upon him, he felt himself most deeply and intensely active and alive. At such moments there is a voice inside which speaks and says,

"This is the real me!" . . . Now as well as I can describe it, this characteristic attitude in me always involves an element of active tension, of holding my own, as it were, and thrusting outwards things to perform their part so as to make it a full harmony, but without any guaranty that they will. Make it a guaranty—and the attitude immediately becomes to my consciousness stagnant and stingless. Take away the guaranty and I feel (provided I am uberhaupt in vigorous condition) a sort of deep enthusiastic bliss, a bitter willingness to do and suffer anything, which translates itself physically by a kind of stinging pain inside my breast-bone (don't smile at this— it is to me an essential element of the whole thing!), and which, although it is a mere mood or emotion to which I can give no form in words, authenticates itself to me with the deepest principle of all active and theoretic determination which I possess.

8

Sigmund Freud: The Vicissitudes of Narcissism

If James's theory of the self was primarily a theory about consciousness, Freud's is primarily a theory about the unconscious. James's great contribution to the understanding of the self is his envisioning of the self as a stream, any segment of which contains and represents all that precedes it, giving the experience of self a continuity and coherence that earlier empiricists denied. Freud's great contribution to the understanding of the self lies in his unparalleled depiction of the self as a house divided, torn by conflict, the sources of which are largely unconscious—or outside of our awareness. Bringing them into consciousness is beyond our ordinary abilities. For Freud, that which we experience as self, or better, as ourself, is but the tip of an iceberg, the vast bulk of which lies out of sight and beneath the waterline.

Sigmund Freud (1856–1939) is a difficult figure to write about. He is known not accurately, but too well. Contemporary American culture has been described as Freudian or as post-Freudian, and it is certainly true that popularized and "media-ized" versions of his theories have profoundly influenced activities as diverse as literary criticism and child-raising. He has importantly contributed to the formation of what Philip Rieff (1959) called "the triumph of the therapeutic" in Western, particularly American, societies, and he has profoundly altered the self-concept of members of those societies, resulting in the emergence of what Rieff called *psychological man* as the dominant character type of our time. Psychological man has replaced *economic man*, who was himself a successor of *religious man*, a descendant of *political man*. Put differently, the classical world produced political man; the collapse of that world, religious man; the Industrial Revolution, economic man; and the 20th century, psychological man. Psychoanalysis, Freud's brainchild, with its unprecedented emphasis on the inner life, created, at least in part, psychological man. Read any newspaper or magazine, go to the movies, turn on the television, and you will hear of projection, Oedipal conflict, psychological repression, denial, and sibling rivalry—all Freudian concepts. Freud did not write about the self per se, but he did write about the ego and about narcissism, and our present understanding of the self would be unthinkable without his contribution.

Freud was born in 1856; 3 years later Darwin published *Origin of Species*, a book that was to profoundly influence Freud. The year 1856 was an interesting one in which to have been born in Eastern Europe. Less than a decade after the defeat of the revolution of 1848, it was a time of rapid change as the face of Europe was irreversibly altered by industrialization. The failure of the revolutionary movement had led to reaction, yet the revolution of 1848 was not completely futile. Governments granted constitutions and made various accommodations to an increasingly powerful middle class. Although the Austrian-Hungarian Empire was anything but democratic, reform was in the air, and not long after Sigmund's birth the last of the restrictions on Jews were dropped, and they were granted full citizenship. The romantic movement was playing itself out, to be replaced by realism in aesthetics and in politics. Science was making rapid strides, and a scientific *Weltanschauung* was making inroads on the consciousness of the educated. The bourgeoisie, although in some ways mired in hypocritical respectability, was creating wealth and gaining influence. Freud was to uniquely integrate opposing strands of European culture, at once a late representative of the Enlightenment striving for classical clarity and simplicity in his literary style, admiring Goethe and Mozart, and embodying the Enlightenment values of demystification, secularism, and distrust of authority, and a late romantic, obsessively exploring the dark realms of the irrational and enacting in his own life the romantic ideal of the isolated hero defying the world. Although deeply committed to the values of scientific objectivity and rigor and empirical verifiability, Freud had a wildly speculative side that was willing to seriously consider telepathy and to philosophize about matters far removed from the realm of observation. A large part of Freud's fascination lies in this amalgamation of classicism, romanticism, realism, and the scientific world view. As a "good European," Freud embodied these tensions in the mainstream of European thought, but Freud was not only European, he was a Jew, and as such he suffered a certain marginality, being both a part of and apart from the general European culture. His Jewishness was just as problematic as his Europeanism. He was both one of the preeminent representatives of the *Haskala*—the Hebrew enlightenment—and more indebted to and unconsciously influenced by Jewish mysticism than he knew. His father had left behind his Hasidic background and become one of the *Maskilim*, "the enlightened ones." Yet he read Hebrew and taught his son the Bible. Freud himself didn't recognize these tensions in himself and in his writings, consciously adhering to science and the enlightenment; yet they clearly are there and make him a richer and more complex thinker. As both European and Jew, he embodies the conflicts of those cultures and struggles to assimilate and make intelligible the speculative, the credulous, the irrational, and the mystical by giving a scientific account of them. Freud reminds me of another of my cultural heroes, Giuseppe Verdi. Both started from modest (at best) circumstances and both achieved world eminence without relinquishing a tough, skeptical, hard-nosed common sense that cast a jaundiced eye on human affairs; neither was overly impressed by human beings and their pretensions, yet neither was bitter; and both retained something of their origins that kept them apart from and critical of high bourgeoisie culture. Both were inordinately ambitious, had a dry wit, and viewed life as tragic, being pessimistic or realistic, depending on one's point of view; neither took power or love at face value; and in their very different ways, each taught us something new about our emotional lives.

Freud was born in Freiberg, Moravia, then a province of the Austrian-Hungarian Empire and now a part of Czechoslovakia. He was born into an economically marginal, strangely constituted Jewish family living in a provincial town; his father was middle-aged, his mother young. He had half brothers as old as other children's fathers, and his nephew, John, was a bit older than he. Jacob, his father, a not very successful wool merchant, had married once or perhaps twice before. There was also a Christian Czech woman who took care of him and to whom he was attached. Freud wrote obsessively of the troubled relations between fathers and sons, but has little to say about a son's relationship to his mother except to say that a mother's love of a son is the only unambivalent love with which he is acquainted. In his account of the Oedipus complex, it is a son's murderous competition with his father, not the son's lust for his mother, that is most salient for Freud. Freud certainly had strongly ambivalent feelings toward his father, but his idealization of his relationship with his mother is suspect. Most of his biographers believe that Amelia, his mother, was a narcissistic, self-involved person who was not emotionally available to little Freud. This is possible, but the evidence is fragmentary.

Eventually, Freud's half brothers moved to Manchester, England, and Freud early developed a love for England and things English. The circumstances of his brothers leaving Freiberg are mysterious, as is the occasion for Freud's immediate family hastily leaving shortly thereafter. The complex and confusing family constellation in which he grew up stimulated the young Freud's speculations on the mysteries of conception and birth.

When Freud was 4, the family suffered some sort of crisis and suddenly departed first for Leipzig and then for Vienna. Whether Jacob Freud's financial position had finally become desperate or whether there was some sort of trouble is not known. Freud's father's brother was later convicted of passing counterfeit money, and some of Freud's biographers think that his father and possibly his half brothers may have been similarly employed—at least for a time. Be that as it may, Freud experienced leaving Freiberg as a profound loss. (Freud loved the countryside around Freiberg, remembering it as a paradise lost and retaining a love of nature all of his life.)

By the time Freud left Freiberg, he had lost a newborn brother, Julius, and seen his nurse driven from the house and arrested for theft. His brother Philip had reported the nurse to the authorities after things were found to be missing from the home. Both these events left indelible imprints on Freud. He apparently had death wishes toward his rival younger sibling, and his depressive side may have been partially determined by guilt over those wishes and their apparent efficacy. The disappearance of the nursemaid puzzled him and left him with a fear that his mother would also disappear.

The family settled in the Leopoldstadt, Vienna's equivalent of New York's Lower East Side. The family was poor, and Freud—who later stated that he hated two things above all, poverty and helplessness—never forgot the deprivations of those years. He was educated by his father and possibly in a Jewish parochial elementary school until he entered the Gymnasium, the European classical secondary school. During the Vienna years, four sisters and a younger brother were born. Probably his most important educational experience was reading the Bible. Old Testament allusions appear frequently in his dreams and much of his imagery is derived from Biblical stories. He identified with the Biblical Joseph, who was also an interpreter of dreams, and with Moses, the archetypal law-giver. Although often seen as, or more pejoratively accused of, being a pan-sexualist, Freud was at least as obsessed with religion as he was with sex, albeit from the stance of a nonbeliever. By the time he entered the Gymnasium, the family was fairly comfortable, possibly because his half brothers sent money from Manchester, where they were doing well.

Freud's secondary school career was spectacular; always at the top of his class, he was the adored darling of his family. He alone had his own room, and when his sisters played their piano, he complained that the noise distracted him, and the piano went. Throughout his life, Freud remained unresponsive to music, with the exception of the operas of Mozart, which appealed to him with their crystalline clarity, knowing insight into the vicissitudes of sexuality, and embodiment of enlightenment values, and Wagner's *Meistersinger von Nürnberg* with its middle-class craftsman artist hero. There is a bitter irony in Freud's enjoyment of an opera set in Nuremberg. Nuremberg became the site both of Freud's meetings with a much-loved friend and of psychoanalytic congresses. It was one of his favorite places. Nuremberg also became the site of Nazi rallies and played an important part in the rise of Nazism. The piano incident showed Freud's power within his family and the relative status of boys and girls within it. Having vanquished his infant rival, Julius (at least in his mind), back in Freiberg, Freud was now clearly the dominant and privileged personality in his home. None of his sisters nor his youngest brother, Alexander, were serious threats to his supremacy, and he retained cordial relations with them throughout adulthood.

Freud's career cannot be understood apart from the changing status of the Viennese Jews. During Freud's life span, the Jewish population of Vienna exploded as the city attracted immigrants from the impoverished villages of the Empire and of Russia. The 1860s were a time of hope for Viennese Jews; liberalism was ascendent in politics as well as in intellectual life in general. Although the liberals maintained power by restricting the franchise through a property qualification, they reformed the educational system, secularized the government, and gave equal rights to minorities, including the Jews. Exponents of laissez-faire capitalism, they also championed rationality, professionalism, and careers opened to talent, science, and culture. Although theoretically egalitarian, in practice they were the party of the middle class, entry into which Freud and his family, along with most of the Jews of Vienna, strove.

The ego of Freud's structural model of the mind was in many ways a psychologicalization of liberalism—a rationalistic arbiter between the increasingly violent protests of the lower classes, particularly the newly created urban proletariat, in politics and the demands of instinctual energies in the psyche, and between the autocratic demands of the aristocracy in politics and the inflexible prohibitions of the internalized parents in the psyche. We shall see more of Freud's attempts to conceptualize the mind, including his structural model, in what follows.

The great slogan of Austrian Liberalism was *Weissen macht Frei*—"knowledge liberates"—a slogan cruelly and barbarically parodied by the Nazis in their sign over the entrance to Auschwitz—*Arbeit macht Frei*—"work liberates." Two of Freud's sisters were to be murdered in Auschwitz, while a third was to die of starvation in Thierenstadt, an Austrian concentration camp. These horrors were inconceivable in the halcyon days of the 1860s and 1870s when Jews in large numbers gained access to professional and business careers and came to play a dominant role in the intellectual and aesthetic life of Vienna. The Freud family had a picture of the "Bourgeoisie Ministry," a cabinet composed of middle-class professionals, including several Jews, that enjoyed a brief reign during Freud's adolescence. His early ambitions were political, and his friend and classmate Heindrick Braun became a leader of the Austrian Social-Democrats.

In a sense, Freud did have a political career, as founder, organizer, and unquestioned leader of the psychoanalytic movement. Although he thought of himself as a scientist, many have accused him of founding a quasi-religious movement, and, indeed, the history of the psychoanalytic movement with its expulsions-excommunications for dissidence-heresy, its charismatic leader, and secret committees is reminiscent of an Hasidic court with Freud as a *Zaddic*, or holy man. Freud may indeed have unconsciously enacted an historical, archetypal, cultural role and cast his movement far more in the role of the Rebbe and his followers than he was aware. Of course, models for such a structure are not lacking in the broader Western tradition, and Freud had no need to revert to the Hasidic model, but his conscious identification as a Jew was strong and his unconscious identification may have been even stronger. Certainly his decision to structure psychoanalysis as an autonomous profession apart from the universities and organized psychiatry was partially determined by the need to create a professional structure and profession that Jews could enter and indeed lead without having to struggle against the barriers and prejudice of the general culture. Freud did, in fact, create a predominantly Jewish profession; however, he was aware that this threatened to undermine its universality, and he very self-consciously strove to bring Gentiles into the movement. His relationship with Carl Jung was importantly determined by this need and by his wish to have a Swiss, a Gentile, and a member of the psychiatric establishment as his successor.

In his senior year at the Gymnasium, Freud heard a lecture on what he thought was Goethe's essay "On Nature" and was so enraptured that he decided to study medicine instead of law. Freud left secondary school with a thorough knowledge of the German classics, a reading knowledge of Latin and Greek, an acquaintance with the masterworks of antiquity, and rigorous training in science and mathematics. A linguist of considerable scope, he was to analyze patients in English, translate French and English texts into German, and get by in Spanish and Italian. Although he claimed to know no Hebrew, it is unlikely that he didn't learn any from his fluent father or his early schooling, and he must have picked up Yiddish fairly well from his milieu. He also left school having formed the first in a long series of intense relationships with father substitutes, the first in the line being his religion teacher, Samuel Hammerschlag. Hammerschlag was a kindly humanist who interpreted scripture in terms of its human and ethical significance rather than supernaturally. Like Jacob Freud, he was an inherent of the *Haskala* and a "reform" Jew. He was one of the few father surrogates with whom Freud did not eventually acrimoniously break.

Freud's university career was prolonged. For a poor boy who needed to establish himself, Freud was strangely desultory in his studies, taking 7 years to complete the 5-year medical course. Freud's early studies were broadly humanistic, and he was to fall under the spell of Franz Brentano. Brentano was an ex-priest and something of a man-about-town. Brilliant and charismatic, he was a professor of philosophy and well known in Viennese intellectual circles. A philosophical psychologist, he influenced not only Freud, but also the young Edmund Husserl, founder of the philosophical school of phenomenology. Brentano was, so to speak, the grandfather of phenomenology. His best known work is *Psychology from an Empirical Standpoint* (1874/1918). Brentano's combination of scientific exactitude and speculative boldness had great appeal for Freud. Brentano was a believer who made belief intellectually respectable. For a time, Freud became a theist, or at least open to the possible validity of religious experience; however, this was not to last. When his involvement with Brentano came to an end, so did Freud's "religious" phase. Brentano taught a doctrine that he called *the intentionality of consciousness*, which was an attempt to overcome or better undercut the bifurcation of reality into conscious subject and extended object that the Cartesian legacy had made almost commonsensical, however problematic, in Western thought. Brentano sought to resolve this dichotomy by demonstrating that thought always had an object, that there is no consciousness that is not conscious of something—so to speak, consciousness reached out and grasped objects in the world. The primary datum of experience is consciousness of something, not consciousness sundered from its objects, that is the result of analysis and is not the data of experience. Freud later developed a theory of *cathexis*, of the grasping by instinctual energy of objects, that is clearly indebted to Brentano. In German, Freud's term is *Besetzung*, which means *to occupy*, as in a military occupation, clearly a notion with more of an aggressive connotation than Brentano's consciousness, which connotes always being consciousness of. More of this later. Freud studied with Brentano for three terms, taking, among other things, seminars on the English philosophical idealist, Berkeley, who maintained that "to be is to be perceived." In later life, Freud expressed disdain for academic philosophy, probably seeing Brentano's espousal of Berkeleyan idealism as a ploy to justify religious beliefs. Most of Freud's disdain for philosophy derived from most philosophers' dismissal of unconscious mentation as self-contradictory. For all of his turning away from philosophy, Freud retained considerable respect for Brentano's intellect.

The greatest influence on Freud during his university career was Ernst Brücke, who came to Vienna from Berlin to found the physiological laboratory. Brücke was a liberal in politics, a foe of the anti-Semites who were then enjoying a resurgence following a financial crisis of 1873 that was blamed on "Jewish bankers," and a leading member of the "School of Helmholtz." The School of Helmholtz maintained that no forces or entities other than the ordinary chemical and physical ones were necessary to explain vital phenomena, so that biology in a sense became physics and chemistry. They stood in opposition to the Vitalists, who believed that life could not be explained without resource to extraphysical principles. Helmholtz was a brilliant and multifaceted investigator: physicist, physiologist, and philosopher of science. The scientific positivism of his school had an indelible impact on Freud. Scientific explanation called for accounts in terms of "forces *equal in dignity* to those of physics and chemistry." The triumph of the Helmholtzian approach to scientific biology was hard won, having long struggled against various mystical explanations of life and of man. It was with great reluctance that Freud turned from "hard science," here meaning rigorous rather than difficult, to investigate such "fringe phenomena" as hypnosis and dreams, but he did so in the spirit of Helmholtz and Brücke, extending the subject matter while attempting to retain the method of his masters. Darwinism, which placed man firmly in the natural order, was part of the same world view, and many of the investigations of Brücke and his colleagues were aimed at gathering evidence in support of or in elaboration of evolutionary theory.

Freud became an assistant in Brücke's laboratory, where he pursued histological research. Interestingly enough for the future discoverer of the castration complex, he spent a summer at the Research Institute in Trieste dissecting 10,000 eels, looking for their testicles. He found them. He also came close to discovering the neuron. Freud's early papers were based on careful empirical research and made substantial contributions to the science of the time. In addition to his study and research, two other events played a key role in his development during his student years: falling in love and discovering cocaine.

Judging from his letters to Martha Bernays, his relationship with her was a passionate one. Among other things, he wrote urging her to try cocaine, which he had discovered to be a wonder drug. He published papers on the therapeutic efficacy of cocaine that ultimately damaged his professional reputation and recommended it to a friend and superior in Brücke's lab, Ernst Fleischl-Marxow, who had become medically addicted to morphine. The results were catastrophic, and Freud's guilt (had he unconsciously wanted to knock off another rival and open a place for himself?) about the incident is expressed in several of the dreams he reported in his masterpiece, *Interpretation of Dreams* (Freud, 1900/1953). In fact, cocaine plays a considerable role in that book. Cocaine is a potent ophthalmalogical anesthetic, and Freud knew this, but his friend Carl Kohler published first and received the credit for the discovery of this property of cocaine. Freud's overvaluation of cocaine was driven by his chronic depression and by his overweaning ambition. He had missed fame in discovering the neuron, and now he missed gaining credit for a legitimate medical application of cocaine. In *Interpretation,* there is a dream in which Freud associates to his father's benefitting from the ophthalmalogical anesthetic qualities of cocaine during a cataract operation and his satisfaction with his part in its discovery. The dream elicited a memory of urinating in his parents' room as a small boy and his father saying, "The boy will amount to nothing." Freud interpreted his dream as saying, "See, you were wrong. I have amounted to something."

At this stage of his career, Freud wanted to be a researcher in the university, but Brücke told him that there was no hope for him in that direction and urged him to finish his medical degree and enter practice. Freud later wrote that medicine was a detour for him, and that he never wanted to be a healer because he didn't harbor sufficient hatred to have to seek a career that was a reaction formation (his term for the psychological defense of turning an emotion into its opposite) to that hatred. This rejection, no matter how kindly intended, by a revered father figure must have been a deeply painful, perhaps even devastating, narcissistic wound to Freud. Be that as it may, he left Brücke's lab, belatedly qualified in medicine, and entered practice, which enabled him to marry. Before he did, he went to Paris on a traveling fellowship to study under Charcot, the leading neurologist of the day. Charcot was the next of Freud's father surrogates. He taught him to "look at the same thing again and again." Charcot was not only a famous neurologist, he also maintained a salon where the literary and artistic luminaries of the time gathered. Charcot's salon introduced Freud, for the first time, to the world of fashion. More important, Charcot took neuroses, in particular *hysteria*, seriously and attempted both to understand and to treat those neuroses. Hysteria was a near pandemic in the late 19th century; it is rarely seen now.

Hysterics suffer a bewildering variety of physical illnesses without physical causes; their ailments are psychogenic. Most physicians dismissed hysterics as malingerers; not so Charcot. Furthermore, he recognized psychological causality and used hypnosis therapeutically. He would hypnotize an hysteric and give her a suggestion that, for example, she could move a limb rendered inoperative by hysterical paralysis. Charcot's method worked; he could both induce and remove symptoms, at least for the duration of the hypnotic state. Here we have the genesis of a new concept of the self. Implicit in both hysteria and hypnotic phenomena is the notion that there are aspects of the self removed from awareness and that there are states of consciousness that do not communicate, that have no knowledge of other states of consciousness. Suddenly the self gains a complexity, including the possibility of disassociation into isolated mutually incommunicative realms, that earlier conceptions of it lacked.

Freud worshipped Charcot. He translated his lectures into German (at roughly the same time he was translating several of John Stuart Mills's essays, including *The Subjugation of Women*), championed his ideas in Austria, named a son for him, and wrote a highly laudatory obituary of him. Back in Vienna, Freud went into private practice as a neurologist. His practice consisted mostly of neurotics, patients no one else wanted and who were not psychotic, yet who suffered from psychological as well as organic disabilities. Freud made important contributions to neurology. His monographs *On Aphasia* (1891/1953d) and *Infantile Cerebral Paralysis* (1897/1968) are classics, the one on aphasia the first evidence of his compelling interest in language and its connection with psychopathology.

In 1885, Freud became a lecturer at the university and he found yet another father—Joseph Breuer. Breuer was a prosperous and highly successful internist with a broad range of cultural interests. He encouraged Freud, loaned him money, and most importantly told him about his treatment of Bertha Pappenheim, a highly gifted neurotic who became known in the psychoanalytic literature as Anna O. Anna, who was the first psychoanalytic patient, suffered from multiple hysterical symptoms. She had fallen ill after the death of her "beloved" father whom she had nursed during his final illness. Breuer listened to her very carefully. Sometimes he induced an hypnotic trance. If Anna recalled traumatic events associated with her symptoms and recalled them with deep feeling, they disappeared. The psychoanalytic cure consisted in "once more with feeling," as my piano teacher used to say. Breuer saw Anna every day, often more than once, and their relationship became intense. Anna, a creative patient if ever there was one, called what they were doing the "talking cure," and the talking cure became psychoanalysis and psychotherapy in general. She also called it "chimney sweeping," an illusion to the necessity of cleaning out the soot and grime of life.

Anna continued to improve as long as her sessions with Breuer continued. The cure was, at least in part, what the modern analyst would call a transference cure. Transference is the patient's projection onto the analyst and the reliving of intense emotions of love and hate first felt for parents or siblings. It is a new edition of an old book. By expressing her (repressed) emotions in the context of an intense relationship, Anna's hysterical symptoms abated. Now trouble arose. Breuer told his wife about his fascinating case and her reaction was to say, in effect, "I'll handle the transference, and transfer you off of this case." And she did. Breuer went on vacation with his wife, and Anna relapsed. The child conceived on that second honeymoon was to suicide 50 years later in New York City after having fled the Nazis. Breuer's sudden departure recapitulated Anna's abandonment (through illness and death) by her (ambivalently) beloved father and was equally traumatic. Her relapse was so severe that she required several hospitalizations. Eventually she recovered and went on to a distinguished career, becoming the founder of social work in Germany. She ended her career by helping Jewish children get out of Germany just before World War II. She became and remained an implacable foe of psychoanalysis.

Freud and Breuer collaborated on "Studies on Hysteria" (1895/1955), the first psychoanalytic text, which included Anna's case history. In it, Freud wrote that "hysterics were suffering from reminiscences," and that "hysterics were suffering from strangulated affect." In both formulations, the self is split into conscious and unconscious segments, and the goal of therapy is to bring the unconscious part of the self with its unconscious ideation into consciousness with the release (abreaction, said Breuer and Freud) of the unconscious strangulated affect. The cure lay in the expression and discharge of repressed energy and feeling. Primal scream therapy and its relatives are the collateral descendents of Freud and Breuer's technique of 1895, albeit in an extreme, un-self-critical form. There is no question that we can and do have repressed powerful emotions that are in some sense "within us," yet not available to our awareness, nor is there any question that the coming into consciousness and the expression of those emotions is therapeutic. The empirical evidence is incontrovertible. But the place and mode of their "storage" is far from clear, and there are many competing, although perhaps complementary, theories to account for these thoughts and feelings.

The mode of storage of affect is a puzzle. Both the expression and experience of affect (emotion) involve somatic (neuromuscular and hormonal) activity. How this could be frozen and stored is far from clear. It may be the case that affect as such is not repressed, but rather that the ideation (thoughts, fantasies, and images) that arouses intolerable affect is what is repressed and that, upon the bringing to consciousness of that ideation, the defended-against affect is triggered and experienced. This seems probable to me. However, there are problems with this. There is the phenomenon of "isolation of affect," in which a thought is conscious but not accompanied by appropriate affect. When therapy succeeds, that isolated affect is experienced. Where was it? Was it "attached" to other ideation? In cold storage? The clinical data are irrefutable—we do "stuff our feelings" and sever feelings from thought. However, there is no totally satisfactory theoretical account of these phenomena.

The idea that we think and feel thoughts and feelings that we don't think or feel is paradoxical, at least on the surface. These phenomena argue for a self with, so to speak, more than one compartment, which are in less than perfect communication with each other. How does the conscious self know what to repress if it isn't aware of it, or how does what Freud would later call a *censor* know what to censor? This is an old and still unresolved problem with Freud's early, and possibly his late, theorizing. Although the abreaction of affect is therapeutically efficacious, Freud came to be suspicious of that efficacy, and later came much more to trust the achievement of insight (the understanding of the realm of the repressed and the defenses we use to bring about that repression) as curative, although he didn't overrate that power, either. Most modern therapists hold that both catharsis and insight are necessary for any lasting therapeutic effect. In his characteristically acerbic manner, Freud wrote in "Studies on Hysteria" that the purpose of psychoanalytic therapy is "to change neurotic misery into ordinary human unhappiness" (Freud & Breuer, 1895/1955, p. 305). Unlike our current panacea hucksters, Freud does not promise too much, an attitude that has much to commend it.

During the same years that Freud was trying to persuade Breuer to publish *Studies*, containing his case history of Anna O. (Breuer was reluctant, especially because of Freud's growing emphasis on the etiological significance of sexuality in neurosis), Freud pursued his practice, became the father of an expanding family (he had six children in all), and published a series of papers on the neuropsychoses of defense (1894/1962a, 1896/1962b) that dealt with the clarification of the dynamics (i.e., inner conflict) and etiology of neurosis, especially of anxiety neurosis. The most salient feature of Freud's theorizing during the 1880s and early

1890s was his recognition of the centrality of sexuality and its vicissitudes in the etiology of the neuroses. Freud's first concern was nosological, to distinguish between organic neurological illness and hysterical symptoms. He further distinguished the actual neuroses from anxiety neurosis. Freud thought that both had a sexual etiology, but that in actual neurosis it was sexual frustration, the physical blockage and lack of release of sexual substances, that caused the anxiety. Freud was not here thinking of semen primarily, but probably what later became known as the sexual hormones and the energy engendered by them. If that sexual energy was not discharged, or *sublimated* (i.e., expressed or discharged in some culturally valuable symbolic form), it, so to speak, went sour, fermented, and became toxic. Thus, the actual neuroses were physiological illnesses with actual (i.e., biogenic) causes and required "actual" cures—an increase in the patient's sexual activity, an increase in the patient's ability to sublimate, or both. The *psychoneuroses* in contradistinction to the *actual neuroses* do have psychological causes and are amenable to psychological treatment. Freud included neurasthenia, William James's malady, among the actual neuroses and, given James's long period of sexual repression, or suppression, this makes sense as at least a contributing factor to James's emotional difficulties.

In the actual neuroses, that which ferments, dements. Not much has been done with Freud's category of the actual neuroses, except by the heavy-handed. Although lack of sexual discharge or its symbolic equivalent certainly contributes to anxiety, life is not so simple, and sex, however intrinsically desirable, has cured few neurotics. Freud knew this. In his paper on the "wild analyst" (1910/1957), he tells of the young but puritanical widow who came to him after consulting a "wild" (i.e., untrained) analyst for anxiety. The analyst told her, "Madame, you must either remarry, take a lover, or satisfy yourself." The patient said she did not wish to remarry, and her voice trailed off. The would-be analysand fled. Freud commented, If she had either been able to take a lover or to satisfy herself she wouldn't have been a patient in the first place; so that the wild analyst's "intervention" was useless.

If not more interesting, then more influential were Freud's accounts of the psychoneuroses. Freud's first theory of anxiety was a toxic one: anxiety is caused by failure to discharge or sublimate sexual energy, hence anxiety neurosis is classified along with neurasthenia as an actual neurosis. Accordingly, psychological intervention alone cannot cure it. Not so hysteria, Freud's "model" for both etiology and treatment by analytic explanation and technique. In his papers on the neuropsychoses of defense, Freud set forth his first conceptualization of the mind and its workings. In them, he depicts a process he sometimes calls *defense* and sometimes calls *repression*. In modern usage, *defense* is the broader term, encompassing not only psychological repression (i.e., the pushing down from consciousness to unconsciousness of forbidden wishes and desires), but also such defenses as regression, the return to an earlier developmental stage; isolation of affect, separating the feeling from the thought; splitting of various sorts, of self and object into all good and all bad, or of consciousness into mutually contradictory states or beliefs; projection of inner states, feelings, and thoughts onto others and onto the world; introjection, placing external dangers within the self so they may be controlled; denial, believing that it isn't so when it is; rationalization, finding seemingly rational reasons to justify emotionally driven or self-serving beliefs and actions; intellectualization, overvaluing cerebration and separating it from affect;

turning anger and hate against the self because directing them against objects is too dangerous; and, finally, reaction formation, the turning of hate into its opposite, love.

Doubtless there are other psychological defenses, but these are the most widely employed. *Repression* is used by contemporary analysts in the narrow sense of driving out of consciousness unacceptable thoughts. Freud's usage is not so consistent: sometimes repression means defense in general and sometimes it means the defense of repression. Freud uses the term *defense* in his early writings, then drops it for an ambiguous use of the term *repression*, only to reintroduce defense with repression as a type of defense in his last writings. Such terminological confusions are common in Freud's voluminous output.

In the preceding paragraph, I used the term *object*. This has a special meaning in psychoanalytic theory. *Object* is of course opposed to *subject*, as it is in much philosophical writing. You are the object of my thought as subject. However, the psychoanalytic usage is much broader. It includes not only people, but things, concepts, and ideals; indeed, any object of my thought. The flag, God, and Sally are all objects, or can be if I think of them. More significantly, psychoanalytic objects are both the things and people out there and my mental representation of them. Hence analysts speak of internal objects, and in many ways are more interested in these internal objects (mental representations) than in the objective correlatives of thoughts (external objects).

Once Freud has a concept of defense or repression, he has a theory of the etiology of the psychoneuroses, hysteria and obsessive-compulsive neurosis (to be distinguished from obsessive-compulsive disorder, which contemporary thinking views and treats as primarily an organic neurological condition). In the 1880s and 1890s, Freud's emphasis was on hysteria. Hysteria is caused by the repressed affect pressing for discharge, in fact, by the failure of repression. If repression is successful, symptoms don't occur; nor does emotional illness. But repression is generally not successful. Furthermore, it requires energy to keep the repressed repressed, to keep it subterranean. Repression is not a one-time act; on the contrary, the psyche (self) is a dynamic organization in which contending forces struggle toward an unstable equilibrium much as in a vector model of contending forces in physics. Symptoms are "the return of the repressed," which find distorted (disguised) partial expression in the illness. Symptoms are simultaneously covert, symbolic representations of forbidden wishes and drives and a punishment for that expression. An emotional illness is a compromise between the forces of repression and that part of the self that desires their expression. *Self* is here equated with the psyche and its dynamic tensions; however, as we shall see, Freud was acutely aware of the saliency of the body as well as of the psyche in constituting the self; it is simply that the emphasis here in his early models is on the mind and its structure.

So now we have the nucleus of the theory of self (of the psyche) as consisting of a forbidding agency, a censor, and an agency pressing for discharge and satisfaction of instinctual energies. In various elaborations, this will be Freud's model of both self and mind.

Here we must ask, "Is the mind the self?" This has been a problem throughout our study. Self theorists vary in the degree of embodiment or disembodiment that they attribute to the self. In our discussions of self, Plato's psyche, mind, spirit, or soul was treated as a self, which is probably faithful to his intent, as was Hume's mind as a theater that doesn't exist. On the other hand, the extreme disembodiment of the Cartesian self was seen to be problematic. Freud is actually a monistic thinker; for him, psyche and soma are two aspects of one reality, so I think we are justified, for the time being, in treating his theory of the mental apparatus of the mind as a theory of self. Freud was a lifelong admirer of Spinoza, the metaphysical monist who believed that there is only one substance whose infinite attributes include thought (mind) and extension (body). The spirit of Spinoza's philosophizing finds expression in Freud's work, though he is not explicitly cited. The School of Helmholtz tended to treat mind as an epiphenomenon of matter and psychology as a branch of biology, which is a monistic point of view, even if one in which dualism is overcome by making mind derivative.

Freud eventually dropped the epiphenomenalism (i.e., the reduction of mind to body of the School of Helmholtz) while retaining its monism. His theory of anxiety is revealing. In it, he describes anxiety as a borderline phenomenon having both somatic (e.g., pounding heart, elevated blood pressure, open pupils, and sweating palms) and psychological (e.g., feelings of dread, doom, and fear) aspects. Pointing out that the somatic manifestations of anxiety in many ways mimic the somatic correlatives of orgasm, Freud concluded that anxiety could be a disguised or distorted sexual expression or satisfaction of the very sexual needs whose repression was causing that anxiety. So here anxiety is both physiological, the product of toxicity caused by repression, and psychological, insofar as it is a symbolic expression in a disguised form of a forbidden wish.

As we shall see, Freud also regarded the instincts as simultaneously somatic and psychic. However, it is not vital that we consider Freud's models of the mind as models of the self. He is a theorist who continually develops and changes, so that in talking about Freud it is always necessary to specify which Freud. In addition to his theories of mind, he has much to say about the ego in its meaning as self and the derivation of that ego from bodily experience.

Let's return to the neuropsychoses of defense (*psychoses* here meaning mental illness in general) and the etiology of hysteria. We are now familiar with the mental structure Freud infers from the illness, but so far I have said little about the nature (content) of the repressed. The Freud of the 1890s maintained that the content of the repressed was always sexual. It was sexual wishes and desires that were driven underground, and the etiology of the psychoneuroses, particularly hysteria, was a partial return of repressed sexuality—both sexual memories and current desires. Freud based this theory on clinical evidence. Patient after patient recovered memories of having been "seduced" in childhood by adults, often parents, or by much older siblings. Freud first took these "reminiscences" as factual; later, although he never denied that incest is a real phenomenon and indeed etiological when it occurred, he came to believe that a great deal of what his patients told him was fantasy derived from childhood sexual wishes.

By the turn of the century, Freud's technique had evolved from the recovery of traumatic memories through the use of hypnosis, which he said he abandoned for the reasons that not everyone was hypnotizable and that he was not very adept at it, to an active technique in which Freud literally pressed a patient's head to squeeze out the repressed memories, to instructing the patient to say whatever came to mind, no matter how embarrassing, inappropriate, or seemingly irrelevant or nonsensical. The latter is the technique of *free association*, and the injunction to say whatever comes to mind is the *fundamental rule of psychoanalysis*. It was suggested to Freud by a patient who essentially said, "Leave me alone." His genius consisted, at a time when the authority of the physician was unquestioned, in listening to her and shutting up. As it evolved, free association became a powerful therapeutic tool in gaining access to the derivatives of the unconscious. It is a way around, or perhaps behind or beneath, defenses. The talking cure, as Anna O. called it, is more than a technique. It is a moral posture. It says that the individual is worthy of meticulous prolonged attention and that the inner life is worthy of our attention. Implicit in it is the belief that self-knowledge is intrinsically valuable— and it and we are worthwhile.

Psychoanalytic technique evolved further when free association became a tool in an art of interpretation that focused on analysis of transference and the resistance, two ubiquitous concomitants of every analytic session. The patient transfers feelings of love and hate toward figures in early childhood onto the analyst, and their interpretation is a means of making the unconscious conscious. As Freud said, the patient "acts instead of remembering" (1914/1958, p. 150): acts in the sense of reenacting the feelings in the present instead of remembering their origins. Resistance, another omnipresent phenomenon, is a manifestation of the patient's defensive struggle to repudiate or keep from awareness painful repressed material. Modern analysts interpret defense before and sometimes in lieu of content.

Hypnosis, although no longer used in modern analysis, played an important role in the history of psychoanalysis. The reality of hypnotic phenomena was compelling evidence for an unconscious, or at the very least a split consciousness. It is still one of our best evidences of the presence and efficacy of the unconscious. Freud had a long-standing interest in hypnosis, which he had studied under two French pioneers in therapeutic hypnosis: Bernheim and Liebecault, whose work he translated into German.

I return to Freud's seduction theory of the etiology of neurosis and his abandonment of it; there is much current controversy surrounding this abandonment. Some of Freud's critics charge that he abandoned the seduction theory, which was true, either out of fear of social disapproval, which was already strong because of his emphasis on sexuality, or because it raised too many personal issues for him, either about his mother's seductiveness or his father's sexual abuse. Nobody accuses Freud of being consciously dishonest, but they do suggest that unconscious conflict led him away from his initial attribution of childhood seduction (i.e., sexual abuse) as the cause of neurosis. The issue is of great importance, theoretically over the existence of unconscious fantasy and the intrinsic unreliability of reality testing, and practically in treatment and in social policy. The tremendous attention that sexual abuse of children has received in the past decade, in the media and elsewhere, is a return to the seduction theory. My own view is that children do indeed have sexual fantasies about their parents and their guilt about this deepens the trauma of actually being "seduced by" an adult. Freud would have agreed with this; he never said, as his critics sometimes state, that childhood seduction and sexual abuse were not a reality, merely that it was not the universal cause of neurosis. One sidelight of this controversy that is directly relevant to our topic of the self is the increasing and now convincing clinical evidence that people who suffer from "multiple personalities" are people who have been traumatically abused, sexually and sometimes physically, at extremely early ages. Multiple personalities are defenses to cope with the traumatic disillusionment and pain of their early experience. Recovery of traumatic memories leads to reintegration of the split and isolated multiples.

There is another aspect to Freud's early belief that the cure of neurosis lies in the remembrance of traumatic experiences. There is no other treatment that so stresses remembering, and there is no religion other than Judaism that makes a religious duty of remembrance of traumatic events. "You shall not forget that your forefathers were slaves in Egypt and you shall teach it to your children and to your children's children" is one of the cardinal commandments of Judaism. The Passover Seder is a dramatization of that traumatic event and the redemption from it, so that it will not be forgotten. The Jew must remember that his forefathers were slaves. Freud repudiated Judaism as a religion and consciously was an atheist who followed no religious practices or ceremonies; however, he never repudiated his identity as a Jew or his cultural adherence to Judaism. On the contrary, he was proud of it. I would suggest that the psychoanalytic emphasis on remembering as the essence of the cure was a return of the repressed or perhaps a return of the disavowed that was in part determined by the unconscious part of Freud's identity as a Jew. This, of course, does not affect the theoretical validity or the degree of practical utility of the cure through remembering, nor does it deny the clinical inspiration for the theory. Theories, like all psychological states and products, are, to use another Freudian concept, overdetermined; that is, they have many causes. The source of an idea has nothing to do with its value; to think so is to commit a genetic fallacy. After I wrote this, I came across Yosef Hyman Yerushalmi's brilliant and moving *Freud's Moses: Judaism Terminable and Interminable* (1991), in which he expresses a similar understanding of the origin of some of Freud's psychoanalytic theorizing.

Breuer, the third of Freud's spiritual fathers broke with him over the issue of sexuality. Love turned to hate, or, more accurately, the flip side of Freud's ambivalence toward fathers came to the fore, and Freud found it necessary to cross the street when he saw Breuer, his presence being so distasteful to Freud. There followed a period of lonely isolation during which Freud met and fell in love with Wilheim Fleiss, a charismatic Berlin internist to whom he was related by marriage. Freud was neither the first nor the last to be fascinated by Fleiss. Confident, successful, and uncritically admired by many, Fliess was just what Freud needed. Brilliant, if erratic and eccentric in his ideas, Fliess was receptive to Freud's otherwise and otherwhere unwelcome theorizing. Fliess had a mesmerizing charm and was probably more than a little crazy. His theory that all illnesses were caused by nasal disorders, the nose being a sexual organ, has found little scientific support, nor has his belief that all natural phenomena could be accounted for by combinations and permutations of the female (28-day) and male (23-day) cycles. Fliess's pseudoscientific numerology probably owes an unconscious debt to cabalistic number mysticism—altogether, an unlikely consort for the Helmholtzian, scientifically rigorous Freud, but the heart has its reasons, and a passionate relationship developed between the two men. Their contact was mostly through their correspondence, occasionally punctuated by *congresses*, Freud's term for their anxiously anticipated meetings, a term that suggests both grandiosity and sexuality. Reading Freud's side of their correspondence, which is all that has survived (Freud, 1985), we get a sense of intense intellectual excitement: here are two men approaching 40 who sound like adolescents who have just discovered the world of ideas, with all the passion and excitement that goes with that discovery. Of course,

Fliess's excitement is an inference from Freud's letters, but it certainly appears to be there. Freud's letters to Fliess are a depiction of life of the educated Jewish middle class of late 19th-century Vienna that have all the vividness and richness of a great novel. Sentences filled with Freud's deep love of children alternate with sarcastic comments on his academic rivals, discussion of current political events, and theoretical "drafts." The overall effect is exhilarating. Freud's early theories about neurosis, anxiety, and the role of sexuality are all given trial balloons in the drafts he sent to Fliess. The most extensive of the drafts is Freud's "Project for a Scientific Psychology" (1895/1950), which he abandoned and never published. It is a brilliant attempt to give a quantitative neurological explanation of psychological states and of psychopathology. It was Freud's last attempt to reduce psychology to physiology. Although he never abandoned the belief that a neurochemical explanation of mental events was possible, he himself turned to purely psychological explanations to account for both normal and pathological events. It is true that his psychological models and accounts retain a physicalistic basis, and much of Freud's theorizing is based on a "hydraulic model" of forces, pressures, flows, and blockages. It is a model based on 19th-century physics. It is also true that his theorizing becomes more and more a theory about meaning, and about relationships, and becomes truly psychological rather than pseudopsychological physics.

During Freud's almost two-decade-long relationship with Fliess, he suffered a "considerable psycho neurosis" (Jones, 1961, p. 198) himself. Freud's emotional pain drove him to undertake his self-analysis, in which Fliess served as a sort of analyst by mail, and more important, was a transference figure eliciting all of Freud's intense feelings of love and hate for his father. Although it is unlikely that the two men were actually lovers, there is no question that Wilheim Fliess was the great love of Freud's life.

In the course of his self-analysis and his relationship with Fliess, Freud "discovered" the Oedipus complex and wrote what is usually considered his most important work, *Interpretation of Dreams* (1900/1953a). In analyzing his dreams, Freud came to see that dreams have the same structure as symptoms. They too are disguised expressions of forbidden wishes. He concluded that all dreams are wish fulfillments. In the course of his self-analysis, he discovered much about himself: about his intense rivalry with and ambivalence toward his father; about his murderous feelings toward his infant brother, Julius; about his drivenness; and about his narcissistic vulnerability.

The dreams reported in *Interpretation of Dreams* make a unique contribution to the autobiographical literature of the West. They expand the account of self to include a new dimension. The self asleep—at least while dreaming—now becomes an integral part of self. Descartes's questions about distinguishing dreams and waking reality as a vital component of reality testing become irrelevant, and Locke's concern about the continuity of self during sleep is seen in a new light: dream consciousness is just as much consciousness, just as integral to the self, as waking consciousness. The injunction "Know Thyself" changes in meaning as the locus of self shifts to that which is not known, to the unconscious as represented in disguised and distorted forms in the dream. The self is now more unknown and unknowable, apart from undergoing the rigors of analysis, than hitherto believed. Freud's technique of dream analysis is double-edged: on the one hand, it gives us a tool for knowing the self; on the other hand, it reveals a new, unknown territory that must be reclaimed before the self can be either known or integral.

Having gone public in a unique, if partial and selective, way, Freud put an important part, by his lights the most important part, of himself up for scrutiny by any and all; and indeed his dreams have been interpreted and reinterpreted in a bewildering variety of ways, both from within and from without the psychoanalytic movement. One of the most fascinating perspectives on Freud's dreams is that of Carl Schorske (1980), who looks at their political meaning and significance and sees Freud as "regressing" from the political (adult's) to the familial (child's) world, from external reality to internal reality, because of the disintegration of the Austrian-Hungarian empire, its series of defeats in war, and growing dissension, corruption, and decadence; also, increasingly virulent anti-Semitism (Karl Lueger was installed as the anti-Semitic mayor of Vienna just as *Interpretation* was published) made action in the outer world increasingly futile and hopeless. Freud's dreams do indeed have many political references, and Freud like Plato before him takes the relation between social classes as representative of, or isomorphic to, the relationships of the parts of the psyche. Additionally, Freud's metaphors of self and mind are consistently political, and even sometimes military: defense, resistance, occupation, and drive.

Schorske interprets what Freud calls the *manifest dream*, the dream as dreamt, which Freud distinguishes from the *latent dream*, which is where his interest lies. In Freud's theory of the mechanism of dreams (which serves as a paradigm for his theory of mind in the sense of self) the dream thoughts that are forbidden childhood wishes, derivative of drives (instinctual energies) striving for discharge, are "converted" by the *dream work* into the manifest dream through the mechanisms of displacement, condensation, symbolization, visualization, and secondary revision. The task of dream interpretation is to work backwards from the manifest dream to the latent dream thoughts by listening to the dreamer's association to each dream element. Secondary revision is the mind's reworking of the dream material to give it more apparent sense and continuity than it possesses, that is, to give the dream a better story line. Dreams make use of current materials (the "day residue") but always equally, or more than equally, represent in distorted form the events and desires of childhood. Dreams are always egoistic. The censor imposes the dreamwork on the latent dream thoughts so they do not arouse so much anxiety as to wake the dreamer.

Freud has now moved from psychopathology to a normal psychological phenomenon, dreaming, and found that dreams are compromise formations in just the same way as symptoms. He is now in a position to expound a general psychology, an omni-applicable account of human nature. In the years following the *Interpretation of Dreams*, Freud went on to apply his paradigm to jokes, art, hallucinations, religion, and culture in general, finding each to have the same basic structure as compromises and disguised wish fulfillments.

In the famous "specimen dream of psychoanalysis," the dream of Irma's injection, Freud for the first time subjects a dream of his own to analysis. In the dream, the dreamer is in a large reception hall receiving guests, including Irma, who is a former patient who is still ill. By the time the dream ends, Irma's continued illness is blamed on at least three other persons, including one who represents Breuer. Freud interprets the dream wish as the desire to be blameless as well as to pay back some old scores. Irma in real life was Emma Eckstein, whom Fliess had operated on for "nasal neurosis" (which was plain madness), an intrusive application of his wild theory to a human being. To make matters worse, he left the packing in, which infected (long before antibiotics) and almost killed the patient, who suffered the torments of the damned and was given psychological interpretation of her difficulties by Freud. Freud told her that her symptoms were a holding onto her illness, which was a manifestation of her negative transference to him. Freud's dream was certainly an attempt to find himself guiltless by projecting blame for Irma's difficulties onto others, but Freud missed the main thrust, the deepest wish, behind the dream: to find Fliess blameless in order to protect his (Freud's) idealized love object from contamination and devaluation. Freud missed the motive power of our need for ideal objects, for perfect lovers with whom we can identify and perhaps merge. Fliess was such an ideal object for him. If Fliess was a transference object, as according to Freud's theory he had to be, then it was his father who was to be protected from the charge of injuring a woman. The childhood wish represented in distorted form in the dream was his wish that Father be perfect and blameless. In light of Freud's revision of the seduction theory, one wonders what the idealized father had to be rendered blameless of. Emma Eckstein held no grudges and became an analyst herself. As far as Freud's relationship with Fliess went, the bloom was soon to be off the rose, and the relationship between the two men became increasingly acrimonious.

In Chapter 7 of *Interpretation*, Freud elucidated his first model of the mind, the topographical model. In it, there are three realms, those of *consciousness*, *preconsciousness*, and *dynamic unconsciousness*. The *descriptive unconscious* includes all that is out of awareness at a given moment: that is, the contents of the preconscious and of the dynamic unconscious. The preconscious is the realm of all that is out of awareness, but that can be accessed by attention or by an act of will. The dynamic unconscious, on the other hand, is blocked from access to storage in the preconscious or awareness in consciousness by the censor. As I noted above, Freud never solved the problem of how the censor knows what to censor. Consciousness is the ego's or self's point of contact with the external world. The normal flow, the normal progression, is from outside to inside, from the senses to consciousness, but the reverse can also be true, and there can be a *topographical regression* in which the contents of the dynamic unconscious—the inside—find (disguised) representation in consciousness, in dreams, and in hallucinations. Regression can also be temporal to that which is earlier in development, or formal, in which structure is simplified or lost and the more articulated becomes less articulated. Topographical, temporal, and formal regression are three aspects of one process.

Consciousness is organized temporally and logically; the law of the excluded middle and the other Aristotelian logical categories are operative; and there are orderly, lawful causal connections between thoughts. Contradictory beliefs cannot be simultaneously held. Freud called this kind of sequential, rational thinking *secondary process thinking* to distinguish it from *primary process thinking*, the mode of operation of the unconscious. Unconscious thought processes are not bound by the rules of logic, contradictory propositions can exist without conflict, causal sequences are irrelevant, and all primary process is timeless, outside of the temporal order. Freud's description of the dynamic unconscious and its primary process mode of operation is strikingly reminiscent of Kant's self-in-itself, the noumenal self, with the important difference that Freud's unconscious is potentially partially knowable through analysis of its derivatives such as dreams, while Kant's noumenal self is knowable, if at all, through moral action. Of course

Freud's dynamic unconscious is, unlike Kant's noumenal self, not the source of morality. Quite to the contrary, it is the source of egoistic drive discharge and wish fulfillment.

Freud has now, so to speak, delineated the anatomy of the psyche, but not yet its physiology. In order to do so, he needs a driving force, and he finds it in his concept of *psychic energy*. Psychic energy is conceptualized as parallel to physical energy—as an underlying force equal in dignity to the forces postulated by physics and chemistry. Psychic energy undergoes vicissitudes just as physical energy undergoes transformations. In both cases, there is a conservation of energy; that is, energy, psychic or physical, can be transformed from one state or form into another, but the sum total of the available energy remains the same, that is, is conserved. Again we can see the parallelism between Freud's theory making and the theories then in vogue in the physical sciences. Freud's concept of psychic energy has been criticized as a metaphysical rather than an empirical scientific notion. It is seen as unoperationalizable (i.e., not measurable; an unverifiable, extrascientific conception), but its defenders view it as an explanatory hypothesis that, like many such explanatory hypotheses in the physical sciences, accounts for the data of observation without itself being observable. Those who think that the notion of psychic energy has conceptual validity point out that we no more see physical energy than we do psychic energy, and that in both cases, what we can see and measure are the presumed effects of these hypothetical forces.

Once he has the concept of psychic energy to work with, Freud sees it as manifesting itself in the form of instinctual drives. These are not instincts in the sense of prepatterned sequences of behavior, but rather are forces pressing for discharge and expression; that is, they are biological drives. Freud sees these instinctual forces as being both mental and physical, but he is most interested in their mental representations and effects—what he calls their *derivatives*. Psychic energy, or instinctual drive power, differentiates itself into two main classes of instincts that are conceptualized as libido and ego instincts by the early Freud and as Eros and Thanatos by the late Freud. Always a psychologist of conflict, a theoretical underpinning (or *metapsychology*, as he called it) that had contending forces intrinsic to it suited Freud perfectly. A dualistic instinct theory made sense of Freud's clinical data, and it was able to account for the irrationality of human behavior. It made sense of the inner life of people as it unfolded on the analytic couch.

Each major instinct has component instincts, thus libido finds expression in orality, anality, sadism and masochism, as well as in voyeurism and exhibitionism, along with its manifestation in genital sexuality. Libido is more like Plato's Eros than like sexual desire in the narrow sense. The *ego instincts* are the self-preservative instincts in which aggression is implicit but not, at this stage of Freud's theorizing, explicit. Ego instincts are much like Spinoza's *conatus*, the drive that every living thing has to maintain itself. Libido and the ego instincts have different goals: libido seeks to join and to preserve the species, the ego instincts seek to preserve the individual as a separate entity. There is a sense in which libido is primordial, for Freud speaks of the ego instincts as being anaclitic—leaning up against—the sexual instincts, but this is a nuance in a dualistic system.

When Freud is talking about the ego instincts, he is talking about the self-preservative instincts. Here Freud is talking about the self. In German, his term for ego is *das Ich*, the I; hence, the ego instincts are the I instincts. When Freud uses the term *ego* before 1923, the date of his second model of the mind, the *structural hypothesis*, *ego* means self in its ordinary usage. This self is the whole person, including the bodily self and the mental self. Freud disliked technical terms, although James Strachey, his English translator, did not, and when Freud said *ego* or *self*, he was not intending anything sophisticated, just the plain man in the street's notion of being a person like other persons who have a mind and body, however the two may be related. After 1923, Freud used *ego* (*das Ich*) either to mean the self in its ordinary connotation or, more usually, to mean an agency of the mind in his structural model. The reader must determine from the context which meaning is intended. Now we have two Freudian notions of the self: the topographical psyche with its instinctual energies and the whole person with all of his or her bodily and mental experiences.

In 1915, Freud wrote one of his most perceptive clinical papers, "Mourning and Melancholia" (1915/1957b). In it, we see the beginning of what was to become object relations theory. Freud looks to compare a pathological phenomenon, depression or melancholia, with a normal one, mourning. In mourning, we suffer the loss of an object and wander about like a dazed, lost child looking for a mother. In Freud's view, what the mourner must do is to introject the lost object, to in some sense make the lost object a part of self, a part of the mourner. The introjected object may be experienced as a foreign body, which indeed it is. Only after introjection can the bonds of libido that tie the mourner to the lost person or lost ideal or value be loosened. Freud says we do this by hypercathecting—investing with an overabundance of libido—each separate memory of the lost one. The intensity, so to speak, breaks the bond, almost like an elastic band being stretched until it snaps. When the last memory is hypercathected, the last band snapped, the tie to the lost object is severed, and libido is free once again to invest itself in a new object. In short, we become able to love again. In melancholia, there is also a loss, but it is often not obvious what has been lost, and there is no working through, no freedom from the lost object achieved.

Freud hypothesized that in melancholia, a hated object is introjected, and the hatred felt for that object that is now within is visited upon the self. In the famous and strangely poetic aphorism, Freud says, "The shadow of the object fell on the ego" (1915/1957b, p. 249), ego here meaning self. Here we have a whole new notion of self, a self as an entity that can contain that which is taken in from the outside by introjection and that can project parts of itself outward onto the environment—onto the world of objects. Another way Freud views introjection is to say that "an object relation [i.e., a relation between the self and another] has regressed to an identification [i.e., an amalgamation of self and other in which the self virtually becomes the other]." Now the hatred felt for the introjected object is visited on the self, and the result is melancholia. Freud is perfectly aware that not all depressions have this mechanism and, indeed, that some are biological in nature, but he captured for all time the phenomenology of one type of psychodynamic depression—the type in which anger is turned inward.

Freud cited the grandiosity and arrogance of the melancholic that is so discordant with the self-deprecation and self-laceration that goes with melancholia as evidence that what looks like self-hatred is really hatred of an internalized other. He goes on to say a seemingly and perhaps contradictory thing, namely, that the only way the ego (the self) can give up its objects is to make them part of itself.

Indeed, "the ego [self] is the precipitate of abandoned object cathexis"; that is, the self is constructed by the identification with and introjection of those we once loved but from whom we have now withdrawn our emotional investment. This is an extraordinary notion of self.

In his much-revised, "Three Contributions to a Theory of Sexuality" (1905/ 1953b), Freud elaborates the libido theory and the vicissitudes of the libido into a developmental scheme in which an objectless autoerotic stage develops into a narcissistic stage, which in turn evolves into the psychosexual stages of orality, anality, and phallicity, and finally into the object-related stage of genitality. In undergoing this development, the component instincts of libido first find expression in oral experience ("love and hunger meet at a woman's breast"); then in anal experience in which sexual pleasure is concentrated in the sensation of the anal mucosa during both retention and expulsion; then in phallic or clitoral sensations in masturbation; and, finally, after a period of latency, in the mutuality of intercourse. In the course of development, the partial or component instincts of masochism-sadism and exhibitionism-voyeurism also find expression. In healthy genitality, the component instincts find expression and satisfaction during foreplay. Freud's libido theory is a precursor to his concept of narcissism, and some understanding of his understanding of the vicissitudes of libidinal development is a necessary prelude to understanding narcissism as Freud conceptualized it.

NARCISSISM

Narcissism is an old concept that has been given a modern meaning or meanings by psychoanalysis. The word *narcissism* comes from the Greek *narke*, to deaden. It is the same root that is found in the words *narcotic* and *narcotize*. Both narcotics and narcissism deaden, attenuate sensation and feeling. That says something interesting about addiction in its relationship to narcissism. The Greek root took on its meaning of deadening from the name of a protagonist of a legend, Narcissus. In the legend, Narcissus is a beautiful youth who becomes so entranced by his reflection in a pool of water that he remains frozen, gazing upon his own face until he perishes. At his death, he was transformed into a flower, the narcissus. His infatuation with self gave narcissism its meaning of self-love. Both *narke* and the tale of Narcissus remind us that there is something dangerous, even potentially fatal, about self-love, yet without it we would also perish. So there must be a healthy self-love (narcissism), which is life enhancing, and a pathological self-love (narcissism), which deadens.

Freud, 2,500 years later, turned narcissism into a scientific concept in his prescient paper "On Narcissism: An Introduction" (Freud, 1914/1957c). In it, Freud distinguishes several meanings of narcissism: as a sexual perversion in which the self is taken as the primary sexual object; as a libidinal component of the instinct of self-preservation; and as the libidinal cathexis of self, cathexis being the investment of an object with psychic energy. He cites a number of phenomena as evidence for the existence of narcissism: the existence of the above-mentioned sexual perversions in which pleasure in looking at, admiring, and fondling the self provides complete sexual satisfaction; the normal and universal love of self; the megalomania of schizophrenia in which all of the libido seems to be directed onto the self; the clinical evidence of the distinction between object libido and ego libido as manifested in the transference neuroses in which a libidinal bond is formed with the analyst and the narcissistic neuroses (i.e., the psychoses) in which such a bonding does not take place; organic illness, in which self-absorption is normal; hypochondria, in which libido is also directed onto the self or fragments thereof; the egoism of sleep; love between men in which object choice is choice of a replica (in some sense) of the self; and parental love with its excesses and denial that the restraints of reality apply to the child, which Freud views as narcissistic love once removed.

In his seminal essay, Freud described a normal developmental process in which there is a progression from autoeroticism (love of isolated body parts) to narcissism (love of self) to object love (love of others). The infant first derives pleasure from body parts, experienced as isolates, not as parts of the self; these sensory experiences are later integrated into a self, or ego, that is experienced as tenuous and unclearly demarcated from the not-self (the world); and this ego is loved. Finally, a portion of this primeval self-love, or *primary narcissism*, overflows and is projected out as object love. Thus, our instinctual energy is first invested in our own body parts, then invested in ourselves before the distinction between self and other has been firmly established, and finally flows outward to emotionally invest (cathect) objects. Narcissistic libido becomes object libido.

According to Freud, disappointment in object love can lead to withdrawal of interest (libido) from the world and reinvestment of that libido in the self. Freud denoted this phenomenon *secondary narcissism* to distinguish it from the primary narcissism of infancy. Freud postulated that normal self-esteem results from a reservoir of self-love that is retained from the stage of primary narcissism and that continues to exist alongside object love. He thought that secondary narcissism was the basic mechanism of psychotic withdrawal from the world, and that the psychotic delusion of the end of the world reflected the reality of the withdrawal of libido from the world of objects and its redirection onto a now impoverished and isolated self.

Few aspects of Freud's thought have born as much fruit as his discussion of narcissism. Narcissism as the libidinal cathexis of the self make sense in terms of Freud's energetic model, and the conversion of narcissistic libido into object libido explains the lowered self-esteem of unrequited infatuation, in which the lover debases him- or herself concomitantly with idealizing the loved object.

Freud uses two metaphors, that of the amoeba with its pseudopodia reaching out to cathect objects in the environment and that of the manometer in which mercury flows out of one side of a U tube into the other, just as narcissistic libido flows outward, changing into object libido. Both the liquid in the manometer and libido can reverse their flow. Overinvestment in love of others leads to impoverishment of the ego (the self) and lowering of self-esteem. The amoeba analog implies considerable aggression in loving; retraction of the pseudopodia corresponds to the withdrawal of libido from the world in secondary narcissism. Freud ingeniously interprets the delusions and hallucinations of schizophrenia as an attempt at creating a restitutive world by the ego (self) that cannot stand the aridity and vacuity of the objectless world of secondary narcissism. If loving too much impoverishes the ego, loving not at all is even worse; it results in megalomania and the secondary symptoms (the delusions, catatonic postures, and hallucinations) of psychosis. Libido must be expended (invested) or it goes sour. Freud trenchantly concludes, "We must love or grow ill" (1914/1957c, p. 85).

THANATOS: THE DEATH INSTINCT

Freud wrote of the vicissitudes of libido, of self-love and object love, immediately before World War I; after that war, he focused on the death instinct. Western man apparently preferred making war to making love. *Beyond the Pleasure Principle* (Freud, 1920/1955) is one of the great tragic visions of human life. In it, Freud revamped his theory of the instincts, replacing the ego instincts with Thanatos, the death instinct. Now the dynamic conflict within us is between love and death. Freud compared his new metapsychology to that of the pre-Socratic philosopher, Empedocles, who wrote of the eternal war between Eros and Strife. Freud postulated that all organic matter, everything that lives, has a desire to return to the quietus of the inorganic. Freud variously called this the Nirvana principle or the death instinct. He cited self-destructive behaviors of all sorts, the deeply conservative nature of human beings who seek endlessly to repeat (relive) past traumas; the games of children in which repetition is a source of pleasure; the negative therapeutic reaction in which the better the patient does, the worse he feels; and the all too manifest horrors of human aggression. If the death instinct is indwelling, then there must be a primary masochism analogous to primary narcissism, and just as libido must turn outward to avert emotional illness, so must Thanatos turn outward in the form of aggression. At its darkest, it is a choice of murder or suicide. Just as secondary narcissism is always a human potential, secondary masochism—the taking back and turning on the self of aggression derivative of the death instinct—is omnipossible. If love is primordial, so is hate. All of our lives we must strive to keep our aggression out front, and in the end we all fail, returning Thanatos to its source within, and die. Freud is here trying to account for therapeutic failure, addiction, suicide, and self-mutilation and their murderous externalizations. He comes up with the notion of the *repetition compulsion*, the inertial force derived from the death instinct that keeps us acting out the same self-destructive patterns over and over. Sameness is like quietus: nothing new happens, and this inbuilt inertial force is in perpetual war with Eros, the life force, that seeks growth, union, and novelty.

Few later analysts have accepted the death instinct, but most have agreed with Freud that aggression is innate. Their dual instinct theories pit libido against aggression rather than Eros against Thanatos. Closely related to the repetition compulsion is Freud's notion of phylogenic inheritance. Freud came to believe that a kind of primitive guilt is inborn, almost as an innate idea. Freud's innate ideas are a kind of template that predisposes us to Oedipal conflicts, guilt, and self-punishment. Freud's theory of the primal crime of the band of brothers killing the tyrannical primal father and sharing the guilt by consuming him in a totem meal, which he developed in *Totem and Taboo* (1913–1914/1953c) led naturally to his theory of the inheritance of phylogenetic guilt. Freud needed this concept to make sense of the ubiquitous masochistic behavior he encountered in his patients and in human history. If human beings are motivated solely by the pleasure principle, which was Freud's original contention, human behavior as he found it is inexplicable. Innate guilt, the repetition compulsion, and the death instinct hardly make for an optimistic view of human nature, but as Freud said in "Thoughts for the Times on War and Death" (1915/1957d), "that which is painful may nevertheless be true."

The template for the Oedipus complex—Freud's label for the complex, ambivalent feelings children have for parents, particularly their death wishes toward the rival, same-sex parent and desire for sexual possession of the opposite-sex parent—is also innate—part of our phylogenetic inheritance. The Oedipus complex is complicated by children's love for the parent they hate and hate for the parent they love. Freud first expounded the Oedipus complex in *Interpretation of Dreams*, where it is the chief fruit of his self-analysis. Freud believed that most psychopathology arises from failure to work through Oedipal feelings and somehow resolve them by renunciation, mourning, identification with, and internalization of the rival parent. In effect, the way out of the Oedipal impasse is "If you can't beat them, join them." That is, successful resolution of the Oedipal conflict entails identification with the ambivalently hated, same-sex rival parent.

Freud's revision of his instinct theory may owe something to Alfred Adler, who advocated the inclusion of an aggressive instinct in psychoanalytic theory; to Sabina Spielrein, a former patient and mistress of Jung, who like Adler participated in Freud's "Wednesday Evening" seminars; and most important, to Otto Weininger, a brilliant neurotic, whose *Sex and Character* (1906) became a sensation in Vienna after he suicided in Beethoven's home at the age of 23. Weininger, who was both Jewish and homosexual, hated both Jews and homosexuals; in his book he advocated a Schopenhauerian renunciation of desire and a seeking for an asexual Nirvana-like state of quietus. Whatever the influence of these three on him, the death instinct is a genuinely Freudian concept; it comes out of clinical concerns, the carnage of World War I, and perhaps an unconscious intimation of the cancer that would soon strike him. Interestingly, it is an oral lesion that Freud and his colleagues are examining in the dream of Irma's injection. Was Freud, even then, unconsciously anticipating his oral cancer, and was that cancer, caused by the smoking that he wouldn't relinquish, a self-punishment for his treatment of Irma and for his death wishes toward Julius, his father, and Fliess? It is at least possible that the man who introduced the death instinct, for all his vitality and life force, was "half in love with easeful death." At the very least, he certainly knew something highly personal about the repetition compulsion and about masochism.

The publication of Weininger's book brought about Freud's final break with Fliess. In the book, Weininger advocated an inherent bisexuality in all human beings. That was an idea that Freud had taken over from Fliess, and Fliess accused Freud of giving it to Weininger without giving Fliess credit. Freud had indeed discussed bisexuality with a patient who was a friend of the demented philosopher, but denied it.

In 1923, Freud published *The Ego and the Id* (1923/1961), literally, *The I and the It*. In it he expounded his second, structural model of the mind. The structural model supplements, or perhaps supplants, the topographical model. Freud sees the mental structure as developing from an undifferentiated state in which impulses strive for discharge. The repository or source of these impulses he denoted the id or it. The id operates through primary process and is unconscious. It is the repository of instinctual energy. Using a spatial metaphor, Freud describes the ego, or I, as arising on the surface of the id at the id's point of contact with external reality. He states that an entity as complex as an I or ego could not exist from the beginning, which is congruent with his description of the ego, here meaning the self, actually coming into being from "islands of self experience" in "On Narcissism." The ego develops into a separate agency of the mental apparatus defined by its functions of perception, reality testing, defense (against both internal, instinctual threats, and external dangers), memory, motility, and judgment. The ego is partly conscious and partly unconscious. The ego defenses are most likely to be unconscious, and much of contemporary analytic therapy is aimed at making them conscious. The ego is sort of the executive, but it is a weak executive, having no energy of its own, deriving its energy from the id, and having the formidable task of mediating between the demands of the id for immediate gratification, the restrictions and prohibitions of the superego, and the constraints of reality. The superego, or the over-I, is both the product of further differentiation of the ego into an ego ideal (that which we would like to be) and the heir of the resolution of the Oedipus complex in which ambivalently loved and hated parents (particularly the boy's father whom he is in love with yet wishes to murder in order to possess his mother) are internalized and made part of self; the ego (self) is the precipitate of abandoned object cathexis. Identification leads to internalization. Now the prohibitions of the parents and of the culture are inside. Freud now defines the goal of analytic therapy as the strengthening of the ego: "where 'it' (id) was 'I' (ego) shall be."

The self is now the structural ego, the agency of the mind that attempts to find a "rational" solution to the conflicts of contending forces rather than the person or bodily-mental self of prestructural theory. The id says, "Give me everything yesterday"; the superego says, "You get nothing ever"; and the poor ego has to squeeze out a modicum of satisfaction today or tomorrow.

Freud tells us that the "ego is in service of the Id"; that is, it tries to satisfy the id's demands while taking into account "recalcitrant reality." Freud says something very interesting about this ego or self; namely, that it is "first and foremost a bodily ego." By this he means that the structural ego, the sense of self, is built up out of bodily sensations, much as the prestructural ego emerges from the autoerotic stage. This is diametrically opposed to the Cartesian notion of the self as pure cognition, in which bodily experience is suspect or unreal. Freud's therapeutic goal is to both strengthen and unify this ego. If we regard it as the self, the self has its origins in bodily experience and only slowly comes into contact with the external world as it evolves into a mental agency that mediates between internal forces and external reality. Further, it is largely unconscious and only comes into full being by becoming more conscious. The self as ego is not a given; it is an achievement.

The ego is in one sense the Jewish professional and middle class caught between the forces of an increasingly violent and anti-Semitic Austrian proletariat and the prohibitions of an authoritarian and increasingly corrupt ruling class. Although having special referent to the Jewish professional class, the ego is in many ways the heir of the goals and values of Austrian liberalism and the class interests that that liberalism represented. Although weak and having no force (army, police, or instinctual energy) of its own, both the ego and the professional middle class represented the ideals of rationality, prudence, intellectuality, and understanding. Insofar as the ego was that class, it certainly was a weak reed; it has since been exterminated. If the structural model is in part unconscious sociology, it is also powerful psychology. Although many have criticized it, particularly for the powerlessness of the ego, the structural model retains an heuristic power to organize and make intelligible a wide variety of human experience, particularly of conflict, that few other models of the mind can rival.

In 1926, Freud revised his theory of anxiety. In his first formulation, we are anxious because we repress (the toxic theory of anxiety); in his second theory, we repress because we are anxious, and anxiety is reinterpreted as a danger signal, a sign that dangerous or forbidden thoughts or wishes are coming to consciousness, in analogy to the way in which we deal with external dangers. The ego, which is now the "seat of anxiety," responds with defenses and represses or otherwise fends off the threatening thoughts or wishes. The concept of *signal anxiety* is clinically useful; the failure to develop it leaves one subject to panic terror, since suitable defenses or actions cannot be instituted when anxiety arises. In *Inhibitions, Symptoms, and Anxiety* (1926/1959), Freud delineates the resistance to recovery from the three agencies of the mind: from the id, the "adhesion of the libido," and the "conservatism of the instincts" resist change; and from the ego the transference (acting instead of remembering), repression and other ego defenses, and the "secondary gains" from the illness mitigate against recovery; but the resistance most difficult to overcome is that of the superego. The patient unconsciously believes that he or she doesn't deserve to be well and holds onto the illness as a means of self-punishment.

Freud now views anxiety as developmental. Anxiety at the earliest stage of life is a panic terror of annihilation, which is followed by fear of loss of the object, which is followed by fear of loss of love of the object, which is followed by castration anxiety, which is followed by fear of the superego, which is followed by social anxiety, fear of punishment by the culture. In the course of that development, anxiety hopefully comes to be treated as a danger signal that can be responded to either with psychological defenses or by actions to modify the external world. Castration anxiety is an important Freudian concept. It refers to the child's fear that the rival parent will punish him by castration for his aggressive wishes toward that parent and his sexual wishes for the parent of the opposite sex. Castration anxiety and the Oedipal complex are two sides of the same coin. Freud thought castration anxiety was the most frequent cause of repression. However, separation anxiety—fear of loss of the object and fear of loss of the love of the object—became extremely important in psychoanalytic theory.

At the end of his life, Freud wrote the paper "Splitting of the Ego in the Process of Defense" (1940/1964a). In it, he describes how the fetishist simultaneously believes that women have penises and that they don't have penises by splitting the self into two selves who, so to speak, don't talk to one another. At the same time, he wrote *Moses and Monotheism* (1939/1964b), a work with many meanings and having many psychological sources. There is a connection between the two works. If polytheism is a projection of unintegrated components of the self onto the cosmos, monotheism represents the human project of the reintegration of the self, the healing of the splits in the ego, which is the final goal of Freud's therapy. Abreaction and insight—self-knowledge—are but tools in that endeavor. The great theorist, in the end, sees the human task as the integration of the conflicting elements of the self, in spite of the fact that he knows perfectly well that it cannot be done. Freud asked what it was that made him Jewish, although he neither believed nor practiced. I submit that the profoundest expression of his Jewish identity lies in his reintegrating the projected monotheistic God of Judaism in the therapeutic goal of integrating the ego—making the self as whole as it can be just as the God of monotheism is a whole.

There is another way of looking at Freud's motivation for writing *Moses and Monotheism*. Freud was a driven man in writing it, and obviously it had many sources in his life and many meanings for him. It was, as psychoanalysts say, overdetermined. At one level, it was a masochistic act of debasement, a desperate attempt to propitiate the violent murderous anti-Semitism of Hitler's Europe by declaring that the greatest Jewish hero, Moses, was in fact a *goy*, an Egyptian. As such, it was an identification with the father who passively stepped into the gutter to pick up the hat the Gentile had knocked off; however, on another level, it was a profoundly proud assertion of all that Freud valued and held dear in his Jewish identity. At the time of the most insane, irrational racism and blind pride of race, Freud implicitly asserted that truth is a transcendent value, overriding all considerations of racial pride. The ultimately Jewish act was to stand by the truth, as he saw it, that Moses, the Jewish hero, was in fact not Jewish, and the assertion of that truth was a statement of his, Freud's, ultimate dignity as a Jew and as a human being. Whether or not Freud was factually correct is here irrelevant. So the act of seeming masochistic debasement becomes a contemptuous challenge: I, the hated and persecuted Jew, relinquish brute narcissism for the sake of scientific objectivity, for the disinterested pursuit of truth, while you, the Gentiles, trample on truth in a desperate attempt to raise your self-esteem through infantile grandiosity and archaic narcissism. Few have thumbed their noses so effectively or so covertly. In doing so, Freud achieved a positive identification with his father and a loving resolution of his Oedipal conflicts.

The episode referred to above, in which Freud's father's hat was knocked off by a Gentile and he passively stepped into the gutter and picked it up without replying was profoundly disillusioning to Freud. He recounts the story in his associations to one of his dreams in the *Interpretation of Dreams,* and the depth of the narcissistic injury he felt at the thought of this big, strong man whom he looked up to and admired being submissive and passive and allowing himself to be debased was profound. A great deal of Freud's adult life was a repudiation of that kind of passivity and an attempt to be active, aggressive, and self-respecting. *Moses and Monotheism* is both an identification with the father's debasement and a repudiation and transcendence of it.

Old and sick, Freud went into exile in England. His books and collection of antiquities were sent to England, where his Viennese study was recreated in his home at Mansfield Gardens, where it can still be seen. A visitor entering the study said, "Professor, it's all here," to which Freud replied, "Ja. Aber Ich bin nicht hier"—"Yes, but I am not here." With this mordant statement, this most complex of our theorists about self made what is perhaps his most profound comment on the nature of self, that to have a self is something other than to exist. Paradoxically, he was never more himself than when he denied his presence as a self.

9

Carl Jung: The Self as Mandala

Fliess was the last of Freud's "fathers." Carl Jung was the first of his "sons." For Freud, the break with Fliess was traumatic. Fliess was more than a substitute or symbolic father, he was partly a brother, partly an idealized love object, partly a professional audience when Freud had none, and partly a companion in the adventure of creativity. His relationship with Fliess was the relationship that caused him more pain than any other. Brücke could not give him a patrimony; Charcot died; Breuer broke with him on the issue of sexuality; his own father died; and his relationship with Fliess ended in bitter acrimony. It was enough of fathers. From here on out, Freud would be the father, not the son. However, being a father worked no better for Freud than being a son. Freud's relationships with his "sons" were at least as conflicted and tormented as his relationships with his "fathers." Almost without exception, they ended in mutual recrimination and hurt. This was certainly true of his relationship with Jung.

Freud's legacy to self theory is rich, encompassing the not necessarily compatible notions that the self is not primordial but develops only slowly; that the self is only partly and not primarily conscious; that the self is built up through internalization of lost objects; that the self is originally and to a great extent remains a bodily self; that the self is suffused with narcissistic libido and love; that the self is prone to dynamic conflict between unconscious drives: sexuality and aggression and their repudiation by conscious and unconscious ideals; and that the self is prone to defensive splitting, the integration of which is a primary goal of therapy. Thus, Jung as "son" had much, perhaps too much, to accept, assimilate, and transmute into something of his own or to reject from his "father." This was the case for all of psychoanalytic theory, but particularly true when it comes to Jung's understanding of the self. As we shall see, the Jungian self is radically different from the multidimensional Freudian self.

Carl Jung (1875–1961) was born in a Swiss village where his father was the dissatisfied parson. The family had produced a long line of clergymen. Jung's father had wanted to become a classical scholar, a university professor, and regarded his actual career as a poor second choice. The relationship between father and son was never close or warm. Jung's mother, although capable of more warmth, was subject to depressions and was not reliably there for him. She also seems to have had ambivalent feelings toward him. The parents did not get along, and there was much dissension in the house. Jung's later theory of the man getting in contact with the woman within (the *anima*) and the woman getting in touch with the man within (the *animus*) and achieving some sort of integration of masculine and feminine elements can be seen as a theoretical derivative of his intense boyhood desire to reconcile his parents. In life, he did not succeed in doing so. He grew up an introspective, socially isolated child prone to withdrawal, avoidance, and psychosomatic difficulties. Like Freud, he was strongly attracted to nature, especially to the Rhine, which had its source near his home, and to the lakes and mountains of Switzerland. Jung early realized that his tendencies to neurotic with-drawal could lead him into great difficulties, and he precociously, self-consciously fought against them, eventually becoming a "successful" schoolboy who enjoyed the respect of his fellows, although it is extremely doubtful that he really felt a part of things. Jung was always an egalitarian from above, and one has the sense of a separation and alienation from his fellows, although he denied this. At any rate, Jung did succeed in connecting with his peers at a manifest level, and this was important for him. It probably prevented him from regressing into the all-too-seductive realm of imagination and fantasy in a perhaps irreversible way. Even as a child, he was deeply engrossed in the inner world of his dreams. In his maturity, Jung emphasized the absolute necessity of the patient remaining in or becoming attached for the first time to the ordinary day-to-day social realities of familial and occupational responsibilities in order to have a secure enough base so that the "journey" into inwardness that Jungian therapy became could be safely under-taken. Jung cited Nietzsche, who strongly influenced him, as a tragic example of the consequences of pursuing inward reality at the cost of loosening one's bonds with external reality. It is too dangerous to enter the cave without someone to rappel for you. Nietzsche's madness was partially organic in etiology; Jung knew this, but he nevertheless believed that psychological factors had cost Nietzsche his sanity. Jung was determined not to suffer a similar fate, nor did he wish his patients to descend into the maelstrom of madness as a consequence of the pursuit of the world of fantasy, imagination, creativity, and solitary contemplation. Ac-cordingly, Jung would not engage a patient in such work unless he or she had such an anchor. If the patient did not have such an anchor in day-to-day responsibilities and ordinary social reality, Jung's first therapeutic thrust was in establishing such connectedness with its concomitant network of validation. Those of my patients who have been most taken with Jung and most interested in "trips" and "jour-neys" have been those with the weakest ties to ordinary social reality; had they read their Jung more carefully, they would have seen that his therapy would not have encouraged this.

Jung himself emphasized the internal life in his 1961 autobiography *Memories, Dreams, and Reflections*, in which he said, "My life is a story of the self-realization of the unconscious" (p. 1). Accordingly, his autobiography concen-trates on dreams. As every analyst knows, what isn't discussed is what is most conflictual, and Jung's waking activities included sleeping with his female patients and playing footsie with Herman Göring. Jung's relationship with the Nazis has been variously interpreted, and his supporters, including many Jewish ones, have vigorously denied that he ever had sympathy for or with the Nazis or that he was an anti-Semite. It is also true that Jung undoubtedly did help many Jewish analysts escape from Germany when the Hitlerian night was growing ever darker. How-ever, he did accept the presidency of the German Psychotherapeutic Society after Göring took it over, although he said he did so to protect Jews. Even if this was true, it is impossible to defend the article he wrote distinguishing an "Aryan" from a "Jewish" science of psychology, just as the Nazis were persecuting Jewish psychoanalysts, and which clearly gave support to Nazi ideology, although it was written by a man who claimed to have discovered the universality of the arche-types that structure and determine all human experience. Whatever the equivoca-tion and ambiguity of Jung's relationship to Fascism, it is unsavory. I do not like the man and see his emphasis on "spirituality" as hypocritical and self-serving, but it is not only that. Having put my bias on the table, I will try and do justice to the things he said about self and about the emotional life. Even if mistaken, Jung's theoretical constructs and insights into self and psyche have been and are widely influential, are frequently original, and throw new light on our tortuous topic.

To return to Jung's earlier life, by the time he reached adolescence, his family had moved to Basel, where he grew up. Brilliant and brooding and a voracious reader, he was strongly attracted to Goethe, to the German Romantics, and to Schopenhauer's and Nietzsche's philosophical psychologies of the irrational, of blind striving of the will, of the drive for power, and of the unconscious nature of those primordial forces within. Jung would have had no trouble understanding George Groddeck's (1923/1930) statement that "the It [id] lives us." (Freud borrowed the term *id* from Groddeck.)

Jung's intellectual interests were not restricted to the German Romantic poets and philosophers. Classical literature had an almost equal appeal for him, and he was far from immune to the allure of the new Darwinian biology. Additionally, theology fascinated him. The diverse pulls of literature, philosophy, theology, and science never left him. His life and works are an attempt to integrate them. Jung first decided to become a classical philologist, perhaps in an ambivalent attempt at an Oedipal victory over his father and a wish to enact for that father the desire that he himself had not been able to fulfill, but he turned away from classical studies to study medicine. He saw in psychiatry a field uniquely integrating the scientific and the humanistic. He had also considered and rejected a clerical career, but his view of psychiatric healing was a pastoral one, so in a sense he did become a sort of clergyman. He has been called "the doctor of the soul," which would have pleased him; it would not have pleased Freud.

Jung was early fascinated with the occult, and would continue to be throughout his life. Though I find aspects of his preoccupation with alchemy, the occult, and the *I Ching* obscurantistic and pseudoprofound, it is also true that his interest in these matters made them accessible to scientific scrutiny and rendered the study of a vast stretch of human experience academically respectable. My tastes apart, Jung took the occult seriously (as Freud did parapsychology), and that interest became a second source of his interest in the unconscious and its manifestations, the first being literary and philosophical. While in medical school, he became involved in spiritualist experiments with his cousin, Helen Preiswerk, who was a medium. He wrote his dissertation on those experiments.

After graduating (in 1900), Jung joined the staff of the Burgholzi, the Swiss state mental hospital, as what we would call a resident. His chief there was Eugene Bleuer, a remarkable man who was totally devoted to his lower-class, psychotic patients. Bleuer, a teetotaler who insisted on total abstinence from alcohol by his patients and staff, is chiefly known for his classic description of schizophrenia, a term that he coined, and his origination of the concept of ambivalence. Bleuer listened to his psychotic patients and took what they said seriously, just as Freud had listened to his neurotic patients and taken what they said seriously. The Burgholzi was a unique institution, pioneering modern psychiatry. The celebrated Forel had preceded Bleuer as director, so a psychologically minded psychiatrist like Jung couldn't have found a better appointment.

While there, Jung read *The Interpretation of Dreams*; it changed his life. He wrote to Freud and quickly became an adherent of psychoanalysis. Reading the two men's correspondence (Freud & Jung, 1974), it is immediately clear that their collaboration was doomed to failure. From the beginning, they lived in different worlds and operated on a different set of conscious and unconscious assumptions. Freud was desperately anxious to recruit Jung. He needed him. Jung was brilliant, Swiss, a psychiatrist, Gentile, and on the staff of the best mental hospital in Europe. He was in a position to make psychoanalysis acceptable to the medical establishment. Jung, on the other hand, was longing for a theory that would help him understand his desperately ill patients, and he was looking for a father. As the logic of transference would have predicted, he had ambivalence toward his new father from the beginning, and ended by enacting an Oedipal revolt against him. (This is not to judge the merits of the substantive differences between the two.) Freud was skeptical, empirical, extremely leery of philosophical speculation, and, most important, adamantly atheistic, viewing religion as a neurosis, while Jung was open to all kinds of investigational techniques, believed that speculative thought could be a source of truth, and, most important, believed that religious experience was meaningful and that it could contribute to mental health. Jung believed in God, although he was never, as an adult, a member of a church. There was no chance that the two could work together for any length of time. To grossly oversimplify, Freud believed that neurosis was caused by repressed sexuality, while Jung believed that it was caused by repressed spirituality. However, 1900 was not 1913, the year of their break, and Jung started out by courting Freud. He went on to become Freud's "crown prince" (Freud's phrase) and president of the International Psychoanalytic Association.

Jung quickly applied psychoanalytic methods to the treatment and understanding of psychotics. He was the first to do so. He soon discovered that psychotic delusions and hallucinations had the same structure as dreams; that wasn't surprising, since Freud regarded both as compromise formations expressing in disguised and distorted form a repressed, forbidden wish; what is more surprising was Jung's discovery that the contents of dreams, hallucinations, and delusions were strikingly similar. Jung, with his religious, metaphysical, and philosophical interests, had become fascinated with mythology. He discovered that myths from disparate cultures, dreams, and psychotic symptoms dealt with the same themes, that they all reflected universal aspects of human nature that were transcultural. Jung was on his way to his formulation of the *collective unconscious* and its *archetypes*.

While at the Burgholzi, Jung also engaged in empirical psychological research, using the word association test. He published his psychological account of dementia praecox (schizophrenia) (Jung, 1907/1909) and rapidly acquired an international reputation. At the same time, he became romantically involved with Sabina Spielrein, a Jewish patient from Russia whom he had treated in the hospital. She did well in therapy, left the hospital, and entered medical school. When her mother protested that Jung as her physician should not be sleeping with her, he replied that since he had received no fee, he was under no obligation to refrain, but if she wished to pay his usual fee, he would stop having intercourse with her daughter. That is sort of prostitution in reverse, and is Jung at his most outrageous. Of course he was not entitled to or even permitted a fee because Sabina was a hospital patient and Jung was on the hospital payroll. Ethics aside, he did "cure" her, and this brilliant woman became an analyst herself. She returned to her native Russia, married a man who later became psychotic, and had a child with him, but always remained in love with Jung. She was shot by the Germans when they invaded Russia. She was apparently the inspiration for Jung's concept of the anima.

In 1909, Freud and Jung journeyed together to America to receive honorary doctorates from Clark University. Before boarding ship, Freud fainted. On awakening, he said that his fainting was a reaction to Jung's death wishes toward him. Not long after, their dissension became overt. In 1911, Jung delivered a series of lectures at Fordham University in which he redefined libido as psychic energy in general, or as a life force rather than as sexual energy per se, and in the same series of lectures denied the universality of the Oedipus complex. Although Freud tried to placate him, the two were theoretically and temperamentally poles apart. Their relationship ended with Jung's resignation as president of the International Psychoanalytic Association in 1913.

After World War I, Jung developed a treatment technique and a system of theory he called analytic psychology. It still has many advocates and practitioners. During the same period, Jung experienced some sort of crisis that he understood as a descent into the underworld. This was a prolonged episode of serious emotional illness, lasting for a decade. During it, Jung resigned his official and university posts and isolated himself as he descended deeper and deeper into the unconscious levels of his personality. It was a period in which psychic reality—dreams, myths, and perhaps hallucinations—were predominant in his life. These experiences have been variously interpreted as a "creative illness" and as a psychotic break. Jung successfully maintained his ties to reality by continuing to see patients and by meeting family obligations. He emerged from his decade-long creative illness with a fully developed theory of personality, including a theory of self. Jung universalized this experience and taught that the second half of life is a time to turn from the mastering of external reality to a journey within. The outcome of that shift in orientation is the emergence of the self. The rest of Jung's long life was spent elaborating his theory of the self and in teaching and practicing psychotherapy. Jung continued to have liaisons with his female patients and students, most of whom remained devoted to him, as did his wife Emma, who herself became a Jungian analyst. He died full of honors, having received honorary degrees from both Harvard and Oxford.

Jung's thoughts on personality and self are complex and difficult to summarize. Although Jung disliked Hegel and regarded his language and style as contaminated by primary process thinking, there is a Hegelian quality to much of Jung's writing, insofar as it is dialectical; there are reciprocal relations between entities and concepts in all of Jungian theory, and nothing can be understood in isolation from the whole. Like Hegel, Jung believed the truth is the whole. Jung sees two explanatory principles as having equal validity: causality and teleology. Human behavior is determined both by the past as actuality and by the future as potentiality. Individual and racial (here meaning the human race) history are causal, while aims and aspirations are teleological. Action is shaped by both; that is, we live by aims and by causes. This allows for a chink in an otherwise deterministic system. Jung here is somewhat Kantian, with the self being both part of the causal chain and free, depending on whether we are viewing the phenomenal self or the noumenal self. He is also echoing Aristotle's analysis of causality with its efficient and final causes.

For Jung, human life is characterized by constant and creative development and by the search for wholeness and rebirth. It is that drive for growth and integration rather than solely the satisfaction of biological drives or compulsive repetition that moves human behavior. Jung here is clearly anticipating the self-actualization theorists like Kurt Goldstein and Abraham Maslow.

Jung's term for the mental self in the everyday sense of self is the *personality*. The personality is everything about a person except his or her body, although the body finds expression in the personality. Jung would deny the body-mind split. For Jung, the personality is archaic, primitive, innate, unconscious, and both universal and racial. That is, everyone's personality has the same structural elements, which are inborn, and phylogenetic inheritance of the experience of the human race determines, at least in part, both structure and content of that personality.

The personality is constituted by the ego; the personal unconscious and its complexes; the collective unconscious and its archetypes, the most important of which are the persona, the anima and animus, and the shadow; the attitudes of introversion and extraversion; and the self. The *ego* is the conscious mind. Its functions include perception, memory, thought, and feeling. It is what gives us feelings of identity and continuity. Jung's ego is the structure responsible for consciousness and is itself conscious. It differs from Freud's structural ego in important ways. Freud's ego is partially unconscious; one of its principal functions, defense, is out of awareness. Not so Jung's ego. Furthermore, Freud's ego is a mediator seeking to balance the demands of instinctual needs, internalized prohibitions, and external reality. Although the Jungian ego is concerned with reality testing and action, it is not a mediator in Freud's sense. Perception and memory are functions shared by the Freudian and Jungian egos. Jung's ego is closer to the realm of consciousness in Freud's topographical model than to Freud's structural ego. There is no question that we have a conscious mind, and there is no reason that Jung should not denote it the ego and make it one constituent of the totality that is the personality.

The *personal unconscious* is like Freud's descriptive unconscious. It is not exclusively the product of repression. It contains repressed, forgotten, unnoticed, and ignored material. Some of this material is retrievable by an act of attention; some of it is not, unless a way can be found to derepress it. The content of the personal unconscious is both those things I ignore and those things I cannot deal with and must keep from awareness: memories of events, feelings, or drive-derivatives that threaten me. They are historical, that is, part of my personal history that was in some way traumatic. So far there is nothing new here, but Jung includes under the personal unconscious its *complexes*. A complex is an unconscious nucleus that organizes experience. For example, if I have a father complex, then I will react to all "fathers" in a rigid, stereotyped way, with submission, defiance, fear, or whatever my unconscious father experience dictates, regardless of the actual behavior of the current father figure with whom I am engaged. My experience of any father figure will be organized and strongly biased by the father complex in my personal unconscious. We all have complexes; however, in pathological instances, the complex may dominate the whole personality. In such a case, we would speak of a *pathological introject*, an internalized father, or whatever, who is experienced as a foreign body and who "takes over," or dominates, important segments of personality and determines the way we think and feel. A pathologically introjected father become a complex could lead to avoidance of all authority figures, crippling a patient's vocational and educational behavior.

The *collective unconscious*, also called the transpersonal consciousness, is a uniquely Jungian concept. The collective unconscious is a repository of the experience of the species—of the human race. Although there are some gender differences, the collective unconscious and its contents are essentially the same for all human beings. Jung is a Lamarckian, one who believes in the heritability of experience, of acquired characteristics, as did the French naturalist, Jean Baptiste Lamarck (1744–1829).

The theory of evolution—with its doctrines of the struggle for existence, of the survival of the fittest, and of "natural" selection and its corollary, the descent from and continuity of man with the animals—was part of the intellectual climate in which psychoanalytic theory was formulated. Darwin did not believe in the inheritance of acquired characteristics. On the contrary, he thought that certain traits were "selected" because they had survival value, and their possessors lived to reproduce and transmit those characteristics to future generations. Few biological scientists then or now have sided with Lamarck against Darwin on this issue. Freud did, an aspect of his teaching accepted by few analysts. Trying to account for the universality, regardless of individual history or of the particulars of early childhood experience, of such manifestations of the darker side of human nature as primordial guilt, the need for and self-destructive enactment of self-punishmnent, and the Oedipus complex, Freud postulated that the *anlage*, or template, for such experiences and behaviors was inborn and an inheritance from the experience of the (human) race. It was a viewpoint with which Jung agreed. Jung did not, however, agree with Freud on what was inherited. To restate, Freud came to believe in the inheritance of certain psychic predispositions that overrode individual experience and hence appeared universally in human beings regardless of families, cultures, or historical eras. Freud theorized that certain experiences, such as the murder of the primal father by the horde of primal brothers, was the source (or, to be more accurate, the guilt over those acts was the source) of religion and morality. Furthermore, that experience was stamped in and passed down through the generations so that all of the conflicts around the desire to murder the father were inborn. Freud was convinced of the necessity for such a theory to account for the irrational elements in human behavior. Why else do people behave so totally contrary to the pleasure principle and detrimentally to their own welfare?

Jung, as I have said, was an adherent of this theory of the inheritance of acquired characteristics or, in his case, of acquired thought patterns, attitudes, and preconceptions, although he did not agree with Freud on the prominence of the self-destructive and aggressive in that inheritance. His notion of the collective unconscious is his account of such inherited predisposition. The collective unconscious is, in a sense, a modern incarnation of the doctrine of innate ideas. What is innate is a predisposition to certain forms of thought, to certain ways of organizing and construing experience. This innateness is more Kantian than Cartesian; it is more structural than specific, more like Kant's categories of the understanding than like Descartes's innate ideas of God and immortality. Jung's collective unconscious is actually somewhere between an innate idea and a category of the understanding, but much closer to the latter. Speaking of the infant, Jung says, "The form of the world into which he is born is already inborn in him in a virtual image."

Freud's topographic (dynamic) unconscious and structural id are repositories of seething biological energy: primitive, archaic, timeless, beyond the restraints of logic and the laws of contradiction, and pressing for discharge regardless of the requirements of external reality. Jung's collective unconscious has this aspect, but is not only, or even primarily, so characterized. Rather, it is the heir of our racial experience, demonic and archaic, as well as sublime and wise. It is not primarily biological; rather, it is primarily object-relational, a repository of self- and object representations or, better, the anlagen for them. What it shares with Freud's id (it) is its impersonality; it is collective, not individual, racial not personal. The collective unconscious holds the potentiality for a multiplicity of experiences and actions, all of which are locked away from the conscious mind. It has at its disposal as subliminal content the forgotten and overlooked wisdom and experience of uncounted generations. The danger of coming into contact with this collective unconscious is the loss of individuality, the engulfment by the universal and transpersonal of the individual, the personal, and the unique. In Jung's view, that is what happens in psychosis. On the other hand, not to come into contact with the collective unconscious is to be impoverished, to be cut off from the wisdom and experience of those countless (not quite) past generations. Individualization involves both differentiation from the collective unconscious and integration of part of its infinite richness.

The structural components of the collective unconscious are the *archetypes*, universal thought forms that "contain" a large element of emotion. They are sort of a die that stamps a given type of experience or, to change the metaphor, a lens through which a given type of experience is refracted. For example, our experience of our own mothers is shaped by, or refracted through, the innate archetype of Mother, derived from the experience of the race with mothers. An archetype is a schema with both emotional and cognitive aspects. Their parallel to Kant's categories of the understanding is obvious. There is, however, an important difference: Jung's archetypes are patterns of self- and object perception and representation; Kant's categories are logical constructs that pattern relationships between objects; they are purely cognitive, lacking affectivity.

Just as Freud came to believe that certain modes of thought were innate because they were universal and cut across cultures and individual experiences, Jung came to believe that certain modes of perception and experience were innate because they too were universal and appeared in every human culture and in every individual human life. He found the evidence for the existence of archetypes, the structural elements of the collective unconscious, in myths, dreams, rituals, symptoms, and art. What he saw was that the same themes, the same characters, the same relationships, and the same narratives found embodiment in the most disparate materials. Jung studied the mythologies of many different peoples and found the same heroes, the same heroines, and the same interactions between them in Greco-Roman, Norse, Hindu, Chinese, and primitive peoples' myths. They reappeared in his own and in his patients' dreams, in neurotic symptoms, in psychotic hallucinations and delusions, and in works of art. Their appearance may be in the manifest or in the latent levels of human experience, but they are always found. (The distinction between *manifest* and *latent* goes back to Freud's dream theory, in which he distinguishes between what the dreamer dreams, the manifest dream, and the underlying meaning of the dream to be unraveled by following the dreamer's associations to each of the elements of the manifest dream.)

Among the archetypes that Jung described are birth, rebirth, death, power, unity, the Hero, the Child, God, the Demon, the Old Wise Man, the Earth Mother, and the Animal. The archetypes are prototypes within us through which we process our experiences of their objective correlatives, but they are also available for projection and realizable in symptoms, religious myths, and art. They are within, yet we largely experience them as external. Once again, "the world is half created and half perceived."

One could argue that these themes and characters appear and reappear in myths, dreams, art, and symptoms because they are universal human experiences that appear in and are lived by each and every generation. Each and all have a mother, is or was and knows a child, and so forth, so of course we write, sculpt, paint, and dream about them, and there is no need to posit an innate mother pattern antecedent to experience of mother. Universality does not necessarily entail innateness. The archetypes, like Plato's forms, double the world—there is the world as experienced and the world as eternal pattern—in the collective unconscious, or in the Platonic Heaven, or in the mind of God. Is this doubling necessary? Does it really explain anything? I have my doubts, although I do not espouse a naive empiricism or a radical nominalism. Aristotle and the conceptualists had it right; we do shape as well as are shaped by experience, and we do that by processing input through conceptual categories, including and perhaps predominantly linguistic ones. But these categories have no existence apart from the objects that embody them. I find Kantian innateness more compelling because it is more structural than Jungian innateness, which is more specifically contential. Be that as it may, Jung's notion of a collective unconscious with its structural analogs, the archetypes, does offer an esthetically appealing way of organizing an enormous amount of seemingly disparate data. It is more compelling as an explanatory hypothesis than as a set of entities to be taken concretely, as Jung apparently intended. Such doubling moves away from concrete human experience and easily contributes to obfuscation and mystification. Instead of looking at my relationship with my mother, with all of its love and hate, sexuality and aggression, fusion and separation, I can get lost in the "mother experience," as exemplified by the Mother archetype. This is not to say that what myths, dreams, and art have to say about mothers may not be useful to me in exploring and understanding my relationship with my mother, but this can all too easily become an intellectual exercise. My objection is both theoretical and clinical. Jungian analysts ask their patients to amplify by evoking mythological conceptions when they are talking about personal matters, and this can easily lead to intellectualization, and away from feelings.

Jung delineated five special archetypes that are the best known of his theoretical entities. They are the *persona*, the *anima*, the *animus*, the *shadow*, and the *Self*.

The persona is a mask; it is "the face I put on to meet the faces that I meet." It is not quite a social role, but the internal representation of social roles. Its nucleus is an archetype, an archetype that has arisen out of the race's experience that social convention and stereotypical roles and representations are essential to smooth social interaction. Community life would be impossible without them. We need easily recognizable cues; we need defenses—a certain distance and formality—to interact with others in other than intimate ways, in the workplace, in the marketplace, and in organizations of all sorts. The particular persona I wear is a product of my personal characteristics, my culture, and my historical situation, but the fact that I easily develop a persona, or personae, is made possible by its preformation in my collective unconscious. I fill in the details, the particulars, but the mask was already there. Thus, the persona as archetype is something within, and the masks I wear that are its derivatives are the outward manifestations of that inner preformation.

More central to Jungian psychology are the anima and the animus. The anima is the female archetype within the man, while the animus is the male archetype within the woman. The anima and the animus are Jung's version of bisexuality.

They are also Jung's version of androgyny. They are derived from the racial experience of man with woman and of woman with man, respectively. The germ of femininity within the man and of masculinity within the woman call to mind the Chinese symbol of the Yin and Yang, ☯, which represents the dialectical unity of the paired opposites, including gender opposites. The black dot in the white half and the white dot in the black half of the circle are anima and animus, as well as the seed of all the other contrarieties embedded in their respective antinomies. Jung was familiar with the Yin and Yang and saw it as an artistic artifact of the archetypical relationships he was describing. It is said that Jung discovered the anima in his relationship with Sabina Spielrein, when he realized that his infatuation with her was partly driven by his projection of his woman within, his anima, onto her. Archetypes are prone to such projection and externalization. Lack of insight into that process makes for all kinds of difficulties in interpersonal relationships, when we treat people as if they were the archetypes rather than themselves. Jungian analysis is importantly concerned with making that unconscious process conscious. Midlife is a time in which men realize their feminine potential and women their male potential, as both sexes move toward androgyny. Individualization requires such an assimilation of the latent other. Some have alleged that the concept of the anima-animus was Sabina Spielrein's and that Jung appropriated it without giving her credit. It is difficult to sort out creative collaborations, and how true this is is up for grabs.

The *shadow* is the archetype most prone to projection. It is the "animal" side of human nature (one wonders if a psychologist who was him- or herself the member of a nonhuman species would come up with the *people* as an archetype of primitive aggression to be projected onto other nonhumans). The shadow is all that is instinctual, biological, sexual, aggressive, and "evil." The shadow is usually projected outward as the Devil or the enemy; it is the source of the doctrine of original sin. Jung's notion of the shadow and its projections is a compelling explanation of prejudice and of intergroup hatred. The enemy (the Jews, the Blacks, etc.), are beastly (cruel, sadistic, inhuman, perverse, immoral, etc.) not me or mine. However, one wonders what is gained by concretizing the projection of that which is unacceptable to us, within us, as the shadow. Why make process substance? Again, why the doubling? According to Jung, the shadow must be integrated, owned, and made a conscious part of me. This too is a goal of Jungian analysis.

This brings me back to our topic, the self. Jung's notion of the self is unique. He sees it in a completely different light from our earlier authors. It is central to his understanding of human life and its purpose.

The *Self* is Jung's master archetype. As such, it is an innate racial inheritance that is an indwelling organization and organizer of experience. Although Jung intended his account of the Self to be descriptive, an account of something that is and has just as much reality as a rock or a mountain, his conception of Self is clearly normative. It is an injunction to engage in a spiritual journey of self-discovery into centeredness. According to Jung, the Self in the first half of life is the total personality, but in the second half of life, the period of introversion, it becomes an archetype representing man's striving for unity and centeredness. The Self is a holistic integration. From Jung's description, it appears that the Self moves from, almost literally emerges from, being a sort of outward envelope encompassing the personality to being an inward locus of balance and harmony.

This change in the nature of the Self parallels Jung's change in his theoretical understanding of the Self. He himself moved from the Self of early adulthood to the Self of maturity, and then expressed this change theoretically. Jung's psychology of the Self is a psychology of total unity, or at least the striving for it. Jung (1945, p. 219) described the relocation of the Self in this way:

> *If we picture the conscious mind with the ego as its center as being opposed to the unconscious, and if we now add to our mental picture the process of assimilating the unconscious, we can think of this assimilation as a kind of approximation of conscious and unconscious, where the center of the personality no longer coincides with the ego, but with a point midway between the conscious and the unconscious.*

The Self is this new centering of the personality, made possible by a preformed propensity derived from the experience of all the human beings who preceded us. When Jung says "midway between the conscious and the unconscious," *unconscious* means both the personal and the collective unconscious.

The Self is life's goal: the search for wholeness, sometimes, but not necessarily, through religion. True religious experience is as close to Selfhood as men come. Christ and Buddha are highly differentiated expressions of the Self archetype.

Jung "discovered" the Self in his studies of the religions of the Orient, in such symbolizations as the Yin and Yang and the Mandala and in the striving for unity and centeredness in such ritualized disciplines as Yoga and Zen.

According to Jung, before the Self can emerge, the various components of the personality must be fully developed and individuated. Human development is a process of differentiation of an undifferentiated mass and the subsequent integration of that which has been differentiated. (Shades of Hegel—this is the cosmic dialectic personalized.) Because the Self cannot come into being antecedent to that differentiation and integration, the archetype of the Self doesn't emerge until middle life, which is, or should be, a time of serious effort to change the center of the personality in the conscious ego to a midpoint between the conscious and unconscious. This midway region is the province of the Self. Failure to do so results in psychopathology—the midlife crisis as illness instead of creative opportunity. Is Jung here confusing *is* with *ought*, description with prescription? He thinks not, but I am not so sure.

The Jungian Self in various manifestations has great currency. The many notions of self-actualization are essentially Jungian in origin. Each urges the realization of an innate potentiality. Such personality theorists as Abraham Maslow and Carl Rogers are not consciously Jungians, and would reject a good deal of what Jung says, yet their notions of self-realization in the second half of life, their confusion of *is* and *ought* and of description and prescription, are strikingly reminiscent of Jung. Their theories lack the complexity of his—they are simpler, more pragmatic, and less "spiritual"—yet they share the Jungian notion of the Self as something that gains realization through development and intensive striving.

Alfred Adler (1870–1937) was another early associate of Freud's who broke with him to found his own school. Adler developed a notion of the *creative self*. The creative self is the unique constellation that each person constructs out of his or her goals, values, style of life, constitutional givens, and experience. It is the principle that organizes experience and stamps it ours. It is essentially teleological—pulled by the future in our projections more than propelled by the past or by the biological. Adler's creative self owes something to Jung and something to William James, but the creative self itself is uniquely his. It too has a hortatory quality and is difficult to evaluate philosophically or scientifically.

Jung contributed several other illuminating ideas to our understanding of our inner world. We owe him the notions of extraversion and introversion. At any given moment, we are either extraverts or introverts, with the nondominant trait latent in our unconscious. Midlife is normally a time of turning inward, of becoming more introverted. The complementarity and dialectical relationship between the two attitudes is quintessentially Jungian. Even if we were to take a non-Jungian view of the self, the notion that that which is not manifest in consciousness is latent in the unconscious and potentially realizable would enrich our concept of self. Jung cited the evidence of dreams to demonstrate that the nonmanifest is nonetheless present.

Jung delineated four psychological functions: *thinking*, whose function is comprehension of self and world; *feeling*, whose function is evaluation of pain and pleasure; *sensing*, whose function is to provide us with concrete facts, perceptions, and representations of the world; and *intuiting*, whose function is perception by way of the unconscious and which is the source of mystical experience. Sensing is phylogenetically and ontogenetically prior; thinking and feeling differentiate out of it. The four psychological functions are not equally developed. We each have superior functions that dominate and inferior functions with which we are much less in contact. The superior functions are conscious; the inferior ones are unconscious and find expression in dreams and fantasies. There are interactions between the functions: one function may *compensate* for the weakness of another; one function may *oppose* another; or one function may *unite* with another to form systems. The complete *actualization of the Self* requires an ideal synthesis in which the four psychological functions acquire equal strength, that is, are equally developed. Jung represented that state of affairs by a circle in which the four functions and the two attitudes of introversion and extraversion are equidistant. The dialectical unity of opposites is brought about by the *transcendent function*. This full actualization of Self is a goal toward which we strive, not a place where we arrive. It is an ideal, not an actuality.

The work of realization of the Self, as well as all other psychological work of the personality, is done by *psychic energy*. Jung's notion of psychic energy is that of a life force or life energy, and although he sometimes calls it libido, it is not exclusively sexual like Freud's libido. Psychic energy is a hypothetical construct, not an empirical observable. Psychic energy fuels biological survival, sex, and the cultural and spiritual by a process similar to Freud's sublimation.

Jung developed a dynamic of personality that is essentially a dynamic of psychic energy in which that energy is subject to laws parallel to the laws of physical energy. The first law is the *principle of equivalence*, which states in parallel to the first law of thermodynamics in physics that psychic energy can neither be created nor destroyed, only transformed. It is a conservation principle. Of more interest is Jung's *principle of entropy*, which parallels the second law of thermodynamics and which states that there is a tendency for a personality to go toward equal values in all of its components. The endpoint of this process is an ideal state in which total energy is evenly distributed throughout the various highly developed systems in the Self. The ego, the personal unconscious and its complexes, the collective unconscious and its archetypes, the attitudes, and the psychological functions all move toward a state of equilibrium and equi-energy. This is what happens in a closed physical system: energy is conserved, but the uniformity of energy states makes further change impossible, and the system is "dead." Self-actualization means that the dynamics of personality move toward a perfect, albeit then static, equilibrium. This is Jung's version of the Nirvana principle or, if you prefer, the death instinct: life moves toward perfect equilibrium that is stasis, pure being and no longer process. That is a state of affairs both wished for and dreaded. Illness is one-sidedness.

Another Jungian notion that has had widespread reverberations in the self-actualization movement is the *principle of synchronicity*, which is the acausal correspondence between manifestations that is neither causality nor teleology. It is reminiscent of Liebniz's "windowless monads," who share states of being because of their preestablished harmony. Jung's synchronicity makes coincidence meaningful.

We are now in a position to see the Jungian Self whole. Essentially, it is the endpoint of the individualization process: that is, the developmental unfolding of the original, global, undifferentiated wholeness into the differentiated aspects of personality described above, followed by their integration into a balanced, dynamic whole whose components are equidistant, equi-potent and equi-energized and whose goal is the realization of the Self. The Self is both that realization and the quest for it. Full development requires the differentiation and expression of all aspects of the personality. That comes about through a complex process of progression and regression. Regression is sometimes necessary for growth and can be creative. The transcendent function unites the fully differentiated parts of the personality into the Self, leading to "the realization, in all of its aspects, of the personality originally hidden away in the embryonic germ plasm; the production and unfolding of the original, potential wholeness." A mandala (the Sanskrit word for circle) is a perfect symbolization of the Self.

The movement toward the realization of the Self is innate, driven by the psychic law of entropy. The fully actualized Self would cease striving, being in a Nirvana-like state of equi-potentiality and stasis that would be a kind of psychic death. But not to worry—nobody gets there.

Do we strive for wholeness, integration, and the realization of all of our our potential? It would be nice to think so, but I don't see much evidence for it. Jung thought otherwise, and believed that he saw such evidence in myths, religions, and Mandalas, as well as in his own life and the life of his patients. Is there anything to be gained by calling this process and its product the Self and giving it archetypal status? I don't think so, although the Jungian Self makes more sense as an explanatory hypothesis than as a substantive entity. If the Jungian Self lacks evidential support and is more of an ought than an is, more of an injunction than a scientific description, is it then of value? Should the goal of life be balance and integration? Is the movement of self from an identification with the conscious ego with all of its willfulness to a full comprehension of that which is unconscious concomitant with the relinquishing of some of our conscious control desirable? You might sell me on that, but that is a value judgment rather than an objective elucidation of the self experience. Has Jung convinced you that his style of self-actualization is worthwhile—in fact, the highest good?

10

Self: Illusion or Our One Certainty? 20th-Century Version

Part 1: Social Psychology and Positivism

The 17th-century intellectual struggle between those who, like Descartes, make the self the basis of their philosophizing and those who, like Locke and Hume, regard the self as either a construction (Locke) or an illusion (Hume) gets recapitulated in the 20th century. In its modern incarnation, the protagonists are the logical positivists and analytic philosophers who have maintained either that the questions "Does the self exist?" and "What is the nature of the self?" are meaningless or that the self is an illusion, and the phenomenologists and existentialists who, in one way or another, place self at the center of their philosophizing, treating it as that which is indubitably known and the one certainty. The players in this drama are Bertrand Russell, Alfred Ayer, and Gilbert Ryle on the positivist side and Edmund Husserl, Martin Heidegger, and Jean-Paul Sartre on the other. Ludwig Wittgenstein, a Viennese who largely worked in England both is and is not a logical positivist; or, to be more precise, he is a positivist with mystical inclinations. He too has some interesting things to say about the self. So does Ronald Laing, an existential psychoanalyst who was much influenced by Sartre and who wrote a book called *The Divided Self*. Alfred North Whitehead doesn't easily fit into either camp, but he too has made contributions to a theory of self.

The positivists are the heirs of the English empirical tradition, particularly of Hume, and are themselves mostly English, while the phenomenologists are the heirs to the European rationalistic tradition, particularly of Descartes, and are themselves mostly continental Europeans. The term *analyst* does not refer to psychoanalyst in this context, but rather to the school of analytic philosophy prominent in England and the United States that conceives of the task of philosophy as the minute and highly precise analysis of language and its relationship to the world. The disagreement about the self reflects a more basic disagreement about the nature of philosophy and of the right way to philosophize. At bottom, it is a disagreement about epistemology and ontology, about how we know and what there is to know. However, I will concentrate on the way in which these almost temperamental differences get played out in theorizing about self. Descartes's *ego cogito*, thinking self, is the starting point for diverse 20th-century reevaluations of the ontological status of the self. Ryle calls Descartes's *cogito* "the ghost in the machine," while Husserl believes that an entire structure of consciousness, of self-experience, is implicit in Descartes's *cogito* awaiting its explication by phenomenology. In addition to philosophic analysts, America has made a unique contribution to self theory from a social psychological or sociological perspective. Charles Cooley and George Herbert Mead are the main actors in this tradition. The self has also been "operationalized" (i.e., defined by the way in which it is delineated in self-descriptions of various sorts). Here self becomes self-concept.

I am going to discuss each of these theorists, and each of their points of view, in rather less detail than I have the major theorists of the previous chapters. I will start with the empirical psychologists; go on to the social psychologists Cooley and Mead; the analysts Ayer, Russell, Ryle, and Wittgenstein; the phenomenologist Husserl; and the existentialists Heidegger, Sartre, and Laing; and finish with Whitehead.

THE EMPIRICAL PSYCHOLOGICAL SELF

American academic psychology tends to be tough-minded. It has little tolerance for the abstract, the speculative, or the psychoanalytic. This is a tendency that goes back at least to the 1920s and James Watson's behaviorism. Behaviorism was a reaction to both introspectionism and psychoanalytic theorizing. Introspectionism was a school of psychology associated with the Cornell professor Edward Titchener that thought that the proper way to do psychology was to introspect, to examine the contents of consciousness and report upon them, rather than to study outward manifestations of behavior. Behaviorism, on the contrary, defines psychology as the science of behavior, of what is public, observable, measurable, and quantifiable. Although cognitive psychology, which deals with thought processes—mental contents—has come to the fore in the past 20 years, academic psychology continues to be hard-nosed. It looks at a concept like self and asks, What is the cash value of such a concept? What does it tell us that we wouldn't know without it? If it is an explanatory hypothesis, what does it explain? If it is a concept, how can it be operationalized? To operationalize a concept is to state how one would measure it. Thus, the self, from an empirical psychological standpoint, would be the operation used to measure it. To talk about measuring the self doesn't make too much sense, so academic researchers rarely talk about the self. Instead they talk about the *self-concept*. A person's self-concept is his or her view of what he or she is. It is the characteristics that a person believes that he or she has. These characteristics may be moral (honest-dishonest); functional (skilled-unskilled or bright-dull); affective (happy-sad); relational (friendly-unfriendly); and any other dimension the researcher comes up with. The self as self-concept introduces a new meaning of self. Now the self is the sum total of my beliefs about myself or that subset of them that I can articulate. The self as self-concept is mediated by language: the self is those words, or that which they denote, that describe me. So the self becomes self-description. I am what I describe myself to be.

The self as self-concept can be operationalized in a variety of ways. Most common is an adjective checklist in which the subject is asked to check those adjectives that describe him or her. There are also a variety of "objective" descriptive psychological tests, such as Cattell's Sixteen Personality Factors test. The person's self-description may be scaled in various ways according to norms on a set of dimensions that have been standardized on a research population. One of the more interesting self-measurements was done by Carl Rogers, the "client-centered" therapist. Rogers (1959) adopted a research technique called Q, developed by Stephenson, to the study of personality. A Q sort is a pack of cards with descriptions on them that the subject is asked to sort into a series of piles on a dimension of *least like me* to *most like me*. The piles at the ends get the fewest number of cards, and the one in the middle the most, creating a statistically "normal" distribution. The normal distribution is the way in which a trait such as height is distributed in a large population. It has been extensively studied by statisticians, and its shape and characteristics are well known.

The subject is then asked to sort the cards to describe his or her "ideal" self, and the disparity between "real" and ideal selves is noted. Rogers thought that the greater the disparity, the more psychopathology, and went on to do outcome studies of psychotherapy in terms of a move toward less disparity. In other words, Rogers postulated that a discordance between ideal and real self would be manifested in symptoms, such as anxiety and depression, and that successful treatment would lessen that disparity. His data supported his hypothesis.

The self as self-concept operationalized as one or another method of self-description has the strength of rendering the self less abstract, less reified, and more contentful, but the self as self-concept fails to grapple with the issues of how the self is experienced or of continuity and discontinuity in the self-experience. It converts a problem in ontology into a problem in methodology. The self as constitutive or as organizational, as developmental or as conflictual, has no place here. There is not even any language in which they can be discussed. The empirical psychologists would disagree and say the self is what is self-described on instrument X on date Y. If it changes at date Z, then it is that which is self-described on date Z on the same instrument. The two can be compared, and that is all that can be meaningfully stated about self.

There are several obvious objections to this. First, subjects can, as research methodologists put it, "fake good" or "fake bad," that is, describe themselves as better or worse than they really feel they are for whatever reasons—for example, to impress or to continue to qualify for a disability benefit—so that their self-description is not really an accurate account of who they really believe they are. But, says the empirical psychologist, I can build in a lie scale by asking the same question in different ways, or use other techniques to detect such deceptions. I would reply, Perhaps you can, and practically that would be of value, but philosophically that doesn't help. If there is a self-concept that is different from the operationalization of it, then that self-concept is mentalistic—something that someone believes but not something that I can necessarily measure. The empirical psychological self and its operationalization is a powerful research tool, but it contributes little or nothing to the solution to the problems about self that I have raised. Further, it operates only on the conscious level. The subject, even if attempting to be totally honest, doesn't know everything about him- or herself and so cannot possibly completely articulate self on an adjective checklist, objective test, or Q sort. This is far from a mystification, as the hard-nosed psychologists might maintain; it is not even speculative. One of the most common experiences in psychotherapy is for a defensive grandiosity to collapse into openly expressed contempt for and hatred of self. It could be maintained that this fact could be perfectly well accounted for by saying that the self-concept changed, without evoking an unconscious self-concept to explain this change. It could, indeed, but only at the cost of doing violence to the data of defensiveness and the acting out of that which is denied, repressed, or otherwise walled off. This is a case where an attempt to be parsimonious is not really parsimonious. The more complex theory that encompasses preconscious and unconscious self-concepts better explains the facts, but in doing so can no longer deem self as the operations performed to measure self-concept.

What about the social psychological view of the self? The social psychologist sees self as the product of social interaction and as always reactive to the social surround. Cooley (1902) believed that we primarily see ourselves through the eyes of others, and form our concept of ourselves from the reaction of others. He called this the *reflected* or *looking glass self*. It has three components: how we imagine others see us, how we imagine others judge us, and our emotional reaction to those imagined judgments. The looking glass is not quite the right metaphor, because Cooley's self is active and constitutive, particularly in constituting an imagined judgment by others. The self is not merely what is reflected back to us; it is our interpretation of it. Cooley recognized this, but even with this caveat Cooley's social psychological self is highly determined by the reaction of the social self to the surround. Of course, the self is in turn reflecting back self-images to other selves, from which they construct their selves. Human life becomes, importantly, the process by which we mutually mirror and are mirrored by other selves, and in this interactive reflective process build selves.

George Herbert Mead (1934) had much the same notion. Self for him is the *generalized other*, rather than the looking glass self, but his description of the development of self is similarly social and interactive. For Mead, language process is essential for the development of self, and since language is a social acquisition, self is necessarily social. The self is not there from birth; rather, it develops in the social matrix in which language is acquired. Eventually, we organize all, or almost all, of our experiences as experiences of self, especially *affective experience*, but this need not be so. Mead's notion that feelings are especially the stuff of self is insightful. As we will see in the next chapter, Daniel Stern, the infant development researcher, thinks that he has demonstrated that affects are the least changing of experiences over the course of a lifetime, so that they are the securest foundations for the experience of ongoingness and continuity. Returning to Mead, he pointed out that we organize our memories on the "string of self." Self is not necessarily involved in the life of the (human) organism. Indeed, we can and do distinguish between body and self. "Self has the characteristic that it is object to itself" (Mead, 1934, p. 136), which is the case for no other object including the body. The self is reflexive; it is both subject and object. How can this be? Further, the individual organism must take account of him- or herself in order to act rationally. (Organism is Mead's term for the total person, including mind and body.) How can this be achieved? It can only happen through a social process of interaction in which the individuals take the attitudes of others toward them and make them their own. This is strikingly similar to Cooley's looking glass self. Since self develops by internalizing the attitudes of many others toward the self, many selves are possible. This is normal; we are all multiple personalities to some extent. However, in health there is a degree of unity that arises out of an identification with and internalization of the "generalized standpoint of the social group as a whole." Thus, the self, insofar as it is unified, is the generalized other—or better, the generalized others' attitudes toward the self. (The terms identification and internalization are mine, not Mead's.)

All of this happens through communication. At first, the self is a dialogue with others; only later is it an internal dialogue—a dialogue of the self with the self. That is how the self becomes object to itself—becomes simultaneously subject and object. The self as object to itself is essentially a social structure; it is communicative, interactive, indeed dialectical, and always mediated by language. The process starts with gestures rather than speech, but self is inconceivable without words. Self is a dialogue I have with myself in which I take the role of a generalized other, or of particular others, and speak to myself as subject as if I were an object of the others' subjectivity. As with Cooley, the process is not passive, for I form the others no less than they form me, and I am as such a part of their internal dialogues, which I influence just as they influence me.

Mead's self that is both subject and object is *self-consciousness*. Self is self-consciousness, mediated by and expressed in language. Developmentally, my relations to particular others and their internalization are prior to relationships with the community or with subsets of it and their internalization as the generalized other that becomes constitutive of self. Without communication with the larger community, a developmental arrest occurs and the self is crippled by particularization. Mead believed that the capacity for abstract thought came from our "conversation" with a generalized other (team, organization, or polity) becoming part of that conversation with ourselves that is the self. Children's play, games, and rituals in which roles are assumed and enacted supplement linguistic communication in the process of developing the self.

Mead distinguishes between the *I* and the *me*. The I is the response of the organism to the attitudes of the others, and the me is the organized set of attitudes of others that become internalized. The derivatives of the attitudes of the others constitute the organized me, and my reaction toward those others is the I. The me makes community possible; the I makes individuality possible. Mead is much more convincing in his account of the me than in his account of the I. If the self is constituted by assuming the reaction of particular others and the generalized others to me in talking to myself as they talk to or about me, then I can see little place for the I. Where does the individual reaction come from if the self that does that reacting is formed by that which it is reacting to?

Sociologist Erving Goffman gave the dialectic of the mirror self an additional twist in his discussion of *impression management*, through which the self creates, or tries to create, consciously or unconsciously, the response of the social surround that in turn is constitutive of that self. Goffman is concerned with *The Presentation of Self in Everyday Life* (1959). Goffman's self is an amalgamation of Jung's persona and Cooley's looking glass self.

Social psychological theories of the self clearly have something true to say. The existence of social bonds and interactions that can be accounted for by biologically determined mechanisms and cooperation for survival clearly is logically and temporally prior to self, and self certainly arises out of a social matrix. Something may be no less true because it is paradoxical, and self can indeed only emerge from a social matrix. Further, the interactive, communicative nature of self and the necessity of such interaction and communication for the development of self has been firmly established by clinical research. Mead is also right in pointing to the importance of gesture as a precursor of linguistic communication and of its continuing role in the communicative shaping of self throughout life. We have seen self as self-consciousness in Hegel and in Kierkegaard, but the self as self-conscious internal dialogue is unique to Mead and new in our history of concepts of the self.

Less successful are both Cooley's and Mead's attempts to account for the autonomy of the self, the degree to which it is neither a looking glass self nor the assumption of particular others' reactions to or view of it, or the assumption of the generalized others' reaction to it. I do, indeed, react in an autonomous way to others' perception of me, but how I can do that is incomprehensible on purely social psychological terms.

THE LOGICAL POSITIVISTS

Whether self is self-concept as operationalized in a self-description for the empirical psychologists or the internalization of reflections from or refractions through others mediated by signs and symbols for the social psychologists, it is a meaningful concept. It can be talked about meaningfully, and its referents are clear. Neither of these types of theorists about the self seriously question that inquiry into the nature of the self is a meaningful activity. Not so for the logical positivists. The focus of their philosophical activity has been clarification, a clarification that has demonstrated, to their satisfaction, that certain philosophical problems, which they call metaphysical problems, are pseudoproblems because the questions they raise have no meaning. From a positivistic standpoint, the question is, is the question "Is there a self?" meaningful? The question about meaningfulness is meaningful, and must be asked antecedently to any attempt to answer the question "Is there a self?"

Historically, positivism has had two sources, one being the English empirical tradition whose 20th-century representatives have been Ox-Bridge academics who were often active in social and political affairs, usually from a liberal or radical standpoint. (Ox-Bridge, of course, refers to Oxford and Cambridge universities.) Russell, G. E. Moore, Gilbert Ryle, and A. J. Ayer are all linear descendents of Hume. The English positivists are sometimes called analysts and their way of doing philosophy is called analytic philosophy. Though not strictly accurate, I use the terms (logical) *positivists* and (philosophical) *analysts* interchangeably. The second source of positivism was the "Vienna Circle," a group of logicians and philosophers of science led by Moritz Schlick who were heirs of Helmholtz and Ernest Mach, a physicist with philosophical leanings. They too were influenced by Hume. Not all the Vienna Circle were Viennese: Polish and other European logicians were strongly identified with the group. Most of its members wound up in the United States after the rise of Hitler. The Vienna Circle articulated the principle of verifiability. A proposition is meaningful if, and only if, there is a course of action that can be taken to verify its truth or falsity.

Let us start with Gilbert Ryle (1900–1976). Ryle was an Oxford philosopher who has been widely influential. His best known book is *The Concept of Mind* (1949), in which he ridiculed Descartes's dualistic metaphysics as a doctrine of the ghost in the machine. In effect, he says that Descartes creates two parallel worlds, an outer, physical one and an inner, mental one, when there is no need to do so. The Cartesian *cogito* is not an indubitable datum as Descartes thought; on the contrary, it is a postulate that Descartes needed to create in order to preserve a realm of moral autonomy exempt from the rigorously deterministic laws of the physical world. In impugning Descartes's motives or, if you prefer, uncovering their unconscious determinants, Ryle does nothing to refute Descartes's argument. Ryle does that by pointing out, as Russell had done before him, that thoughts do not necessitate a thinker. That is what Ryle would call a *category mistake*. Ryle's example of a category mistake is the visitor to Oxford who sees all the Colleges and then asks to see the University, as if it were an additional member of the class of colleges rather than the organization of the Colleges. Of course, the University *is* something different from the Colleges. Ryle recognizes this, but doesn't seem to realize that the organization of the Colleges into the University is an entity just as real, albeit of a different kind, as the Colleges themselves. By analogy, Ryle asks, once we have enumerated our thoughts, feelings, wishes, and so on, why do we ask to be shown the thinker, feeler, and wisher as if something additional was needed? But Ryle goes further. He is not merely attacking the notion of self as substance. He is radically questioning the existence of a private, inner world that is the domain of thinking substance: soul, mind, or self as something that exists over and above my public observable behavior. Ryle believes that such errors arise partly for psychological reasons, but mostly because we misunderstand how language works and look for substantives corresponding to nouns. The import of all this is to reduce the mental to the physical. The ghost disappears, but the machine remains. Ryle essentially reduces the inner to the outer, collapses the Cartesian dichotomy into a monist realm of the observable. If I want to know about allegedly "mental acts" like willing, desiring, or pondering, what I do is observe those who are alleged to be "having" those "mental" experiences. Ryle is not quite a radical behaviorist; he does not maintain that all private mental events are really publically observable bodily states and events—behaviors, but the realm of the private is radically reduced and of little interest to him.

> *To talk of a person's mind is not to talk of a repository which is permitted to have objects that something called the "physical world" is forbidden to have; it is to talk of the person's abilities, liabilities and inclinations to do and undergo certain sorts of things, and of doing and undergoing of these things in the ordinary world." (Ryle, 1949, p. 199)*

That is a behaviorist theory of mind, or of what was formerly thought to be mind. I know another person's mental attributes by observing his or her actions.

Ryle's notion of self follows directly from his notion of mind. It is contained in his discussion of self-experience. Essentially, he says that we discover ourselves by observing ourselves exactly as we observe others. There is no such thing as self corresponding to the noun *I*; rather, *I* is an index word that locates a certain event of experience. In many instances, *I* can be replaced by *my body*, but not in all. In most other cases, *I* can be replaced by my attending to my unuttered utterances. Although there is no intrinsic reason why nonbodily self-experiences have to be unspoken speech, all Ryle's examples are of such unspoken utterances. Essentially, I know myself in the way I know other people, with the important additional knowledge of the thoughts I speak to myself. There is nothing else to say about self; it is self-experience as here described, and to ask for more is to ask to see the University after having seen the Colleges. The word *I* refers not to substance but to particular actions at particular times, as in "I am walking down the street." The only function of *I* is to locate me in a time and place, performing a publicly observable action. The whole thrust of Ryle's argument is linguistic, consisting of a detailed, painstaking analysis of how *I* and *me* are used by speakers of the English language. His method is as significant as his conclusion. It is the examination of ordinary usage in an attempt to demystify philosophical inquiry. It is a method highly characteristic of analytic philosophy. Ryle's disciples are known as ordinary language philosophers.

Ryle is convincing in his demonstration that regarding the self as a mental substance that is a ghost in the machine does nothing to clarify the problems inherent in the unraveling of the nature of the self; our doubling the self into a bodily self and a mental self, that operate in different realms by different rules, is indeed a dubious procedure. Furthermore, Ryle is probably right in attributing this to a category mistake. His notion that we must examine how we use language very carefully to make sure that our philosophical problems, including questions about self, are not pseudoproblems is heuristic, and it is certainly true that we obtain a great deal of our self-knowledge by observing our own behavior and/or its publicly observable impact on others, and that another large chunk of our self-knowledge comes from attending to words we say to ourselves but do not speak; however, there is something reified and incomplete about Ryle's account of the self. I think that the central problem is that the University is *not* the Colleges and that the self is not self-experience, or not merely that. Rather, it is the organization of those self-experiences that is itself experienced with just as much reality as the individual self-experiences. Ryle does not seriously contend with either the University or the self, although he does have much that is illuminating to say about the Colleges and about self-experience.

Bertrand Russell (1872–1970) was a protean thinker whose restless energy took him everywhere. He was a mainstay of the anti-Vietnam War movement in his 90s; an early supporter of women's suffrage; a pacifist in World War I, for which he was jailed; an advocate of a freer sexual morality, for which he was fired from City College; and in general a supporter of liberty and freedom always. For this, he is rightly admired. However, our interest is not in his moral and political writings, nor in his educational theory, but in his technical philosophy. Here his influence has been enormous. In a sense, the entire movement of philosophical analysis is his creation. At the very least, he pioneered its methods and techniques. A wonderful stylist, his work is characterized by precision, lucidity, clarity, and simplicity. Russell may be wrong, but you always know what he is saying.

Russell's first interest in philosophy was in the foundations of mathematics. He was troubled by the fact that Euclid's axioms were unproven and that the whole structure of arithmetic and geometry might be arbitrary. His first solution to this problem was a kind of neo-Platonism in which numbers and their relations were seen as universals already existent—where or how is not clear. But he soon abandoned Platonic realism and instead tried to give mathematics a certain foundation by reducing mathematics to logic; that is, he developed a logical system from which he deduced a real number system and its relations. He did this in collaboration with Alfred North Whitehead, his former math tutor, and the results were published in their three-volume classic, *Principia Mathematica* (1910–1913). The proofs he and Whitehead deduced are said by mathematicians to be beautiful and elegant.

In the course of his work on the foundations of mathematics, Russell developed an interest in more general philosophical problems, particularly in the nature of sense perception and the ways in which we construe both physical and mental reality. In the course of that work, he made a distinction between *knowledge by acquaintance* and *knowledge by description*. Those things we know by acquaintance we know directly while those we know by description, we know only inferentially. In his original formulation (Russell, 1912), objects of acquaintance included one's self, one's current mental states and acts, sense data, and acts of memory. In different language, the self is a direct intuition, and Russell's view of self is not substantially different from Kant's notion of the phenomenal self as revealed by the inner sense. However, Russell changed his thinking about self, and when he published *The Analysis of Mind* (1921), he thought of the self as a series of experiences. We have knowledge by acquaintance of those experiences, but not of the self, which is a logical construction from them and known only by description. Russell does not mean to say that our subjective experience of self is that of building a logical structure, but that that is its logical status. He is making a logical, or perhaps epistemological, statement, not offering a psychological description.

A Russellerian notion of some interest to self theory is his *theory of types*. The theory of types grew out of technical problems in the philosophy of mathematics. What it says essentially is that a class is not a member of that class. To assume it is, is to get involved in a paradox. Hence the class of self-experiences is not itself a self-experience, at least not of the same type.

Russell's theory of types leads to a hierarchy, so that a metalanguage is necessary to speak of a primary language. The relevance of Russell's theory of types to Ryle's discussion of category errors is obvious. Russell's solution to the paradoxes of his logic has been criticized as really solving nothing, but as simply bringing in an extraneous postulate from outside the system. In a sense, he is back where he started when he questioned Euclid. There is, in effect, an axiom that cannot be proved from within the system. Kurt Godel, who was a member of the Vienna Circle, later proved that it is impossible to prove the consistency and completeness of a logical system from within that system—that can only be done by bringing in an assumption (postulate) that is not part of the system. Godel was not writing about Russell's theory of types, but in a sense his theorem vindicates it. Russell's theory may be aesthetically and logically unsatisfactory, and indeed emotionally unsatisfying, yet it may be the case that classes of events can only be meaningfully spoken about on a level of discourse above the level that applies to the members of the class.

In our case, it may not be possible to speak of the class of self-experiences as itself an experience of self. That raises the question of how, then, we can speak of it, and what is it? Russell's contention that the self is a logical construction seems to violate the subjective experience of selfhood. To say, as he does, that he is making a logical, not a psychological, statement somehow doesn't solve the problem. I certainly do have knowledge by acquaintance of the logical construction that is the self in his later theory, and I am not at all sure that I have knowledge by description of it. At least, Russell does not provide one. The strength of Russell's theory, as was the case for Ryle, lies in the method rather than its result—in the careful analysis of what is meant by self and of what kinds of experiences are self-experiences, as well as the suggestion that they are not all on the same logical or epistemological level.

A. J. (Alfred Julius) Ayer was the *enfant terrible* of logical positivism. In *Language, Truth, and Logic* (1936/1952), Ayer claimed to have solved the problems of philosophy—largely by demonstrating that they are pseudoproblems, and much like his hero, David Hume, turned to more broadly cultural interests. Although Ayer became less fiery as he aged, and somewhat trimmed his sails, he never really repudiated the radical stance that he took in his 20s. What is that stance?

According to Ayer, there are only two types of statements that are not nonsense (i.e., meaningless). These are analytic statements in which the predicate is contained in the subject. Analytic statements are tautologies that tell us about how we use a symbol system, be that symbol system logic or mathematics or an analytic truth, such as "cats are animals." The truth or falsity of analytic statements can be tested by the means of *truth tables*, a device of formal logic developed by Wittgenstein. The truth of analytic statements can be established with certainty because they do nothing but spin out the meanings implicit in their premises. They may be psychologically novel (i.e., show us a relationship we didn't know to exist), but logically they reveal nothing new. We can know analytic truths with certainty, but they tell us nothing about the world; indeed, they are not about the world.

Empirical hypotheses *are* about the world. They are meaningful if, and only if, I can state what actions I would take to verify them. Verification means verification in principle: I cannot now verify the existence of certain states of affairs in distant galaxies, but since they are verifiable in principle, statements about them are not meaningless. Furthermore, *to verify* means to increase the probability that a statement is true (or false), not to establish it beyond a doubt. The principle of verification is a theory of meaning—or, better, of meaninglessness—espoused by the Vienna Circle and by Ayer. There are no synthetic a priori statements that are meaningful. Any statement that is not an analytic or empiric hypothesis subject to verification in principle is meaningless (literally, without sense). Statements that are neither analytic nor empirically verifiable may arouse emotions or induce aesthetic experience, but they have no truth value. They are neither true nor false. By this criterion, all of metaphysics is eliminated as senseless nonsense. Ayer, like Hume, would consign all volumes not concerned with relations of ideas or matters of fact to the flames.

There are difficulties with the verification theory of meaning. Is the verification principle itself verifiable? It certainly isn't analytic, since it is not logically absurd to maintain that a statement without truth value is nevertheless meaningful, nor does it seem to be an empirical hypothesis, since there doesn't appear to be any observation we can make, even in principle, that would be evidence of the probability, let alone certainty, of its truth. Ayer would probably answer that the verification principle is a definition, and that the business of philosophy is to provide definitions by analyzing language and how we use it. Such definitions are held to be neither descriptive nor prescriptive, but to be outcomes of philosophical analysis. But this either begs the question or introduces a third type of knowledge that the verification principle would not allow. Be this at it may, Ayer and the logical positivists' verification criterion of meaning has application to our theories about self.

From the positivist point of view, the question "Is the self substantive?" is neither true nor false; it is literally meaningless. "The self is substantive" is not analytic, since "the self is not substantive" is not self-contradictory. Nor is it an empirical hypothesis. What operations, even in principle, could add to or detract from the probability of its being true? The same would apply to "the self is an illusion," "the self survives the body," "the self is our one certainty," and "the self is the foundation of knowledge." Although I don't altogether subscribe to the principle of verifiability and have noted that it itself is not verifiable so that there must be meaningful statements that are neither analytic nor verifiable empirical hypotheses, the theory is salutory in that it forces us to be attentive to the possibility that we are asking meaningless questions or raising pseudoproblems (*meaningless* and *pseudoproblems* here meaning problems without solution, beyond our capacity to know). Ayer states that he is doing something different than Kant did when he "eliminated" metaphysics by showing its conclusions to be contradictory (see Kant's transcendental dialectic); that he, on the contrary, is analyzing language and how we use it. However, the result is the same. Some kinds of speculative questions are seen to be without sense, and this is all to the good. It demystifies and directs our attention to questions that can be fruitfully approached. The trouble with the principle of verification is that it has no place for organizing principles or explanatory hypotheses that are not directly empirically verifiable. The self may be fruitfully and meaningfully conceived of as an organizing principle, an explanatory hypothesis, or both.

Although the principle of verifiability renders some kinds of statements (or questions) about self meaningless and consigns them to the flames, Ayer does have a theory of self.

> We know that a self, if it is not to be treated as a metaphysical entity, must be held to be a logical construction out of sense-experience. It is, in fact, a logical construction out of sense-experiences which constitutes the actual or possible sense-history of a self. And, accordingly, if we ask what is the nature of self, we are asking what is the relationship that must obtain between sense-experiences for them to belong to the sense-history of the same self. And the answer to this question is that for any two sense-experiences to belong to the sense-history of the same self, it is necessary and sufficient that they should contain organic sense-contents which are elements of the same body. (Ayer, 1952, p. 125)

Ayer has already said that sense contents are neither mental nor physical, although the objects that are logically constructed out of them are. All of this is far from clear. What exactly is a logical construction of our sense contents? Ayer says, "We are not saying that it is actually constructed out of those sense-contents, or that the sense-contents are in any way part of it, but are merely expressing . . . the syntactical fact that all sentences referring to it are translatable into sentences referring to them" (1952, p. 126). If I follow this, what it seems to mean is that self is a logical construction out of sense contents that is not really a construction but merely a statement that any proposition I can assert about the members of a class of sense experiences will be true for the class itself. This is an odd kind of self. Is the statement that the self is a logical construction, in this special sense, analytic? A verifiable empirical hypothesis? It seems to be neither. By Ayer's criterion, it is meaningless, but I am willing to accord it meaning; I simply don't understand it.

So far, Ayer seems to be in accord with Hume that the self is nothing but a bundle or collection of different perceptions, but he doesn't want to say that. Hume fell back on memory as a unifying principle, but then rejected it because what I can't remember is just as constitutive of self as what I can. So Hume, in the final analysis, can't see any connection between perceptions that would make them oneself. Ayer thinks he has solved this difficulty. He does this by defining personal identity as bodily identity and by defining self as the sense experiences of that body; or, to be more precise, that the self is reducible to the sense experiences of that body. "To say anything about self is always to say something about sense-experiences." Now what a logical construction is makes more sense. What Ayer seems to be saying is that I have a self that I know because any statement I can make about it is a statement about the sense experiences of the body. So the self as a logical construction of sense contents doesn't mean that I construct the self, but only that I can analyze any statement I might make about self into a statement about a sense experience of my body. That makes it uniquely mine, because the statement that sense experience belongs to more than one body is self-contradictory. As much as Ayer struggles from construction to linguistic analysis, his notion of self is still that of a collection of self-experiences that belong to one body. The belonging to one body is the glue that makes them one self.

Ayer's position seems to be that when I say something about myself, I am saying something about a sense experience with a given sense content that occurs to my body. That does not make it a bodily experience (or a mental one), merely an experience somehow attached to my body. But how do I know that my body is the same body I had at birth? Or yesterday? Isn't the statement that I have the same body itself a construction? But Ayer would say that it is an empirically verifiable hypothesis. I could, for example, compare fingerprints or chromosomes in infancy and adulthood. The sameness of the body is verifiable in principle. That leaves the question of how sense experiences with their sense contents are related to (attached to, or occur to) that same body. Bodily identity is there and empirically verifiable, but is the belonging of sense contents to that body analytic or synthetic, logically necessary or empirically verifiable? Again, this is not clear.

So the self is a logical construction that is not a logical construction of sense experiences belonging to the same body. The vector is from self to sense experience, not from sense experience to self. Ayer is talking about logical analysis, not about empirical synthesis. In that case, it is not clear why we need a notion of self at all. I suppose that Ayer would answer that we have one firmly embedded in language and that it is the business and only business of philosophy to give a "definition in use," to analyze how a term is used. Having done so, the philosopher has done his job. Ayer is content to say that he is not doing psychology and is not making a statement about the relationship of sense experience to sense content, so that he is not committed to Hume's atomistic psychology or to any other psychology. So the degree to which the subject organizes sense experiences, is active and constituent rather than passive and receptive, is a question for cognitive psychology, not for philosophy.

For Ayer, the self is subjective and private. Yet anything we say about it must be in principle verifiable. For me, the most salient feature of the Ayerian self is its connection with the body. Clearly the body does have continuity, and reducing the continuity of self to the continuity of sense experiences of that body has the virtue of simplicity and face validity. Nevertheless, it is schematic and leaves much unanswered.

It is interesting that even so "antimetaphysical" theorists as Ryle and Ayer feel a need to give an account of the self. In effect, they apply Ockham's razor to knowables rather than to entities, that is, their application of Ockham's injunction to not multiply entities beyond what is absolutely needed to account for the world is to what we know rather than to what there is. They are parsimonious epistemologists rather than parsimonious ontologists; nevertheless, in spite of their denials, they do wind up doing a kind of ontology, and among the objects held to exist is the self. But that does not prevent them, especially Ayer, from at least implicitly declaring many questions about self and its nature meaningless. What is left in the positivist's account of self is an analysis of how we use the word *self*. From this point of view, the question "Does the self exist?" is meaningless, but the question "What do we mean when we use the word *self*?" is meaningful and, indeed, the focus of a rigorous philosophical analysis. In more current language, Ayer deconstructs the self. What Ayer comes up with is that whenever we say *self*, its only meaningful referent is to some sort of self-experience, contained in some sort of self-content, a self-experience being a sense experience of some sense content that is experienced as part of the sense history of one self. This is obviously circular, and Ayer tries to get out of the circularity by saying that self is the sense history of my body—and therein lies personal identity. Reducing self to the sense experience of the body is in itself circular: don't I need an experience of self in order to experience body as *my* body? *Self* is now defined as a logical construction out of the sense (experience) history of my body, with logical construction merely meaning that I can analyze statements about self into statements about sense experiences that are part of the sense history of my body. Clearly Ayer is talking about how we use the word *self*, not about an entity (experience, organization, or organizer) denoted by that word. Ayer would deny that; he thinks that he is not merely talking about language and its use, but about sense experience and how it is organized. That brings us to a philosopher who was obsessed with language, its limitations, and the ways in which we are confined by it: Ludwig Wittgenstein (1889–1951).

Wittgenstein is one of the most intriguing figures in the history of philosophy. Tormented genius; arch-romantic; rigorous positivist, at least in one highly salient aspect of his philosophizing; language analyst; logician; mystic; and creator of a method of philosophizing intended to put to rest the agony of the need to philosophize, he is a figure of paradox, conflict, and antithetical *Weltanschauung*. His work is often oracular and obscure, and most of it concerns matters remote from our concerns. However, Wittgenstein does have something explicit to say about self in his early book, the *Tractatus Logico-Philosophicus* (1922), and his later work has implications for a theory of self.

Wittgenstein was born into a wealthy, highly cultured Jewish family who had converted to Catholicism. There were multiple suicides in the family; two of his brothers had killed themselves before he was grown and a third did so when his regiment failed to obey him in World War I. The Wittgensteins were musical. Brahms had been a family friend; brother Paul, who tragically lost an arm in World War I (he continued his career as a performer of piano works for the left hand) was a concert pianist, and father stipended composers. Musicales were part of the ambiance. The Wittgenstein fortune was derived from manufacturing, and Ludwig was denied the classical Gymnasium education customary for his class, instead attending a technical high school in Linz—Hitler's home town. Wittgenstein went on to study engineering. Music and engineering continued to supply models for Wittgenstein throughout his life—models of reality and its relationship to symbol systems. He was fascinated by gadgets and mechanisms of all kinds, and the relationship of musical thought to score to performance resonated for him, suggesting analogous relationships between language and world. The phonograph, with its grooves isomorphic to the electrical oscillations it produces, which are in turn isomorphic to the sound waves they produce, synthesized the mechanical with the musical to provide Wittgenstein with yet another model for the relationship between symbol system and reality. When he wrote that language is a picture of the world (or a portion of it), he must have had the musical score and the phono-graph record in mind. The mechanical and the musical constituted the parallel sources of this thought in yet another sense; the mechanical was the source and prototype of his vigorous analytic side, while the musical was the source and prototype of his mystical side.

A brilliant, sensitive adolescent in a home dominated by a tyrannical father and marred by tragedy, the young Ludwig was enthralled by the pessimistic, other-worldly philosophy of Schopenhauer. The 1906 appearance of Weininger's *Sex and Character* could hardly have been better timed for Ludwig. We have met the neurotic, brilliant, exhibitionistic, self-destructive Weininger before. Freud and Fliess's final break was over Fliess's accusation (partly true) that Freud had given Weininger Fliess's concept of bisexuality. Weininger, who was Jewish and homo-sexual, hated Jews and homosexuals. Much of his book is a "demonstration" that Jews and homosexuals are "feminine," a degraded state of being. Weininger apo-theosizes the romantic hero in his concept of the "duty of genius." The duty of genius is to follow its unique and lonely way, regardless of the cost to self or others. The duty of genius is to be utterly ruthless. The impact of *Sex and Charac-ter* was amplified by Weininger's histronic suicide at Beethoven's house. There was much for Ludwig to identify with here; he was Jewish (by descent), intellec-tual, homosexual, self-loathing, and a genius who felt compelled to realize his genius. He became obsessed with suicide, having both Weininger and his brothers for models. His survivor guilt must have been very strong. The part of Weininger that influenced Wittgenstein most was the former's injunction "genius or nothing," and all of Wittgenstein's life was a search for the superlative. He felt despair when he couldn't reach that superlative.

Wittgenstein went off to study aeronautical engineering at the University of Manchester. He is said to have designed a jet engine there. The seven years he spent in Manchester were spent struggling against suicidal depression. During that period, he became fascinated with the "foundation of mathematics" and with mathematical logic. He visited Frege, the great German logician who anticipated Russell and Whitehead's *Principia Mathematica* by 30 years, but who remained relatively unknown. Frege sent him to Russell.

Wittgenstein showed up on Russell's doorstep one day and the two spent 10 hours talking about logic and the foundations of mathematics. Although formally Russell's student (having transfered to Cambridge to study philosophy), Wittgen-stein was quickly recognized by Russell as his peer and heir apparent. Wittgen-stein's intensity eventually wearied Russell, and the two men were temperamen-tally incompatible, the one liberal, rational, and skeptical and the other conservative, strongly attracted to the irrational, and in search of belief and salva-tion. Nevertheless, their close if often strained relationship bore fruit. After sev-eral years of total concentration on the problems of logic as a Cambridge under-graduate, Wittgenstein suddenly left England and built himself a hut in a remote part of Norway where he went to live. He had fallen in love with David Pinsent, who was probably much less in love with him. Pinsent's premature death nearly shattered Wittgenstein. The *Tractatus* is dedicated to Pinsent. Wittgenstein, under the influence of Tolstoy, signed his fortune over to his sisters and joined the Aus-trian Army as a private at the outbreak of World War I. Eventually, he was cap-tured by the Italians, and he finished the *Tractatus* while in a prisoner of war camp. After the war, Russell arranged for it to be published. Believing that he had solved all of the problems of philosophy, Wittgenstein became an elementary school teacher in an Austrian village. Overintense as usual, he was accused of physical abuse of the children and, although acquitted, resigned and returned to Vienna, where he designed a strange, austere, cubistic home for his sister.

At Russell's urging, Wittgenstein returned to Cambridge, where he earned a PhD, submitting the *Tractatus* as his dissertation. Both *Principia Mathematica* and the *Tractatus* are, at one level, attempts to formulate a "logically perfect" (i.e., unambiguous and complete) language based on a system of logical symbols. The later Wittgenstein repudiated this ideal and turned to the examination of "ordinary language" with all of its complexity and ambiguity as a vehicle for the discovery of philosophical truth. What does the *Tractatus* say? That is not an easy question to answer. It is written in an oracular style as a series of numbered propositions that are often epigrammatic. Basically, Wittgenstein's position is that the world is a world of facts. It is composed of *atomic facts* or *states of affairs*. Wittgenstein gives no examples of atomic facts, and his commentators have outdone themselves in attempts to elucidate and concretize the concept of atomic facts. Their efforts notwithstanding, it is still far from clear what would constitute an atomic fact. The best that Wittgenstein can do is to say that an atomic fact is what is represented by an atomic proposition. That seems to make language prior to reality, somewhat as Ayer unwittingly does. Atomic facts are independent; there is no causal nexus between them. Thus, all that we can legitimately do with language is to "picture" atomic facts or demonstrate the tautological relations between molecular (composite) facts. Thus, "grass is green or grass is not green" is a molecular proposition that is true because it is the case regardless of the truth value of "the grass is green." In logical notation, the generalization of the above proposition would be $P \lor \sim P$. Where P is any statement whatsoever, the $\lor$ is a symbol for weak disjunction (i.e., at least one of the propositions connected by the wedge is true), and the $\sim$ is a sign of negation. Now if P is true, $P \lor \sim P$ is true, and if P is not true, P or not P is still true; so $P \lor \sim P$ is a tautology. The example may be banal, but all analytic truths are tautologies of this type. They are true regardless of the truth value of their components. They tell us about the meaning of our logical symbols, but nothing about the world, since they are the case no matter what the state of affairs pertaining in reality (in the world).

The purpose of language is to reflect the logical structure of molecular facts, complexes of atomic facts. "We make to ourselves pictures of facts" [2.1] (Wittgenstein, 1922, p. 14). A linguistic proposition is such a picture of reality. In the picture and the pictured there must be something identical in order that one can be the picture of the other at all. What the picture must have in common with reality in order to be able to represent it after its manner—rightly or falsely—is its form of representation. [2.16 and 2.17] (1922, pp. 15–26). In other words, the representation must be isomorphic, as a mathematician would put it, with what it represents. In a slightly different mathematical simile, it must be possible to *map* a representation through a *transformation* (formula) into what is represented and vice versa. "The gramaphone record, a musical thought, a score, the waves of sound, all stand to one another in that pictorial internal relation which holds between language and the world. To all of them the logical structure is common" (4.014). The purpose of philosophy is not to build a system of propositions about the world, but rather to make propositions clear. Most propositions and questions that have been written about philosophical matters are not false but senseless. We cannot, therefore, answer questions of this kind at all, that only state their senselessness. Most questions and propositions of philosophers result from the fact that we do not understand the logic of our language [4.003] (1922, p. 37). Wittgenstein goes on to describe tautologies. "A tautology is a proposition in which the truth value of the conclusion can be deduced from the truth values of the premises" [4.004]. It is Wittgenstein's elucidation of analytic propositions. A conclusion of a tautology is true no matter what the truth value of its premises, while in a contradiction, the conclusion is false no matter what the truth value of the premises is. Tautologies are true regardless of the state of affairs of the world; propositions are true when there is a state of affairs in the world corresponding to that proposition; while contradictions are never true no matter what the state of affairs pertaining in the world. The first is certain, the second possible, and the third impossible. Wittgenstein elucidates the nature of tautology through the construction of truth tables, which show that the truth value of their components is irrelevant to their tautological certainty.

According to Wittgenstein, most of the statements in the *Tractatus* are "meaningless nonsense," at least insofar as they are statements about the nature of things (e.g., "the world is a world of [atomic] facts"). Wittgenstein says that when he is making such statements he is speaking nonsense, and only when he is analyzing (i.e., clarifying) that nonsense is he not speaking nonsense. Wittgenstein says that the nonsense of the *Tractatus* is "important nonsense" and compares it to a ladder that we must climb to get to the top of a floor to get the view, after which we should discard the ladder. The purpose of getting to the top floor is to get a synoptic view, a view of the whole, but Wittgenstein says that anything we can say about the whole is nonsense, and that the only meaningful propositions picture states of affairs, or are tautologies. Philosophical discourse clarifies the logical structure of language. Those parts of the *Tractatus* that are ontological are nonsense. His notion of important nonsense is paradoxical and unsatisfactory, yet he may be right. Wittgenstein goes on to say that we can "show" what we cannot (meaningfully) say. So perhaps Wittgenstein is here able to show us what he cannot meaningfully say.

Wittgenstein has some important nonsense to show (say) about the self. But before we can look at his "theory" of self, let Wittgenstein tell us what he is doing. He is here defining philosophy, and his comments on self are presumably philosophy.

> *Philosophy aims at the logical clarification of thought.*
> *Philosophy is not a body of doctrine but an activity.*
> *A philosophical work consists essentially of elucidations.*
> *Philosophy does not result in "philosophical propositions," but rather in the clarification of propositions.*
> *Without philosophy thoughts are, as it were, cloudy and indistinct: its task is to make them clear and to give them sharp boundaries [4.112]* . . . .
> *Theory of knowledge is the philosophy of psychology [4.1121]. (1922, p. 49)*

Wittgenstein rarely argues for his position in the *Tractatus*; rather he simply states it. Since he believed (at that time) that he had solved the problems of philosophy, he is presenting his solutions and but little of the way in which he arrived at those solutions. His presentation is somewhat reminiscent of Spinoza's in the *Ethics*, which has the form of geometric proofs, but the content of which is but tenuously related to those proofs. Much of Wittgenstein's concerns are technical ones that I am not competent to judge, but one can't help but notice how often Russell is criticized, often in a highly polemical way. At some level, the *Tractatus* is a transferential playing out of Wittgenstein's ambivalence toward his father, reenacted in his homage to and savaging of Russell. This, of course, is a commentary on the psychodynamic meaning of the *Tractatus*, not on its truth value.

Wittgenstein's discussion of self is intertwined with his discussion of language.

> The limits of my language *means the limits of my world [5.6]. . . . The world is my world: this is manifest in the fact that the limits of* language *(of that language which alone I understand) means the limits of* my *world [5.62]. I am my world . . . [5.63] . . . There is no such thing as the subject that thinks or entertains ideas.*
>
> *If I wrote a book called* The World as I Found It, *I should have to include a report on my body, should have to say which parts are subordinate to my will, and which are not, etc., this being a method of isolating the subject, or rather of thinking that in an important sense there is no subject; for it alone could* not *be mentioned in that book [5.631].*
>
> *The subject does not belong to the world; rather, it is a limit of the world [5.632]. (1922, p. 117)*

What Wittgenstein has done here is extraordinary. At first he seems to be doing what Ryle does, deconstructing the self into the body, but precisely at that point he turns his argument on its head and puts the self as subject as the limit of the world. Because this self is not in the world (as experienced) but the limit of that world, it cannot be meaningfully discussed propositionally (by discursive language) so it cannot be "said"; however, it can be "shown," and Wittgenstein does show it by the use of a visual analogy. He draws an eye and its visual field to demonstrate that the eye is not part but rather the limit of that field [5.6331]. Thus he shows us what cannot be meaningfully said. What can be shown and not said is that the self is that which has a world but is not in the world.

> *Thus there really is a sense in which philosophy can talk about the self in a non-psychological way. (The psychological way would be a set of contingent propositions which are logical pictures of states of affairs and belong to science.) What brings the self into philosophy is the fact that "the world is my world." The philosophical self is not the human being, not the human body, or the human soul, with which psychology deals, but rather the metaphysical subject, the limit of the world—not part of it [5.641]. (1922, p. 117)*

The logical analyst ends in a position strikingly similar to Kant's, with language replacing the transcendental aesthetic and categories of the understanding and the metaphysical subject coming preciously close to Kant's noumenal self. It too is a thing in itself, beyond the only world that I know, the world of my language. Again like Kant, Wittgenstein winds up a sort of empirical realist and transcendental idealist. For someone who sets out to demonstrate that metaphysics is nonsense, Wittgenstein turns out to be quite a metaphysician. To say that he is talking important nonsense won't quite do. As his friend, the incredibly brilliant logician Frank Ramsey (who tragically died in his 20s) said, If Wittgenstein's analysis of language and its limitations is correct, we should take it seriously and make no distinction between important and unimportant nonsense and act on the famous conclusion of the *Tractatus*; "What we cannot speak about we must consign to silence" (Ramsey, 1923, p. 478). One suspects that what one cannot speak about includes hatred of fathers, homosexuality, and the suicide of brothers. Wittgenstein's theory of the self reflects his isolation—his existential position of being not in the world—just as his disconnected atomic facts reflect the lack of integration of his experiential world.

Wittgenstein eventually rejected the *Tractatus*, at least the part of it that set out to construct a logically perfect language more or less a priori by examining the foundations of logic, and instead turned toward a painstakingly minute examination of ordinary language. In the course of doing so, Wittgenstein devised the concept of *language games*, and invented many such games in his exploration of how language actually works. In the course of his analysis of language games, Wittgenstein came to relinquish his view of propositions as logical pictures of atomic facts that are independent of one another. The existence of "simples" is a function of the *rules* of our language games, which we are free to modify. How connected or unconnected states of affairs may be is indeterminate.

For our purposes, the salient thing about language games is that we always play them; there is no standpoint outside of, above, beyond, or beneath the language games we play from which we can examine reality. The favorite philosopher of the later Wittgenstein was St. Augustine. Like Augustine, Wittgenstein experienced himself as radically incomplete but, unlike Augustine, never found a sense of completion through belief. Of course, Wittgenstein's critique in the limits of knowledge leaves open the possibility of religious belief; God would be outside the world and not knowable, but perhaps capable of being shown.

Wittgenstein was also influenced by his fellow Viennese, Freud; he was fascinated by dreams and their interpretation, and his language games are importantly concerned with how we use the term *unconscious*. In fact, Wittgenstein's philosophizing is a kind of psychoanalysis aimed at freeing the sufferer from the torments of philosophizing (i.e., of asking meaningless questions), by demonstrating to the sufferer that he is playing a language game. The aim of philosophy is "to show the fly the way out of the fly-bottle." "Philosophy is a battle against the bewitchment of our intelligence by the means of language" (Wittgenstein, *Philosophical Investigations*, 1953, p. 109). If he were here, Wittgenstein would doubtlessly try to get out of the fly-bottle of our quest for the self. Wittgenstein would certainly have understood Freud's comment that "when one asks the meaning of life one is already sick."

In his *Philosophical Investigations* (1953), Wittgenstein comments on William James's analysis of the self of selves as bodily sensations in the neck and head, and concludes that James failed to analyze the meaning of the word self, but, rather, noted the state of his attention while trying to so analyze it. Wittgenstein thinks that this is intrinsically valuable, but that James is not doing what he thinks he is doing.

Wittgenstein suffered deeply from guilt, and at one point, arranged a sort of public confession to his friends. Among the things he confessed was virulent anti-Semitism, an aspect of self-hatred that he successfully overcame, and his mistreatment of schoolchildren when he was a schoolmaster in rural Austria following World War I. Wittgenstein was appointed Professor of Philosophy at Cambridge, where he became a cult figure. He directed his disciples away from academic life into "practical" careers, and himself served as a menial worker in a hospital in World War II. Eventually, he resigned his professorship and spent his last years as a wanderer. He died of cancer relatively young, without having gotten out of the fly-bottle.

11

Self: Illusion or Our One Certainty? 20th-Century Version

Part 2: Phenomenology, Existentialism, and Process

In our discussion of self, we must indeed be careful not to say what cannot be (meaningfully) said and to be aware that that which cannot be said can perhaps be shown. Wittgenstein's analysis of the limits of language and of the world placed the self outside of it. In a strange way, his view of self coincides with that of our next thinker about self, Edmund Husserl (1859–1938), the founder of phenomenology.

Husserl's *transcendental ego* is also outside of the world and, in some sense, constitutes that world. Like Wittgenstein, Husserl's initial interest was in the foundations of logic, and only later did he become concerned with "philosophical" issues per se. The language analyst's and the phenomenologist's views of self have much in common, but Husserl finds a way to say a great deal about that which we must remain silent. He does this by "bracketing" the world and holding in suspension any judgment about the reality of that world as we experience it. In his elucidation of our experience of the world, whatever the ontological status of that world may be, Husserl elucidates the structure of the self. At least he believes he does so.

Husserl studied under Brentano, and phenomenology owes a great deal to Brentano's doctrine of the intentionality of consciousness, the doctrine that the essence of consciousness is its being directed toward an object that may or may not objectively exist. We have met Brentano before, as Freud's philosophy professor who almost made religious belief an intellectually respectable option for the adolescent atheist and whose theory of intentionality was transmogrified into Freud's theory of libidinal investment (cathexis) of objects. According to Brentano, consciousness intends in three ways: by grasping objects without intellectual judgment so they appear in consciousness without judgment of their truth or falsity or external reality or lack of it; by acts of intentionality in which an intellectual judgment is made about the object of consciousness; and by acts of intentionality in which an affective judgment is made. In other words, consciousness intends objects neutrally, with judgments of truth or falsity, or with judgments of goodness or badness. This schema was intended as the basis for an empirical psychology whose evidence would be both experimental and introspective. However, Brentano put the emphasis on introspection, on *acts* of consciousness, perceiving, judging, and experiencing, not on the correlatives of consciousness. That is, he was interested in exploring what we are actually aware of, not whether anything corresponds to it in the world; he was interested in mentation rather than in judgment. Brentano is an introspectionist. Husserl was to turn this way of psychologizing into something quite different.

Husserl's first book was on the philosophy of arithmetic. It gave a primarily psychological account of mathematics; that is, it described the mental processes by which mathematics is done. Brentano's influence pervaded Husserl's account of the foundations of arithmetic from a purely "psychological" point of view, yet Husserl did devote attention to the mathematical objects intended by mathematical consciousness. Nevertheless, his emphasis was on the mental activity of the mathematician, not on numbers and operations. Gottleib Frege, the German mathematical logician who sent Wittgenstein to Russell, criticized Husserl's psychological account of mathematics. Husserl listened to these criticisms and for a while took the position that all acts of consciousness intended "real" objects. Like the early Russell, Husserl became a Platonic realist, that is, one who believed that mathematical objects were real, that "two" for example, exists somewhere, and that we "see" it and its relations with our mind's eye. However, Husserl did not long remain a Platonic realist. His interests shifted back to consciousness and its intentionality, an interest that evolved into his mature philosophy, which he called *phenomenology*. Husserl's first explication of this point of view was in his *Ideas for a Pure Phenomenology*, but my comments below are based on his late work, *The Cartesian Meditations* (1931), which were originally lectures delivered at the Sorbonne.

Phenomenology, especially the phenomenology of *The Cartesian Meditations*, is important to our inquiry because it puts the self, here called the transcendental ego, at the center of a system of thought and makes it the central datum of philosophy. The philosophical analysts, however reluctantly, all wound up discussing the self, but for them it is tainted by a history of metaphysical (i.e., meaningless) speculations about it, and they either reduce self to body or give a linguistic account of how we use the word *self*. Not so Husserl; the transcendental ego, the thinking (in Descartes's sense of thinking: judging, willing, or feeling) I, is the one certainty, and the logically necessary basis for any *apodictically certain* knowledge. Husserl's phenomenology is the explication of the I (ego) and its consciousness in all its modalities and ramifications. Husserl's starting point is Cartesian radical doubt, a radical doubt that leads to the *cogito*, the self as thinker, as consciousness, as the only possible starting point for philosophical knowledge. Husserl embraces the Cartesian methodology but believes that Descartes missed an opportunity to build a science of consciousness that his procedure of radical doubt made possible.

In his lectures, Husserl enjoined his audience to engage in Cartesian radical doubt, to, like Descartes, doubt all that can be doubted until a foundation for knowledge that cannot itself be doubted be found, if there is any to be found. As Husserl engages in the Cartesian attitude with its attendant anxiety, he, like Descartes before him, comes to see that the existence of the external world, of his body, and of his mind as an object of scientific study—as the psychologists envision it—are all not indubitable. On the contrary, they could be the product of illusion, a dream, a hallucination, a fantasy, or a distortion.

So far, Husserl and Descartes are in precise agreement. They remain so in the next step, the discovery that doubting implies a doubter—that thinking, in the sense of consciousness now, is indubitable. So is the thinking self. This raises several questions. Why the need for certainty? Why not the tentative, the probable, the likely, the approximate? In general, Anglo-American empiricists tend to be willing to settle for less than certainty, while the continental rationalists seek it.

John Dewey, the American pragmatist, wrote a book called *The Quest for Certainty* (1929) which critiques that quest for making an impossible demand and rejecting the actual in search for the ideal, while Husserl, positioning himself as the heir of the founder of rationalism, insists on certainty whether in his philosophy of logic and mathematics or in his phenomenological psychology. Several thinkers, including Alfred North Whitehead, have pointed out that mathematical deduction in its apparent certainty may be the wrong model for philosophy and speculative thought in general. Be that as it may, Husserl started out as a philosopher of mathematics and, although not a great mathematician like Descartes, remained entranced by its apparent certainty. There is an irony here; modern philosophers of mathematics tend to believe that mathematics is certain because it tells us nothing about the world, that it is tautological, to use Wittgenstein's term, and in a sense, Husserl achieves certainty by suspending all judgment about the world and what is in (or not in) it.

The second question raises a more fundamental issue. Both Descartes and Husserl go from the indubitable datum "thinking (consciousness) now" to thinker, transcendental ego, and believe that the latter is as certain as the former. As I said in the case of Descartes, this is not a valid inference, its legitimacy being particularly in question if thinker is interpreted as thinking substance. Husserl's way of handling this is different from Descartes's. Descartes is simply certain that thinking implies thinker, and for all the radicalness of his doubt, he does not question it or argue for it. It is his first principle. Not so Husserl. Rather, he argues that consciousness is consciousness *of*, and consciousness of consciousness of (i.e., awareness of being conscious of), and that unless there is an ego, or I, a consciousness that is a consciousness of being conscious of, we would be in an infinite regress in which there would have to be a conscious conscious of being conscious of being conscious *ad infinitum*. So he postulates a transcendental ego, an I beyond, in the sense of being logically prior to, experience, experience always being experience of being conscious of. It is the transcendental ego, the beyond-I, that does phenomenology, that is the phenomenological investigator. The transcendental ego is strikingly similar to Wittgenstein's self as the limit of the world. For both thinkers, the world is my world but the my is not in it.

Husserl emphasizes the difficulty in truly engaging in radical doubt. The habits of a lifetime, biological survival mechanisms, psychological defense mechanisms, common sense, and the need for security (however illusionary) all mitigate against sticking with it. Radical doubting engenders too much anxiety. Try it. What may start out as an intellectual exercise can quickly transmute into an intensely affective experience. But with Descartes's example before us, it can be done. In Husserl's version, this is not a one-time activity; quite the contrary, it is an ongoing enterprise that requires constant effort. The endpoint of radical doubting, the bedrock that cannot be doubted, is radical doubting itself and the transcendental ego.

Husserl makes radical doubting the foundation of his phenomenology. He does that by institutionalizing it, by making it the *sine qua non* of philosophy and philosophizing. He does this by suggesting that "we put the world in brackets," that is, make no judgment about its ontological status, its reality or irreality, its substantiality or phantasmagorality. When we do this, we assume the attitude of *phenomenological reduction*, which Husserl also calls *phenomenological epoche*. To maintain an attitude of phenomenological reduction, of suspension of judgment, is counterintuitive and meets resistance. We are intrinsically naive ontologists, and to refrain from ontological judgment is a far from easy task. The injunction for the phenomenologist to maintain an attitude of epoche has been compared with the fundamental rule of psychoanalysis: to free associate, to speak whatever comes to mind without regard for its sense or nonsense or the embarrassment or anxiety it entails. Just as the analyst analyzes the patient's resistance to free association, the phenomenologist recalls the thinker (who may be himself) to the attitude of epoche.

Once the world is in brackets, we see that there is always consciousness (thinking) and that consciousness is always consciousness of. We can now describe either pole of consciousness of—the consciousness or the object of consciousness—and we can do it with what Husserl calls apodictic certainty (i.e., the same level of certainty one would have of the truth [validity] of a logical or mathematical proof). This is reminiscent of Kant's analysis of the transcendental aesthetic and the categories as a priori (i.e., as requisite to any possible thought), but Husserl thinks that he is not making an a priori argument, a transcendental deduction in Kant's terms, but is simply describing consciousness without judging the ontological status of the objects of consciousness. Given Husserl's understanding of what he is doing when engaging in phenomenological epoche and describing that which appears to consciousness, it is not surprising that the slogan of phenomenology as a movement became "back to the things themselves," the things as experienced rather than as judged or prejudged.

In Husserl's view, Descartes had been on the verge of founding phenomenology, but didn't see the implications of his *cogito*. It remained an abstraction, and after establishing the certainty of his clear and distinct ideas—those as clear and distinct as the *cogito*—by "proving" the existence of a good God who would not deceive him, Descartes left off radically doubting and went on, to his satisfaction, to establish his dualistic metaphysics. Husserl thinks Descartes missed the boat. The *cogito* is not an abstract thinker about whom nothing can be said beyond his activity as a cogitator. On the contrary, once we establish the *cogito*, there is an enormous amount we can say about the self as thinker and about that thinking. As long as we maintain the attitude of phenomenological epoche, of bracketing the world, what we say about the structure and activity of the *cogito* as cogitator will be as apodictically certain as my existence as a thinker is certain. The activities of the *cogito* are not necessarily clear and distinct; they may or may not be, and Descartes's use of clearness and distinctness as an epistemological standard misled him. It was perhaps the major reason Descartes missed the opportunity to found phenomenology. Such is Husserl's view. Descartes, however, was not interested in founding phenomenology; he was looking to secure a place, epistemologically and politically, for physics and mechanistic psychology. Husserl is aware of this, and in no way minimizes its value, but believes that the historical mission of Cartesianism as originally conceived has been and is being fulfilled by the "positive" sciences, and that now is the time to actualize the potential for a descriptive phenomenology that is implicit in Descartes' procedure and conclusion.

What is the enormous, indeed virtually infinite, descriptive phenomenology of the Cartesian *cogito*—of "consciousness of"—of which we can be apodictically certain? What things do we find when we go back to the "things themselves"? We can look at "consciousness of" from the side of consciousness or from the side of what which is intended, the object. The first Husserl calls a *noetic* description, the second a *noematic* description; they are, respectively, descriptions of experiencing and of the experienced. As long as we stick to descriptions of our consciousness and the objects of consciousness (i.e., maintain the phenomenological attitude of parenthesizing the world and the psychophysical self), we can describe with apodictic certainty the structure of knowing, doubting, willing, affirming, perceiving, and feeling, regardless of whether or not these cognitions are "about" what they name, about what the naive (pre-epoche) ego would regard as physical objects, mental objects, our own consciousness, or the consciousness of others. For example, if we analyze any act of perceiving, we "discover" as a pure description of how one perceives that any act of perception entails an anticipation of further perception; that when I perceive red, I expect to continue seeing red if I divert my gaze, or if I see the front of an object, I anticipate that I can see its side by moving my position. As Husserl puts it, perception always has horizons, and moves toward those horizons. This is now known to be true a priori, and will be true for any possible perception of a "physical object," quite apart from the objective existence of physical objects, if there be such; or the hallucinatory nature of physical objects, if they be such; or the constitutive nature of physical objects, if they be such. All of this sounds Kantian to me, although Husserl does not think it is; it seems to come down to my being only able to perceive the world in the way in which I perceive it, in this case as having horizons, regardless of what the thing-in-itself may be. Husserl wishes to avoid splitting reality into the phenomenal and the noumenal, and thinks that he is describing the phenomenal. It is Kant without the thing-in-itself, belief in metaphysical ultimates having been suspended.

Further phenomenological analysis, descriptive of the consciousness of, of the transcendental ego, reveals that all acts of consciousness have temporal horizons, look toward the future. The anticipation of the horizons already implies this. Husserl's program for phenomenology is that of an exhaustive analysis of the structure of each form of cogitating. Thus, there would be a phenomenological description of willing, desiring, affirming, objecting, believing, doubting, and so forth. So far this seems to be more program than substance, and Husserl doesn't get much beyond methodology. It is his program, not his findings, that are of interest.

The transcendental ego is transcendental because it is not in, but logically prior to, any experience of the world, and that experience of the world is always my experience of the world. Husserl is surely right in maintaining that the world is always my world—it could hardly be otherwise—and that the self as transcendental ego, as the I beyond (logically prior to) any possible experience has to be the starting point for any epistemology—of any endeavor to explain how we know and experience. Husserl's return to subjectivity is salutary in an ambience of behavioristic denial of the possibility of saying anything about consciousness. With the rise of cognitive psychology in academia during the past two decades, Husserl's corrective is less needed. However, historically it has been extremely important.

The notion that the self (transcendental ego) that constitutes my world, the only world that exists for me, is not in that world is uncanny. Although apparently true in some sense, there is not much you can do with it. Husserl's program notwithstanding, it remains rather abstract. Although there is no intrinsic reason that the phenomenological description of the ego states of the transcendental ego cannot include states of affectivity (Brentano's doctrine of intentionality included affectivity) Husserl does little in that direction.

The *Cartesian Meditations* led Husserl to an awareness that he was in danger of being interpreted as a solipsistic idealist, and he is anxious to avoid this. He does this by describing the way in which any subjectivity (his or anyone else's transcendental ego) is conscious of another subjectivity. He thus establishes a "bracketed" intersubjectivity. We experience others as other subjectivities, just as we experience some objects of consciousness as physical objects, and the phenomenologist can describe the structure of intersubjectivity just as well as he can describe the structure of perception of a physical object. Other subjectivities are just as real intentional objects as any others, and as long as we suspend our naive faith in their objective (i.e., objectively subjective) existence, we are on safe, indeed certain, ground in describing how we are conscious of them.

For all his disclaimers, Husserl winds up a metaphysician of sorts. In his discussion of intersubjectivity, he invokes Liebniz's notion of monads: self-contained nodal points with a greater or lesser degree of awareness (i.e., greater or lesser degrees of consciousness). The Husserl of the *Cartesian Meditations* comes across as a philosophical idealist. For him, ideas and consciousness of them are the ultimate reality. This is hardly surprising. Brentano's most popular course was a seminar on Bishop Berkeley, who demonstrated that Locke's primary qualities were in the same boat as Locke's secondary qualities, and that both had reality only as ideas. Berkeley concluded, "To be is to be perceived." Husserl never quite says this, but there is a strong tendency inherent in his position to see consciousness and its ideas as the ultimate reality. As soon as he makes consciousness of his starting point, it is hard for him not to wind up as a philosophical idealist, a philosophical idealist being one who believes that the ultimately real is thought. To maintain a metaphysical position including the idealistic one is to cease to be a phenomenologist, and Husserl did not want to do that. There is a tension in him between the phenomenologist and the metaphysician.

The elucidation of the complex structure of the self as transcendental ego was mostly left to Husserl's disciples. There are phenomenological psychoanalysts and psychological theorists who "describe" pathological states without offering dynamic or mechanistic explanations of those states. *Dynamic* here refers to Freudian explanations of pathological states in terms of drive derivatives, instincts, and conflicts between elements of the structural self. Rather, they strive to present without judgment or preconception the subjective experience of those suffering from these pathological conditions. In psychiatry in general, phenomenology has come to mean a description of the disease without consideration of etiology.

American descriptive psychiatry, although it does not totally ignore affect and cognition, tends to be behavioristic in its descriptions of various pathological syndromes, while the phenomenological psychiatrist or psychoanalyst is exclusively concerned with the subjective experience of the patient. Phenomenological psychologists have elucidated such phenomena as the experience of space and time in various pathological states, although they might be loath to use the word *pathological*. Rather they would simply say they were describing alternate modes of being conscious. For example, in depression the experience of time is slowed down, and it was a phenomenological psychoanalyst who first brought this to our attention.

The most influential of Husserl's disciples was and is Martin Heidegger. Heidegger's task was to fill in the details, to make the transcendental ego concrete rather than abstract. Whether or not he did so is up for grabs. Before we turn to Heidegger, it is worth relating a perhaps apochryphal story about a visit of Gilbert Ryle to Husserl. While Ryle was waiting to see the master phenomenologist himself, Husserl's wife engaged him in conversation. During the course of the discussion, she turned the conversation toward Husserl's reputation in England. Ryle was silent so she asked, "Is my husband regarded as a worthy successor of Descartes?" Ryle said nothing. "Of Kant?" Ryle still said nothing. "Of Hegel?" "Oh yes," said Ryle, "your husband is regarded as every bit the intellectual equal of Hegel and as of equal importance as a philosopher." Mrs. Husserl beamed as English tact had its day.

HEIDEGGER AND *DASEIN*

Martin Heidegger (1889–1976) was a thoroughly despicable human being. Character aside, his philosophy is intriguing. Some believe that Heidegger was basically a charlatan who hid behind obscurity and pomposity and was pseudoprofound. There is certainly that aspect to him, but some things he has to say about self are worth looking at.

To start with the man: Heidegger was born into a peasant family in the Black Forest and retained a love for the region and the soil throughout his life. In later life, he withdrew to a hut in the Black Forest to ponder and to philosophize. Heidegger studied philosophy at the University of Freiburg under Husserl, becoming his disciple and the leading phenomenologist of his generation. Husserl was Jewish; so was Hannah Arendt, the political and social philosopher with whom Heidegger had a long affair, and so was one of Heidegger's most brilliant colleagues, who converted to Catholicism and became a nun. She was dragged from her convent by the Nazis and murdered in a concentration camp. In spite of, or perhaps because of, his close links to Jewish intellectuals, including the man who was his philosophical mentor, Heidegger became a Nazi. With the advent of National Socialism, Husserl lost his post and the right to teach in Germany. Heidegger succeeded him as Professor of Philosophy at Freiberg. He was soon appointed rector of the university, on the occasion of which he gave a speech embracing Nazism as the fulfillment of his philosophy. It is true that he soon resigned his rectorship and played no further political role during the Third Reich, but he never resigned from the party and never repudiated his Fascist leanings. Considerable evidence has recently come to light that Heidegger never relinquished his Nazi beliefs and that he held them long before Hitler came to power. It is, to say the least, difficult to take his writings on authenticity and truth, published during the Nazi regime, seriously. His supporters say, by way of extenuation, that his embracing of Nazism was merely opportunistic. Aside from the fact that this is apparently not true, it puts forward the thesis that it is all right to advance one's career by complicity in murder. Such "excuses" have been made for Herbert von Karajan and others; I don't find them persuasive. In addition to his complicity in Nazism, Heidegger's Greek etymologies, upon which he bases much of his late philosophizing, are at best fanciful, or ignorant, which is not likely, and so, at worst, dishonest.

Be this as it may, we will ignore the messenger and look at the message. What follows is based on *Sein Und Zeit* (*Being and Time*), Heidegger's 1927 tome. *Sein Und Zeit* is dedicated to Edmund Husserl, "in friendship and admiration." In it, Heidegger says that he is interested in elucidating Being, but that before he can do so, he must elucidate our experience of Being. Being is to be distinguished from beings, the individual things that are, and that presumably arise out of and are grounded in Being itself. Exactly what this might mean is not clear. Perhaps Being is one of those things about which we cannot speak. After the War, Heidegger published a volume called *"An Introduction to Is Metaphysics"* (1953/ 1961) in which he asks, "Why is there something rather than nothing?"—a question that evokes emotion but is unanswerable; Heidegger proposes no answers in his book.

Heidegger's entire career has been seen as an attempt to elucidate Being, but he can say but little about it. This seems a long way from the phenomenological injunction to return to the things themselves. Presumably the things themselves are beings and not Being. It is significant that Heidegger doesn't use phenomenology in a subtitle, and his book is usually classified as part of the existential tradition. Heidegger has said that he isn't an existentialist. As a preliminary to his discussion of Being, which never occurs, Heidegger gives a phenomenological description of what he calls Being-there, or *Dasein*. *Dasein* is Heidegger's term for the concretely existing human being. To be human is to be there: to be a part of a surround, to already be part of a world. For *Dasein*, there is no subject-object dichotomy.

For our purposes, *Dasein* is a self. The essence of this self is that it has a world. In no way is it a disembodied, solipsistic subjectivity. Such a subjectivity is an abstraction; the concrete lived reality is always the reality of connectedness, of emergence in, of being a part of. To be a self is to be-there, and to be-there is to be in the world. It is only upon analysis that the distinction between subject and object arises. This notion of *Dasein* obviously owes something to Husserl and to Brentano. Just as there is no consciousness devoid of an object, there is no existence devoid of a world. So far, so good. Heidegger is right. Nobody experiences himself as a Cartesian *cogito* unless he is philosophizing. *Dasein* would appear to be a psychological notion, but Heidegger wants to make it an ontological one. Human existence is Being-there because Being is primary. Being and beings stand in the relation of figure and ground.

Another way of conceptualizing *Dasein* is as the center of a field in the same way a magnet is the center of a field. This is an imperfect analogy, because the fields of force of *Dasein* and of the world are mutual. They emanate both ways; their interconnectedness is intrinsic. *Dasein* is the field of force or, better yet, a nodal point within it. The world is already "at hand"; there is no isolate of a self that builds or perceives or needs to connect with a world; the self is *Dasein*, is already in and of a world. Subject and object are abstractions, the result of analysis of the concrete reality of the human situation. *Dasein* and *cogito* are polar opposites. More divergent concepts of self would be hard to imagine, and indeed Heidegger is self-consciously criticizing Descartes, whom he believes to have been totally mistaken.

According to Heidegger, the first fateful decision in Western thought occurred when the ancient Greeks lost or greatly attenuated their contact with Being and focused on beings, on things rather than the source of things, on figure rather than ground. That decision was a corollary of an antecedent "decision" about the nature of truth. According to Heidegger, the etymological root meaning of the Greek word for truth is "unconcealing." He also says that the root meaning of truth is "standing forth." Truth is noninvasive and nonmanipulative. It is an allowing of Being to be present, and to be unconcealed, rather than a correspondence in which truth is the agreement of a proposition with a state of affairs. Put differently, we in the Western tradition pursue truth through the use of scientific inquiry and experiment, which involves aggression, separation, and experimental manipulation, while truth as unconcealment, as allowing to stand forth, has much more to do with a state of receptivity, a kind of passive creativity that allows that which is to manifest itself.

Heidegger believes that the shift in the meaning of truth, already implicit in the pre-Socratic nature philosophers, was carried further by the Pythagoreans with their mathematization of nature (the ultimate reality is number), and completed in certain epistemological doctrines of Plato adumbrated in the *Theaetetus* and parts of the *Republic*. This shift in the meaning of truth reflects or perhaps actualizes a shift from Being to beings. This shift made the development of science, the defining characteristic of Western culture, possible, but only at the cost of losing contact with Being. Descartes completed and exacerbated this process by his bifurcation (into extended substance and thinking substance) and further mathematization of nature. Again, a gain for science entailed a further loss of contact with Being. Now the ultimate becomes beings, regarded as extended substance in motion described by mathematical equations. intellectualization and abstraction, rather than lived emergence and embeddedness. Man came to live in a world of concrete things that he sought to control and manipulate, rather than to experience himself as a part of the totality of things, as grounded in Being itself. We no longer listen to the silent, awesome reverberations of Being itself; instead we are lost in a sea of objects.

Elsewhere, Heidegger says that in our era "God is absent." Unlike Nietzsche, he does not say that God is dead, merely absent. Our loss of contact with Being itself is loss of contact with the absent God. At least that is a reasonable reading of Heidegger. It is difficult to know what to make of Heidegger's notion of Being. It seems to be something antecedent to rationality, with which direct contact is possible. Although Heidegger would not like the label, it seems to me to be a mystical notion. However, unlike the experience related in most mystical traditions, there is no experience of fusion with the totality of things, the one and ultimate reality, but rather a quiet sensing of its omnipresent reality as the source and ground of all that exists.

There is a connection between Heidegger's obsessive languishing for Being and his welcoming the rise of Fascism, between his ontology and his politics. Heidegger's critique of rationality harkens back to the German counter-Enlightenment and its espousal of the irrational, the mystical, and the primitive community. In his inaugural speech as rector of the University of Freiberg, Heidegger welcomed the New Order as an incarnation of the mystical German folk, as a return from beings to Being. There is something about Heidegger's style of irrationality—he would deny that he is an irrationalist, rather maintaining that he is seeking the ground of both rationality and irrationality in his search for Being—that is exceedingly dangerous. It all too easily becomes confused with the archaic emotionality of mass movements: the primitive and precivilized. To return to Being becomes a return to bestiality.

Heidegger does not really argue his account of the forgetting of Being and the pursuit of the control of beings in Greek thought, nor does he justify his account of the change in the meaning in the concept of truth in Greek thought with any sort of scholarly presentation. He is not at all clear on what it would mean to return to the thinking of the pre-pre-Socratic Greeks. Presumably, it would involve some sort of un-self-conscious, prescientific state of receptivity of the awesomeness of the created universe. How that notion with its implication of a state of awe and wonder became confused, as it does in his inaugural speech, with the hyperemotionality of a nationalistic regression is difficult to understand, yet that confusion seems to exist in Heidegger.

I return to Heidegger's discussion of *Dasein*, which we are interpreting as self. Self as *Dasein* is embedded and interrelated, rather than a solitary, unconnected thinker. Heidegger's *Dasein* is reminiscent of the ethological concept of the *Umwelt*, the around world, or surround. For the ethologist, the animal is understood not as a biological isolate, but as a creature embedded in the environment as a part of his *Umwelt*.

The European school of psychoanalysis called *Daseins Analytics*, or sometimes existential psychoanalysis, derives from Heidegger. This school is mainly associated with Ludwig Binswanger, a Swiss psychoanalyst who maintained a lifelong friendship with Freud in spite of their total disagreement about human nature and therapeutics. One suspects that the friendship lasted because Freud did not take Binswanger's theories seriously. Binswanger elaborated on Heidegger's conceptualization of *Dasein* and described three dimensions or aspects of Being-there as a person: namely, relatedness to the *Umwelt*, the *Mitwelt*, and the *Eigenwelt*; the surround, the with-world, and the value-world. These are not external relations, but rather are intrinsic to *Dasein*. The first is the relation to the encompassing natural world; the second the relationship with other *Daseins*, with people; and the third *Dasein's* relationship with itself. There is no human existence apart from relationship to nature, people, and self. To be a self in the sense of being a *Dasein*—a concrete, real existence—is to be a part of and apart from nature, a part of and apart from a human community, and to have a reflexive and reflective relationship with self. The ways in which these three aspects of human existence, of selfhood or *Dasein*, get played out determines the life of that particular human existence and its unique mixture of health and pathology.

(Another philosopher, whom we will shortly meet, who also talks about an experience of Being is Alfred North Whitehead. His language and style of philosophizing is completely alien to that of Heidegger; yet, when in his theory of perception he talks about a mode of knowing that is pre- or nonverbal and nonpropositional, which he calls *causal efficacy*, the silent awareness of the power of the surround, he is alluding to something strikingly similar to Heidegger's call of Being.)

After Heidegger's preliminary discussion of Being, the rest of *Sein Und Zeit* is devoted to the elucidation of human Being-there—of the existential situation of the self. This is why Heidegger is so frequently classified as an existentialist, his protests notwithstanding. Most of what he wrote is descriptive of human existence. Like all the existentialists, he maintains that existence precedes essence, so there should be no human nature to describe, no essence of *Dasein*. Heidegger resolves this dilemma, to his satisfaction at least, by saying that he is going to give a description of the *Existentialia* of *Dasein*, of the conditions of existence of human Being-there, of the intrinsic modalities of selfhood. So to speak, the dimensions of human Being-there are describable and are the same for all, while the way they are lived is unique to each self. We are what we become; there is no preformed essence that gets actualized in human existence, but the lines, or *existentialia*, along which we become what we become are the same for all. The self is what it becomes, but it can only become that in certain ways that are ontological and intrinsic to *Dasein*.

For Heidegger, the existentialia are Mood, Understanding, Speech, Anxiety, Care, Truth, Finitude, Temporality, and Historicity. Each of these existentialia can be lived authentically or inauthentically. Heidegger's emphasis on the centrality of Anxiety and Finitude also puts him in the existential camp. Let us take a brief look at each of Heidegger's existentialia.

For Heidegger, Mood, the German word also meaning attunement, is intrinsic to *Dasein*. There is no human existence or moment of existence that is not characterized by a mood. One's Mood may be quiet and low key, subliminal so to speak, yet there always is one, one that sets the tone of our experience of nature, people, and self. Of course, one Mood may come to the forefront and become painfully and unignorably present, but mostly we do not attend to our moods. To characterize self as intrinsically moody, in the sense of always having a mood, is to come a long way from the self as cogitator, or indeed from any of our previous characterizations of self.

Understanding is also intrinsic to *Dasein*. There is no human existence, or a moment of human existence, that does not entail or is not, in part, constituted by Understanding. Understanding, like Mood, is intrinsic to Being-there, to human existence. The self is a self that is engaged in Understanding, the unconcealment, the standing forth, the revelation of Being. Acts of intellectual understanding, of propositional knowledge, are derivatives, particularizations of the existentialium of Understanding. The same is true of Speech. To have a self is to have language. To exist as a human being who is already there in the world is to have Speech. Heideggerian speech is there before particular words; it is the intrinsic, linguistic communicability of *Dasein*. It exists before, in both the logical and temporal senses, language acquisition.

To be a self is to have Mood, Understanding, and Speech. Coming from a very different perspective and philosophical stance, Noam Chomsky's *generative grammar*, the innate substrate, the template, of all speech and all language acquisition, is a notion close in content if not in spirit to Heidegger's *Reade*—speech as an existentialium.

Mood, Understanding, and Speech stand in relation to particular moods; acts of understanding, comprehension, or knowledge; and acts of verbal communication in a manner parallel to the relationship of Being to beings. There is no moment of human existence that is not perfused by a mood, by some level of comprehension, and by some sense of being in communication.

Dasein is intrinsically anxious. *Angst* is an existentialium. Human existence, the self as *Dasein*, is ontologically anxious; that is, anxiety is built into the very self structure itself. There is no way to be and no moment when the self is not anxious, because it is constituted by Anxiety, just as it is constituted by Mood, Understanding, Speech, and the other existentialia. It isn't that the self as *Dasein* is anxious; rather, it *is* Anxiety and the rest of the existentialia. The existential theologian and philosopher, Paul Tillich (1952), made a distinction between neurotic anxiety and ontological anxiety. Neurotic anxiety is a product of psychological conflict, particularly of unconscious conflict between desire and prohibition. It is the anxiety Freud elucidated in his second theory of anxiety when he said we repress because we are anxious, and drive thoughts and feelings from consciousness because they are too threatening, even though they reappear as inhibitions, acting out, and symptoms, all of which are manifestations of the ineluctable return of the repressed. Neurotic anxiety can be "cured," or at least radically attenuated, by making the unconscious conscious, by integrating the repudiated, defended against, rejected aspects of self. Not so ontological anxiety; it is built in (ontological), and arises out of human finitude, the limits of existence, particularly our mortality. According to Tillich, ontological anxiety has three facets: the anxiety of fate and death; the anxiety of emptiness and meaninglessness; and the anxiety of guilt and condemnation. The anxiety engendered by the brute facticity of life and of death; the ineluctable feeling that life is "a tale told by an idiot full of sound and fury signifying nothing"; and the inexorable guilt and self-condemnation consequent on the aggression inherent in living are all givens, all woven into the very structure of human existence, of Being-there. The self *is* ontological anxiety— among other things. Tillich maintains that neurotic anxiety is exacerbated by defenses against ontological anxiety that repress, reject, or deny it. Neurotic anxiety is not only caused by unconscious Freudian conflict; it is caused by failure to withstand, in the full light of consciousness, ontological anxiety and to come to terms with it in whatever way we can. Neurotic anxiety arises from a failed attempt to cheat, to escape the ontological anxiety that is inescapable. All such attempts at cheating are doomed to failure, and those who engage in them get paid back in spades—or in symptoms. To take nothing away from Tillich, or the creativity of his analysis of anxiety, all of this is quintessentially Heideggerian.

According to Heidegger, angst is ontological because Nothingness is part of Being, including human Being-there. Nothingness is part of our very selves, and there is an experience of Nothingness. Understanding encompasses Nothingness just as it does Being: as Heidegger puts it, *"Das Nicht nichts,"* the Nothing nothings. You can imagine what the verification people—the positivistic and analytic philosophers—did with that one, but that doesn't make Heidegger wrong. There *is* an experience of Nothingness, of feet walking on my grave, of uncanniness. Nothingness is the source of ontological anxiety with its three components of death anxiety, dread of meaninglessness, and dread of condemnation.

Another way of conceptualizing the self as angst—angst intrinsic to the intrinsicality of Nothingness, the Nothingness within the self and within the universe—is to see the self as finite, and Finitude is another existentialium. *Dasein is* Finitude, and the realization of my Finitude, my limitations, and my certain termination; of the Finitude that is me engenders, triggers, awareness of the angst that is also me. There is another aspect of Finitude: not only will my existence as a self end, it has a beginning, and that beginning is *utterly arbitrary*. It is radically contingent, and that contingency is a part of my Finitude. Heidegger's name for the contingency of *Dasein* is *Geworfenheit*: "thrownness." Why I was born here and now, rather than there and then, indeed why I was born at all, is utterly contingent. There is no sufficient reason for me to have been born, let alone to have been born here and now. I have simply been thrown into existence here and now, and the experience of this thrownness, or the defense against it, engenders, or actually constitutes, part of the angst that constitutes, or partly constitutes, me.

My encounter with Nothingness, with my Finitude, and with Anxiety overwhelms me, and I ineluctably defend against those awarenesses; I defend by a flight into *Everydayness*, an attempt to get lost in anonymity by becoming one of the crowd, by becoming *Das Mann*, The One, one like all the others, living daily life with the least possible awareness. When I experience myself as The One, as impersonally as possible, as one among rather than one as a finite, anxious, contingent self, I am in a state of *Fallenness*. Fallenness, too, is an existentialium. Every *Dasein* experiences Fallenness; it is an ontological aspect of self, a mode of Being-there that is unavoidable because the full consciousness of angst is not possible, at least not on an ongoing basis. The most powerful drive to Fallenness, its primordial source, is the depersonalization of and loss of anxiety about death when I realize, as an abstract proposition, a bit of intellectual awareness, that "Man dies." That is not threatening, in the way that the emotional experience of my Finitude, *my* death, and of footsteps walking on my grave is anxiety-provoking— anxiety-provoking in the highest degree. The knowledge that everyone dies is the polar opposite of the realization that my death lies within me as a facet of my intrinsic Finitude. It is not that I will die some day: it is the stark realization that the death within me can become actual, now, at this very moment—that Nothingness confronts me now and always. The experience of Nothingness is captured by Hemingway (1933/1970, p. 32) in *A Clean, Well Lighted Place*:

> *Turning off the electric light, he continued the conversation with himself . . . what did he fear? It was not fear or dread. It was nothing that he knew too well. It was all a nothing and a man was nothing too. It was only that and a light was all it needed and a certain cleanness and order. Some lived in it and never filled it but he knew it was all nada y pues nada y nada y pues nada. Our nada who is in nada, nada be thy name, thy kingdom nada thy will be nada in nada as it is in nada. Give us this nada our daily nada and nada us our nada as we nada our nadas, and nada us nada into nada but deliver us from nada; pues nada. Hail nothing full of nothing, nothing is with thee.*

Or as Samuel Beckett put it, "Nothing is more real than nothing!"

It is interesting that Heidegger, who was himself attracted to a mass movement that incarnated and epitomized the flight into the anonymity of the one, *Das Mann*, so acutely analyzed the mechanism of such flights. It is almost as if he had read Erich Fromm's *Escape From Freedom* (1941), which was published 20 years after *Sein Und Zeit*. In *Escape*, Fromm analyzes the appeal of totalitarian movements in terms of the avoidance of the anxiety of human contingency with its precariousness, and fatedness, and, on the flip side of the coin, its radical impossibility of grounding decisions in rationality, and its termination and death, along with the responsibility of being free and making choices in the face of that radical contingency. That is, Fromm is saying that people are so overwhelmed by the responsibilities of freedom, which flow out of the radical contingency of human life, that they flee into the certainties of Fascism and Communism or other dogmatic belief systems. There is, however, an important difference between Heidegger and Fromm. Fromm's analysis is political and psychological; Heidegger's is phenomenological and ontological. One is talking about concrete, human historical reality in the 20th century, the other is talking about the very nature of self and of Being.

Heidegger's analysis of Finitude as my death, with the possibility of its actualization now, as within me, also has parallels with Freud's theory of the death instinct, Thanatos, which is also within the self, within me. It is noteworthy that both Freud and Heidegger wrote immediately after the carnage of World War I. Again, if there are similarities in concept, there are also differences. Freud's is a tragic view of internal conflict and of the eternal struggle between love and death, Eros and Thanatos, while Heidegger's vision is a metaphysical one of the worm of nothingness in the apple of Being, of the yawning abyss within that I strive not to see. As we will see, Heidegger also has a concept, care, that is somewhat parallel to Freud's eros, yet very different from it. The antithesis of Fallenness is *Resolute-ness*, and the antithesis of flight into the anonymity and depersonalization of The One is *Sein Zum Tod, Being-toward-death*, in which I own the death within me, feeling the nothingness within and without, and fully feel my Finitude. It is only through Being-toward-death that *Authenticity* becomes possible. Being-toward-death is Authenticity; Fallenness is *Inauthenticity*. Heidegger is not writing ethics here, is not being moralistic, and is not maintaining that Authenticity is a "better" state of being than Inauthenticity. On the contrary, he is being descriptive, elucidat-ing the structure of *Dasein*, the structure of the Heideggerian self. Fallennness and Being-toward-death and Authenticity and Inauthenticity are equally existentialia. Since they are structural, they are not to be avoided. That man partakes of Fallen-ness and Inauthenticity is a facet of and consequence of Finitude. Any particular *Dasein*—you and I—oscillates between Authenticity and Inauthenticity; the balance varies, but tension between the two poles is always there for everybody. One wonders about Heidegger's disclaimer of doing ethics. Fallenness suggests the Biblical Fall and is in its way Heidegger's version of original sin; or perhaps his abjuration of the ethical and his focus on the inevitability of Inauthenticity is somehow implicit in his political amorality.

Heidegger is certainly right in highlighting the dialectical tension within *Dasein* between acceptance and denial of death. I have often thought that our insane destruction of the environment is motivated and driven by more than rapacity, greed, and political stupidity. Our behavior is too irrational. It is so in denial of reality that I believe its underlying motivation is an unconscious, magical convic-tion that science and technology can confer immortality. To acknowledge the limi-tations of technology is to see that this God isn't omnipotent. It is to be made anxious, because such acknowledgment carries with it the (unconscious) realiza-tion that science isn't magical and can't confer immortality. During the past dec-ade, things have become so bad that some reality has seeped through, and the current revival of fundamentalist, dogmatic religion has something to do with replacing this failed God.

Sorge, or Care, is the existentialium of commitment to and involvement with other *Dasein*. It too is structural. We cannot help but be intrinsically intertwined with the being of others and to take some kind of responsibility for them. This involvement with the *Mitwelt* is structural. There is no human Being-there that is not so related. Care comes out of the awareness of the Finitude of others, but I have *Sorge* toward myself as well as toward others. I defend against Care by detachment and distancing, and both Care and defenses against it are structural components of self.

The self is intrinsically temporal. Time too is within *Dasein*. Every moment of lived time has three *ex-tases*, three *standing outs*: that of the past, that of the present, and that of the future. There is no experience of *Dasein*, of the self, that is not temporal, and that temporality always involves the pastness of the past, the nowness of the present, and the futurity of the future. I am always pushed by the past and pulled by the future. The pastness of the past and futurity of the future are interpretations and anticipations, respectively, and are not passively received givens, but lived choices. I am always constructing a living and lived past out of the facticity of what has occurred, which then either pulls me back toward it or, as is more usual, propels me forward. Similarly, my projections onto the future, my anticipations, pull me forward, and the present is always permeated by them. I cannot help but do this; the temporality of existence, with its three *ex-tases*, is within me. Augustine anticipated Heidegger in his account of time in the *Confessions*.

The injunction to "stay in the now" is futile; I cannot sustain doing so. The now is not an isolated, detached moment; it is a dynamic fusion and tension between past, present, and future. To be a self is to live in time so conceived. *Dasein's* temporality is not the same as public time, or scientific time, the time we measure by natural regularity, with our clocks, watches, calendars, and chronometers. Public time, the objectively measured flow of uniform duration, is derivable from the temporality of *Dasein*; it is a kind of "fallen," "everyday" representation of that temporality, flattened out, spatialized, and homogenized.

Heidegger owes something here to another Jewish thinker, Henri Bergson, and his distinction between *temps* and *durée*—measured time and experienced time— but Heidegger, with the exception of his references to the Greeks, Descartes, and Kant, gives no credit to anyone as the sources of his analysis of *Dasein*, unless his dedication to Husserl be taken as such an acknowledgment. This is odd in a thinker who makes Historicity one of his existentialia. *Dasein* is intrinsically, structurally historical. He is permeated by Historicity, the awareness that he is part of a community of *Daseins* who have a past and that that past is part of him. The self cannot help but experience itself as a part of human history. Positive history, the kind we read in textbooks and study in school, is derivative from and only possible because of the Historicity of *Dasein*. The existentialium of Historicity is what allows *Dasein* to write history.

One might say that Heidegger has only elaborated in a ponderous and pseudo-profound way the obvious, that men die and that they know it, and that that knowledge makes them anxious; in a sense this is true. However, Heidegger does more than that; he delineates the structure of the self as embedded, encompassed, attuned, comprehending, linguistic, in contact with the unconcealed and the hidden, anxious, finite, concerned, thrown, contingent, dialectically authentic and inauthentic, temporal, and historical. Heidegger would not accept this characterization; to say that he elucidates the structure of the self is too essentialistic for him. Rather he would say that he is naming the existentialia of human Being-there. This, however, is a distinction without a difference (to me), and the Heideggerian self is a highly structured self, a complex self, a real as opposed to an abstract self. Heidegger succeeds in saying something about the self that none of our previous thinkers about the self have done. His self is the Kierkegaardian self, systematized, extended, enriched, secularized, and updated.

JEAN-PAUL SARTRE: THE *COGITO* GROWS MORE ANXIOUS

The literary and philosophical movement of existentialism is closely identified with Jean-Paul Sartre (1905–1980). The existentialist movement was a post-World War II European phenomenon that emphasized the radical contingency of human life, the absence of ultimate sources of value and rationality, and extreme conditions of human existence. It focused on the dark side of human life, on death, anxiety, meaninglessness, and despair. It dwelt on the "absurdity" of the human situation and of human existence and on the irrationality of life and the choices entailed by life. Although its content was surely depressing, the response to its insights was not necessarily despair. On the contrary, it was often heroic defiance. Sartre's philosophy was such a heroic defiance. Although there are religious existentialists, such as Buber, Tillich, and Marcel, existentialism is identified with atheism and its two leading exponents, Sartre and Camus, were atheists. Although the postwar existentialist movement has historical antecedents and there are existential elements in much of literature and philosophy, even in such a rationalistic philosophy as Plato's, the modern variety has a unique urgency and poignancy. It speaks to us with a directness and power that its ancestors lacked. Existentialism's remote ancestor is the philosophical and logical doctrine that "existence precedes essence," which goes back at least as far as Aristotle. This doctrine underwent further development in Dun Scotus and other medieval nominalists and continues to find support in nominalistic versions of positivism. More directly relevant than its logical and ontological predecessors are the persistently reoccurring strands of irrationalism in Western thought. Tertullian, an early church father and philosopher, who wrote *"Credo ad absurdum"* ("I believe because it is absurd"); Lucretius' vision of a universe consisting of atoms in motion without value, meaning, or purpose; Pascal's "These immense spaces terrify me"; Luther's "Reason is a whore"; and Kierkegaard's entire output come to mind, as do Schopenhauer's view of reality as blind striving and Nietzsche's analysis of morality as the irrational, unconscious manifestation of the will to power. We have encountered these modes of thought before. Of even more immediate import in the development of existentialism is European phenomenology, with its methodology for the descriptive analysis of consciousness, and the work of Martin Heidegger just reviewed. Sartre was heavily indebted to Heidegger and his analysis of the existentialia of *Dasein*, and since Heidegger so well dealt with these existentialia, I will not go into Sartre's but slightly different statement of them. Sartre, however, is not Heidegger, and his notion of self is radically different from the notion of *Dasein*. Perhaps the greatest influence on existentialism, especially Sartre's, was not intellectual but historical and political. Sartre's existentialism came out of the experience of the collapse of European liberalism, the moral and military bankruptcy of France, the rise of Fascism, the triumph of Hitler, the Holocaust, and the dropping of the atomic bomb. Sartre was profoundly affected by the position of the French during the Occupation. He wrote:

> We were never more free than during the German Occupation. We had lost all our rights, beginning with the right to talk. Every day, we were insulted to our faces and had to take it in silence. Under one pretense or another, as workers, Jews, or political prisoners, we were deported en masse. Everywhere, on billboards, in the newspapers, on the screen, we encountered the revolting and insipid picture of ourselves that our suppressors wanted us to accept. Because of all of this, we were free. Because the Nazi venom seeped into our thoughts, every accurate thought was a conquest. Because an all-powerful police tried to force us to hold our tongues, every word took on the value of a declaration of principles. Because we were hunted down, every one of our gestures had the weight of a solemn commitment. . . .
>
> Exile, captivity, and especially death (which we usually shrink from facing at all in happier days) became for us the habitual objects of our concern. We learned that they were neither inevitable accidents, nor even constant and inevitable dangers, but they must be considered as our lot itself, our destiny, the profound source of our reality as men. At every instance we lived up to the full sense of this commonplace little phrase: "Man is mortal!" And the choice that each of us made of his life was an authentic choice because it was made face to face with death,

because it could always have been expressed in these terms: "Rather death than . . . " and here I am not speaking of the elite among us who were real Resistants, but of all Frenchmen who, at every hour of the night and day throughout four years, answered "No." (1945, as cited in Barrett, 1958)

The philosophy of extreme situations grew out of an extreme situation. The self, for Sartre, is pure consciousness and consciousness is nothingness: no-thingness, pure negativity. Sartre's understanding of self is ontological, a concomitant of his metaphysical schema. The subtitle of *Being and Nothingness* (1950) is *An Essay on Phenomenological Ontology.* By *phenomenological ontology*, Sartre means a description of what exists, of what is real, insofar as we experience it. So Sartre is describing phenomena, not noumena, at least formally, and is taking a Husserlian stance of epoche, of bracketing our experience of reality, of "merely" describing it. But the epoche doesn't play much of a role in *Being and Nothingness*, and Sartre's phenomenological ontology is presented as if it were a metaphysical (ontological) ontology, as if he were describing the things-in-themselves. So to speak, he forgets his Husserlian qualifications. Perhaps Sartre feels that it really doesn't matter, that for us phenomenological ontology is a description of the ultimately real, or at least the only ultimately real that we will ever know. Although Sartre's language is Hegelian, he is a modern Cartesian. There are two kinds of stuff in the world: *en soi*, being-in-itself, and *pour soi*, being-for-itself. This terminology is derived from, indeed directly borrowed from, Hegel, but used somewhat differently, and there is no Hegelian dialectical synthesis of being-in-itself and being-for-itself. On the contrary, Sartre's ontology is radically dualistic.

In the Hegelian dialectic, Nothingness is the antithesis of Being. Being being unarticulated solidity, without Nothingness Being would be the One of the pre-Socratic Greek philosopher Parmenides, whose One is a plenum, a One forever fixed and static. In Parmenides, change and process are reduced to illusion. But for Hegel, process is, in a sense, the ultimate reality. The Absolute may have been pure Being when it existed only as potentiality, but it only becomes actual—real— in its unfolding. So to speak, the initial great ball of wax articulates itself by generating its antithesis, Nothing, and their synthesis is Becoming, the reality of process and development, the unfolding and actualization in history of that which was implicit and potential. Hegel's is a sort of Big Bang theory without the bang.

My metaphorical analog of the big ball of wax or of the Big Bang are, in an important way, misleading. The ultimately real, potentially and actually, for Hegel is thought, not stuff; idea, not material. As we have seen, Heidegger has beings emerging from the ground of Being with Nothingness intrinsic to both Being and human Being-there. Sartre's version of the Hegelian categories of Being and Nothingness and of their dialectical relationship is neither Hegelian nor Heideggerian, neither idealism nor an attempt to reconnect with Being. On the contrary, Sartre's analysis is quintessentially existential. It is totally rooted in the analysis of human existence. Heidegger has said he is not an existentialist, he is a philosopher of Being, and he is right. Sartre has no place for the search for Being; he is wholly absorbed in the concrete experience of human beings.

To return to Sartre's phenomenological ontology, being-in-itself is solid, self-consistent, dense, and totally without awareness. It is thingness. It is stonelike. Being-for-itself is no-thing. It is consciousness. Consciousness negates. Consciousness creates distance, distinctions, articulations, categories, and types. It says no. It is not consistent with itself. Neither has it solidity. Nothingness came into the world with consciousness. "Man is the being through which Nothingness came into the world" (Sartre, 1956, p. 241). This is an extraordinary notion, radically different from anything we have encountered before. Nothingness is here not a logical category (Hegel), nor a part of reality, nor an experience, but rather a creation of human consciousness. Consciousness is negation: emptiness, vacuity, and insubstantiality. Is this consciousness that is no-thing, that is negation, the Sartrian self? Yes and no. What he calls the ego is my awareness of the states of my consciousness. It is reflexive and it is a synthesis. That ego is Sartre's version of the empirical self, which is in many ways thinglike, although not material. It is not the for-itself. The self-for-itself is not in the world, is not thinglike. On the contrary, it is pure freedom, always trying to transcend itself. It is this self as pure freedom, as radical contingency, as choosing and creating, as negating and denying that is the uniquely Sartrian self. My relationship to my body is much like my relationship to my ego. It too is a thing in the world, but that is not how I experience my body. I am not that body, or my experience of it. So the self, although it has aspects as ego—the product of self-reflection and synthesis and of body as object and as synthesis—is neither of these, but rather pure negativity. The self is no-thing; the self both *is*, and is the source of, Nothingness.

Consciousness is always reflexive. It is never simply, or at least for long, conscious of anything without being aware of being conscious of it. This makes for a special kind of alienation, an inability to be what one is even for a moment. This contributes to the insubstantiality of consciousness. Sartre's example is of being sad, then being aware of being sad, which is not the same as being sad. He calls this the *metastability of consciousness*. The for-itself is forever oscillating between experience and awareness of experiencing. Consciousness is not only no-thing, it is not even self-consistent awareness of, but only awareness of awareness alternating with awareness. This is another aspect of its pure negativity.

At one level, the Sartrian no is the no of the Resistance fighter who refuses to speak to the Gestapo. In his short story *The Wall* (1948), Sartre depicts a political prisoner about to be shot. Even in the moment of execution, the protagonist remains free, and his freedom lies in his potential to refuse affirmation of his oppressor, to say no. Sartre is right. The ability to say no is the basis of human freedom. Usually a child's first word is *no*! It is the assertion of individuality and autonomy. But Sartre is doing more than pointing to the possibility of heroic—or even more ordinary—resistance to the will of others. He is identifying the self with negation and the ability to negate. Conceptual thought depends on negation—on discrimination and separation. Language is negation. The political and the psychological have become ontological. The resistance no and the child's initial no have become the no of consciousness and part of the structure of what is.

For Sartre, there is no dialectical synthesis of Being and Nothing, no reconciliation of being-in-itself and being-for-itself. For him, this is impossible because it is self-contradictory. To be the thing that knows it is a thing cannot be—things do not know; and to be a consciousness that has solidity, substantiality, also cannot be—consciousness is nothing. Yet the desire to be the thing that is conscious that it is a thing, or to be a thinglike consciousness, is intrinsic to human life. We are free to be or do anything, but we are not free to become the thing-in-itself-for-itself: the consciousness that is a thing, the thing that knows it is a thing. How we attempt to actualize this impossibility is our *project*. All of human culture and of human history, all personal relationships, all individual accomplishments, and all psychological conflicts are derivatives of our projects. Since the most basic human drive is to bring about a synthesis that cannot be, Sartre concludes, "Man is a useless passion" (1956, p. 615). The Cartesian bifurcation of nature into extended substance and thinking substance is reconstituted as a tragic tension: a dualistic metaphysics becomes the preeminent and ineluctable human impossibility. Ontological bifurcation results not, or not only, in an interior psychological split; it is on the basis of an alienation that cannot be healed. The self as futile passion trying to be a thing when it is not a thing yet unable to do so and the self as pure freedom and pure negativity are new in our considerations of theories of the self.

Sartre is every bit as much a psychologist of conflict as Freud; it is simply that the conflicts are seen differently. Being a futile passion is intolerable or nearly so, so human beings engage in all sorts of deceptions to escape that futility. They attempt to reduce other consciousnesses—other for-selves—to objects, to things, to in-itselves. If you are an in-itself to my for-itself, I have in some sense become the thing-in-itself, for-itself. But this is not possible because the Other can only be an Object of my consciousness by choosing to be such an Object, and such choosing is an act of consciousness. Similarly, I cannot solve my dilemma by becoming an object of another's consciousness because I can only do so by an act of consciousness. As the sadist said to the masochist who asked to be beaten, "I refuse." Man is a futile passion. And women too. All of the maneuvers and manipulations, all of the attempts at domination or submission (Sartre can't seem to conceive of an interpersonal relationship that doesn't have such a dynamic), all of the self-deceptions in the service of becoming the thing-in-itself-for-itself, are acts of *bad faith*. Bad faith is Sartre's version of inauthenticity. It too is ontological, intrinsic to human existence.

Although Sartre cannot give any reason why it is better not to be in bad faith, and indeed bad faith is unavoidable, he is clearly being a moralist whether or not he wishes to be. Even if one cannot escape bad faith, one can cop to it. The ultimate act of good faith is to acknowledge one's bad faith, one's attempts to become the in-itself-for-itself, or one's attempts to fool oneself into thinking one has realized one's project.

Sartre, unlike Heidegger, is an existentialist, and self-consciously so. Existence precedes essence, and self is what self becomes. "Existentialism is a humanism." Since God would be the thing-in-itself-for-itself, there can be no God (presumably, God is bound by the laws of logic and cannot be self-contradictory), and man is alone in the universe. That makes man responsible. There are no external ultimates, no divinely given guidelines, indeed no logically necessary reasons for our actions or choices and no grounding in rationality of our moral choices. This is the sense in which man is "condemned to freedom." It is absurd that we live, that we exist; there is no rational reason for our being here. It is we who give meaning or attempt to give meaning to our lives through our however futile projects. Here we are as far from Hegelian rationalism as it is possible to get. If for Hegel, "the real is rational and the rational real," for Sartre (human) existence is irrational (has no ultimate justification or sufficient cause), and that irrationality is the essence (pardon the word) of (human) existence.

Sartrian freedom does not ignore or deny the causal nexus of the world. What Sartre calls my *facticity*, the givenness of my situation and of my body, is "real" enough, but in no way diminishes my freedom. In a sense, the givens of my life are contingent, have no sufficient reason, or simply are, and in that sense, self is radical contingency. But neither the facticity nor the contingency of human existence changes the fact that I choose, choose a project however unconsciously (Sartre doesn't believe in the unconscious, saying this is a self-contradictory notion; however, he does say that consciousness is not necessarily awareness which seems to me a distinction without a difference) and makes moral choices that cannot be justified, let alone be entailed by universal norms. Sartre's example of the the son with a sick mother who wants to join the Resistance and who tries to apply Kant's categorical imperative to make a decision illustrates perfectly the uselessness of looking outside the self for moral justification. Using Kant's criterion, can I choose fighting tyranny for all humans? Yes. Can I choose protecting sick mothers for all humanity? Yes. The categorical imperative doesn't help. So here is another sense in which the self is condemned to be free. Moral choice has no ultimate, external justification and is not determined by the "moral law within." There are no moral laws. The consciousness that is nothingness cannot escape its freedom, although it can, in an infinite variety of acts of bad faith, attempt to do so. In a sense, Sartre's analysis of the radical freedom of the self that gives meaning to facticity and contingency is not very different from Kant's assertion that "man as phenomenon is determined, while man as noumenon is free," yet they are utterly disparate. Kant is writing from an Enlightenment perspective that the world is intelligible, that its rationality can be understood by the human mind, however unknowable the thing-in-itself. The freedom of the self as noumena makes morality possible and makes human beings responsible, but in no way lessens the objectivity, the reality, of the moral law within. Sartre is writing during a total eclipse of the moral law, during the glorification of irrationality and brute force and in the face of torture and murder, and whatever his technical philosophical reason for describing the freedom of the self as he does, it is a self living in the midst of hideous evil and constant crisis. Sartrian freedom has a grandeur that also has a quality of desperation. It is a magnificent no to the Gestapo, to the torturers, to the murderers, to the collaborators, and to bourgeois complacency; it is also a cosmically lonely, intrinsically frustrated, interpersonally conflicted awareness of the impossibility of knowing why we are here, what we should do, and who we should be by appeal to anything—religion, ideology, or love—outside of self. It is indeed a self *condemned* to be free.

Sartre also wrote of an existential psychoanalysis that would not analyze in a deterministic way the forces driving patients into symptoms and pathological behavior, but rather would try and make the patients aware of their bad faith and of their avoidance and denials of their radical freedom and the responsibility that that entails, as well as to bring to full awareness the patient's basic project. It is a psychoanalysis that does not recognize a structural unconscious, but that acknowledges that all is not in awareness. On its more psychological side, the in-itself is presented as a viscous, sticky stuff that envelops and engulfs. For Sartre, it seems identified with femininity, while the for-itself is illumination, penetration, space, and openness and is identified with masculinity. Here the impossibility of the in-itself-for-itself becomes the impossibility of successful union of man and woman, which is also implied in the dialectic of the struggle to turn the other into an in-itself for one's for-itself. Sadomasochism is the human lot, and denial of it is bad faith.

One cannot help but wonder how Sartre negotiated the developmental stage of separation-individualization (see Chapter 12). Is the radical disjunction of in-itself and for-itself and the radical freedom of for-itself a theorization of a phobic fear-wish for a (re-)fusion experience? Is there hidden in Sartre, under all that forbidding Hegelian language, a terror of the seductive pull of merger and a defense against it? The psychoanalyst in me wants to say, "Tell me more about your mother." Of course, the truth value of a theory is not to be judged by its emotional origins, but still the man does protest too much, and one wonders why.

In the famous passage in Sartre's novel *Nausea* (1938/1964), the hero Roquentin is gazing at the gnarled, twisted, overly elaborated roots of a giant tree and becomes nauseated at its sheer excess; it is *de trop*—too much. All this messy organicity, all this viscosity, may trap me. The organic world is like quicksand, and my reaction to it is nausea. This is "the world is too much with us" with a vengeance.

Sartre had an ambivalent and highly conflicted lifelong relationship with the Communist party, and his late technical philosophy tried to reconcile Marxism and existentialism. Sartre's Marxism is the search of the for-itself for connectedness, for human solidarity in the face of its ineluctable need to reduce others to objects. The closest to good faith that human beings can come is through "engagement" in the human struggle to be (externally) free. There is no reason to engage rather than to be disengaged, and it would be bad faith to pretend that there is. But to be engaged is to have a project that is freely chosen. I recall Raymond Kablansky, one of my philosophy professors at McGill University in the 1960s, telling his ethics class of a friend who voluntarily returned to occupied Europe to help others escape. He was caught by the Gestapo, tortured, and killed. Professor Kablansky, who was a European refugee, asked, "Who was more free, he who returned to die or I who did not and am sitting here?" Who indeed? The professor's friend was engaged.

Although I am not competent to judge the matter, most critics feel that Sartre failed in his attempt to reconcile Marxism and existentialism. After a period of being the leading intellectual in France, Sartre fell out of fashion. Old and ill, he remained independent and courageous in politics, breaking with the Communist party over the Soviet occupation of Hungary, criticizing the French involvement in Algeria, and attempting to enter into some sort of alliance with the student rebels of the 1960s. He was supported to the end by his lifelong companion, Simone de Beauvoir. Theirs was a relationship marked by spectacular mutual infidelities that did not seem to interfere with a more basic fidelity. Sartre felt that marriage was a bourgeois hypocrisy and, for this reason alone, would not have married.

Sartre left us a new notion of the self, a notion of self as almost unbearably responsible, as tragically unfulfilled, as without essence or justification, as radically contingent, as inevitably and ineluctably free, as a giver of meaning to absurdity, and as unavoidably in flight through acts of bad faith from these realities. It is a self not without nobility. More than any of our other theorists about self, Sartre, with whatever romantic adolescent posturing, pinpoints the ultimate aloneness of the self, with its essence consciousness (including self-consciousness) separating and alienating it from the world, from itself, and from others.

RONALD (R. D.) LAING:
THE ONTOLOGICALLY INSECURE SELF

R. D. Laing (1927–1989) was a Scottish psychiatrist and psychoanalyst who became a student counterculture hero in the 1960s and 1970s. While difficult to classify, Laing was deeply influenced by Continental thought, in particular by Sartre's existentialism and by phenomenological psychiatry, yet he was clearly part of the English object relations school of psychoanalysis. Laing's interest was largely in psychosis. He came to see the madness in what is usually called sanity and the sanity in some forms of madness. He was exquisitely sensitive to the ways in which people are driven mad and pioneered the study of the family dynamics of psychotics. Although in danger of romanticizing mental illness, he saw some things that are clearly true. When he asks who is crazier, the mental patient who believes that the atom bomb is within her or the statesman who prepares to drop the bomb and the societies who support atomic saber-rattling, we cannot ignore his question. Laing founded a refuge for seriously disturbed young people called Locksley Hall. It was a cross between a crash pad, a half-way house, and a commune. Its residents tried to talk out their conflicts in an atmosphere of total acceptance.

The sanity in madness lies both in the unexpected insights the "mad" sometimes have and in the "sense" that their madness makes in the context of their lives. They are psychotic because their psychosis is the only way they can protect whatever residual sense of self they have. The relatives (usually parents) of Laing's young patients described their descent into illness as a progression from "sad to bad to mad." They could not understand their children's madness or their part in causing it, nor could they see the desperate attempt at vitality in their children's "badness." Laing could and did. His treatment essentially consisted in affirmation of the sense of the patients' world view. He saw psychiatry as all too frequently the agent of a crazy society rather than as an ally of the patient's struggle for affirmation, transcendence, and ecstasy. In an era where psychosis is officially understood as genetically transmitted neurochemical deficit, Laing's exploration of the inner world of his patients and of the relationship between their experience with others, particularly in the family early in life, and those inner worlds is salutary. Even if the organicists are right and psychosis is a neurological and neurochemical illness, the people who become psychotic grow up in families, and the dynamics of those families profoundly affect the manifestation of that neurochemistry.

Laing is very much a self theorist. For him, psychopathoplogy is self-pathology. Illness is the outcome of the self's struggle to preserve its autonomy in a situation that would deny and destroy that autonomy. Unfortunately, the life-saving (in the sense of the psychic life) defense itself self-limits, deforms, and diminishes the very self it is invoked to save. Laing is the first of our theorists about self who is frankly normative, who distinguishes between the healthy and the pathological self. For Freud, illness and health are on a continuum, and the neurotic self differs merely in the degree of conflict, dissociation, and repression from the healthy self. Structurally they are the same. Not so for Laing. The schizoid self is structurally different from the neurotic or healthy self. The essential differences lie in *ontological security* or the lack of it. The ontologically secure self is certain of its existence, of its differentiation from the world and from others, of its aliveness, of its realness, and of its embeddedness in the body. The ontologically secure self is a bodily self. The ontologically insecure are not like this at all. Their existence is in question; their autonomy, continuity, and identity are precarious; their hold on reality is tenuous; and their experience of emptiness and deadness is of the essence of their selfhoood. More saliently, they experience themselves as disembodied. Their selves are not coextensive or importantly coextensive with their bodies; they are not who they seem. The experience of disembodiment and of having a "real" self that is different from the self that speaks, acts, and behaves is more than an extreme of a "normal" self-experience, although the normal self-experience can encompass all of the above states; rather, it is a structurally different self. To have a self that is disembodied is to be ontologically insecure in a way that the embodied self that has an "out-of-body" experience is not. It is to live in a state of perpetual fear of engulfment, implosion, and petrification. Engulfment is fear of losing self in other; implosion is fear growing out of the sensation of inner emptiness, fear of shattering, of breaking into pieces; while petrification, which Laing adopted from Sartre, is fear of being turned into a thing by the gaze of the other. The ontologically insecure person cannot win. The dreads of engulfment, implosion, and petrification lead to schizoid defenses of detachment, distancing, posturing, posing, isolation, and avoidance. The result is estrangement, alienation, and cosmic loneliness. There is no possibility of "being alone together" as the best human relationships make possible; there is only "being alone alone." The ontologically insecure self is caught between the terror of being destroyed by the other and the terror of absolute aloneness. Whether or not one is ontologically secure or ontologically insecure is largely determined by one's experience with other people. That is why Laing's theory of self is an object-relational as well as an existential theory of self, object relations being the internal representations of interpersonal relations. Some childhoods lead to the formation of a false self to protect the real self, which goes into hiding or is "dead." Those are the childhoods that result in ontologically insecure selves. Laing took the concept of the false self from Winnicott, an English psychiatrist whom we shall meet in the next chapter.

Now for the first time we have a theory of self that does not describe a self that has certain lineaments, certain characteristics, certain properties that are invariant, and that are the same for all selves. Each of the philosophical, metaphysical, phenomenological, or psychological selves adumbrated by the earlier self theorists was abstract in this sense. Even in developmental theories, that development of self was described in universal terms. Not so for Laing. The Laingian self is concrete; its structure and its subjective experience of itself are the products of its particulars, unique and individual interactions with parents and siblings. The kind of self that results makes sense in light of the particular person's struggle to maintain psychic aliveness in a particular environment. This is a new notion in the history of self theory. Laing does, of course, delineate the broad categories of the ontologically secure and the ontologically insecure self (a theorist cannot help but abstract), but he never loses sight of the concrete experience of particular lives developing securely or insecurely. He keeps his vision concrete rather than abstract by listening to his patients and trying to see things as they must see them, to see them from their unique standpoint. His is a clinical rather than a theoretical theory, and that is why he can see that not every self is constituted in the same way.

WHITEHEAD AND THE SELF AS PROCESS:
THE SELF AS ORGANISM

Alfred North Whitehead (1861–1947) did not write about the self as such, nor does he comfortably fit into our positivist-analyst/phenomenologist-existentialist dichotomy of 20th-century philosophy. Whitehead does not use the term *self*; rather the self for him is a metaphysical entity within his exceedingly complex cosmological schema, rather than an aspect (physical, mental, or experiential) of, or the totality of, personhood. Whitehead does not fit into the analytic-existential rubric because his mature philosophy is an attempt to give an extremely general account of the universe—of the totality of reality. He variously calls this cosmology and metaphysics. Cosmology is the study of the cosmos (literally of the world) and, by extension, of the universe. Metaphysics is an attempt to describe the "ultimate" nature of reality. It is roughly interchangeable with ontology, but its connotation is of something broader. An old Elaine May-Mike Nichols routine comes to mind. She plays an awed ingenue attending a lecture by the learned Herr Doktor Professor. He says, "Today I vil speak upon the universe," upon which she asks, "Why the universe, Professor?" He replies, "Vat else is there to talk about?" The term *metaphysics* is an artifact of the arrangement of Aristotle's lecture notes by his pupils after his death. The lectures on ultimates were placed after the lectures on nature (*phusis*), hence *metaphysics*, after or beyond the nature lectures. The exact order of the lectures has been forgotten, but the notion of metaphysics, that which is beyond physics, antecedent to that science, has remained. Whitehead is very much a metaphysician in this sense. A mathematician, he had a consummate knowledge of mathematical physics and used that knowledge to construct a conceptual scheme of the maximum generality that would be able to account for the data and constructs of not only physics, but also of history, aesthetic experience, and religion. Plato wrote in the first comprehensive cosmology, the *Timaeus* (1961c), that the function of such a cosmology was to "save the phenomenon" (i.e., to give an account of, an explanation of, that which appears). That is exactly what Whitehead tries to do. As a metaphysician in an antimetaphysical era, Whitehead, his techical work in mathematical logic excepted, is out of the mainstream of 20th-century philosophy. In fact, his influence has been far greater on theologians than on professional philosophers.

Why, then, include a cosmologist among our thinkers about self? There are several reasons: first, Whitehead's analysis of two errors in thought which he calls the *fallacy of misplaced concreteness* and the *fallacy of simple location* has great relevance to the clarification and possible resolution of the paradoxes of the self and the discrepant accounts of self we have encountered. Furthermore, his account of perception in what he calls a "mode of causal efficacy" illuminates our experience of the agency of the self; and perhaps most important, his notion that the "process is the reality" and his elaboration and specification of it in what he calls "the philosophy of organism" may give us a way of understanding our sense of ongoingness and continuity in the face of mutability and flux and a way to give an account of a self that is not the same self from moment to moment, yet remains the same self. Whitehead is a difficult author who eludes summary, but I shall try to give a reasonably clear rendering of those of his notions that are relevant to self theory.

Whitehead was born into a clerical family in a peaceful, backwater town replete with a medieval church and town green not far from the Thames. It was an environment of Victorian respectability and rectitude. The Whiteheads were solidly upper middle class, and it was assumed that Alfie would take his place in the upper clergy or in the professions. Although Whitehead was born shortly after Freud and lived through the same period, two less similar lives, sets of assumptions or environments would be hard to imagine. The Whiteheads were apparently not warm. If Alfred had strong feelings toward his mother, he left us no record of them; his relationship with his father and brothers was warmer and closer. There was a conservative side to Whitehead's character, beliefs, and values that separated him from his early collaborator, Bertrand Russell, and is reflected in his return to a theistic metaphysics, albeit a highly unorthodox one.

Whitehead left his stable and secure, if emotionally tepid, world to attend a 1,200-year-old public (i.e., private) school. Again, he was in a highly provincial setting that paradoxically had direct ties to the world of power. As he comments, he knew men who became the rulers of the British Empire or the leaders of its professional class at a time when the sun didn't set on that empire. It was a world that was to cease to exist by the time Whitehead developed his philosophy of organism. The same was true of his intellectual world: the seemingly immutable truths of Newtonian physics that he learned were to prove totally inadequate as ultimate explanations of the nature of things during his lifetime. The collapse of these "certainties" profoundly influenced him. At school, Whitehead excelled at mathematics and sports. He became the head prefect, the student leader of the school. A kindly man, he wrote half a lifetime later how upset he had been, in his capacity as head prefect, to have to flog a student who had committed theft. Whitehead went on to Cambridge University, eventually joining the faculty as a mathematics tutor—again, a part of a parochial yet highly privileged and influential society. He married a woman whose flamboyant, sometimes histrionic, and sometimes hypochondriacal behavior complemented his staid, placid temperament. His union with Evelyn was a happy one. Although Whitehead published well-regarded mathematical works, his work was not earth-shattering. His collaboration with his erstwhile student, Bertrand Russell, changed that. Together they produced the *Principia*, already discussed in our examination of Russell, in which they were able to deduce all of arithmetic and algebra from a few simple notions, such as conjunction, disjunction, and implication. The reduction of mathematics to logic had philosophical as well as mathematical implications. Its enduring influence on Whitehead resided in the notion that science requires a foundation—that there is something more ultimate. Just as the *Principia* founded mathematics on logic, the philosophy of organism provided physics and science in general with such a foundation—at least such was Whitehead's intention. During his years at Cambridge, Whitehead had accumulated an extensive library of theology, which he ultimately sold, deciding that it was all worthless gibberish. Thus, in his middle years, he shared Russell's atheism—however, without Russell's passion and polemical verve.

Whitehead's middle years were troubled ones; he suffered from chronic insomnia and apparently a considerable degree of neurotic conflict and depression. Since Whitehead was reticent and not in the least self-revealing, we can't be sure what his midlife crisis was about: perhaps the loss of religious faith, along with the collapse of what seemed a certain account of the physical world with the discoveries of relativity and quantum mechanics, had shattered a basic security. His mature thought as expressed in his philosophy of organism can be seen as an attempt to reconcile, by encompassing both in a broader synthesis, science and religion. The God Whitehead returned to was certainly the "God of the philosophers" rather than the "God of Abraham, Isaac, and Jacob," but a God nevertheless.

Although Whitehead was a liberal—active in politics and a courageous supporter of women's rights at a time when that was not fashionable—and greatly admired Russell's intellect, he did not share Russell's political and social radicalism, or his pacifism. Some biographers think that Russell had an affair with Whitehead's wife, but if that is so, Whitehead managed not to know it. Whitehead was in his 40s by the time the third volume of the *Principia* appeared, and by then a professor. For reasons somewhat similar to Wittgenstein's a generation later, Whitehead resigned his post. Both men found Cambridge too insular and ultimately stultifying. Undoubtedly there were also personal reasons that remain a mystery.

Whitehead moved to the University of London, where he became an educational administrator pioneering in what we would now call adult education. Instead of participating in the education of an elite, he was one of the leaders of an institution serving the lower middle and working classes. An educational theorist as well as educator, he was in a way returning to the family tradition of the clergyman-educator. His experiences in London broadened him. Whitehead lost a son, an aviator, in World War I. It profoundly saddened him, and it is said that his wife never recovered from the loss. He may have had this son in mind when he wrote that one of the difficulties of youth is that it has "no memory of disaster survived." Whitehead was in his 60s when he left London to become a professor of philosophy at Harvard. It was there that he publisheand *Science in the Modern World* (1925), *Process and Reality* (1929), and *Adventures of Ideas* (1933), the works for which he is remembered. Whitehead was highly successful at Harvard; a beloved teacher, he died a revered wisdom figure. His reputation has suffered greatly since his death, and except for the *Principia*, which is not much read, he tends to be dismissed by academic philosophy. That is unfortunate. Suspicious of "final truths" and of dogmas of all sorts, Whitehead characteristically stated, "The universe is vast." His system is an attempt at a tentative illumination of that vastness. It rejects nothing and attempts, in the face of Whitehead's knowledge that it is not possible, to encompass everything.

Let us start with his analysis of perception. Characteristically, his approach is historical, looking at attempts to understand perception in the philosophical tradition, seeking out the limitations and blind spots, and only then developing what he hopes is a more adequate account. In this sense, Whitehead's method of philosophizing is a dialogue with his great predecessors—in this case, with Hume and with Kant. In Whitehead's reading of them, both Hume and Kant see only one mode of perception, one that Whitehead denoted *presentational immediacy*, and mistakenly regard it as primary when in fact it is a symbolization, not a direct cognition. Presentational immediacy gives us a *display*, almost in the sense of a computer display. It is vivid, colored, sharply defined, at a distance, and representational. It is also cold, empty, and intrinsically meaningless. It is a projection of a bodily state. Sight is a paradigmatic exemplification of presentational immediacy. There are no internal connections, no necessary connections between the bright bits of color or the sounds or the smells of presentational immediacy. Causal connections are not part of the display. Both Hume and Kant, and their 19th- and 20th-century heirs, take presentational immediacy as primary and ask, Where do the connections come from? Each, in his own way, put the connection inside us, made it subjective, Hume, by the appeal to custom and habit, and Kant, by the categories of the understanding. According to Whitehead, both Hume and Kant and the philosophical traditions emanating from them erred in taking a highly specialized, high-level phenomenon—presentational immediacy—as primary, when in fact it is the privileged possession of higher level organisms in their moments of maximum consciousness. Presentational immediacy is never so effective as in a state of alertness. It has been built into the higher organisms in the course of evolution because its symbolizations and their interpretations, although fallible, have, on the average, survival value. It is an instrument of great practical utility but not necessarily the best source of insight into the ultimate nature of things, not the best tool with which to do metaphysics. If we limit ourselves to presentational immediacy, the events of the world have only external connections, if any; it reveals no intrinsic linkages or causal sequences. It simply displays that which is contemporaneous. Not so for what Whitehead calls *causal efficacy*. Causal efficacy is just as much a mode of perception as is presentational immediacy. In fact, it is more basic in the sense that it characterizes lower grade organisms and dimmer states of consciousness. It is causal efficacy, not presentational immediacy, that is the preeminent mode of perception in the sense that it gives us our experience of the causal nexus, which is the world. It is the source of our sense of the power of things, of their ability to impinge on us, of their agency and activity. As such, it has great survival value, and it too was built in by the evolutionary process. We get our experience of causal efficacy by defocusing; it is vaguer, more premonitory, more likely to be felt in the dark, in states of semiconsciousness as upon awakening, or in the hypnagogic state preceding sleep. It is the sensation that there are powers around us, and that they can act on us, that they have causal efficacy. The paradigmatic case of causal efficacy is the sense of the brooding presence of things in a dimly lit room as we emerge from sleep. Somewhere Whitehead says that the data of philosophy, at least of cosmological metaphysics, must include all of our experiences, waking and sleeping, going to sleep and awakening, rational and insane, scientific and religious, ill and well, sharply focused and dimly perceived, highly abstract and irredeemably concrete, and brute fact and flight of fancy. All are grist for the philosopher's mill. To ignore any aspect of human experience is to philosophize with less than a full deck, and Whitehead implicitly criticizes philosophers for having done so. The notion of a mode of perception like causal efficacy comes from attention to these philosophically neglected aspects of experience. Whitehead points out that if the causal nexus were to be found in the mode of presentational immediacy, it should be revealed by the highest magnification and the most intense illumination, but the opposite is the

case. The vivid is the most disconnected; it provides (potentially) aesthetic pleasure but not a demonstration of the power of events to affect one another. That is
only revealed in the philosophically disavowed, vague, dim, unfocused, lower
level experience of the power of things to affect us. Whitehead's turning to the
philosophically disreputable is reminiscent of Freud's and psychoanalysis's attention to the "sordid" details of life, and to such "unscientific" data as dreams and
jokes. Is Whitehead right? Do we perceive in the mode of causal efficacy? His
appeal is to direct experience. Have you had such sensations of the power of your
surround to act on you? If so, there is no reason to make any mode of perception
privileged and to discard and ignore this one. If we take into account all of our
direct experience, the problem of causality, in the sense that necessary connection
is nowhere to be found in "objective" experience and must be supplied subjectively, disappears.

The mode of causal efficacy makes us aware of the *withness of the body*, that I
see with my eyes, hear with my ears, smell with my nose, and taste with my
palate. The withness of the body is primordial, given in direct experience. Is that
true? Are you in contact with seeing with your eyes when you see? Is that a direct
experience? I think it is, at least when I make an effort to focus on something, but
does that direct experience validate the existence of a mode of perception in which
the causal efficacy of things, events, and powers is a given? I am not sure, but be
that as it may, Whitehead has put the proprioceptive sensations of our sense organs
in action (presumably the source of the direct experience of the withness of the
body) at the center of our experience of causal power. Perhaps he is not talking
about proprioceptive perceptions, of movement of the eye muscles, and so forth,
but of some other direct experience. If so, it is difficult to conceptualize. One is
reminded of William James's (who greatly influenced Whitehead) self of selves as
the subliminal sensation of the glottal movements of the muscles between the head
and the body. Both James's self of selves and Whitehead's witness of the body
suggest, in somewhat different senses and in a different way than Freud, that "the
ego [self] is first and foremost a bodily ego [self]." Furthermore, the entire notion
of the perceptual mode of causal efficacy has implications for self theory. The self
in the mode of presentational immediacy has aspects of the Cartesian *cogito*; the
cogito's cognitions are in the realm of presentational immediacy, albeit, in the
initial stage of radical doubt, without symbolic reference to an external world. It is
also a spectator in the Humeian theater that doesn't exist, the data of presentational
immediacy being the show in that theater. While on the contrary, the self in the
mode of causal efficacy is an interactive self, having direct experience of its power
to causally affect (act on) its own body and the world and of the world's power to
causally affect (act on) it. It is a self that is a part of the stream that is the process
that is the universe. It is radically different from the *cogito* as thought "bifurcated," to use Whitehead's word, from the world of extension. Whitehead's entire
analysis of perception (and indeed his metaphysics) is importantly shaped and
determined by his critique of Descartes's bifurcation of nature into thinking substance and extended substance, a bifurcation partly resultant from solely focusing
on the vacuous display in the mode of presentational immediacy of the realm of
extension (if there be one) in the cognition of the solipsistic subject to the neglect
of the mode of causal efficacy, which would reveal in direct experience the connectedness, even perhaps the oneness in manyness, of thought, thinker, and world.
As we shall see, the Whiteheadian self itself is a living organic unity whose flow is

interactive with the flow that is the reality of the other real things in the universe. This way of looking at self has complex derivatives in Whitehead, but his analysis of perception is one of them.

Perception is not the exclusive property of higher organisms like man, although the perceptual mode of presentational immediacy is. Perception in the mode of causal efficacy is the property of all "actual occurrences," the ultimate "real objects" of the universe. Whitehead's universe is a universe of organisms interactive with one another. Such perception does not necessarily involve consciousness. There are grades of awareness and of self-consciousness in the *real entities*, or *real events* that are Whitehead's *ontos on* (ultimate being). This will be further elucidated, I hope, in our discussion of Whitehead's metaphysics, but for now I would like to point out, as Whitehead himself does, the similarity of his notion to Liebniz's (the 17th-century philosopher and mathematician) concept of *monads*, the ultimate real entities that constitute reality for him. Liebniz's monads are also organic unities, although more immaterial substance than process and strikingly similar to Whitehead's ultimates, events. They too have different levels of awareness (consciousness). They differ by being substances rather than events and by being "windowless." They are not interactive, but coordinate because God has created their "preestablished harmony." In a sense, each is a clock wound up and set to run in harmony, in coordination with each other. They do not "perceive" each other, they only act as if they did. Whitehead's events do have windows, and the model for those windows is human perception, especially perception in the mode of causal efficacy.

Perhaps a more interesting parallel, and one that neither man was aware of, is that between Whitehead's modes of perception and the psychoanalytic developmental psychologist Rene Spitz's distinction between *co-enesthetic sensing* and *diacritic perception*. Spitz is best known for his work on *hospitalism*. Babies removed from London during the B-2 attacks in World War II and raised in institutions where their physical needs were met, but where they were not held or fondled, sickened and even died. Love turns out to be a biological as well as a psychological need, and without it, the symptoms of *marasmus*, the loss of vitality and even of life itself, develop. Spitz (1965) went on to conduct some of the first infant observational research and concluded, among other things, that the earliest mode of perception was co-enesthetic sensing, or sensing with (cf. Whitehead's the withness of the body)—experiencing on a level of deep, primarily visceral, global, or totalistic sensibility, which is largely superseded in adult life by the mode of diacritic perception, which is perception at a distance through the specialized sense organs of discrete sensa—colors, sounds, tastes, and smells. The "vague" (a word used by both Spitz and Whitehead) intimations of co-enesthetic sensing (sensing with the mother and with the surround), the vague but powerful awareness of presence, is clearly a close relative of Whitehead's causal efficacy, and diacritic perception is clearly a close relative of presentational immediacy. Spitz believes that those adults who retain the greatest capacity for co-enesthetic sensing are the artists and creative thinkers of the race. Co-enesthetic sensing is the basis of intuition and of feelings of connectedness and interaction—of causal efficacy. It is preeminently an affective mode of perception, while the diacritic is preeminently a cognitive mode. Feelings rather than high-level abstract thinking give us our most intimate and veridical experience of the ultimate nature of things, that experience being grounded in the experience of connectedness, indeed, of oneness with mother, as well as apartness and separation from her. Whitehead could not agree more with the importance of this vague affective sensing as a guide to ultimates. The bridge between the co-enesthetic and the diacritic is the experience of being held on the breast with nipple in mouth and looking at Mother's face. The vague, richly affective sensations of tactile merging with Mother are coordinated with the more cognitive presentation at a distance through sight of Mother's face. Affect is the bridge. Whitehead too writes of the interaction of the two modes of perception, but it was Spitz who found the biological, developmental linkage in the nursing experience. Thus, Whitehead's bimodal theory of perception finds support in psychoanalytic developmental psychology.

Whitehead also wrote of two cognitive errors characteristic of much of Western thought. He called them the "fallacy of misplaced concreteness" and the "fallacy of simple location," respectively. In a sense, both stem from the naive and uncritical assumption that the subject-predicate syntax of the Indo-European languages is isomorphic to, and an adequate guide to, reality and its ultimate nature. Like Wittgenstein, but with a different emphasis, Whitehead is trying to free us from "the bewitchment of language." The subject-predicate distinction imported from grammar to logic and metaphysics at least as far back as Aristotle has been the basis of Western philosophical thinking until the recent past. Aristotelian logic has been under assault in various ways at least since Hegel's development of a triadic dynamic logic. Whitehead's immediate predecessors in this regard were William James in such works as "Does Consciousness Exist?" and Henri Bergson. Subject-predicate syntax and its philosophical derivatives see reality as comprising some sort of solid stuff—substance—that has enduring qualities, attributes, or characteristics that somehow adhere in that enduring substance. Substances and their accidents, (i.e., individual characteristics) are the ultimate. The idea of an underlying substance that is the permanent substrate of the surface flux of things stems from the pre-Socratic Greek philosopher Thales's statement that "all things are water," water being the permanent underlying substrate. Thales's water becomes Anaxamander's air; Empedocles' air, earth, water, and fire; and Democritus's atoms. In one way or another, the basic model of underlying stable stuff of some sort having qualities that endure "beneath" or "behind" the ever-changing surface resurfaces repeatedly in the history of philosophy, each time having weathered intermittent criticisms until the late 19th century, when new developments in physics made it a more dubious "account of what appears." Whitehead is concerned to lay it to rest once and for all.

Aristotle understood process as the resultant of four forces or causes, which he called the material cause, the formal cause, the efficient cause, and the final cause. Western scientific thought and its philosophical derivates largely dispense with final causes, with the teleological, with the idea that things happen because of some ultimate purpose or design, God's plan or what have you, but retain the other Aristotelian causal entities in one form or another. In our thinkers about self, only Jung incorporated final causes as a part of his ontological description of self. Whitehead retains the notion of final cause in his metaphysics, but radically reinterprets material and formal cause. Aristotle's material causes, underlying permanent stuffs, become events and energy undergoing transformation, while Aristotle's formal causes—the universals embedded and embodied in particulars, which is his version of the Platonic forms—become Whitehead's *eternal objects*, permanent potentialities that exist nowhere until they appear in actual occurrences. They are omnipossible but only actual when they occur, unlike Platonic ideas or forms, which always and everywhere exist and from which particular things take their reality. Efficient causes are causes in the ordinary sense of cause (A causes B), ubiquitously present in scientific explanation and uncritical common sense. Naive realism, Hume's devastating critique notwithstanding, is very much alive. Whitehead is to preserve the notion of efficient cause, invoking as evidence the perceptual mode of causal efficacy as a source of direct experience of that causality. Hume's critique becomes irrelevant, since it is based on the assumption that presentational immediacy is the only mode of perception. Of course Whitehead is aware that the subject-predicate mode of construing reality has great pragmatic utility, that it is a rough-and-ready yet adequate guide to action, and that is why it is incarnated in the syntax of ordinary language. Like Newtonian physics, it is not so much untrue as true only under restricted circumstances; it is adequate for many purposes, but is of insufficient generality to be a useful tool in metaphysics, the most general account of what is. The Newtonian physics that Whitehead learned in his youth turned out not to be an eternal verity as had been thought, but the description of a special case, albeit one of great practical import to humans. Ordinary language, with its simultaneous imprecision and overgeneralization, also turns out to be a veridical guide to a special case, again one of great practical utility, but not a veridical guide to insight into the ultimate nature of things. The *Principia*, the chief work of Whitehead's youth, is an implicit critique of language for its imprecision and an attempt to derive a more precise mathematical language, while the philosophical work of Whitehead's maturity can be understood as a critique of language for the misleading consequences of its generalizations to a description of the universe. In this prelude to my discussion of Whitehead's analysis of linguistic fallacies, I have virtually summarized his metaphysics, which must seem odd. But it is not; rather, it is a consequence of the seamless web of Whitehead's thought. If one understands his analysis of perception and of language, one already understands his metaphysics. The ultimate connectedness of the universe is reflected in the connectedness of his thought.

The fallacy of misplaced concreteness is the error of eating the menu instead of the steak (or these days, the menu instead of the sushi). It is mistaking our abstractions for the individual concrete existents, or mistaking conceptual analyses for the realities. One of Whitehead's examples is the empirical tradition from Hume on, mistakenly taking discrete *quala* (individual sense experiences) for the givens of perception, when they are not. To the contrary, they are the products of high-level intellectualization, of the conceptual analyses of perceptual givens, and of then wondering how these discrete *quala* can mean anything or be interactive or interconnected in any way and reaching a skeptical conclusion. The whole problem is a pseudoproblem, arising from an error of misplaced concreteness. The same is true of the whole question of how qualities adhere in substances. We take substance, either naively from the grammatical structure of our language, or sophisticatedly, from the high-level abstract reasoning of philosophy as a given, as a concrete reality when it is not. In Whitehead's view, a good deal of philosophical error and puzzlement comes from taking our abstractions from the concrete givens of experience as the concrete things themselves. Symbol systems are not the symbolized. To abstract is to take away from, to strip down. Accordingly, abstractions tend to be bare, and a metaphysics based on mistaking abstractions for direct experiences ineluctably results in a picture and understanding of reality that lacks meaning and in which connectedness and causal sequence is problematical.

In the case of the self, the self as a static, substantial "thing," an entity, is an abstraction—the product of extensive intellectual analysis, not a given. To mistake this abstraction for the reality lands us in the pseudoquandary of how the ever-changing, evolving, mutable self can be the same self. There is no same self; that is our abstraction. There is only the self in flux. The self is that flux, albeit with relatively enduring patterning that itself changes. We look at the self "cross-sectionally," as a slice in the temporal flow, and wonder how the succession of such slices relate to one another. There are no such slices; they are products of thought, thought that freezes process and turns it into a thing. It is a case of misplaced concreteness, of eating the menu. Looking at our usual notion of self to determine if we are mistaking abstraction for experience frees us to see that the self is flow, is process, and that our experience of ongoingness is just as primordial as our experience of change. Neither requires a "substantial" self in any of its variations to account for either the ongoingness or the mutability. Both are primordially given.

The fallacy of simple location is the error of assuming that events are things that exist only at a place specifiable by a system of coordinates, when the reality is that events are field phenomena in the same way in which electromagnetic events are field phenomena. They are in fact emanating throughout the universe. It is the pebble-in-the-pond phenomenon. Its waves radiate asymptotically throughout space time. Not only, as in Heidegger's concept of self as *Dasein*, do I have the world at hand, I am the energy radiating from my epicenter into that world. Seen in the light of the error of simple location, the dilemma of how self interacts on world and world on self becomes a pseudodilemma. I am my interactions with the universe and the universe's interactions with me. Skin is no longer a boundary of self. Self is energy and patterns of energy emanating from a center that can be specified in a coordinate system, but is not, or not simply or only, that epicenter. Whitehead is not saying that boundaries are not important, or do not have pragmatic utility or some sort of reality, but rather that boundary phenomena are restricted special cases, abstractions, of a concrete reality that is the emanation of patterned energy. Just as Whitehead's category of misplaced concreteness illuminated and to some extent dissolved the paradox of sameness amidst change across time, giving us a new way of looking at the temporality of *Dasein*, his category of simple location gives us a new way of understanding *Dasein*'s relationship to its surround. The Whiteheadian self is self as flow of relatively but not permanently enduring patterns, and self as not so much embedded as it is interactive energy exchanges. Since for Whitehead space and time are not different "things," not anything apart from events, it is more accurate to say that the self is one of the events comprising space time. From a more restricted, less general standpoint, the self is both a temporal flux and a spatial flow. The latter is a more abstract account than the former; it is further removed from the concrete actual entity.

This brings us to a discussion of Whitehead's metaphysics per se. His is an exceedingly complex system, and I will not attempt to present that complexity but only those aspects of it most salient for a theory of self. According to Whitehead, metaphysics is not a deductive procedure in which truth is inferred from a few apodictically certain premises. That is the way in mathematics, which has seduced and deceived philosophers. What metaphysics should do is to give an extremely general account of experience. "Speculative philosophy is the endeavor to frame a coherent, logical, necessary system of general ideas in terms of which every element of our experience can be interpreted" (Whitehead, 1929, p. 4). Such a system must "save the phenomenon" by giving an account or an interpretation of "brute fact" in which individual brute facts are given context. Since he is not reaching any deductive conclusions that go beyond experience, the trashing of metaphysics by Hume, Kant, and the positivists should not invalidate his procedure.

Whitehead's ultimately real are "actual occurrences," also called "actual entities" and "actual events." Such "a real individual is an organizing activity fusing ingredients into a unity, so that this unity is the reality." Events are interdependent—mutually immanent. Events come into being and then perish. One is reminded of Locke's statement that "time is perpetual perishing," and Whitehead tells us that his philosophy of organism owes much to Locke's *Essay on Human Understanding*. But in perishing, actual occasions are preserved by being "prehended" by other actual occurrences, by new events. The living are alive in virtue of incorporation of the dead. Whitehead calls this *objective immortality*. But all is not determined by the past; there is a "creative advance" of the universe; novelty is real. Shades of William James. The universe strives for vividness and value. What is, is the "consequent nature of God"; the creative advance in novelty is the "primordial nature of God." Whitehead's distinction between the consequent and primordial nature of God is reminiscent of Spinoza's distinction between nature natured and nature naturing, nature natured being the actual, individual, real entities and nature naturing being their ground and their totality. The parallel is inexact. Spinoza is a strict determinist, and Whitehead is not, so his primordial God is the source of creativity and novelty.

An actual occasion is the prehension of its real antecedents, and of *eternal objects*: permanent possibilities waiting to be actualized in actual occurrences. This coming together of antecedents and eternal objects in actual occurrences Whitehead calls *concrescence*. Eternal objects are Whiteheadian, disembodied universals; they do not exist anywhere until they are actualized. Actual occurrences or events prehend each other, so that the universe is a mutual grasping of the contemporaneous, a mutual immanence, and a successive incorporation of those events that are perishing. Thus there is a causal push and a teleological pull.

Self is a "society" of actual occurrences, a patterning of those that are contemporaneous and a patterning of those that are successive. The creative advance of the self is that of coming into being by reaching back and grasping—prehending—that which is perishing, thereby making the dead part of the living. In so doing, the actual occasions that constitute the society that is the self both change (perish) and endure. Thus the self can be the same yet different. The process is the reality. In the course of emergence of new actual occasions, permanent possibilities of organization and of quality come into being as part of that which is prehended by those actual events. Experience is experience of an enduring organism in a world of organisms. Our most immediate environment is constituted by our body, hence the witness of the body. Experience is activity, and Whitehead's self is activity: activity initially aware of its own organism and sequentially of the organisms that constitute the universe. The self is a society of actual occasions, or societies of societies of actual occasions, depending on the level of complexity from which we view it. The self is a real individual and a real individual is an organizing activity fusing ingredients into a unity.

What I find most convincing in this admittedly most animistic metaphysic is the notion of the uptake of the perishing past by the living present so that the paradox of endurance admist change is resolved; the centrality of bodily experience in self-experience; and the patterning that is that which endures in the evolving society of actual occurrences that is self. No longer cut off in schizoid isolation or solipsistic splendor, the self is a monad with windows, wide-open windows, through which the mutuality of the contemporaneous is fully as constitutive as is the unique strand of successive patterned events that is the creative advance—that is us.

Is all this too poetical? Perhaps. Whitehead's metaphysical system with its implicit account of self is almost ineffable; language can't quite catch it. Is the whole thing an old man's attempt to reconstitute the secure world of his youth—secure in its scientific notions, secure in its social relations, and secure in its religious beliefs—in a vague, wordy, barely understandable "system"? Is it an old man's attempt to give himself some solace from the pain of loss so intense that he said that the words of his beloved romantic poets trivialized his feelings after his son's death through a doctrine of objective immortality? Probably all true. Whitehead's system does suffer from vagueness, overcomplexity, wishful thinking, and a yearning and a desire to bring back meaning and significance into a universe where they may not exist. Yet, somehow it *feels* right. The process is the reality. Although the theistic aspects of Whitehead's system are less than convincing, his allover vision of the ongoing process of the individual entities, the actual real events, organized into societies and societies of societies, incorporating, prehending, and radiating their vibratory energetic patterns to each other, makes some kind of sense. The evolving self perpetually perishing and perpetually incorporating that which has perished resonates. It has affinities to William James's stream of consciousness and Freud's ego as the precipitate of abandoned object cathexes. Whitehead's system is a high-level intellectualization derived from his analysis of relativity theory, quantum theory, and the history of philosophy. In the next chapter, I look more microcosmically at the developing human being, seen through the microscope of psychoanalytic scrutiny, and see how the poles of oneness and separateness, of ongoingness and of fragmentation, have been seen by the theorists of the psychoanalytic experience.

12

Contemporary Psychoanalytic Theory: The Self as Developmental

Psychoanalytic theories of the self are developmental theories that trace the emergence of self from some sort of primordial, undifferentiated state, the understanding of which varies among theorists. For a long time, analysis avoided discussion of self because the term carried metaphysical, unscientific connotations. That has changed, and one of the most active of contemporary analytic schools is *self psychology*, which focuses on self rather than on drives or mental structures. A persistent difficulty in analytic *metapsychology* (theoretical formulations) is in providing a "container," an integrator for drives, instincts, dynamics, and structures so that the psychoanalytic self doesn't wind up, like Hume's, a nonself, a bundle of stuff without a cord to tie it together. In tracing the analytic understanding of the self, we will trace the history of analysis, albeit in microcosm.

As we have seen, Freud doesn't use the word *self*, but rather talks about the ego, often confusing the various meanings of ego so we cannot be sure whether he is talking about the psychosomatic self, the person, or an agency of the mind. For all the terminological and more than terminological confusions in Freud's writings about self, he did leave psychoanalysis with a sometimes explicit and sometimes implicit notion of self that is complex and multifaceted. For him the self is not primordial—"an organization as complex as the ego cannot exist from the beginning"—but only develops in the course of maturation. The English analyst Edward Glover (1956) spoke of *ego nuclei* (bits of self experience) that coalesce in the course of development, forming the ego. Although Freud didn't put it that way, his notion isn't very different from Glover's. Glover's "islands of ego [self] experience" correspond to Freud's autoerotic stage of development in which there are affective experiences of pain and pleasure in body parts not yet experienced as integrated into a whole. Although Freud sees the self as developing out of these sensations, he has another notion of the emergence of the self in which the ego develops out of the id in the area of the id's contact with external reality. Here self is equated with the structural ego, not with the person as a whole. There is some confusion here, but the two conceptions are complementary, not in conflict. Self develops out of isolated sensations experienced as mine, albeit before there is a me, and self develops out of the encounter with the external world in which the desire for instinctual (biological) drive discharge and gratification is modified to take into account the constraints of reality. So self first arises from encounter with nonself and the resistance of that nonself (the environment or the world). In short, frustration creates the self. Now Freud has two complementary notions of self-development corresponding to the two meanings of ego: one a maturational one in which there is a progression from autoeroticism (love of isolated body parts and their sensations) to narcissism (love of self) as self coalesces out of these isolated experiences of sensation, and the other in which self arises out of contact with the environment. One is a preprogrammed biological sequence; the other is object relational. I just mentioned narcissism (self-love), and, as we shall see, you can't discuss psychoanalytic theories of the self without discussing psychoanalytic theories of narcissism. The psychoanalytic self is an affective self. It cannot be understood apart from the feeling of that self for itself.

In addition to these developmental notions of self, Freud stressed the origin of self-experience in bodily experience ("the ego is first and foremost a bodily ego"); the building of self through the internalization of others ("the ego is the precipitate of abandoned ego cathexes"); the depth and extent of unconscious determinants of self; and the need for integration of split, repressed, and projected aspects of self into a coherent whole—a task never to be completed.

The early Freud and the early analysts espoused what has been called an "id psychology" that emphasizes repressed drives, desires, wishes, and instincts pressing for discharge and the precarious hold we have on our sexuality and aggression. It is a view of self and of human nature as biologically, not rationally, determined. The late Freud and his successors put more emphasis on the ego, that frail rationalist who tries to mediate between biological pressures, internalized prohibitions, and reality and whose frailty is often exacerbated by the internal saboteur of maladaptive unconscious defenses, maneuvers, and mechanisms that, whatever their original intentions, come to be hindrances rather than helps in getting a modicum of satisfaction out of life. The study of the (structural) ego and its defenses became what is known as *ego psychology*, while the study of the building of an internal world of representations through identification and introjection became what is called the *object relations* school of psychoanalysis. In this chapter, we are going to look at what these ego psychologists and object relations theorists have to say about the self. The psychoanalytic literature is voluminous, and many have contributed theoretical insights and clinical understanding to the psychoanalytic tradition, but we are going to focus on a few main actors: Heinz Hartmann, Edith Jacobson, Margaret Mahler, and Erik Erikson among the ego psychologists and Melanie Klein, Ronald Fairbairn, and Donald Winnicott among the object relations theorists. Otto Kernberg is heir to both ego psychology and object relations theory. We are also going to look at an important recent development in psychoanalysis, the self-psychology of Heinz Kohut, and at the infant observational theorist Daniel Stern.

I return to Freud before leaving him. His self is a construct, the components of which are identification with those we love and bodily sensations. Self is not primordial, but rather is an integration of my sensations and experiences. It is ongoing and developmental.

HEINZ HARTMANN

Heinz Hartmann, whose background was as a biologist, is usually regarded as the father of ego psychology. Hartmann's structural ego is not as weak as Freud's. It has inborn *apparatuses of primary autonomy* that, in healthy development are "conflict free." These autonomous ego apparatuses make possible perception, thinking, judging, memory, language, and intellectual development. They are maturational potentialities that are inborn and that in health at least, are not caught up in the dynamic conflicts of Freudian man. That only occurs in severe psychopathology. This is an ego that is not totally derived from id. In fact,

Hartmann reformulates Freud's developmental sequence, making the first stage the *undifferentiated matrix*. Both ego and id differentiate out of the primal undifferentiated matrix, and id is no longer primordial. Thus, Hartmann harkens back to Hegel and Jung in seeing development as differentiation and integration. Hartmann still has the problem of supplying the ego with energy. He does this with his concept of *neutralization* of drive energy; that is, in normal development, some of the biological energy that serves for the fulfillment of biological needs is neutralized and made available to the ego to do its work. Hartmann doesn't quite say how that happens, and the concept of neutralization remains fuzzy and metaphysical, in the pejorative sense of that word. Be that as it may, Hartmann's structural ego is not nearly as frail as Freud's; it is not derivative from the id, does not attain its energy from it, and has its own autonomous apparatuses that enable it to do the work of *adaptation*, of "fitting into the environment," in such a way that its needs are met with a minimum of conflict.

Hartmann (1958, 1964) developed the notion of self nascent in Freud and clarified some of the confusion caused by Freud's lack of a consistent terminology. Hartmann did this by distinguishing between *self, self-representation,* and *ego*. For Hartmann, *self* is one's—yours or mine—bodily and mental existence. It is what I see in the mirror and my stream of consciousness insofar as I identify it as mine; I recognize you as a self because I see your body and dialogue with your mind. The self is something that exists in the world and is public, or at least potentially so. Not so my *self-representation*. It is neither my body nor my mind; rather, it is my mental representation of them. My self-representation is a construct around which I organize experience. It is related to but not identical with the empirical psychological notion of a self-concept, which is operationalized as various forms of self-description: adjective checklist, Q sort, and the like. The self-concept is conscious or preconscious, while Hartmann's self-representation can be dynamically unconscious (i.e., unavailable to consciousness because of psychological defense). For example, one's goodness or badness may be unavailable to consciousness because awareness of them would be too threatening. So Hartmann's self-representations may be conscious, preconscious, or dynamically unconscious. There may be more than one self-representation, and these competing self-representations are not necessarily consistent. Hartmann's *ego* is Freud's system ego, that is, the ego as an agency of the mind, but with important differences: being stronger and more autonomous.

The environment and the organism's adaptation to it are stressed much more by Hartmann than by Freud. In Hartmann's view, the neonate comes into the world equipped to "fit into" the "average expectable environment." In spite of the forbidding terminology, the average expectable environment is Mother, an ordinary, "good enough" mother, and Hartmann, the ego psychologist, becomes something of an object relations theorist in stressing the interactive nature of ego development.

Hartmann's clarification of self, self-representation, and ego is salutary, and subsequent psychoanalytic literature is indebted to him. Furthermore, his notion of the self-representation is original and has borne fruit. It is, however, not unproblematic. Psychoanalytic theory will go on to build an entire (internal) *representational* world. But where do these representations live? In my head? In my mind? (Note the inevitability of spatial metaphors in discussing the self.) What is their mode of being? Clearly, they are cognitive structures of a sort: cognitive structures that serve to organize experience and are, in that way, like Kantian categories or Piaget's conceptual schemata that both shape and are shaped by experience. This is a notion that has great intuitive appeal. I have a not necessarily conscious notion, idea, or representation of me that I can potentially make conscious and articulate, and this notion, idea, or representation is constitutive of my experience. It influences how I act, how I respond to others, and how I relate to myself.

I like the notion of self-representation as a constituent gestalt, as a cognitive structure that both assimilates and accommodates (shapes experience and is shaped by it), but I am not quite sure how self-representations subsist. As an explanatory hypothesis or a theoretical construct, mental representations, including self-representations, are heuristically powerful; they account for much data about the experience of self, but Hartmann (and I) want to say that the self-representation is more than, or different from, a theoretical construct and to say that, in some sense, they exist somewhere in consciousness (or is it unconsciousness?). It appears that the ontological status of self-representations is just as vexing as the ontological status of the self.

One way to demonstrate the "existence" of self-representations is to demonstrate their effect on behavior, affect, and thought, and that is exactly what much of the ego psychological clinical literature attempts to do. Having seen, and indeed seeing on an almost daily basis, the power of unconscious representations to disable my patients and the emergence of these unconscious representations into consciousness during treatment, I would have to hold that self-representations subsist somewhere, however obscure their neurological or mentalistic housing and mode of storage. The self-representation is a concept that makes sense out of clinical data and human behavior in general.

EDITH JACOBSON

Edith Jacobson (1964) built affectivity into Hartmann's theory of the self-representation. She modified and made more precise Hartmann's formulations, defining self as the whole person of the individual, including body, psychic organization, and their respective parts, while defining self-representations as the conscious, preconscious, and dynamically unconscious endopsychic representations of the physical and mental self in the system ego. They are never purely cognitive but always have an affective quality.

According to Jacobson, in the initial stage of human development there is a *primal psychophysiological self* that is the undifferentiated psychosomatic matrix from which psyche and soma, mind and body, self-representations and object representations, as well as the libidinal and aggressive drives, differentiate. Prior to this differentiation, there are no self-representations (or object representations), and the basic drives are fused. Jacobson is a dual-drive theorist, holding that libido and aggression are innately programmed manifestations of biological energy. Once self-representations arise, they are always cathected by one of the two basic drives. Cathexis, as you will recall, is James Strachey's translation of Freud's *Besetzung*, which literally means "occupation." In Freud's model, psychic energy flows out from the self and grasps hold of objects in the environment. They become emotionally invested. Jacobson reformulates Freud's picture of cathectic action. In her version, it isn't objects that are cathected, but rather self-representations and object representations. This cathexis may be by libido or by aggression, so that the self-representations are always, to some degree or another, loved or hated. The self as experienced has now become the self-representations. These representations are multiple and are contents of the system ego, may be conscious or unconscious, and are affectively colored (i.e., loved or hated). The multiplicity of self-representations opens up potential for conflict between self-representations, particularly between conscious representations and unconscious representations. This puts a new light on or is a different way of conceptualizing Freud's splitting of the ego (self) for the purposes of defense.

Jacobson also modified Freud's notion of narcissism. Freud had described the normal developmental process in which there is a progression from autoeroticism (love of isolated body parts), to narcissism (love of self), to object love (love of others). The infant first derives pleasure from body parts, experienced as isolates, not as parts of a self; these sense experiences are later integrated into a self, or ego, that is experienced as tenuous and unclearly demarcated from the nonself (the world), and this ego is loved; and finally a portion of this primeval self-love, or primary narcissism, overflows and is projected out as object love. Thus, our instinctual energy is first invested in our own body parts, then invested in ourselves before the distinction between self and others has been established, and finally flows outward to invest (cathect) objects. *Narcissistic libido* becomes *object libido*.

Disappointment in object love can lead to withdrawal of interest (libido) from the world and reinvestment of that libido in the self. Freud denoted this phenomenon secondary narcissism. Freud postulated that normal self-esteem results from the reservoir of self-love that remains from the stage of primary narcissism and that continues to exist alongside object love.

Jacobson critiques the notion of primary narcissism, and indeed Freud's whole concept of narcissism, as confused. Since she sees the initial stage of human development as an undifferentiated psychosomatic matrix, the *primal psychophysiological self*, in which neither self- and object representations nor the libidinal and aggressive drives are yet differentiated, Jacobson does not believe it makes sense to speak of narcissism, or self-love, at this stage. Therefore, she defines narcissism as the *libidinal cathexis* of the self-representation. Analogously, object love is seen as the libidinal cathexis of an object representation. In severe psychopathology, there is a regressive fusion of self- and object representations and reality testing is lost, since the patient isn't sure where he or she ends and the object world begins. Jacobson's primal psychophysiological self corresponds to Freud's state of autoeroticism but evolves into a representational world of self- and object representations rather than into a stage of primary narcissism.

The salient aspect of Jacobson's conceptualization of self is the notion that, experientially, self is the self-representation in all its complexity and affectivity. Being a (biological) drive theorist, Jacobson believes that affectivity quality comes from the cathexis of the self-representation by libido, which is the source of narcissism, or by aggression, the source of self-hatred. Jacobson's theory has the merits of clarity and of focus on the affectivity of the self but leaves unanswered the question of how and why the self-representations are cathected with libido and aggression. Is relative strength of these drives constitutional or a result of experience? For all of its clarity, Jacobson's formulation is too schematic.

Hartmann's background was biological, so it is not surprising that he focused on the adaptation of the organism to the environment and on the constitutional givens that make that adaptation possible in his account of the self. Jacobson was a clinician who specialized in severe psychopathology, particularly psychotic depression, so it is not surprising that she focused on two determinants (in her view) of psychotic depression: the regressive fusion of self- and object representations, so that reality is lost, and the cathexis of the self-representation by aggression. This account is her version of Freud's "the shadow of the object fell on the ego" (1915/ 1957, p. 249). For Jacobson, it isn't the shadow, but the loss of distinction, of differentiation from the hated object, that brings about depression. Our next psychoanalytic theorist of self, Margaret Mahler, spent her life treating childhood psychosis. Like Jacobson, she believes that psychosis involves a fusion of self- and object representations, but she sees both development and psychopathology differently.

MARGARET MAHLER

Mahler (1968; Mahler, Pine, & Bergman, 1975), basing her conceptualization on clinical experience with children, describes a developmental sequence of *autism*, *symbiosis*, and *separation-individuation*. This is her way of describing the establishment of a sense of autonomous identity—of selfhood—a description that parallels Freud's and Jacobson's but has a different slant. In Mahler's view, the infant starts life without a sense of self or of objects: there is just need and its gratification. This is the autistic stage. The world of the neonate, is, in William James's words, "a blooming, buzzing confusion." Out of this primordial state of sensation without a sensor, of archaic perception without a perceiver, comes a nascent sense of being and a dim sense of others, primarily Mother, who attend that being. At this stage, there is a nascent stage of separateness, but it doesn't last because it is too frightening, too overwhelming. Ineluctably, frustration and overwhelming feelings of helplessness lead to hallucinatory union with the mother, and the stage of symbiosis is reached. Mahler's autistic stage is parallel to Freud's stage of autoeroticism, Hartmann's undifferentiated matrix, and Jacobson's primal psychophysiological self. Mahler's stage of symbiosis is her unique contribution, although the notion of infantile hallucinatory wish fulfillment goes back to Freud.

According to Mahler, the child acquires a sense of selfhood—of enduring identity as a person apart from Mother—by going through a complex developmental process that she calls separation-individuation, which is characterized by four substages: *differentiation*, *practicing*, *rapprochement*, and finally separation-individuation proper. Her stages are both behavioral and endopsychic. Thus, the development of locomotion and speech enhance the process of separation leading to differentiation: "I am different from Mother." This is both enacted and reflected in a change in the internal representation of self. Differentiation is tested and affirmed through practicing, the toddler's exploration of the world; rapprochement is the developmentally vital opportunity to regress in the face of pain and frustration and to reunite with mother both interpersonally and intrapsychically. Sufficiently gratifying rapprochement experiences build ego strength, so the child can finally "hatch" and become a separate person with a sense of identity, including gender identity, a firm sense of being male or female. In the final substage of separation-individuation proper, I become not only separate from Mother, I become me; i.e., I individuate. By age 4, the child achieves personhood, the sense of being a unique individual with boundaries and characteristics. Both behaviorally and intrapsychically, a self has emerged. Mahler is interested in the genesis of that self but doesn't have much to say about the self that emerges. Mahler has given us a whole new notion of self. Self is no longer something that develops from ego nuclei, or by differentiation from the id; *par contra*, it develops by differentiating itself from a symbiotic union with Mother. The self is that which comes into being with separation; union is primordial. *Symbiosis* is a term Mahler took from biology, where it means beneficial, mutual dependence of organisms. She sees psychopathology, at least in its more severe forms, as either resulting from failure to successfully negotiate the process of separation-individuation or as regression to preindividualization. Such psychopathology is the loss of the self. Mahler's notion is reminiscent of Jung's fears of being swallowed up by the collective unconscious, but here it is the "urge to merge" that results in deliquescence of self. Defenses against this urge to merge can lead to defensive isolation, which in itself is highly pathological.

OTTO KERNBERG

Otto Kernberg (1975), who is medical director of Cornell University's Payne Whitney Psychiatric Clinic and one of the most prominent current psychoanalytic theorists, uses Jacobson's concept of self- and object representations to delineate four stages of object relations development. Kernberg derives from both the ego psychology and the object relations traditions, object relations here referring to internal objects. Kernberg, like Hartmann and Jacobson, starts with an "objectless," undifferentiated matrix. In his second stage, self- and object representations exist but are not yet differentiated; instead there are endopsychic structures that he calls *self-objects*, which are conscious, preconscious, and unconscious mental representations of the predifferentiated self. Instead of having a self-representation, the infant in this stage has a representation in which self and object are amalgamated. The self-object representations are always affectively colored—loved or hated. Memory traces of gratification result in positive (libidinally cathected) self-object representations, while memory traces of frustrating experiences result in negative (aggressively cathected) self-object representations that do not differentiate between the I and the not-I, between self and world. In normal development, gratifying experiences predominate in early infancy.

Fixation, failure to further develop and mature, at either of these first two stages, results in psychosis. Without a distinction between self and world, sanity is not possible. In Kernberg's third developmental stage, the positive and negative self-object representations are differentiated, resulting in four endopsychic structures: a positive (libidinally cathected) self-representation, a negative (aggressively cathected) self-representation, a positive (libidinally cathected) object representation, and a negative (aggressively cathected) object representation. Self and object are now differentiated, but self- and object representations reflecting gratifying and frustrating experiences are not yet integrated. Thus the object (usually Mother) who both gratifies and frustrates is experienced as two separate objects, the "good mother" and the "bad mother." Similarly, there is a "good self" and a "bad self" that are not experienced as the same self. Fixation at this stage, or regression to it, results in *borderline personality disorder*. Borderline personalities have severe difficulties in interpersonal relationships, chaotic emotional lives, and poor impulse control and are prone to acting out. Kernberg's clinical work has been largely with borderlines, and his theory of the development of self reflects that experience.

Kernberg's fourth stage involves the integration of good and bad self- and object representations. Successful completion of this process results in a stable self-representation and in *object constancy*. With the achievement of object constancy, frustrations are tolerable because there are stable representations (internal objects) of loving, albeit humanly flawed, caretakers and a stable representation of self. The attainment of object constancy indicates that there is a libidinal cathexis of the constant mental representation of the object, regardless of the state of need. In less forbidding language, I am now able to love people even when they are frustrating me. Similarly, there is a predominantly libidinal cathexis of a self-representation, resulting in a firm sense of identity.

In normal development, psychic structuralization resulting in the establishment of the ego and the id as separate psychic systems emerging from the undifferentiated matrix of earliest infancy proceeds concomitantly with the establishment of differentiated, affectively complex self- and object representations. Self- and object representations (the internal objects) are components of the system ego. In emotional health, these images integrate the gratifying and frustrating aspects of experience and are differentiated from each other.

Kernberg distinguishes between healthy and pathological narcissism. He conceptualizes *healthy narcissism* as the predominantly libidinal investment of the self-representation that cannot occur before successful completion of his fourth stage of object relations development. Those who have not done so suffer either borderline or narcissistic personality disorder. In *pathological narcissism* there is a pathological self-structure he called the *grandiose self*. The grandiose self is a pathological condensation (fusion) of ideal-self, real-self, and ideal-object representations. Another way of saying this is to say that the grandiose self is a confusion and amalgamation of who I would like to be, who I think I am, and who I would like you to be. It is not a stage in normal development. Narcissistic personalities typically relate to others not as separate people, but as an extension of themselves. They do not really experience others as other, but rather as projections of their grandiose selves. Hence, what appears to be object relations are really relations of self to self.

Characteristic defenses of narcissistic personalities include primitive idealization of self and object, projective identification of parts of self onto objects in order to control them, splitting self- and object representations into all-good and all-bad, and devaluation of objects. In one way or another, these defenses distort the object to meet the needs of the narcissistic. These mechanisms are thus in the service of omnipotent control. True dependence on another human being, experienced as separate and autonomous, would entail the risk of intolerable emotions of rage and envy toward the person depended upon. Thus, what appears to be dependent relating in the narcissistic personalities is, in reality, another manifestation of their need for omnipotent control. Such a pseudodependency cannot possibly meet the real dependency needs that are part and parcel of the human condition, and a vicious cycle of need and failure to meet it is set up. Kernberg's distinction between normal and pathological narcissism is important. Without self-love, we sicken and die, but the wrong kind of self-love is equally detrimental. Rabbi Hillel, the sage of antiquity, summed it up well: "If I am not for myself, who will be for me? If I am only for myself, what am I? If not now, when?"

ERIK ERIKSON

Erik Erikson is another psychoanalytic theorist whose work is relevant to the understanding of the self. Usually considered an ego psychologist, Erikson is a half-Jewish Dane with a confused family history who started out as an artist and became a member of the bohemian avant garde who were attracted to Freud's Vienna and to psychoanalysis. He was analyzed by Freud's daughter, Anna, with whom he also ran an experimental school; became an analyst; and eventually wound up a Harvard professor without having set foot in a university. Always sensitive to the *sturm und drang* of adolescence, he became a counterculture hero in the 1960s. Both his focus on "identity diffusion" and on the need for a developmental "moratorium" before assuming a fixed adult role seemed relevant.

Erikson (1968) speaks of identity and the sense of identity rather than of the self. Identity is not self, but a vital component of self. We ask children, "What do you want to *be*?" as if they didn't exist before assuming a culturally defined and sanctioned role. Self seems to encompass or to be defined by the answer to two questions: "What am I?" and "Who am I?" Identity seems to be concerned primarily with the answer to the latter. Erikson's central notion is that identity comes from *identification*. So to speak, we are or, better, we become an integrated composite of our identifications with people: parents, siblings, peers, public personages, historical and fictional figures, causes, movements, and ideals. So for Erikson there is an almost infinite number of possibilities for identification, a plenitude of material out of which to build an identity. Obviously some sort of selection occurs. The possibilities are narrowed in several ways: one's historical, economic, and cultural situation is limited. As much as I might admire, idealize, and seek to emulate a Comanche warrior, an identity as an Indian brave is not possible for me. Here it becomes clear that for Erikson, identity is both an intrapsychic construct and a social-political-economic-cultural role, or set of roles. Furthermore, my possibilities for identification are limited by my genetic endowment, by my early object relations, and by my family constellation. I can only become what my culture and what my historical situation allows, even if I am an extraordinary individual who creates a new identity. Erikson is interested in creative individuals who forge new identities and thereby create new possibilities for identification. He has written studies of Luther, Gandhi, Freud, James, Hitler, and Maxim Gorky illustrative of the process of identity formation in cases in which a new identity comes into being. Erikson emphasizes the dialectical interplay of personality and culture in the formation of an identity. Once an individual creates a new identity, it becomes available for identification by the next and succeeding generations. A new identity can be constructive (e.g., psychoanalyst) or demonic (e.g., storm trooper).

Erikson (1950/1963) has an epigenetic developmental scheme in which each stage is folded into the succeeding stage. No developmental battles are won once and for all; on the contrary, the process of identity formation is lifelong and provides creative opportunities as well as the potential for disastrous regression over the life span. Although adolescence is the stage for identity formation *par excellence*—a period of detachment from family, of search for idealizable models, or heroes, to serve as raw material in the creation of self through selective identification—the process of identity formation is inherent in every life stage. Erikson's stages are discrete periods of challenge during which the self changes for better or for worse. Consolidation occurs during the intervals between crises. In this formation, self only becomes self through realization in the world, and that which is realized is the outcome of an interaction between culture and personality. Identity may be integrated or diffused. *Identity diffusion*, sometimes called *identity confusion*, is a form of self pathology in which there is no centeredness, nor any superordinate identity that unifies the identity fragments formed through identification. In its more severe form, identity confusion is pathognomic of borderline personality disorder.

Erikson's epigenetic stages are dichotomous: the first of each pair of developmental possibilities is dominant in the healthy self, but the second possibility is to some extent inevitably realized and expressed, and the minor key is no less needed than the major. This lends a richness and complexity to the evolving self. Erikson's stages are basic trust versus basic mistrust, autonomy versus shame, initiative versus guilt, industry versus inferiority, identity versus identity confusion, intimacy versus isolation, generativity versus stagnation, and ego integrity versus despair. They characterize the oral-sensory, muscular-anal, locomotive-genital, latency, puberty and adolescence, young adulthood, adulthood, and late maturity life stages, respectively. Although basic trust predominates in health, we would be in trouble without the capacity for mistrust. *Mutatis mutandis*, the same is true for each succeeding stage. Failure to successfully complete an earlier stage handicaps the developing self in facing each succeeding stage.

The self is more than an identity, more intrapsychic than sociological, yet Erikson's conception of identity evolving over a series of life stages with their unique potentialities for maturation, identification, and objective realization, eventuating in affirmation of the "one and only life that has been possible" (i.e., an affirmation of one's self in the final stage of ego integrity) (Erikson, 1968, p. 139) is a new and significant way of understanding self. Erikson, the refugee, the wanderer, and the poly-careerist, has much in common with William James, who also saw self as complex and as evolving. Although Erikson's view is uniquely his, it clearly owes something to both Freud ("The ego is a precipitate of abandoned object cathexis") and to the American sociologists Meade and Cooley ("The self is the generalized other"). Erikson's theory, however, in common with social psychological theories in general, doesn't adequately address the nature and origins of the self, that core that does the identifying and that must, in some sense, exist antecedently to the choosing of objects with which to identify, be that choosing conscious or unconscious. Erikson does not really see this problem, nor does he address it; however, he was the first to see that the self develops throughout life, and we are in his debt for pioneering the study of adult development.

MELANIE KLEIN

Ego psychology is generally identified with American psychoanalysis. Although some started as Europeans, Hartmann, Jacobson, Mahler, Kernberg, and Erikson all did the bulk of their work here and have had their greatest impact here. You can't get through an American social work school or a clinical psychology program without studying ego psychology. Clinically, it is highly useful in understanding the vicissitudes of separation and individualization, and most contemporary clinicians focus more on separation than on castration (which is, after all, separation from one's genitals) anxiety. Object relations, on the other hand, have been predominantly an English phenomenon. Melanie Klein, who is generally considered the founder of object relations theory, emigrated from the Continent to England after being analyzed by Freud's disciple, Karl Abraham, and remained influential in the British Psychoanalytic Society throughout a long and bitter rivalry with Anna Freud. Abraham had anticipated Freud's proto object-relational constructs adumbrated in *Mourning and Melancholia*, where the internalization of the lost object plays such a key role. Abraham undoubtedly influenced Klein, who like Erikson was an intellectual without a higher education who was attracted to analysis in its early, wide-open days. There was a Mr. Klein somewhere, but he doesn't seem to have played much of a role in her life. Klein worked mostly with children, whom she analyzed exactly as one would analyze an adult, in contrast to her rival, Anna Freud, who pioneered play therapy in the analysis of children. Klein's theories developed out of her clinical work with children and are less in danger of adultomorphic distortions of infantile experience, or projecting adult pathological states understood as developmental arrests onto infants, than developmental theories derived from clinical work with adults—at least, one would think that should be the case.

Klein is not a facile or clear writer, and she is difficult to follow. Her collected papers (1975a, 1975b) are best supplemented by her disciple Hanna Segal's (1973) lucid summary of Klein's theoretical and clinical work. Melanie Klein and her followers are virtually the only analysts who subscribe to Freud's death instinct. It is her starting point. We come into the world with a death instinct within us, where it would drive us toward Nirvana, the quietus of the inorganic—toward death—if it were not externalized, that is, moved from inside to outside. There are two ways this can be done: the death instinct can become aggression and attack external objects, an option not readily available to the neonate, or it can be projected, or projected in fantasy, onto the environment so that it is experienced as external instead of internal, so that which would kill me if it remained inside me is now able to kill me from its position in the environment. At least that's the way it would be experienced according to Klein. A dubious gain, yet Klein thinks that this projection of the death instinct is a universal developmental phenomenon. Once the death instinct is projected outside, the environment becomes persecutory. The death instinct, no longer recognized as mine, now hovers over me and characterizes my objects. They become persecutors, and I am in the *paranoid-schizoid position*. The Kleinian *positions* are developmental stages other than the psychosexual ones described by Freud or the stages in the development of libido also described by Freud. Klein originally called the stage following the projection of Thanatos the paranoid position, but modified its denotation when Ronald Fairbairn pointed out that the response to persecution is defensive withdrawal, hence the paranoid-schizoid position. So far, it sounds like Klein is an instinct theorist, which she really isn't. Once Thanatos has been projected, it plays no further role in her developmental theory, which becomes an object-relational one.

Projected Thanatos adheres in objects, particularly in Mother, the first object, and those objects are now dangerous persecutors, "bad objects." To control them, these bad objects are now (re-)introjected, and the persecutors are now, once more, within, but no longer as highly dangerous as the preprojected death instinct; now they are merely internal bad objects. These internal bad objects can be (re-)projected onto the environment; alternately, the "goodness" within may be projected outward to protect it from the inner badness. The world of the Kleinian paranoid-schizoid position is a Ping-Pong game with good and bad objects flying across the net, where they change from internal objects to gratifiers and persecutors. Reintrojection propels them back across the net again. Herein lies a problem (as if there were no others) with Kleinian theory. At this stage of development, there is no net, no boundary, because the developmental task of separation from symbiotic union with the environment, chiefly Mother, which Klein does not discuss, has not been completed. If the ego psychologists are right about development of the self, this is indeed a strange Ping-Pong game; not only is there no net, but both players are on the same side of the table. Be that as it may, this is Klein's vision of early life.

You may well imagine that the paranoid-schizoid position is not a comfortable one, and it is, in fact, pervaded by anxiety of psychotic proportions, which engenders all sorts of defensive maneuvers. It is a stage characterized by *rage* (why not if the world is persecutory?), *envy* (since my goodness is projected out, I must envy it), and *part objects*. Part objects are objects like Mother and Father, who are regarded as breasts (only) and penises (only), respectively. Objects are reduced to part objects, in part, to make them manageable, but they also exist because integration into whole objects has not yet taken place. Now my internal bad objects, which were created by my internalizing the objects "spoiled" by my original projection of the death instinct, are reprojected onto that part object, Mother's breast, which becomes the "bad breast." Similarly, my good internal objects are projected to protect them from my internal badness onto Mother's breast, creating a second part object, the "good breast." But I envy the good breast, so I must "spoil" it—destroy it with my envy, greed, and rage—turning it into a bad breast. The splitting of the breast into the good breast and the bad breast is reinforced by the ineluctable frustration of the infant's needs. No mother is always there. Interpersonally, the good breast feeds, while the bad breast refuses to gratify. Although Klein realizes that environmental provocation makes matters worse, she doesn't much pursue the role of the environment.

If Freud is notorious for his concept of penis envy, Klein is equally notorious for her concept of *breast envy*. From her pictures, it appears that she was more than amply endowed, and I don't know how much, if any, that amplitude influenced her belief that infants envied Mother's breast. Her whole theory is a theory about the child's aggressiveness toward the mother, and she sees normal biological functions such as feeding and excretion as acts of aggression. I want to bite, piss on, shit on the good breast because I envy it. In real life, Klein had exceptionally awful relations with her own children, and I don't know what impact, if any, this had on her theorizing.

Klein puts so much emphasis on aggression against the good breast and defenses against it that it led me to wonder if the origin of the laws of *Kashrut* (the Jewish dietary laws enjoining, among other things, not eating milk and meat together) lies in a reaction-formation against the desire to bite the (good) breast that provides the milk. Separating the eating of milk and meat would make such aggression against the breast impossible.

If things weren't bad enough in the paranoid-schizoid position, they are about to get worse. At some point in development, I (the infant) realize two things: first, that the good breast and the bad breast are one, and second, that I have created the bad breast by aggressing against the good breast out of envy and hatred. These realizations move me into the *depressive position*, at about age 2. I defend against this realization by using the psychological defense of *splitting* to keep good and bad (part) objects separate. When Kernberg and the other ego psychologists talk about the achievement of *object constancy*, when good and bad self- and object representations coalesce into one complex self- or object representation, they are talking about the same phenomenon that Klein denotes the depressive position. The depressive position is the developmental stage in which good and bad internal and external objects become just objects, with all of the ambiguity of reality, and in which part objects become whole objects.

The depressive position is depressing because I feel guilty about spoiling the good breast, and the way I deal with my guilt is by making *reparation* for my aggression. The notion of reparation is central to Kleinian theory and practice. What happens to my innate envy that has been causing all this difficulty? I overcome it with *gratitude*, another key Kleinian notion. Instead of envying, I feel grateful for the good breast and its successors, and I more or less spend the rest of my life working through the depressive position. Klein goes no further in her developmental scheme. The task of working through the depressive position is the task of integration and of owning that which is being projected.

One response to the depressive position and its guilt-induced pain is to institute a *manic defense*. The notion of mania and its derivatives as a defense against underlying depression is a Kleinian contribution. Klein puts great emphasis on early fantasy, moving the Oedipus complex back into the first 6 months of life. She claims to have found support for her entire schema in the fantasies of her child patients.

There is a phenomenon known as *postschizophrenic depression*, which sometimes results in suicide. It is usually understood as a neurochemical phenomenon: the overabundance of certain neurotransmitters, such as dopamine, during a psychotic episode leads to their depletion, a phenomenon that may be exacerbated by the neuroleptic (drug) treatment of the psychosis. Depletion of dopamine, by either mechanism, brings on depression. Postschizophrenic depression has also been understood as a consequence of the realization that one has a chronic and seriously disabling condition. Kleinian developmental theory offers an alternate explanation. The drugs used to treat schizophrenia may bring about a chemically induced integration that precipitates the patient from the paranoid-schizoid world of psychosis into the depressive position, in which aggression is owned and guilt becomes overwhelming; this occurs without adequate preparation. The suddenness of the change of position works against its being worked through. I guess we could call this theory of the etiology of postschizophrenic depression "Melanie Klein and the catecholamines."

Is Klein's theory a fantastic fairy tale that, far more than Freud's placing sexual fantasies within the mind of the child, makes children monstrous? Thinkers as diverse as Augustine and Freud have emphasized the innateness of aggression, but nobody but Klein has developed this aspect of the self to this extent. In a way, you can see her theory as the psychoanalytic version of the doctrine of original sin, with the death instinct and its derivatives playing the role of original sin. Perhaps, and I certainly find Klein less than persuasive. Yet history is one long record of bloody and barbaric aggression and man's inhumanity to man seems to know no bounds, so we cannot rule out Klein's understanding of the death instinct and its vicissitudes. Further, the defenses of splitting, projection, and introjection are prominent in both psychopathology and health.

What about the self in Kleinian theory? Perhaps that's the most bizarre feature of the whole thing. There is no self. There are only instincts and their projection to create objects. Presumably the self is built up out of the internalized reintrojected objects, and this is part of the working through of the depressive position. However, Klein herself doesn't discuss this. The Kleinian notions of reparation and gratitude do have relevance for self theory. The Kleinian (non)self is fragmented by its biological givens, and the only way it can be reintegrated, both its goodness and badness made once more part of self, is through reparation for damage unwittingly caused by projection. Gratitude reduces the need to attack and to project, which facilitates the integration of internalized objects into a self. Klein's developmental theory makes very clear the need for some sort of notion of the self, if human life is not to be seen as merely a chaotic confusion of projection and reintrojection of impulses, drives, and objects.

RONALD FAIRBAIRN

Ronald Fairbairn, who suggested the label paranoid-schizoid position, was a Kleinian who went his own way. A Scot who practiced in Edinburgh and who had a phobia about urinating in public that restricted his travel, he was isolated physically and intellectually from the mainstream of British analytic thought. Not surprisingly, his clinical interest was in schizoid phenomena (a schizoid being one who phobically isolates and avoids intimacy). He alone among psychoanalytic thinkers believes that the self, which he calls the ego, is primordially integral. Only later, and for defensive reasons, is it "split" into a *central* ego, a *libidinal* ego, and an *antilibidinal* ego. The central ego is the relatively rational residual of the originally integral ego, the libidinal ego is the loving part of that ego, and the antilibidinal ego is the self-critical part of that ego. The similarity to Freud's structural model is obvious, the central ego being Freud's ego, the libidinal ego being the id, and the antilibidinal ego being the superego, but it is an importantly different notion because Fairbairn's self has its own energy, and is not a mental apparatus. It is actually a self that splits into these aspects for defensive reasons. Fairbairn objected to the dichotomizing of structure and energy in Freudian theory, where the drives are energetic and the ego without power. Hence Fairbairn's ego, or self, does have power and need not borrow it through such dubious theoretical constructs as neutralization. The Fairbairnian self in its three aspects relates to three objects: the neutral object, the exciting object, and the rejecting object, respectively. The primordially integral self is only split in this way because the environment is not sufficiently, or consistently, supportive. This is the exact opposite of Klein's vision; it isn't badness but goodness that is primordial for Fairbairn. The task of Fairbairn's psychotherapy is the healing of the splitting of the self, which to some extent will occur in any environment since parents are never perfect, and a return to its primordial integrity.

D. W. WINNICOTT

Donald Winnicott is not a systematic thinker. In some ways more of a poet than a scientist, his insights into the self are diffused throughout his deceptively simple papers. A pediatrician who later became a psychiatrist and psychoanalyst, he never ceased practicing pediatrics. From the beginning, he was concerned with mothers and babies and their interaction. The Winnicottian self emerges from that interaction. Influenced, as were all object relations theorists, by Klein, he maintained his independence from her. Winnicott's thinking about self encompasses a developmental scheme, a notion of self pathology, and an object-relational notion of self. Developmentally, Winnicott postulates three stages of ego development: *integration*, *personalization*, and *object relating*. Though he explicity disavows that he is using *ego* to mean the self and says he is using the term in a structural sense as opposed to *id*, it is clear that Winnicott's ego stages are self precursors. To steal a phrase from the title of one of Winnicott's books, ego development comes about through the interaction of *The Maturational Processes and the Facilitating Environment* (1965). Winnicott's notions of ego and self are object-relational; they come into being only in the presence of and through interaction with others. As he says, "There is no such thing as a baby," meaning that there are no babies unrelated to mothers. Thus, self is defined in relation to others from the outset or, to be more precise, before the inception of self. That is, the precursors of self are already related to others. The first stage of ego development is integration. Integration is the process by which the paradoxically undifferentiated and unintegrated infant begins to differentiate from the experience of merger, which Mahler calls symbiosis, into separateness. It is the beginning of the separation of me from not-me. This me is fragmented, consisting of isolated me experiences, which, following differentiation, begin to cohere or integrate into an I. During integration, and indeed during all of Winnicott's developmental stages, the experience of continuity and "going-on-being" is vital to the establishment of a healthy self. Going-on-being is threatened by *impingement*, traumatic disruptions that fragment self-experience. Impingement is the precursor and prototype of narcissistic injury. Adequate (good enough) maternal care minimizes impingement and establishes going-on-being. Self-cohesion comes from continuity of care.

Winnicott's notion of "good enough" parenting is reassuring to anxious parents intent on being perfect. He says, speaking about parents and therapists, that since frustration is necessary for development, "We succeed by failing." I remember that when everything seems amiss in my practice.

Personalization is the achievement of psychosomatic collusion, of living in the body rather than in fantasy. What Winnicott calls the *holding environment*—initially literal holding, later symbolic holding, provided by maternal handling—enables the infant to feel whole rather than a collection of parts. Winnicott's account is strikingly similar to Kohut's notion (see below) that to move from the stage of the fragmented self to the stage of the nuclear self is dependent on the experience of being treated as an integral self, cohesive in space and continuous in time, by loving caretakers. I gain a sense of being one self that continues to be that self, and that can initiate action, by being treated as a unit that endures and acts rather than as a collection of distress signals. The establishment of psychosomatic collusion, the sense of being one with my body, is vital for mental health; failure to succeed to do so leaves one prone to experiences of depersonalization. In this stage, the body comes to be experienced as a "limiting membrane," as a boundary, further establishing the distinction between me and not-me. The move from integration to personalization is a move from *I* to *I am*, to some sort of affirmation, or preverbal recognition, of personal existence.

In the third stage of ego development, object relating, complex processes, starting with the experience of fantasized omnipotence and progressing through the destruction of the fantasy objects created by that fantasized omnipotence, primarily Mother and her replacement with a real mother, lead the infant into the depressive position. In Winnicott's version, this is a developmental stage in which separateness is consolidated and ambivalence accepted. Winnicott's depressive stage is much less depressing than Klein's. Rather than guilt, he focuses on what he calls the acquisition of the "capacity for concern." It is the stage in which the capacity for empathy and healthy interpersonal relating is acquired.

The child's experience is now "I am alone," but "there are others I can relate to and make part of me" (as internal objects), so that being alone is tolerable, even enjoyable. In one of his most beautiful papers, "The Capacity to Be Alone" (1958), Winnicott tells us that the acquisition of the capacity to be alone, which is an achievement and not a native endowment, is a paradox. It arises out of the experience of being alone with another, another who is not impinging. If we are fortunate enough to have spent sufficient time as toddlers "alone" with Mother, Father, Grandfather, or Grandmother while Mother, Father, Grandfather, or Grandmother "let us be," we internalized that loving caretaker and acquired the capacity to be alone, because now when we are alone, we are not alone because whoever spent that time with us is now a part of us. The Winnicottian capacity to be alone has nothing to do with schizoid defensive isolation; it is its opposite, and is a prerequisite to mental health and to creativity.

In the process of ego development, the id comes into being as the source of id experiences come to be felt as internal rather than as external, as part of me rather than as part of the environment. Paradoxically, I cannot internalize Mother until I separate from her, experience omnipotence over her, destroy her as a fantasy object, reconstitute her as a real object, make restitution or reparation for my aggression against her, and experience her as one person who both gratifies and frustrates. In the process, I too become one person. In the course of ego development, the infant and the toddler goes from the not-I (fragmentation and merger) to I, to I am, to I am alone but related, and so comes into being. This self is the product of an interaction between biological maturation and the human environment, facilitative or otherwise.

The achievement of identity through separation is facilitated by the use of *transitional objects*. Linus's blanket in the comic strip "Peanuts" is the quintessential transitional object. Fantasy turns the inanimate, a teddy bear or a blanket, into a substitute for Mother, and permits me to separate from her. It isn't the teddy bear, per se, but the teddy bear suffused with meaning, meaning that I contribute through an act of creativity, that constitutes the transitional object. In Winnicott's view, all of human culture is a transitional phenomenon derivative from that blanket or stuffed animal. Winnicott emphasizes playfulness, and the creation of transitional objects is play; so is therapy, and so is creativity. Therapy provides a *transitional space*, in which transitional objects can be created as the patient struggles to proceed with his or her development.

Winnicott turns Descartes on his head, saying, "*I see that I am seen, therefore I know that I am*" and "*When I look, I am seen, so I exist.*" This is a thoroughly object-relational notion of self. Self is not a lonely cogitator; on the contrary, self is established by refraction through another. Being held and being seen are the basis for ontological security, the experience of selfhood and of identity.

This brings us to a final Winnicottian concept, that of the *true self* and the *false self*. The true self is the self with all of its feelings, drives, and id derived instincts striving for expression. The true self is messy, egocentric, unsocialized, and filled with hate and envy and destructiveness, but it is also the repository of love, gratitude, and creativity, as well as the repository of yearning and the desire to be loved. The true self is not the id, but includes id as owned, as personalized. It is *it* become *I* without being deinstinctualized. If the true self is unduly threatened by a nonfacilitating environment, particularly one that cannot accept its aggression (its need to destroy the fantasized object), it goes into hiding deep within the recesses of being to be replaced (as far as social reality is concerned), by a false self, a compliant, "people-pleasing" self that looks for approval at all cost. The false-self organization often leads to outward success, especially in intellectual pursuits, but at the cost of vitality and feelings of aliveness and genuineness. The experience is of hollowness, an absence of deep satisfaction. However, the true self has not been destroyed; it is merely in hiding. The true self contains within it, and protects, all that is felt to be threatened by destruction. It is consistent with this notion of the need to protect that which is valued from harm that Winnicott defines God as "the repository of the good aspects of the self, which we need to project outward to protect them from our inner badness." Successful therapeutic intervention surfaces the true self, establishing experiences of wholeness, aliveness, genuineness, and worth.

In summary, Winnicott sees the self as coming into being during the process of ego development, through interaction with loving caretakers who treat the child as a self and reflect back their experience of the child's selfhood. So important is the environment that some forms of psychopathology, the personality disorders, are seen by Winnicott to be "environmental deficiency diseases." In health, the true self is secure enough to express itself freely; in disease, the false self predominates striving to keep the true self safe.

KOHUT AND SELF PSYCHOLOGY

Heinz Kohut, founder of the psychoanalytic school called self psychology, was not primarily a theorist; he was a clinician. His theory of self arose from his work with a group of patients he called narcissistic personality disorders, and out of his observation of how they related to him as extensions of themselves. These narcissistic patients were not psychotic but were more ill than and "felt" different from neurotic patients. His theory is an inference from clinical data, particularly data derived from transference phenomena.

Kohut (1970, 1977) defines the self as a unit, both cohesive in space and enduring in time, that is a center of initiative and a recipient of impressions. It can be regarded either as a mental structure superordinate to the agencies of the mind (id, ego, and superego) or as a subordinate content of those agencies. Although Kohut believed these conceptions were complementary rather than mutually exclusive, he emphasized the self as a central or superordinate principle in his later writings. Kohut borrowed the notion of complementarity from physics, where electromagnetic phenomena are understood as both waves and particles, and saw the same complementarity as pertaining to the self as an overarching, central psychological construct and as a representation in the agencies of the structural model. Some phenomena are best understood as waves (superordinate self) and some as particles (subordinate self.)

The self as superordinate is, so to speak, the organized and organizing center of human experience, which is itself experienced as cohesive and enduring. How does this sense of an I (self) that coheres in space and endures in time develop? According to Kohut, the infant develops a primitive (fragmented) sense of self very early. That is, each body part, each sensation, and each mental content is experienced as belonging to a self, to a me, as mine; however, there is no synthesis of these experiences as yet. There are selves, but no unitary self. Nor are there clear boundaries between self and world. Kohut designates this stage as the stage of the *fragmented self*; it is the developmental stage at which psychotic persons are fixated or to which they regress. Kohut also observed regressive, temporary fragmentation in his narcissistic patients when they became highly anxious. His reasoning went from clinical data to metapsychology. He also cites such evidence as hypochondriasis, in which the integrity of the self fails and isolated body parts become the focus of self-experience, as evidence for the existence of a stage of fragmentation in self-development. Although there are important differences, Kohut's stage of the fragmented self corresponds to Freud's stage of autoeroticism; it is another way of understanding the stage of human development that precedes the integration of the infant's experienced world.

According to Kohut, at the next stage of development an *archaic nuclear bipolar self* arises from the infant's experience of being related to as a self rather than as a collection of parts and sensations. This self is cohesive and enduring, but it is not yet securely established. Hence, it is prone to regressive fragmentation, to "going to pieces" or "falling apart." It is nuclear in the sense of having a center, or nucleus, and it is archaic in the sense of being a primitive precursor of the mature self.

The development of the nuclear self from the fragmented self brings to mind the story of the man who goes to the doctor and says, "Doctor, my feet hurt, I have a dreadful headache, my throat is sore, my bowels are about to burst, and to tell the truth, I myself don't feel so well either." The "I myself" is the nuclear self, while the aching feet, head, throat, and bowels are the fragmented self.

The archaic nuclear self is bipolar in that it contains two structures, the *grandiose self* and the *idealized parental imago*, the internal representation of the idealized parent as part of self. In this stage, there is a differentiated self, which is experienced as omnipotent, but there are no truly differentiated objects. The omnipotence comes from the grandiose self and the undifferentiation from fusion with the idealized and internalized parents. Objects are still experienced as extensions of the self, as what Kohut calls *self-objects*. Self-objects are representations in the same sense as self-representations and object representations, except in this case the representation is that of a fused, undifferentiated amalgamation of self and object. The child's grandiose self attempts to exercise omnipotent control over his self-objects, and indeed is an inference from such behavior.

Kohut's notion of the self-object is confused. Sometimes he uses the term as Kernberg does, to denote the internal representation of nondifferentiation, as I defined it above, but more often he seems to use self-object to means persons, the people who provide what he calls self-object functions, that is, who meet my needs, particularly my needs for self-esteem regulation, modulation of anxiety, soothing, and self-cohesion. It is as if they were extensions of me or were totally under my omnipotent control. In self-object relating, I either treat you as part of me, so of course you will (should) be perfectly under my control, or I merge with you and participate in the omnipotence I endow you with through *idealization*.

Idealization is an important Kohutian concept; he regards the need for idealization as both stage-specific and an enduring need throughout life. Kohut arrived at his concept of the bipolar archaic nuclear self by examining the transferences of his narcissistic patients to him. They either treated him as an extension of themselves whose function was to perfectly mirror them, to reflect back their glory, which he called the *mirror transference*, or they merged with him conceived of as an all-perfect, all-powerful ideal object. This way of relating he called the *idealizing transference*. Thus, the bipolarity of the nuclear self is an inference from the behavior of adult patients.

What Kohut calls *psychic structure* is built through the process of *transmuting internalization*, the piecemeal, grain-at-a-time internalization of not objects, but the functions performed by (self-)objects, through "optimal" or nontraumatic failure of the self-object to perform its functions. The notion is that if my needs are perfectly met, then I have no reason to acquire the means of meeting them through internalization, nor would I have any sense of separateness. If, on the other hand, my needs are so poorly met that it is traumatic, I have little to internalize and am too anxious to do so. In either case, that which was originally outside fails to get inside and become part of me, and a self-deficit results. Concretely this means that I am unable to do certain things, such as soothe myself, maintain my self-esteem, or experience myself as cohesive, that is, as a healthy mature self. If I fail to acquire the capacity, through transmuting internalization, to provide myself with a sense of cohesion, continuity, and stable self-esteem, I must look to the outside and find people to provide them. So when Kohut is talking about structure, he is really talking about capacity, the ability to do certain things, experience certain things, and carry out certain tasks, particularly those tasks having to do with the self.

Transmuting internalization sounds like a fine notion, but is it "word magic"? What is actually denoted, and how do those "grains" get inside?

Kohut puts great emphasis on "mirroring," the age-appropriate approving reflection of infantile grandiosity by self-objects, otherwise known as parents. Jacques Lacan (1977), who believes that the ego (self) is a defensive illusion, has another notion of mirroring. In his version, the child looks in the mirror, real or metaphorical, and sees a being far more bounded, whole, cohesive, and in control than he "knows" himself to be, and feels alienated because his "real" self is there in the mirror outside of himself. In this tragic vision, there is no internalization, and self, instead of being within, is always the "other."

The internalization of psychic structure is codeterminous with the formation of the archaic nuclear, bipolar self. As Kohut puts it, "The rudiments of the nuclear self are laid down by simultaneously or consecutively occurring processes of selective inclusion and exclusion of psychic structure" (1977, p. 183), so it would appear that the archaic nuclear self with its bipolar structure comes from both inside and outside, is maturational in the sense of being a development out of the stage of the fragmented self, and yet is also the product of internalization, the transmuting internalization of psychic structure, and the internalization of the idealized parent. Or perhaps this is not quite so, and the idealization is an idealization of a parent primordially experienced as part of self. That is, the self-object structure comes first and differentiation later, rather than the amalgamation resulting from the internalization process. Kohut is not clear about this. The grandiosity that is a manifestation of the grandiose self, however, seems to be maturational and inborn. That is, it doesn't seem to depend on environment, but universally comes into being at a certain stage of development. Here Kohut may be creating additional difficulties by turning process into substance; the grandiosity certainly is there, but one wonders if anything is gained by attributing that grandiosity to a structure, the grandiose self.

Just as Melanie Klein's developmental theory ends with the achievement of the depressive position, in a sense Kohut's developmental theory doesn't go much beyond his description of the archaic nuclear, bipolar self. However, he does have some things to say about the mature self, which he conceives of as a development out of the archaic nuclear self and which continues to be bipolar. In maturity, the grandiose self develops into realistic ambitions, while the idealized parental imago, now depersonalized, develops into ideals and values. Maturation of self is a process of depersonalization in the sense that attributes and functional capacities that were acquired from others take on an autonomy and become integrated into us in such a way that they are no longer identified with those from whom they were acquired. This is important to a healthy sense of selfhood. I need to feel I can soothe myself, maintain my self-esteem, modulate my anxiety, and maintain my sense of ongoingness, initiative, and boundaries even in the face of great stress. If I cannot do these things, I am subject to regression to the stage of the fragmented self. Such a regression is in essence a loss of self, and its threat leads to panic terror.

Not surprisingly in a theorist so obsessed with narcissism, Kohut's theory is a narcissistic one. In his view, I don't internalize the people I love and who love me, as in Freud's view and to some extent in Klein's; on the contrary, I acquire what I can from them, and in a sense use and discard them when they no longer are necessary to me. The fact that others once did things for me, before I was able to internalize the things they did as psychic structure, as the capacity to do them, is now irrelevant.

According to Kohut, I do not lose or outgrow my need for self-objects (here meaning persons who relate to me in a certain way) in maturity. However, the mode of my self-object relating does change and take on mature forms. Exactly how is rather murky. In Freud's view, narcissistic libido becomes object libido; not so in Kohut's. For him, object libido and narcissistic libido have their own *developmental lines*; that is, each continues throughout life, with infantile narcissism developing into mature narcissism, characterized by realistic ambitions, enduring ideals, and secure self-esteem.

There are serious problems with Kohut's developmental theory of self in that it concretizes process and turns it into substance, so that the self becomes thinglike. This is particularly true of the archaic nuclear, bipolar self that plays such a large role in his theorizing. Kohut tells us that he developed this theory by observing the two types of narcissistic or self-object transferences. The clinical data are irrefutable, but it is a long way from such interpersonal behavior to a bipolar structure in the system ego, or a bipolar structure as a superordinate construct. As long as Kohut is talking about ways of relating, about manifestations of grandiosity, about narcissistic needs, he is on firm ground, but when he tries to convert these into a metapsychology, he becomes less than clear and, to some extent, less than convincing. His problems are compounded by the confusion and ambiguity in his use of *self-object*, sometimes as a representation and sometimes as a person. This fuzziness in Kohutian self theory mars it. However, Kohut himself wouldn't be much bothered by this. He wrote, "All theorizing is tentative, provisional, and has an aspect of playfulness about it" (1977, p. 237).

My reservations notwithstanding, Kohut's theory is interesting. Implicit in it is the notion that the self arises both from the inside and from the outside. The grandiose self seems to be preprogrammed to emerge organically from fragments of self-experience, while the idealized parental imago is an identification with and internalization of idealized parents. Both the grandiosity and the idealization are related to and reactive from the sense of infantile helplessness. The delusional, but phase-appropriate normal, beliefs that I am omnipotent and that those who love me are omnipotent provide the security for emotional growth to proceed.

Kohut's theory introduces a new dimension to the understanding of the self: cohesion and its opposite, fragmentation. The self can be more or less cohesive and more or less subject to regressive fragmentation. Although Kohut recognizes self as a self-representation in the id, ego, and superego, his emphasis is on the sense of selfhood, the lived experience of wholeness, and the human interactions leading to that experience, as well as on the vicissitudes that result in the malformation of the self. Although Kohut does not style himself an object relations theorist, his theory is clearly object-relational. As with Winnicott, "I see and feel that I am seen and felt," therefore, "I know that I am," and further, "I see and feel that I am seen and felt as a whole person who is continuous in time, bounded in space, and is capable of initiating actions." And because I see that I am seen and held as if I were a self so conceived, I come to experience myself as that kind of self.

The Kohutian self always has a self-object aspect, as well as an individual aspect. I am always a part as well as apart. But Kohut's being a part means making you part of me, or me part of you, not relating as a separate person to you as a separate person, although in healthy maturity I also do that.

For Kohut, pathological narcissism is the regression-fixation to the stage of the archaic nuclear, bipolar self. It is characterized by the presence of a cohesive, but insecure self, which is threatened by regressive fragmentation; grandiosity of less than psychotic proportions that manifests itself in the form of arrogance, isolation, and unrealistic goals; feelings of entitlement; the need for omnipotent control; poor differentiation of self and object; and deficits in the self-regulating capacities of the self. Furthermore, affect tolerance, the ability to experience and stay with feelings, is poor. The tenuousness in the cohesion of the self makes narcissistically regressed individuals subject to massive anxiety that is, in reality, fear of annihilation. The fragmentation of the self is annihilation of the psychic self. Those suffering from narcissistic personality disorders are also subject to "empty" depression, reflecting the emptiness of the self, the paucity of psychic structure and good internal objects.

Kohut emphasizes the normality of our narcissistic needs and the deleterious consequences of repression or disavowal of those needs. For him, a healthy narcissism is a vital component of mental health, and it is at least as important as object relating or the ability to achieve instinctual gratification. Kohut is highly critical of what he calls the "maturity morality" implicit in much of psychoanalysis, which he views as unaccepting of the narcissistic needs of the self. He is equally critical of the denial of the legitimacy of our need for self-affirmation by the Judeo-Christian religious tradition that condemns "self-centeredness." He sees many factors working to deny or disapprove of the fulfillment of narcissistic needs and believes, as with any repression, it will fail and the repressed will pop out sideways. If narcissistic needs are not met in healthy ways, they will certainly be met in unhealthy ways, including the expression of *narcissistic rage*, the response to narcissistic injury, with its unquenchable desire for revenge, and the idealization of demonic leaders such as Hitler and the Reverend Jim Jones.

Kohut states that early analytic patients, the patients of Freud and his associates, were what he calls *guilty man*. They were primarily suffering from conflict between desire and conscience. They were caught between the pressures of the id and the prohibitions of the superego. The central issue in their treatment was making their desire and their guilt conscious, so they could find a way to live with them. The contemporary patient, in contrast, is what Kohut calls *tragic man*. Tragic man is not suffering from internal conflict; rather, he is suffering from narcissistic injury, from lack of a cohesive self, from lack of fulfillment and inability to feel whole, integral, or securely there. Kohut quotes with approval Eugene O'Neill's lines in *The Great God Brown*, "Man is born broken. He lives by mending. The grace of God is glue" (Kohut, 1977, p. 287).

DANIEL STERN

Daniel Stern, who was a student and associate of Mahler's, differs importantly from other psychoanalytic developmental theorists in denying the existence of an autistic, fused, merged, symbiotic stage out of which separateness, autonomy, and self emerge. On the contrary, he maintains that the template for the organization of experience into self-experience and non-self-experience is innate, and that it is meaningful to talk about self-experiences occurring in the infant from the age of 2 months on. For Stern, selfhood is an epigenetic development of four types of self-experience: *emergent, core, subjective*, and *verbal*, which are successive in time, distinct and discrete, yet coexistent from about the age of 4, when the verbal self is established, to the end of life. Thus, there are four selves: the emergent self, the core self, the subjective self, and the verbal self, each contributing its harmonies and disharmonies to the symphonic structure of the adult self in which the components retain their uniqueness, yet blend into a unitary experience.

Stern based his theory largely upon the infant-observational and empirically experimental research of the past two decades, taking note of psychoanalytic clinical notions, the validity of which he does not deny, yet insisting that they are adultomorphic, retrospective projections onto the infant. What Stern does validate in the psychoanalytic notions of the self is their emphasis on the reality, indeed the saliency, of inwardness and of subjective experience, in contradistinction to the outwardness and the behavioristic bias of most empirical psychological work. Stern certainly believes in an unconscious, but he doesn't much deal with it.

For Stern, the self is experiential. Explicitly, he defines it as the sense of agency, the sense of physical cohesion, the sense of continuity, the sense of affectivity, the sense of a subjective self that can achieve intersubjectivity with another, the sense of creating organization, and the sense of transmitting meaning. Definitions are prescriptive as well as descriptive, and Stern opts for a self or series of selves that are sensate, vaguely inchoate or sharply experienced sensations and organizations of sensations. These selves are essentially preconscious most of the time, although for the most part they can emerge into consciousness without difficulty. It is not clear how or how much the Sternian selves are dynamically unconscious. Perhaps figure and ground is a better metaphor than conscious and unconscious: Stern's selves most commonly serve as ground, albeit an active and organizing ground, but they can indeed become figure in some situations.

Let us look at Stern's selves in a bit more detail. They correspond to discontinuities—quantum leaps in development. The sense of the *emergent self* comes into being during the first 2 months of life. It is a "sense of organization in the process of formation" (Stern, 1985, p. 38). Stern emphasizes the experience of the process more than he does the product. This process is an ongoing organization of bodily concerns resulting in experiential cohesion of the body, its actions, and inner feeling states. These will form the core self that is now emerging. The emergent self is both the process and the product of forming relations between isolated events. It is the giving of cohesion. In adult life, the emergent self is the basis of creativity and potential for ongoing development.

In the next stage, that of the *core self*, there is a consolidation of that which has emerged from the emerging self. The core self is characterized by experiences of *self-agency* (I can do things), *self-cohesion* (I have boundaries; I am a physical whole), *self-affectivity* (I have patterned inner qualities of feeling that are the same across experiences), and *self-history* (I endure, go-on-being, because there are regularities in the flow of my experience, in the stream of my consciousness). These four self-experiences of the core self are preconceptual. They are "senses of," not concepts, cognitive knowledge, or self-awareness. They are not reflexive or reflective. The core self is a self without self-consciousness. In normal development, it is consolidated at about 8 months.

Stern's inclusion of affectivity as one of the most salient aspects of self-experience has important implications for the experience of the continuity of the self. Stern maintains that affect is the most constant experience we have, in the sense that affects remain more the same across time than any other experience. That is, my experiences of anger, sadness, joy, and pain are essentially the same in infancy, in childhood, in adolescence, in young adulthood, in maturity, and in old age. Therefore, my experience of affect very importantly determines and is constitutive of my experience of going-on-being. There is a clinical implication in this as well, in that putting the patient in contact with his or her feelings, his or her affects, in addition to whatever else it may do, should increase his or her sense of self-cohesion and self-continuity.

The *subjective self* develops from 8 to 15 months. Essentially, it is the discovery that there are inner subjective experiences—thoughts and feelings—that are mine alone. Simultaneously, or slightly later, the infant "discovers" that others also have minds (i.e., thoughts and feelings that are potentially the same as his or hers). This opens up the possibility of *intersubjectivity*. I can share (or not share) or connect (or not connect) with other creatures who are subjects like me, who have an inner world of sensations, feelings, and thoughts. For Stern, self and objects are coemergent, not from a symbiosis, but from genetically and temporally prior, less organized, inwardly experienced experiences of self and others. There is a prior primitiveness of self and others (primitive in the sense of less organized and less self-aware), but no prior confusion or merger. In the state of the subjective self, the subjectivity of the other is also established, and multitudinous possibilities for relatedness come into being. It is only now that merger or symbiosis becomes possible, but only as a union of that which was initially experienced as distinct. The distinctness of self and other, self and world, are preprogrammed, as is the development of the four selves. Of course, Mahler maintains that autism precedes symbiosis, but her notion is rather different than Stern's.

However, development does not take place in a vacuum; it takes place in a social matrix, and there is a dialectical relationship between the emergent selves of the infant and the responses of the adult caretakers. As the child changes, the response he or she elicits changes, which in turn elicits further changes in the child. Here Stern's notion is similar to those of Winnicott and Kohut, but the balance is more on innateness and response to it than on environmental provision (being treated as a self) creating a self. The emphasis is different, but all these thinkers see both innate and environmental input as necessary for the formation of the self.

During the second year of life, the *verbal self* comes into being. Now the self can be represented as a narrative: the story one tells to oneself about who and what one is. The narrative self is reminiscent of Freud's notion of the secondary revision of dreams, the process by which the dreamer gives the dream more cohesion and a better narrative line than it actually has. In a sense, the verbal self is a secondary revision of the dream that is one's life. The verbal self opens up new possibilities for interpersonal experience, but language also increases the possibilities for deception and concealment. The verbal self cannot adequately represent the other selves. It creates a world of concepts and abstractions that carry with them the danger of alienation from the vividness, uniqueness, and vitality of the preverbal experience characteristic of the emergent, core, and subjective selves. Thus, the four selves are equally necessary; the temporally later does not supplant the temporally earlier; rather, they provide different self-experiences. The four selves endure and mutually enrich each other across the life span. In the full flower of the Sternian self, it is simultaneously the experience of coming into being, the experience of being, the experience of interiority of self and others, and the experience of having and creating a history verbally, a narrative.

There are two main disagreements between Stern and the other psychoanalytic theorists that we have surveyed. Stern does not believe in an autistic stage or an emergence from symbiosis, although he does agree that some sort of merger experience does occur between mother and infant subsequent to the experience of separateness. From an evolutionary perspective it makes sense that both the template for discrimination between self and non-self *and* the potential for and drive to bond are inborn. Both have survival value. They are the *anlage* of the *twin poles of separateness and relatedness* of the self. From the evidence of dreams, art, ritual, myth, literature, and human behavior as manifest in activities as diverse as love, politics, and transferential phenomena, it is clear that merger experiences are an indelible part of the human psyche. The psychoanalytic dispute is over how they should be understood and interpreted. However, the difference between Stern and the other theorists is not as great as it seems. It is about timing and sequence more than anything else. From the evidence of infant research, it is highly likely that Stern is basically right when he maintains that separateness is innate and primordial and that the autistic (autoerotic) stage as previously understood does not exist *and* that bonding, subjectively experienced as merger, is just as primordial. Whatever the balance of these tendencies at birth and in the earliest months of life, completion of the developmental task of separation-individuation is prerequisite to the formation of a healthy and mature self.

The second disagreement between Stern and the other theorists concerns "splitting" and the existence of good and bad self- and object representations. Stern does not believe that infants so simplify their worlds and he brings experimental evidence to bear in support of his view. Rather, he believes that the infant has a more average experience of less than perfect gratification that is reflected in an averaged representation. Inferences from infant observation and experiment to infantile subjective (and probably unconscious) experience are, to say the least, fallible, just as are reconstructions of the infant's inner world from the evidences of adult behavior, psychopathological or otherwise. So we cannot be sure of the nature of the infant's representational world. However, all of human history, collective and individual, is a record of the belief in gods and devils, or in God and the Devil, in all good and all bad. Our entire lives we struggle to transcend this invidious oversimplification and distortion of ourselves and our objects (the historical and clinical evidence is here irrefutable) and to perceive and react to the world and ourselves in a way commensurate with the subtlety and complexity of reality. Does this mean that we start with unintegrated good and bad object representations? Or do we split already "averaged" representations for defensive purposes? One can't be sure at the present state of knowledge. Self- and object representations are cognitive structures and as such, are theoretical constructs that can't be observed; however, their manifestations can and the evidence, experimental and clinical, is that we both split and integrate.

13

Integration

It has been a long journey. For you, for me, and for the self. The self has evolved in two senses: the self itself has probably changed over historical time, and our understanding of the self has evolved. There is a dialectical relationship between the two. If the self did indeed change in the course of history, mankind's understanding of that self necessarily changed also, and at the same time, the historical change in the understanding of the self changed the self itself. Since the self is, in at least one of its aspects, an experience, it like all experiences is partly constituted by our anticipations and our conceptualizations. As Wordsworth (1850/1910) puts it, "the world [including the self] is half-created and half-perceived." There were probably two changes in the nature of the self in the course of history. Both involved an increase in interiority, in the experiential insight that I have an inner life that is constituted by awareness and is private. Jaynes (1976) postulated the first change as an owning of what had been "experienced as voices," experienced as coming from the environment, from an animistically perceived world. That owning moved the voices of the gods from the outside to the inside. The voices were experienced in much the same manner as the schizophrenic experiences command hallucinations. Jaynes cited literary evidence in his analysis of the *Iliad*, the Bible, and primitive myth, as well as interpretations of the meanings of archaeological artifacts to support his contention that man had evolved from a bicameral creature who experienced his own subjectivity as external into a creature with a subjective mode of inner experience, usually called consciousness. He sees consciousness, experienced as self-consciousness rather than as sensory awareness, as coming into being in relatively recent historical times, and tries to demonstrate this change in his analysis of later Greek literature and the cultural products of other peoples. This increase in awareness of consciousness as self-consciousness and its resonance "within" was certainly a self-experience, and the change, if there was one, was certainly a change in the self. Now there was a me who was something more, or something different than, a body who perceived.

Socrates and Plato increased the interiority of selfhood, paradoxically by developing a notion of discovery of self interpersonally through dialogue, through what Plato called dialectic. The Delphic "Know Thyself" meant know thyself in relation to the cosmos; the self of Platonic philosophy always has relatedness as well as inwardness. Augustine deepened this inwardness, giving it a new narrative dimension through autobiography. Separateness and the anxiety of separateness is increasing, as is the disharmony, the conflict, or the awareness of it, within the self. At least that would appear to be the historical development.

Any development has both continuity and discontinuity. Within the continuity, there are moments when something new comes into being. Rene Spitz (1965), who did some of the initial infant observational research, saw this in individual development in which new "organizers of the psyche" came into being as sort of quantum leaps during the first year of development. Something similar happens in historical development, and Taylor (1989) highlighted the next quantum leap of self, the emergence of a greater and socially more widespread sense of individuality and apartness in the 17th century. The Renaissance, the Reformation, the breakdown of belief in the great chain of being, and increased privacy all played a role in yet another increase in the interiority of self. Perhaps there is no more eloquent expression of this interiority than the Shakespearean soliloquy, which is roughly contemporaneous with these developments. The Cartesian self, the *cogito*, is, of course, the philosophical expression of this new self. Real selves live in real worlds, and I am sure that what self is, as well as how self is understood, continues to evolve and is always, at least in part, conditioned by culture, by technology, by intellectual development in general, and by ideology. The degree to which the self is a we-self rather than a me-self is indubitably contingent upon culture, and the self of the West, with its strong sense of autonomy and strong sense of alienation and estrangement, is not the only possible self-experience. Not only historically, but contemporaneously, not only across time but across space, different cultures produce different selves, although that is not to deny the indubitable commonality and universality of some aspects of self.

Whatever the historical and cultural variations in the self, there are always two poles, those of isolation and relatedness, aloneness and connectedness, to be dealt with, experientially and theoretically. Some of our theorists—Descartes, Kierkegaard, and Sartre—have emphasized almost to the point of exclusiveness the pole of aloneness. Others—Meade, Cooley, Winnicott, and to a lesser and more conflicted extent James and Heidegger—have emphasized the relatedness, the we-ness of the self. The psychoanalytic accounts of self, more than any of the others, have tried to provide a bridge between aloneness and connectedness through the notions of internalization (which is itself problematic; it's a great word but what, if anything, does it denote?) and of object-relatedness, particularly the interpersonal and intrapsychic relationship of mother and child.

Although I am not enough of an historian to be sure, it appears that the self, as well as the understanding of the self, has changed across time, and is probably still changing, and it also appears to be the case that the self varies across contemporaneous cultures, and these variations in the self itself account for some of the controversy and disagreement among our theorists of self. However, there are also conceptual difficulties and disagreements that do not arise from the possibility of the self changing over time or being different in different places. How are we to account for these controversies? Partly on the basis of differing temperaments and basic assumptions and of the intrinsic difficulty of the questions raised by "self." However, I am not sure that these conceptual difficulties are all real. On the contrary, they are importantly semantic: theories of the self are in disagreement because theorists are talking about different things.

I do not believe the self is one thing, so that it cannot be any other. Rather, our different theorists are really talking about different things, each of which has to be considered in its own right. What are the different meanings of self? Can these semantic confusions be sorted out? I am not sure, but I am going to try. In what follows, *self* means the word *self*, and self is what is denoted.

Self sometimes means a *soul*, or something like a soul.

Self sometimes means a *substance*, or an *underlying substrate*.

Self sometimes means an *activity*; self as an organizer, organizing experience, consciously or unconsciously; and self as that which performs the synthesis that gives cohesion and continuity.

Self is sometimes an *explanatory hypothesis* rather than something ontological. Self here is a construct.

Self sometimes means a *cognitive structure*, as in the psychoanalytic notion of self-representations.

Self sometimes means a *verbal activity*; here self is either an index word locating experience or a narrative.

Self sometimes means an *experience*: conscious or unconscious experience of differing degrees of cohesion, continuity and agency.

Self sometimes means a *process*: the flow of experience.

Self sometimes means something *normative*, as in "the more consciousness, the more self," "the realization of self is the task of the second half of life," or "where it was, I shall be." Here the self is something to be attained, with the theorists usually enjoining us to attain it.

Let us look at each of these meanings of *self* and see what seems useful and valid in each.

The self as soul—the Atman, the "eternal" within, the rational part of the psyche (Plato), the *Logos* within (the Stoics), and its variations in both Eastern and Western religions—is an enduring, ever-resurfacing conceptualization. I do not judge it, but neither do I choose to use the word *self* to denote any of these understandings of soul. I think it is better to make a distinction here and have a different signifier for the eternal part, if there be one, however understood, of human beings, and for the experiential interiority and individuality of human beings. The first is best denoted *soul* and the second *self*.

What about the self as substance, as an enduring substrate? I think Hume, James, the logical positivists, and Whitehead, among others, have taken care of this one. It adds nothing but mystification to our notion of self; empirically you can't find it and conceptually there are better ways to account for the continuity of self-experience.

Our next meaning of *self* is self as activity: activity as organizer or as agent. There are two notions here: one, the self as doer, as a center of initiative, and two, the self as organizer. I think both are useful and meaningful uses of *self*. We do experience ourselves, one hopes, as agents capable of initiating action, quite apart from whether or not we in reality have free will. But to call this agency the self, rather than to see it as an aspect of self otherwise construed, seems limiting. The other meaning of *self* as activity is self as synthesis and synthesizer. This meaning seems highly salient. Here *self* means both the organizing and the organizer. The experience of continuity, of ongoingness, of going-on-being, is accounted for by it. How the self brings this about is, however, far from clear. Locke's attributing this synthesis to memory makes some sense, but his insistence that this task is exclusively a function of consciousness is untenable. For all the mystery here, I do opt for the legitimacy of self as activity in both of the above senses. However it does it, self *is* self-constituting—in a sense, the self *selfs*—and it provides us with our sense of continuity in time. Ontologically there may be something illusionary here; experientially there is not.

The self as explanatory hypothesis is up for grabs. I can see no reason why a thinker cannot use self as a theoretical construct as long as he or she is clear about what is being done. Often theorists are not, and there is a confusion in a given thinker between construct and something substantive or something experienced. Both Kant's transcendental unity of the apperception (I have trouble with this phrase because I always think of an Isaac Bashevis Singer short story in which an overly serious, rather pompous, scholarly recluse is in a rage because the typesetters have mixed up his manuscript for a philosophical journal with copy for a lurid tabloid, and "The janitor got drunk and raped his daughter" appears where "the Transcendental unity of the apperception" should appear. Perhaps I identify) and James's Pure Ego, in one of its aspects, are such explanatory hypotheses, or at least they can be understood as such. They are postulates of thought. The "I think" that accompanies (not necessarily consciously) every thought (act of mentation) is a construct. Hume's account of the unfindability of the self is here irrelevant. This self isn't an empirical discoverable; it is an explanatory hypothesis, and according to Kant a logically necessary one. As such, it needs to be judged pragmatically and instrumentally. Does it help "save the phenomena," that is, give an account of what needs to be explained? In this case, it does: both Kant's transcendental unity and James's pure ego work, as long as they are understood as being what they are rather than as thinglike substances. Other uses of *self* as explanatory hypotheses need to be clarified and judged for their utility on a case-by-case basis. Here is one place where semantic clarification of *self* really helps.

Self meaning cognitive structure makes sense to me. It certainly isn't the only useful way of regarding self, but the various accounts of self-representation, their development out of innate templates, out of undifferentiation, or out of symbiosis, in interaction with the environment, resonate. They too can be regarded as theoretical constructs rather than as entities, but either way they entail activity, processing, assimilation, and sorting of experience into me and not-me. The empirical psychological notion of the self-concept is less dynamic, but also makes sense. *Self* as a cognitive structure is a necessary feature of any account of self. Here the inadequacy of Locke's reliance on consciousness becomes even more clear; perhaps memory is the synthesizer, but self-representations are not always conscious, yet they always influence behavior, affect, and mood. Here, for once, we have empirical evidence.

Self meaning a verbal activity makes perfect sense. I have no problem with the usage, but I do have trouble with the positivists' exclusivity when they maintain that this is all self meaningfully means and that all other usages are meaningless. Self can usefully be understood as *I* used as an index word that locates and sorts out experience into mine and thine, but other usages are clearly possible and meaningful.

That self is also that which is constituted by an internal monologue—by the story I tell myself about who I am, who I was, and how who I was became who I am—is indubitable. We all do it, and self is indeed constituted, or, following Stern, one of our selves is constituted, by this narrative, this secondary revision of the dream that is life. In fact, there is an infinitude of narratives I can tell myself about myself, and one of the most profound ways in which I can change myself is to change the story I tell myself about myself. Psychotherapy is importantly about facilitating changes in this narration by making more material available for storytelling and by changing perspective.

Self meaning experience, or an experience, is to me the single most salient connotation of self. It is less problematic, less metaphysical, and closest to what is actually lived than any other meaning of *self*. The trouble with some accounts of self is that they are actually talking about the self as experience but confuse it with self as something substantive, freezing and concretizing experience. We have reviewed many accounts of self as experience, some emphasizing anxiety and dread and some emphasizing connectedness, centeredness, and ongoingness. How adequate any account of self as experience is, is an empirical question.

Self can mean process; self as experience and self as process overlap. *Self* is usefully understood as process; many conceptual difficulties in accounting for the self come from mistakenly looking at it in cross-section and wondering how these slices connect and flow into one another, when the flow is the actuality and the slice is an abstraction. Both James's "stream," in which each succeeding segment encompasses the preceding segments and represents all the others, and Whitehead's "objective immortality," in which the past is prehended by the present, are illuminating accounts of the self as process. There is no reason there cannot be other accounts of self so understood.

Finally, we come to *self* meaning an injunction to value or do something, a normative statement. I have no quarrel with this usage of *self*, except when a thinker confuses *is* with *ought*. Kierkegaard, Jung, Heidegger, Sartre, and perhaps Freud do this, although some of them deny that that is what they are doing. I too believe that the integration and owning of that which is denied, repressed, disavowed, or projected is desirable and that increasing one's sense of continuity, centeredness, initiative, ongoingness, self-awareness, cohesion, and differentiation is desirable. In fact, my professional activity is to help people move in these directions. But to denote these value judgments *self* is only to cause confusion. *Is* and *ought* are best kept conceptually apart.

Our understanding of self is undergoing yet another revolution; there is currently a very active pursuit of a new understanding of the self through cognitive psychology, neurophysiology, and cybernetics. Exactly what notion of self will emerge from these new sciences and new conceptualizations is not yet clear; however, there is probably something exciting in the horizon of our understandings of self.

Dennett (1991), a leading cybernetic theorist, makes a first approximation to such an understanding when he defines self as a biological self that is prewired to distinguish between self and world, inside and outside, and a "narrative center of gravity," which is an abstraction in the same sense as a physical center of gravity is an abstraction. Dennett's center of gravity self is reminiscent of Stern's averaged self-representations. It is the center of multiple narratives that *spin us*. Dennett is anxious to avoid a ghost in the machine that does the narrating. Rather, his notion is that of multiple perspectives generating multiple narratives—narratives without a narrator. So to speak, words create the self. His is a formulation that is, as he says, counterintuitive.

I turn from the theoretical to the personal. Certain kinds of experience increase my sense of ongoingness, of continuity in time, of being the same self now as I was then. I enjoy those experiences; they feel good. I value them and find that experiencing myself more integrally is intrinsically worthwhile. Writing this book gave me such an experience; it integrated many of my interests, and much of what often feels like disconnected aspects of my life, disconnected over time and disconnected in the moment, came together. So many disparate activities, so many episodes and experiences stretching back at least to adolescence integrated and felt both one and mine as I pursued this task. Certain kinds of aesthetic experiences, the ones I go back to again and again, also give me a feeling of cohesion and continuity. Rereading or reseeing Shakespeare, Chekov, and Freud; rehearing Beethoven, Mozart and Verdi; and looking at certain pictures gives me the feeling that I am the same person, that I have been here before, and that I have endured, and at the same time give me the sense that I have changed, that I am understanding, hearing, or seeing differently. I like that feeling. The last time I felt it really strongly was looking at a Rembrandt self-portrait in the Metropolitan Museum of Art. It was wonderful—both the portrait and the sense that I was the same person I was the first time I visited the Philadelphia Museum of Art at 9 or 10, but somehow different. Nature can give me the same feeling. Walking in the mountains, in certain moods especially, gives me an indelible feeling of being one with the child who wandered the hills of upstate New York. That too feels good. All of these experience are self-conscious ones, yet I wonder about the paradox that I am, and I am sure that you are, as well, most myself, most centered, most there, when I am least self-conscious. I know this is so, but I don't understand it. It is a mystery. Perhaps the self-conscious sensations through memory of continuity and sameness induced by art, by nature, by a feeling, or by a person have to do with ongoingness, with development through time, while the un-self-conscious feeling of being here now has to do with uniqueness of the emergent moment, with the eternal now. I value them both.

If certain kinds of self-experience seem good to me, can I provide them for my patients? How does psychotherapy strengthen the self? I believe that everything that happens in dynamic psychotherapy contributes to a better self-experience: derepression and integration into consciousness of the disassociated, disavowed, or projected aspects of self increase its integrity and extensiveness; putting people in touch with their feelings increases their sense of continuity because affect is an experience that remains essentially the same throughout life; the holding environment of the therapeutic session and "holding" by the therapist give the patient the experience of being treated as integral, bounded, ongoing, worthwhile, alive, and capable of initiative, all which is potentially internalizable, just as it ideally should have been early in life; and finally, the construction of new and more comprehensive narratives about self enriches self and increases the capacity of the self to synthesize. The new memories uncovered by de-repression provide new material with which the narrator enhances continuity. Here *self* is normative, a decision that all of the above is valuable and worthwhile.

What finally have I come to believe about self? Self is *developmental*; self is *emergent*, emergent from an innately programmed template and from experiences of merger; it comes out of a preselfhood; self is *affective*; self is *not body but not disembodied*; self is *conflictual*, in conflict with various components of itself and with the environment, but not only conflictual; self is *object-relational*, coming into being through interaction with others and always mediated by such interactions; and self is *constitutive*, a synthesizer and a synthesis.

Self is experienced as, and indeed is, an interaction between innate potential and environmental response. Feelings of aliveness, cohesion, agency, continuity (ongoingness), and self-worth come from both within and without. I agree with Winnicott's and Kohut's beliefs that the feelings of being coherent, enduring, and worthwhile, indeed of existing, come, at least in part, from the outside. I become a self by being treated as a self. I learn who and what I am by the ways in which I am treated. Self is both organizer and organization. It always has an affective quality; it is never purely conceptual; it encompasses verbal and preverbal levels;

it is more or less consistent and coherent (the degree of which can only be empirically determined); it is unconscious as well as preconscious, and less frequently conscious; it is a construct and a synthesis; it is a fiction (narrative) and a reality (experience); it is a dialectic of conflict and reconciliation with others and with itself carried out by projection, identification, and introjection; it is partly dependent on memory; it evolves over a lifetime; and it is subject to injury. If you wish to "tune in next week," those injuries, narcissistic wounds, and their treatment will be the subject of my next book.

References

Alford, F. C. (1991). *The self in social theory*. New Haven, CT: Yale University Press.

Ayer, A. J. (1952). *Language, truth, and logic*. New York: Dover. (Original work published 1936)

Barrett, W. (1958). *Irrational man: A study in existential philosophy*. New York: Doubleday.

Brentano, F. (1918). *Psychology from an empirical standpoint* (2nd ed.). Leipzig, Germany: Duncker & Humbolt. (Original work published 1874)

Cooley, C. F. (1902). *Human nature and the social order*. New York: Scribner.

Dennett, D. (1991). *Consciousness explained*. Boston: Little, Brown.

Descartes, R. (1951a). *Discourse on method*. (L. J. Lafleur, Trans.). New York: Library of the Liberal Arts. (Original work published 1637)

Descartes, R. (1951b). *Meditations on first philosophy*. (L. J. Lafleur, Trans.). New York: Library of the Liberal Arts. (Original work published 1642)

Dewey, J. (1929). *The quest for certainty*. Boston: Minten, Balch.

Erikson, E. (1963). *Childhood and society* (2nd ed.). New York: Norton. (Original work published 1950)

Erikson, E. (1968). *Identity, youth, and crisis*. New York: Norton.

Freud, S. (1950). Project for a scientific psychology. In J. Strachey (Ed. and Trans.), *Standard edition of the complete psychological works of Sigmund Freud* (Vol. 1, pp. 294–397). London: Hogarth Press. (Original work published 1895)

Freud, S. (1953a). Interpretation of dreams. In J. Strachey (Ed. and Trans.), *Standard edition of the complete psychological works of Sigmund Freud* (Vols. 4 & 5, pp. 1–628). London: Hogarth Press. (Original work published 1900)

Freud, S. (1953b). Three contributions to a theory of sexuality. In J. Strachey (Ed. and Trans.), *Standard edition of the complete psychological works of Sigmund Freud* (Vol. 7, pp. 125–243). London: Hogarth Press. (Original work published 1905)

Freud, S. (1953c). Totem and taboo. In J. Strachey (Ed. and Trans.), *Standard edition of the complete psychological works of Sigmund Freud* (Vol. 13, pp. 1–162). London: Hogarth Press. (Original work published 1913–1914)

Freud, S. (1953d). *On aphasia: A critical study* (E. Stengel, Trans.). London: Imago Publishing. (Original work published 1891)

Freud, S. (1955). Beyond the pleasure principle. In J. Strachey (Ed. and Trans.), *Standard edition of the complete psychological works of Sigmund Freud* (Vol. 18, pp. 1–64). London: Hogarth Press. (Original work published 1920)

Freud, S. (1956). The ego and the id. In J. Strachey (Ed. and Trans.), *Standard edition of the complete psychological works of Sigmund Freud* (Vol. 19, pp. 1–66). London: Hogarth Press. (Original work published 1923)

Freud, S. (1957a). Observations on "wild" psychoanalysis. In J. Strachey (Ed. and Trans.), *Standard edition of the complete psychological works of Sigmund Freud* (Vol. 11, pp. 219–230). London: Hogarth Press. (Original work published 1910)

Freud, S. (1957b). Mourning and melancholia. In J. Strachey (Ed. and Trans.), *Standard edition of the complete psychological works of Sigmund Freud* (Vol. 14, pp. 237–258). London: Hogarth Press. (Original work published 1915)

Freud, S. (1957c). On narcissism: An introduction. In J. Strachey (Ed. and Trans.), *Standard edition of the complete psychological works of Sigmund Freud* (Vol. 14, pp. 67–104). London: Hogarth Press. (Original work published 1914)

Freud, S. (1957d). Thoughts for the times on war and death. In J. Strachey (Ed. and Trans.), *Standard edition of the complete psychological works of Sigmund Freud* (Vol. 14, pp. 273–302). London: Hogarth Press. (Original work published 1915)

Freud, S. (1958). Remembering, repeating, and working-through. In J. Strachey (Ed. and Trans.), *Standard edition of the complete psychological works of Sigmund Freud* (Vol. 12, pp. 147–156). London: Hogarth Press. (Original work published 1914)

Freud, S. (1959). Inhibitions, symptoms, and anxiety. In J. Strachey (Ed. and Trans.), *Standard edition of the complete psychological works of Sigmund Freud* (Vol. 20, pp. 75–174). London: Hogarth Press. (Original work published 1926)

Freud, S. (1961). Some dreams of Descartes's: A letter to Maxime Leroy. In J. Strachey (Ed. and Trans.), *Standard edition of the complete psychological works of Sigmund Freud* (Vol. 21, pp. 199–203). London: Hogarth Press. (Original work published 1929)

Freud, S. (1962a). The neuro-psychoses of defense. In J. Strachey (Ed. and Trans.), *Standard edition of the complete psychological works of Sigmund Freud* (Vol. 3, pp. 43–62). London: Hogarth Press. (Original work published 1894)

Freud, S. (1962b). Further remarks on the neuro-psychoses of defense. In J. Strachey (Ed. and Trans.), *Standard edition of the complete psychological works of Sigmund Freud* (Vol. 3, pp. 159–188). London: Hogarth Press. (Original work published 1896)

Freud, S. (1964a). Moses and monotheism: Three essays. In J. Strachey (Ed. and Trans.), *Standard edition of the complete psychological works of Sigmund Freud* (Vol. 23, pp. 1–138). London: Hogarth Press. (Original work published 1939)

Freud, S. (1964b). Splitting of the ego in the process of defense. In J. Strachey (Ed. and Trans.), *Standard edition of the complete psychological works of Sigmund Freud* (Vol. 23, pp. 271–278). London: Hogarth Press. (Original work published 1940)

Freud, S. (1968). *Infantile cerebral paralysis* (Lester A. Russin, Trans.). Miami, FL: University of Miami Press. (Original work published 1897)

Freud, S. (1985). *The complete letters of Sigmund Freud to Wilhelm Fliess 1887–1904* (J. M. Masson, Ed. and Trans.). Cambridge, MA: Harvard University Press.

Freud, S., & Breuer, J. (1955). Studies on hysteria. In J. Strachey (Ed. and Trans.), *Standard edition of the complete psychological works of Sigmund Freud* (Vol. 2, pp. 1–306). London: Hogarth Press. (Original work published 1895)

Freud, S., & Jung, C. (1974). *The Freud/Jung letters: The correspondence between Sigmund Freud and C. G. Jung* (R. Manheim & R. F. C. Hull, Trans.; W. McGuire, Ed.). Princeton, NJ: Princeton University Press.

Fromm, E. (1941). *Escape from freedom*. New York: Harcourt, Brace.

Glover, E. (1956). *On the early development of the mind*. New York: International Universities Press.

Goffman, E. (1959). *The presentation of self in everyday life*. Garden City, NY: Doubleday/Anchor Books.

Groddeck, G. (1930). *The book of the id*. New York: Nervous and Mental Disease. (Original work published 1923)

Hartmann, H. (1958). *Ego psychology and the problem of adaptation*. New York: International Universities Press.

Hartmann, H. (1964). *Essays in ego psychology*. New York: International Universities Press.

Hegel, G. W. F. (1929a). *Introduction to the philosophy of history* (J. Sibree, Trans.). In J. Loewenberg, (Ed.), *Hegel: Selections* (pp. 338–443). New York: Scribner. (Original work published 1837)

Hegel, G. W. F. (1929b). *Outline of Hegel's logic* (W. T. Harris, Trans.). In J. Loewenberg (Ed.), *Hegel: Selections* (pp. 98–129). New York: Scribner. (Original work published 1812–1814)

Hegel, G. W. F. (1931). *The phenomenology of mind* (J. B. Baillie, Trans.). New York: MacMillan. (Original work published 1807)

Heidegger, M. (1927). *Being and time* (J. MacQuaurie & E. Robinson, Trans). New York: Harper & Row.

Heidegger, M. (1961). *An introduction to metaphysics* (R. Manheim, Trans.). New York: Anchor Books. (Original work published 1953)

Hemingway, E. (1970). A clean, well-lighted place. In *The snows of Kilimanjaro and other stories*. New York: Scribner. (Original work published 1933)

Hume, D. (1911a). Autobiography. In *A treatise of human nature* (p. viii). London: Dent & Sons/Everyman Library. (Original work published 1775)

Hume, D. (1911b). *A treatise of human nature*. London: Dent & Sons/Everyman Library. (Original work published 1738)

Husserl, E. (1931). *The Cartesian meditations* (D. Cairns, Trans.). The Hague, The Netherlands: Martinus Nijhoff.

Jacobson, E. (1964). *The self and the object world*. New York: International Universities Press.

James, W. (1902). *Varieties of religious experience. A study in human nature.* London: Longmans, Green.

James, W. (1909). *A pluralistic universe.* New York: Longmans, Green.

James, W. (1912a). Does consciousness exist? In *Essays in radical empiricism* (pp. 1–15). London: Longmans, Green. (Original work published 1904)

James, W. (1912b). *Essays in radical empiricism.* London: Longmans, Green.

James, W. (1912c). *Pragmatism: A new name for some old ways of thinking.* London: Longmans, Green. (Original work published 1907)

James, W. (1956). *The will to believe.* New York: Dover. (Original work published 1898)

James, W. (1980). *The selected letters of William James* (E. Hardwick, Ed.). Boston: Godine. (Original work published 1920)

James, W. (1983). *The principles of psychology.* Cambridge, MA: Harvard University Press. (Original work published 1890)

Jaynes, J. (1976). *The origin of consciousness in the breakdown of the bicameral mind.* Boston: Houghton Mifflin.

Jones, E. (1961). *The life and works of Sigmund Freud* (L. Trilling and S. Marcus, Eds. and Abridgers). New York: Basic Books.

Jung, C. G. (1909). *Uber die psychologie der dementia praecox* [The psychology of dementia praecox]. Zurich, Switzerland: Halle. (Original work published 1907)

Jung, C. G. (1945). The relations between the ego and the unconscious. In *Collected works* (Vol. 17). Princeton, NJ: Princeton University Press.

Jung, C. G. (1961). *Memories, dreams, and reflections* (R. Winston and C. Winston, Trans.). New York: Vintage Books.

Kant, I. (1949a). *Critique of pure practical reason* (C. J. Friedrich, Trans.). In *The philosophy of Kant* (pp. 209–264). New York: Modern Library. (Original work published 1786)

Kant, I. (1949b). *Religion within the limits of reason alone* (T. Green & H. Hudson, Trans.). In *The philosophy of Kant* (pp. 363–411). New York: Modern Library. (Original work published 1793)

Kant, I. (1952). *The critique of judgement* (J. C. Meredith, Trans.). Oxford, England: Oxford University Press. (Original work published 1793)

Kant, I. (1953). *Prolegomena to any future metaphysics that will present itself as a science* (P. Lucas, Trans.). Manchester, England: Manchester University Press. (Original work published 1783)

Kant, I. (1959). *Foundations of the metaphysics of morals* (L. W. Beck, Trans.). New York: Liberal Arts Press. (Original work published 1785)

Kant, I. (1986). *Perpetual peace* (L. W. Beck, Trans.). In *Immanuel Kant: Philosophical writings* (pp. 270–311). New York: Continuum. (Original work published 1795)

Kant, I. (1990). *Critique of pure reason* (J. M. D. Mieklejohn, Trans.). Buffalo, NY: Prometheus Books. (Original work published 1781)

Kernberg, O. (1975). *Borderline conditions and pathological narcissism.* New York: Jason Aronson.

Kierkegaard, S. (1940). *Stages on life's way* (W. Lowrie, Trans.). Princeton, NJ: Princeton University Press. (Original work published 1845)

Kierkegaard, S. (1941a). *Concluding unscientific postscript* (D. Swenson, Trans.). Princeton, NJ: Princeton University Press. (Original work published 1846)

Kierkegaard, S. (1941b). *Fear and trembling* (W. Lowrie, Trans.). Princeton, NJ: Princeton University Press. (Original work published 1843)

Kierkegaard, S. (1944a). *The concept of dread* (W. Lowrie, Trans.). Princeton, NJ: Princeton University Press. (Original work published 1849)

Kierkegaard, S. (1944b). *Either/Or, a fragment of life* (W. Lowrie, Trans.). Princeton, NJ: Princeton University Press. (Original work published 1843)

Kierkegaard, S. (1944c). *The sickness unto death* (W. Lowrie, Trans.). Princeton, NJ: Princeton University Press. (Original work published 1849)

Klein, M. (1975a). *Envy and Gratitude and other works 1946–1963.* New York: Dell.

Klein, M. (1975b). *Love, guilt, and reparation and other works 1921–1945.* New York: Dell.

Koestler, A. (1941). *Darkness at noon.* New York: MacMillan.

Kohut, H. (1971). *The analysis of the self: A systematic approach to the psychoanalytic treatment of narcissistic personality disorders.* New York: International Universities Press.

Kohut, H. (1977). *The restoration of the self.* New York: International Universities Press.

Lacan, J. (1977). The mirror stage as formative of the function of the I. In *Ecrits* (A. Sherman, Trans., pp. 1–7). New York: W. W. Norton.

Locke, J. (1946). *A letter concerning toleration*. In *The second treatise of government and a letter concerning toleration* (pp. 125–167). New York: MacMillan. (Original work published 1667)

Locke, J. (1959). *An essay concerning human understanding*. New York: Dover. (Original work published 1690)

Lucretius. (1951). *The nature of the universe* (R. E. Latham, Trans.). Baltimore, MD: Penguin.

Mahler, M. (1968). *On human symbiosis and the vicissitudes of individuation*. New York: International Universities Press.

Mahler, M., Pine, F., & Bergman, A. (1975). *The psychological birth of the human infant: Symbiosis and individuation*. New York: Basic Books.

Meade, G. H. (1934). *Mind, self, and society from the standpoint of a social behaviorist*. Chicago: University of Chicago Press.

Pascal, B. (1966). *Pensées*. (A. J. Krailsheiner, Trans.). London: Penguin.

Perry, R. B. (1935). *Thought and character of William James* (2 vols.). Boston: Little, Brown.

Plato. (1961a). *Phaedrus* (R. Hackforth, Trans.). In *Plato: The collected dialogues* (pp. 475–525). Princeton, NJ: Princeton University Press.

Plato. (1961b). *Republic* (P. Shorey, Trans.). In *Plato: The collected dialogues* (pp. 575–844). Princeton, NJ: Princeton University Press.

Plato. (1961c). *Timaeus* (B. Jowett, Trans.). In *Plato: The collected dialogues* (pp. 1151–1211). Princeton, NJ: Princeton University Press.

Ramsey, F. P. Critical notice of L. Wittgenstein's "Tractatus Logico-Philosophicus," *Mind*, XXXII, No. 128 (October 1923), pp. 465–478.

Rieff, P. (1959). *Freud: The mind of a moralist*. Chicago: University of Chicago Press.

Rogers, C. (1959). *A theory of therapy, personality, and interpersonal relations*. In S. Koch (Ed.), *Psychology: A study of a science*. New York: McGraw-Hill.

Russell, B. (1912). *The problems of philosophy*. London: Home University Library.

Russell, B. (1921). *The analysis of mind*. London: Allen & Unwin.

Russell, B., & Whitehead, A. N. (1910–1913). *Principia mathematica* (3 vols.). Cambridge, England: Cambridge University Press.

Ryle, G. (1949). *The concept of mind*. London: Hutchinson.

Saint Augustine. (1961). *Confessions* (E. P. Pusey, Trans.). New York: Collier Books.

Sartre, J. P. (1948). *The wall*. In *Intimacy* (pp. 59–81). New York: Berkley.

Sartre, J. P. (1956). *Being and nothingness: An essay on phenomenological ontology* (H. Barnes, Trans.). New York: Philosophical Library.

Sartre, J. P. (1964). *Nausea* (L. Alexander, Trans.). New York: New Directions. (Original work published 1938)

Schorske, C. (1980). Politics and patricide in Freud's *Interpretation of dreams*. In *Fin-de-siecle Vienna: Politics and culture* (pp. 181–207). New York: Knopf.

Segal, H. (1973). *Introduction to the works of Melanie Klein*. New York: Basic Books.

Smith, A. (1937). *The wealth of nations*. New York: Modern Library. (Original work published 1776)

Spinoza, B. (1951). *Ethics demonstrated in geometrical order* (R. A. M. Elwes, Trans.). In *The chief works of Benedict De Spinoza* (Vol. 2, pp. 44–277). New York: Dover. (Original work published 1677)

Spitz, R. (1965). *The first year of life*. New York: International Universities Press.

Stern, D. (1985). *The interpersonal world of the infant*. New York: Basic Books.

Taylor, C. (1989). *Sources of the self: The making of modern identity*. Cambridge, MA: Harvard University Press.

Tillich, P. (1952). *The courage to be*. New Haven, CT: Yale University Press.

Weininger, O. (1906). *Sex and character*. Vienna, Austria: Heinemann.

Whitehead, A. N. (1925). *Science in the modern world*. New York: MacMillan.

Whitehead, A. N. (1929). *Process and reality: An essay in cosmology*. New York: MacMillan.

Whitehead, A. N. (1933). *Adventures of ideas*. New York: MacMillan.

Wilson, E. (1972). *To the Finland station: A study in the writing and acting of history*. New York: Farrar, Straus, & Giroux. (Original work published 1940)

Winnicott, D. W. (1958). The capacity to be alone. In *The maturational process and the facilitating environment* (pp. 29–36). New York: International Universities Press.

Winnicott, D. W. (1965). *The maturational process and the facilitating environment* (pp. 29–36). New York: International Universities Press.

Wittgenstein, L. (1922). *Tractatus logico-philosophicus* (D. F. Pears & B. F. McGuinness, Trans.). London: Routledge & Kegan Paul.

Wittgenstein, L. (1953). *Philosophical investigations* (G. E. M. Anscombe & R. Rhess, Eds.). London: Blackwell.

Wordsworth, W. (1910). *The prelude*. In *The poetical works of Wordsworth* (pp. 631–752). New York: Oxford University Press. (Original work published 1850)

Yerushalmi, Y. H. (1991). *Freud's Moses: Judaism terminable and interminable*. New Haven, CT: Yale University Press.

Yovel, Y. (1989). *Spinoza and other heretics* (2 vols.). Princeton, NJ: Princeton University Press.

Index